SEA FOX

WITH

ATTILA

BY

PETER CHESTNUT

Sea Fox with Attila

Acknowledgements

A very special thanks to Bob Cawley, my teacher and mentor, for his unselfish encouragement and help through the publishing process.

To my neighbor, Keith Bettinger for his editing skills and grammar help. To my many friends who encouraged me through the tough times when writer's block raised its nasty head.

And of course to Attila, my real-life Siamese cat, where much inspiration came from.

About this book

Published a few years ago under the title of: "*Attila & the Battle Cruiser*". I decided for several reasons to republish with a different Title. The story is virtually unchanged. The only noticeable difference is the change from Battle Cruisers to Battleships. And the much improved grammar and punctuation. *I didn't do well in High School with this and it showed.* LOL

I received many glowing reviews the first time around and they are there for your perusal on the next pages. Thank you very much.

Reviews for Attila & the Battle Cruiser
Renamed   *Sea Fox with Attila*

Keep them coming. *Attila & the Battle Cruiser* was great. You have the talent. All the best
Clive Cussler – New York Times Bestselling author

. . . .

Although air warfare takes much of the imagination in World War II, the seas were still an important field of conflict. *Attila & the Battle Cruiser* is a novel surrounding great sea battles between Germany and Britain during this most dire of conflicts. Could the presence of a Siamese cat name Attila be giving Germany an edge in these skirmishes? "Sea Fox with Attila" is a fine military fiction read.
MIDWEST BOOK REVIEW

. . . .

Here is a delightful piece of naval fiction, not quite Patrick O'Brian, but darn close. KMS battleships *Scharnhorst* and *Gneisenau* in the Battle of the Atlantic, with an amazing cat on board the *Scharnhorst*. Story setting is early WWII, with several facts different, yet entirely plausible and explained by the author; German radar utilization in particular, an asset which was neglected and never appreciated until too late. Personnel changes in the German High Command as well.

Tribute is paid to the great '50s film "The Sea Chase"; John Wayne's character Karl Ehrlich appears here as X.O. of *Gneisenau*, as well as a scene involving a certain flag before the climactic battle episode. It is said that Hitler fought WWII with the Nazi Luftwaffe, the Prussian Army, and the Imperial Navy.

Here is a vivid portrayal of the Navy. Do allow yourself a window to read continuously; this book is hard to put down, and cat lovers should have their feline companion alongside, for Attila, the Siamese cat shines here as well. Highly recommended as a "keeper" for all navel fiction fans
Mike and "Scamp" SC Coast

. . . .

Like a master chef, Chestnut has skillfully served a tasty bit of historical World War II Atlantic sea battles with a clever blend of fiction. The cunning secret weapon of the German Navy "Attila" is a key ingredient reminiscent of the X-Files
Aaron Kingsley — Author "Visions Revealed"

. . . .

I was given your book as a Christmas present from Gary and Blanche Rever in Las Vegas. I started reading it and could not put it down, but did not finish it until 1 Jan 2012 because of Christmas and family parties. It is a great book, with thrilling battle episodes described in great detail. I enjoyed it very much and want to thank Gary and Blanche for giving it to me. I was so impressed that I had to check out the history of the *Scharnhorst, Gneisenau* and *Prince of Wales.* Your descriptions of the scenes at the British Admiralty were excruciating and probably painfully accurate. Thanks again for a great read,
Donald E. Nieser

. . . .

I just finished reading *Attila & the Battle Cruiser* and I thoroughly enjoyed it. Can't wait for the next one.
Jim Moss – Dallas, TX

. . . .

If you are looking for a good book to read try, *Attila & the Battle Cruiser* by Peter Chestnut. It is a naval fiction story with the ships cat Attila being the hero. It is on a par with naval fiction by Charles D. Taylor and David Poyer. I highly recommend it.
Scott W. Jetter - Illinois

. . . .

Refreshingly different, intriguing, full of action. All told, a great read
Kevin Los Angeles

. . . .

It is a book I have to get. Peter and I share more than a Christian name, a love of Sir Winston and the sea stories of WWII. Not for the evil, but for the good qualities that surface between worthy adversaries doing their duty...a notion that later generations seem to have filtered from their value set. Fortunately, my father, and his three brothers all returned safely from their duty.
Peter Ware

. . . .

I liked the character development and, of course, the premise. Attila & the Battle Cruiser is a fine alternate history story based on the naval battles between Great Britain and Germany circa 1941. It is an excellent example of the cat and mouse games played by warships hunting each other at sea.
I hope this is the beginning of a long line of alternate history stories for you.
D. Carlson, Fire Control Technician (Guns) Rank FTG2, USN

Sea Fox with Attila

The North Atlantic
April 1941

Scharnhorst smartly elevated her gleaming, brass-tipped 5.9 inch guns and slowly tracked the plodding merchant marine oil tanker that lay silhouetted just at visibilities edge; 5,000 meters to the west and waited. The wait was not to be very long. Captain Peter Kastanien gently, but with an ingrained firm conviction, spoke the single, simple word that carried an almost certain death sentence.

"Fire."

The great battleship heeled slightly as four projectiles belched from the gracefully tapered 5.9 inch barrels. *Scharnhorst* had three of these secondary 5.9 inch batteries, but Captain Kastanien had opted to use only two batteries as he was prudently parsimonious with his ammunition. He had learned from tough experience that a battleship that ran out of her deadly missiles went from being the feared hunter to a toothless target for the enemy.

Then for an instant, the cordite and smoke from the port twin double-turrets partially blinded *Scharnhorst*. In less than two seconds the stinging, pungent stench of the strong charges that had hurled the twenty-five kilogram explosive shells was swept away.

On the bridge anxious eyes snapped the huge Zeiss binoculars upwards—glued them into their eye sockets and waited. The wait was short, as was the first shot from the forward 5.9 inch turret. But the second shell slammed like a small, sleek meteorite right into the heart of the rolling tanker. A second later the aft 5.9 inch turret's first shell also came up a bit shy. The aft's number two shell clipped the foredeck and plunged into the inky black sea before exploding and creating a violent water volcano reminiscent of a miniature Vesuvius.

The huge glass eyes that seemed physically attached to *Scharnhorst's* watchers stared. The tanker's midsection seemed to puff up a little in size and caught fire. The blast seemed surrealistic in the darkened twilight. Then the minor shock wave hit the *Scharnhorst* like a tiny tap from a rubber hammer. Just seconds before the brilliant flash of the fireball, the almost invisible dim lights of another ship was spotted by the uncannily sharp eyes of the lookout on the bridge tower towards the northeast. The shape was very faint—only a slightly darker black against the night sky.

Being at a fairly long distance, he could not make out exactly what sort of ship it was. Just that there was a dim light and shape where there wouldn't be any if the ocean was empty of human incurrence. Then the slight concussion hit him and he was short of breath for several seconds. When his breath returned, lookout Heinz Alder immediately called the bridge and reported to First Officer Herman Gott. *Scharnhorst's* captain was at once informed. Captain Kastanien instantly called the radar room.

"Mr. Molter. Do you *'see'* any other ships on your machine?"

"Yes Sir. I have just this minute picked up a very tiny blip that could be a ship or a surfaced submarine. I will inform you as soon as I can ascertain a better idea of what we have here."

"Thank you Molter. I want the information as soon as you can make a better estimation."

Kastanien replaced the intercom and pondered for a brief moment.

"It could be another ship in convoy," Captain Kastanien spoke aloud to no one in particular but the bridge officers knew that he was thinking hard and did not want any opinions at this time.

"And then again in these northern waters, far from the normal convoy routes, maybe a horse of a different breed."

Captain Kastanien then turned his gaze back to the burning merchant ship.

"She doesn't seem to be slowed down much and the fire is small. Let us wait a few more moments. Close up to 3,000 meters," Kastanien said with his normal quiet authority.

With almost twenty knots superior speed *Scharnhorst* closed the now four kilometer gap in only six minutes. The merchant was still plodding along, her speed apparently hampered only slightly. The fire was nearly out. The *Scharnhorst* was now slightly ahead of the merchant ship on her starboard side sliding by fairly quickly.

"Open fire with the aft eleven-inch turret when ready. One volley only," Kastanien ordered.

The long, very long barrels of "C" turret, affectionately called Caesar in all German Navy capitol ships, made only slight adjustments as they had been routinely tracking the vessel all the while. In mere seconds three nearly 400 kilogram shells blasted from the rear of the ship. At only 3,000 meters, it was virtually point blank range for the incredibly accurate gunnery of the gun crews headed by Gunnery Officer Erwin Rost.

The first shell slammed into the merchant just a few centimeters above the waterline and exploded in the boiler room. Shells two and three slammed into the deck just aft of the bridge structure and the innards of the merchant ship blew into the darkened sky like Chinese fireworks.

The mortally stricken ship immediately lost steerageway and promptly slowed to a stop. With alarming speed the huge gaping hole at the waterline flooded the ship. Within three minutes she was listing to starboard over fifteen degrees. Kastanien then turned away from the doomed ship; faced his First Officer Gott and snapped a quick order.

"Change course to oh-four-five and let us close the gap on our new-found friend before she gets too far away for our radar to track in the night. Speed twenty-four knots. We will shadow her until dawn and then see what we shall have for breakfast. We will hold station with her when we are twenty kilometers behind. Make sure that we also stay five kilometers off her starboard beam. We do not want to run into any nasty mines that they might be dropping off to deter us from our destiny."

The orders were rapidly repeated and the mammoth battleship heeled into a sharp starboard turn then settled into the light cross-sea at twenty-four knots. The burning tanker illuminated the darkened, restless sea enough for *Scharnhorst's* new night vision rangefinders to determine the prey's course to be east-northeast. When Kastanien was obviously finished giving orders, First Officer Hermann Gott informed him that the radar operator had just confirmed that the vessel was well on the radar screen and on a heading of fifty degrees with a speed of about twelve knots. Kastanien called the radar room and received further confirmation that the ship was on a heading of fifty degrees and ponderously plodding along at about twelve knots. He requested to know what the distance was but the radar operator apologized for not having accurate information yet. The radar operator promised he would inform him the instant that he knew. After a minute or two of deliberate calculation the radar room called back that the ship was thirty-two kilometers distant. The night vision rangefinders had also estimated this same distance a few seconds before.

"Steer course oh-five-oh. Maintain full ahead until we are in the proper position, twenty kilometers behind her. Again make very sure that we are five kilometers off her starboard side. Then hold that position until further orders. Secure from battle stations and do not darken ship. Repeat DO NOT darken ship. I want our friend up ahead to know that we are here," Captain Kastanien ordered. Then, glancing towards Executive Officer Schmidt he said, "Mr. Schmidt, you have the ship. I will be in my cabin shortly. If anything about this vessel's actions strikes you as rather unexpected or odd, fetch me at once."

"Yes Captain," replied the executive officer in an almost revered tone to the hero that Kastanien was to him. Then Captain Kastanien turned and strode towards the passageway that led to his cabin.

"Second Officer Mueller. Please fetch Attila from his battle station and bring him to my cabin," Kastanien quietly asked his second officer.

Kastanien's orders were always delivered in a tone more like a request than a military order. However, not a single crew member ever thought his standard, gentle way of command was a sign of weakness. Rather, they revered him for his humanity and unwavering respect for all the officers and crew members alike.

There had been one—and only one—time that an officer had not taken the captain's quiet command seriously and was much too slow to implement the order. After several minutes, Kastanien's green eyes had blazed white-hot fire and the public reprimand became a legend throughout the German High Seas Fleet within days. The crew of the *Scharnhorst*, of course, knew of the chastisement instantly. They had muttered in small groups about how they should treat the offending officer. Not a single crew member of the ship's compliment of 1,669 had the slightest shred of sympathy for the officer. Their dilemma was solved when the ship's gossip mechanism repeated with uncanny accuracy and without the normal embellishment (neither negative nor positive) a quiet conversation between the captain and the offender on the bridge.

The captain had simply told the offending officer that he was now a trifle suspect to his fellow officers and crew, therefore it would be best for him to carry out all future orders given by superiors efficiently, expeditiously and—most importantly—without question. The officer instantly became the role model for all his fellow officers; especially the newer ones who had not previously served with Kastanien. The gossip surrounding the incident withered and died like a summer flower when the first frost came. But it was never forgotten by anyone and from that day forth when the soft-spoken captain issued an order, there was never a quizzical look or even an errant thought of questioning his judgment.

"Right away Sir," Mueller replied.

"Begging the Captain's pardon Sir, but what about survivors?" First Officer Herman Gott asked as the captain passed close by. Kastanien stopped and turned to the officers on the bridge, a knowing smile traversing his face.

"Fret not, my gallant officers. U-3200X has been our constant companion for the past few hours and she will pick them up quite smartly," Captain Kastanien patiently explained his apparent lack of gallantry on the high seas to all the bridge officers.

The *Scharnhorst* along with her sister ship *Gneisenau* were grudgingly respected by the British Royal Navy for their adherence to this unwritten gentleman's code of sea ethics. *Scharnhorst* and *Gneisenau* had put their ships in great peril more than once by virtually stopping in mid-ocean. Not only a very dangerous thing to do but not quite totally forbidden by the Kriegsmarine High Command either. *Scharnhorst* and *Gneisenau* were unflagging in their efforts to rescue all possible survivors. The captains of these two magnificent battleships were of a common mind in that war was fought by men with machines but after the battle had been decided loss of life should cease.

Then Kastanien turned and vanished into the dim passageway. It was only a few steps to the cabin but it seemed to be a different world as he silently entered his darkened cabin then turned on a light. The room was large by any naval standards and quite nicely appointed. Adolph Hitler had demanded that his new navy would be the envy of the entire world. So, all of Germany's newest major warships were the fastest in their class, with clean graceful lines and almost classical interior outfitting for the captain's quarters. The walls of Kastanien's quarters were satin-finished walnut with burled cherry wood wainscoting.

A highly-polished rich mahogany oval conference table complete with comfortable leather chairs stood proudly in the centre of the room. Off to the right side of the conference table a matching mahogany captain's desk faced a huge map of the North Atlantic. Kastanien's desk was clear of any clutter except for a leather-fringed green desk blotter. To the left of the entry door was a bunk trimmed in beautifully polished matching cherry wood. Behind the head of the bunk (which in itself was quite large for a naval officer's resting spot) was a rather spacious closet to hold all the various uniforms that a high ranking captain of the German Navy required for shore duty whether in home ports or foreign. At the foot of the bunk was a three-tiered shelving unit spanning the entire width of the bunk also made of highly polished cherry wood.

On the upper shelf was a glass case containing a beautiful Leica camera with a small brass plaque stating that it was number three of a limited edition of only sixty ever made. The middle shelf displayed detailed models of Kastanien's first ship and his last command—the *Emden,* a WWI armored cruiser. The lower shelf was the tallest of the three with five silver matching framed photographs securely fastened to keep them in place when the going got a bit rough. The center photo was of Kastanien's family taken in front of the Reichstag slightly more than two years ago when Kastanien had been summoned to Berlin to receive his commission as captain of the new *Scharnhorst.* Broad grins filled the four faces of his wife Andrea and his three children—Erik, Katrina and Patricia. Kastanien himself looked rather dour.

He explained later to everyone that he was now the captain of a majestic warship and did not deem it fitting to look like a vacationer with an attendant silly grin. That brought on a raucous bout of laughter from all. The celebration afterwards at a spectacular and very expensive restaurant was a different matter altogether. There he was very outgoing and enchanted the entire establishment; patrons and staff alike. For his gregariousness he was rewarded by the restaurant's manager trading him their wondrous meal for his autograph on a precious eight by ten inch glossy print of the *Scharnhorst* he had purchased a few weeks previously.

Kastanien delighted in signing his name for the very first time as captain of the *Scharnhorst.* Every time he reclined on the bunk and looked at this picture, his chest felt a warm and electric pride surge through it.

On the immediate left of the center photo was one of him and the lovely Andrea. Invariably he would let his mind recall beautiful memories of their life together. Occasionally the recollections brought up some of the difficult times but they rapidly dissipated to be replaced by more pleasant thoughts. Unlike a lot of husbands, Kastanien never forgot their anniversary. He regretted very much that he would not be able to hold her in his arms in a few weeks on their twentieth anniversary. The second photo on the left was of his son Erik with an almost impossible huge grin casually leaning against the fuselage of his *Messerschmitt* BF109. In the upper left corner directly under the cockpit were two small French Tricolor flags and two Union Jacks. Four kills so far. One more and he would be an Ace.

A brilliant war record for an eighteen-year-old boy who would turn nineteen in but a few days. Kastanien knew that with the fall of France last year, his son would now be up against a much more worthy adversary in the British *Spitfire* with their very talented and superbly well-trained pilots when the air war restarted in earnest very soon. But then again, he already had downed two *Spitfires* so his fatherly apprehension was reduced somewhat. On the right of center were individual portraits of his two daughters that he had taken in his home studio.

They were two very beautiful girls and their lovely features were further enhanced by his artistic combination of soft diffuse window-daylight for backlighting and reflected fill-in lighting from his studio lamps.

Adjacent to the bunk and its shelving were more matching cherry wood shelves that contained the serious books of warfare along with his map cases and navigational instruments. Adorning the middle of the three shelves was a stunning two-meter long wooden model of his beloved *Scharnhorst*. The model had been made by his lifelong friend Johann Bach. When Bach had learned of his friend's new commission, he immediately cajoled one of his navy buddies out of detailed exterior drawings of the wondrous battleship and began his labor of love.

Johann had suffered the loss of his right leg from the knee down courtesy of a British Maxim machine gun at the horrific battle of the Somme in WWI. With such a restricting injury he could not serve in any combat zone so after working a desk job for a rather sour Wehrmacht colonel during the day, he came home in the evening and made models. Widowed a few years early, he hadn't remarried so model building became his total passion. His models were exquisite with their painstaking attention to even the smallest detail.

The *Scharnhorst* model he had presented to his friend Peter Kastanien was considered by his many admirers to be his best work to date. This model was truly a work of love and passion that even his few detractors could not find any fault with. Behind the model was a rather large porthole. When the sun shone in striking the glistening paint and metal, the model was transformed into a radiating ethereal piece of art that seemed to breathe a life of its own.

Rounding out the comfortable room beside the wall map was an almost hidden door to his private bathroom. Even this bathroom was above and beyond what anyone would expect on a warship. There was everything a man needed but a bathtub. And, most important, it was not crowded but spacious enough to enjoy one's daily ablutions. The only minor irritation was that it took quite a bit of time for the hot water to reach the shower as Kastanien had learned with a disagreeable shock his first time to use it.

Kastanien doffed his highly-polished boots and placed them neatly by the bunk. He then removed his cap and jacket, carefully hanging them on carved cherry wood coat-hangers in the open closet as he proceeded to lie down on the bunk. He was propped up by three pillows that the steward had left when he was tidying up a few hours ago.

There came a light knock on the door.

"Come in," was Kastanien's immediate response. The door opened and Second Officer Mueller, with Attila cradled in his arm, crossed the short distance to the captain's bunk and gently passed him to Kastanien.

"Thank you Mueller for bringing me my friend and our good luck charm. I shall consult with him then chart our future actions accordingly."

Kastanien then winked at Mueller and bade him goodnight. Just as Mueller was reaching for the cabin door Kastanien quietly ordered, "Officer Mueller, go to the radio room and bring me all the outgoing and incoming transmissions from our latest sinking plus any messages to and from the mystery ship we are following."

"Right away, Captain."

Attila immediately curled up on the captain's chest and began to purr. The cat tucked his front paws under his chest but kept the back feet spread slightly askance to maintain a steady platform in the up and down, back and forth slight corkscrewing of the ship. This was common practice for the feline who also strode throughout the ship with his legs spread a bit further apart than any normal *land-bound* cat. Kastanien and the crew quickly came to characterize this slightly different gait as feline *sea-legs.*

"Ah, Attila' your little purr motor is as sweet a sound as our ship's great engines. Let us both close our eyes for a few precious minutes to contemplate tonight and tomorrow morning's actions," Kastanien softly whispered in his cat's ear.

Attila silently acknowledged the captain's quiet voice with a twitch of his head continuing to vibrate on his human's chest. Peter Kastanien closed his eyes but not his mind. Attila slowly let his eyes close and continued to purr with the total contentment that only a cat can have.

Attila was an anomaly in the German Navy. As far as anyone knew, he was the only cat that sailed with a warship from any nation. The entire crew, even those who didn't like cats, had come to adore Attila. And like all felines, Attila basked in the adoration—garnishing every advantage possible from it. To a man, the crew knew that this cat was the good luck charm that had brought them such phenomenal success and had—more importantly—kept them out of harm's way many times. They put Kastanien's unorthodox strategies and brilliant tactics in second place. Needless to say no one had ever uttered this universal belief to the captain. However, Peter Kastanien simply knew (as all great captains knew) the pulse and inner thoughts of their crews.

When he first realized that he took second place to Attila, he smiled a satisfied smile to himself and carried on without divulging even the slightest hint that he was aware of his lowered status.

Just then, the dull throbbing from the great engines dropped to an almost silent whisper as *Scharnhorst,* reaching her position behind the unknown vessel had slowed to match the lumbering twelve-knot speed of her possible, nay probable, next prey. At this slow speed the roll of the battleship noticeably increased as she now puttered on heading slightly off-straight-on into a rolling sea with widely spaced two-meter swells.

The *Scharnhorst* and her virtually identical sister ship *Gneisenau* had triple screws driven by twelve boilers generating 151,893 horsepower. With their very sleek design the two ships were capable of thirty-two knots when their incredibly powerful engine rooms went to battle speed. Full speed was twenty-eight knots, which was faster than all but a few capitol ships of the British Royal Navy. When *Scharnhorst* went to battle speed her thirty-two knot speed exceeded all of the Royal Navies battleships except the *Hood.* And the much older *Hood* could only barely match this high speed when pressed to the maximum.

*   *   *   *   *

The Hood *was the pride of the British Royal Navy.* Hood *was launched in 1918 at the then monstrous displacement of 47,430 tons. When* she was officially commissioned in 1920 she held the distinction of being the largest warship in the world. Not only was she the biggest warship but she was believed to be one of the most beautiful ships ever built as a weapon of war. This icon of the British Empire made a ten-month tour of the world in the early twenties visiting many of the far-flung British possessions and dominions as well as the United States.

Accompanied by the battle cruiser Repulse and several escorts this grand tour was purportedly nothing more than a goodwill gesture of support but it also made very certain that the world knew the British Royal Navy was still the undisputed king of the high seas.

She sported (eight) fifteen-inch guns that could hurl a 1,900 pound shell over twenty miles with reasonable accuracy and packed one tremendous wallop to even heavily armored enemy battleships. Hood's additional armament consisted of (twelve) five-and-a-half inch, (four) four-inch guns and (six) twenty-one inch torpedo tubes. The sloped armor belt (which was a major upgrade to prevent a repeat of the heavy losses suffered at Jutland) added needed protection and enhanced the graceful lines.

The additional weight of the armor created a bit of bother in a heavy sea when she was at speed. She sat a trifle too low in the water and was predisposed to plough through the waves rather ungracefully.

Her worst weakness was her deck armor, which was a mere three inches thick—woefully inadequate protection for the magazines. She was modernized twice—once in 1929 and again early in 1939. These modernizations did little to reduce the weight problem and a third modernization was scheduled for later in 1939 with the sole purpose of reducing redundant weight. The latter was never done as the war broke out too soon and every British warship was immediately pressed into action.

* * * * *

Kastanien gently stroked the perfectly relaxed cat while his mind methodically mulled over the events of the day.

The Admiralty, London
A fortnight earlier.

The Right Honorable Ian McLeod, First Lord of the Admiralty, stood at the end of the beautiful ancient conference table.

The table was at least two centuries old but had very little battle damage considering the innumerable times it had been used by the very, very senior members of the Royal Navy. The table was made of prime heartwood oak from the legendary Sherwood Forest and in the subdued lighting of a late spring day, the deep polish of lemon oil and beeswax that had been applied almost every week for 200 years made the beautifully grained wood seem to glow with a life of its own.

Those who had entered the room for the first time felt that the ghosts of the many lords and admirals who had made momentous decisions here still lived on. The table was twenty feet long and six feet wide which easily accommodated the eight chairs on each side and one—sometimes two—on each end. The two and a half inch thick planks were cleverly fastened together and matched so perfectly that most newcomers to the room at first glance thought that it was a single slice of a majestic tree that had brought forth this grand wonder. Because of its length and depth there were none of the more modern style leaves that to a purist would have simply ruined the subtle grace of such a stately piece of elegant furniture and history.

The edging of the table was gracefully carved to a near perfect rendition of a large hemp hawser—a perfect finishing touch that did not distract from the grandeur of the 120 square foot top. The very substantial weight of the tabletop was supported by six equally sturdy pedestals. The pedestals had been intricately carved by several old retired sailors who had a penchant for carving when they were in the service. Although the pedestals were generally carved the same, the central bulbous globe on each depicted different naval scenes. The three foot height of each pedestal ended in bronze lion's paws quite literally the exact size of the real thing.

The chairs matched the table perfectly with the luster only countless polishing with lemon oil and beeswax can attain. But the deep maroon leather held in place by shining brass octagonal studs did seem a trifle past what courteous gentry would call shopworn. Many a comment had been made over the decades since the leather had been new. The derogatory comments had mostly been made by first time newcomers to this most sacred room of all in the British Admiralty. These newcomers were universally pompous what with their newly acquired exalted status. But it did not take but a brief few minutes after they uttered their almost sacrilegious comments for the wrath of King Neptune in the guise of the more senior longstanding guests of the room to castigate and properly put these unweaned *pups* in their place.

Now, one must keep in mind that precious few of these so-called *pups* who had entered the room over the many years had been under the age of fifty and all had served many long, arduous years with the Royal Navy; thereby earning the right to be here. However, derisive comments were simply not tolerated by anyone.

The room itself was on the second floor of the Admiralty building which was located on Whitehall. The building was begun in the mid-19th Century but required a major design change at the turn of the century to create much more office space to accommodate the needed expansion of personnel that would deal with the threat of the rapidly expanding navy of the German Empire.

A red brick building with white stone trimming in a classical Queen Anne style, it is located but a few short blocks from number Ten Downing Street—the residence of the current Prime Minister—Winston Spencer Churchill. Churchill himself had served as First Lord of the Admiralty during the First World War and held the post for most of the years between the wars until recently when King George VI had requested he assume the role of Prime Minister.

The walls stretched up a massive fourteen feet and were also made from the same beautiful oak that the table was. They did not have the deep glow of the table since they were waxed but once a year and dusted down a few times in between. The walls on both sides of the central table were beautifully proportioned into five panels each. Each of the panels stood out from the blank wall with half-rounded two-inch wide deep, rich mahogany accent furring strips. Inside the vertical center panels on each side, which stretched from three feet off the floor a full eight feet up, hung two beautiful oil portraits—one of His Royal Majesty King George VI, and on the opposite wall—Lord Viscount Horatio Nelson.

Nelson was one of the few *pups* who had been a first-timer here when he had barely turned forty. Nelson had the good fortune to have become a member of the elite when the leather on the chairs had just been replaced a few months earlier. The remaining eight panels were horizontal and contained spectacular oil paintings of classic historical sailing warships of the Royal Navy. Two paintings of Nelson's flagship HMS *Victory,* with guns blazing away at Trafalgar, bracketed his portrait.

All of the paintings were comfortably ensconced in ornate and very intricate Victorian-era gold frames. The British Admiralty, like most navy personnel from maritime nations worldwide, still had the romance of sail in their blood and although they were proud of their steel leviathans; tall-masted ships invoked the most nostalgia.

Beneath the oils on both sides of the room were two matching sideboards made from the richest, deepest-toned British Honduran mahogany. On each of these four sideboards a rather mixed bag of a dozen or more silver platters silently awaited their calling. Each held a different style and size of exquisite, spotlessly clean Waterford crystal glasses and goblets. At first glance the non-uniformity of the silver platters seemed rather out of place in such an orderly, august setting, but when one started reading the swirling engraved messages each contained, it became blatantly obvious how precious and thought-provoking these historical treasures truly were. All had obviously been lovingly cared for and brilliantly polished to a mirror finish for untold decades.

The styles had changed little considering that some dated back to the mid-18th Century when the room was new. The largest of the platters was fully three feet long and two wide. Needless to say this was the centerpiece. It depicted the monumental battle that saved the world at Trafalgar. Although used rarely and only on special joyous occasions, the secret innards of the sideboards contained a complete serving set for twelve of the finest Royal Albert English bone china.

At the far end of the room behind where Ian McLeod stood were two almost-medieval windows that provided a soft and subdued light. The windows, along with the great conference table, had been removed from the Old Admiralty building and reinstalled at this new complex. Tradition was very long and as strong as Sheffield steel in the Royal Navy—so it was never questioned in anyone's thoughts that so much of the old should grace the new. The top brass in the Royal Navy (to a man) all felt in their heart of hearts that the mixture of old and new gave solid credence to the timeless strength of the Royal Navy.

The old Admiralty building had quite willingly given up its cherished memories of these nostalgic treasures to let them begin a new life in a new building.

The windows were hinged and opened outward to occasionally give the room some quite questionably fresh London air. The light was not all that bright today as the gloomy gray skies that perpetually came to London at this time of the year cut short much of the sun's brilliance. Then the rather poor light began to fade somewhat as the sun began its daily descent. Most of the quite old, rather small, panes of glass were not very clear so the view of the outside world through them was a trifle distorted. The lead metal frames that held these three inch by five inch panes showed many, many battle scars; testimony to the countless times the glass had been replaced over the many decades.

The newest panes that were less than thirty years old were of a much clearer glass and a few of them were actually at a height that made viewing through them much easier to see the storied courtyard below and a minute portion of the great city of London—stretching further on into the distance until the vision was swallowed up by smoke, fog and whatever the air over London possessed at any time. Even on the clearest days, which were notably few these days, the vista seemed endless.

The First Lord of the Admiralty was not gazing out the window. He was leaning heavily on the table supported by his hands which were balled up into tight fists. His head was bowed to the horizontal and his shoulders had a definite droop to them. It was almost like the he was being crushed by the weight of the endless bad news that came his way—what with the war going rather poorly for his side. The First Lord was fighting off waves of helplessness and despair. He had been appointed by Churchill nearly a year and a half ago when his lifetime friend Winston had taken the supreme office in the land. His was no appointment lightly given to a close boyhood chum. Ian McLeod was a razor sharp thinker and had a well-deserved reputation for his uncanny ability to pull rabbits out of a hat—seemingly at will.

Churchill considered the man to be a leader who would not shrink or fade under the intense pressure that he knew, even back then, that would be shortly forthcoming. Churchill also felt that McLeod's post during the First World War as Deputy Minister of Defense would be invaluable. It was a giant plus for McLeod that he had also served several non-elected posts in the governments between the wars and was well-armored with incredibly thick skin to fend off the incessant peacock political posturing of those he was bound, of necessity, to deal with on a daily basis.

He had called today's meeting of the senior heads from all the military branches to come up with a solution to the deteriorating situation in the North Atlantic. The sinking's were gravely affecting incoming critical supplies to keep England afloat as the last holdout in Europe free of German occupation. His inner emotions were so varied and tumultuous that they simply would not focus on a single solution. These roiling emotions would never show in public view in the slightest, nor would even his closest relatives and friends even suspect that he had tremulous moments of indecision fueled by fear of failure. He was well born of a prominent political family—raised sternly in the nasty art of politics.

His tenure at Sandhurst had solidified and polished this dynamic man's rather outstanding raw character into the classic epitome of a polished political leader that carried on regardless; seemingly without pause or reflection. This physically unimpressive sixty-one year old was exactly what King and country needed now. McLeod knew that an awful lot was expected of him with much of it going to have to be conjured up with a magic wand to succeed.

Shortly after his appointment, Churchill had warned McLeod of the childish bickering that went on between the services. It was up to him to convince these schoolboys to put aside their petty posturing in order to be unified for the defeat of the Germans. Churchill, after this private pep talk with McLeod, sensed more so than noting any outward signs, added a postscript to his order with a knowing smirk on his classic rotund face.

"Ian, please remember always that the only real enemy is the Germans. The others are simply figments of their own very overactive egotistical imaginations."

McLeod instantly grasped the cryptic witticism and suddenly laughed rather loudly which caught Churchill off guard. Then Churchill chimed in with his own laughter as the two old friends shook hands all the while laughing heartily as they parted company.

That meeting many months ago, and especially the parting words, had never been forgotten by McLeod. He knew deep down in the private inner sanctum of his soul that today would see something of a resolution. He prayed it would be the correct one. First Lord McLeod had suffered through countless meetings with each of the participants who were about to arrive and had listened with the patience of a saint to excuse after excuse why the battles were going badly. He had called this special assemblage of all the heads of every military branch in what he considered a Herculean effort to attain a cohesive plan of defense and hopefully counter attack.

The First Lord of the Admiralty Ian McLeod suddenly threw off the yoke that had bowed him then stood as erect as a telegraph pole. With a slight shrug and a shake—akin to a lion on awakening—McLeod walked briskly over to the portrait of Nelson and stared up at it for a long moment. He then rounded the table standing before the newer portrait of his beloved King George VI for the same amount of time. Being as McLeod was a regular churchgoer it would be no surprise that his silent thoughts were a beseeching prayer for help and guidance from the Almighty.

Turning sharply, he then returned to the recently departed head of the table and, standing ramrod stiff, stared down the length of the room. Then slowly in a quiet voice tinged with Sheffield steel, he uttered the two words that had for untold thousands of his ancestral English warriors been their altar of strength and bulldog determination.

"Hold fast." Then again Ian McLeod repeated the phase with the volume notched up a bit. "HOLD FAST."

McLeod repeated the two-word phase several more times, each being louder and stronger than the previous until virtually shouting the words of defiance. The tall, delicate Waterford crystal-fluted champagne glasses actually reverberated with a rather pleasant resonance. The high-pitched singing from the stemware registered on Ian McLeod and he glanced over to the sideboard where the glasses were and a slightly askew knowing smile grew slowly on his face.

The controlled outburst and the pleasant response from the silent sentinels brought McLeod back from a reverie. After a brief second's pause he strolled down the starboard side of the table and approached the control panel tucked unobtrusively in a small enclave. The light from outside had been the only source of illumination since he had entered the room a short quarter-hour earlier. But now it was rapidly diminishing as a dark, gloomy, rain-laden overcast arrived. Ian McLeod flipped a couple of switches and the brass-framed sconces made from gracefully carved satin glass came to life. He then flipped one more switch and the three spectacular Irish crystal chandeliers, suspended over the long table, burst forth with a dazzling brilliance equaled only by South African diamonds.

The lighting quite simply brought a life to everything in the room including the First Lord, who perked up noticeably, as an intense pensive look came over his countenance.

McLeod strode back to the head of the table. If there had been witnesses to his demeanor, they would have sworn to Almighty God that they could hear the gears turning beneath his slightly balding iron-gray hair. Then McLeod glanced up at the clock quietly moving inexorably to the hour for the meeting he had called. He noted that only three minutes remained before the room would be host to the five most senior officers in the British Armed Forces. The Minister had prayed and beseeched Almighty God, King George and Lord Nelson that the senior officers would work out a plan that had a chance, however slim, of success.

McLeod strode purposefully back down the port side of the table and opened the door. Leaving the door open he walked tall, very purposely about a hundred feet, and down a wide staircase to the comfortable waiting area on the first floor. The waiting area was also irreverently referred to as the holding tank. Waiting patiently stood the famous five officers. They gave but a cursory glance toward the First Lord and continued to engage in what appeared to be quite amiable chit-chat. After a brief pause to assimilate this rather unexpected scene; Ian McLeod simply announced in his best politician's voice.

"Gentlemen, please come upstairs and let us begin." The five, as one, turned smartly, mounted the twenty-two steps and marched into the room without jockeying for position.

Placards had been placed in front of the five seats at the furthest end of the table near where McLeod had been standing only a few brief moments earlier. The placards were used for virtually every meeting simply to prevent any conflict regarding rank or stature that could easily be perceived by personages of high rank. All five of the men had been here before and understood the gut-wrenching mental ordeal that the seemingly simple act of placing these cards entailed. Everyone in the room had done it themselves. It never got easier.

In calmer times before the war some of these gentlemen had attended a state dinner or two at Buckingham Palace and had chuckled amongst themselves that to lay out *those* placards would be nigh onto impossible to get it correct to meet the King's approval. With not a second thought about whether they warranted their own position at the table, the five high ranking officers promptly seated themselves without uttering a sound.

First Lord of the Admiralty Ian McLeod did not sit down. Rather he launched into what appeared to be an impromptu short but stern speech. Deep frown lines were emphasized with his very deliberate pronunciation.

"Gentlemen, I have called this meeting on very short notice and rather late in the day because Winston is *demanding* some *immediate* action in the war at sea. When I came from him only three hours ago, he gave me that look and very strongly told me to get the troops together to hash out a plan. As some of you are aware our losses in merchant ships has not only reached unacceptable levels but has of late dramatically passed that benchmark."

The assembled brass sat silently as McLeod strongly strode the few paces to the right of the windows and pressed a discreetly placed button. The quiet whirring of electric motors commenced as the heavy maroon drapes that were housed in recessed alcoves began to close thus shutting off the outside world. Slight clouds of dust puffed from the heavy velvet drapes and refracted in the rather weak light beams streaming through the windows.

None of the assembled men had ever been in the room when the drapes were closed. It was an unwritten very old protocol that the windows remain open to the world of inner city London at all times. The protocol was so ancient that no one knew what had prompted it in the first place. However, the thought of changing it never even entered the minds of those who passed through.

By the time the drapes were closed, McLeod had moved to a covered, rather substantial, easel to the left of the now draped windows. With a flourish akin to a magician's cape he lifted the covering gray muslin sheet up and over the back of the board without saying another word. Then he stood off to the side of the board to let its contents sink in. The razor-sharp quick minds of the men read the numbers instantly as they simultaneously inhaled an incredulous gasp. Before anyone could utter a word McLeod resumed his narrative.

"As you can see, the situation is rather grim. The Germans are sinking our merchants at more than double the rate we can build them. And that is including the *Lend Lease* ships that President Roosevelt is sending over for us. Our main culprits are the U-boats of which the enemy has plenty of. Their few surface ships are sinking an alarming number of our merchants as well. I probably need not bring up the fact that the Germans will have twice as many surface ships loose very soon and their U-boat production is at least four times that which we are sinking. In short gentlemen, at the present rate, the time is rapidly approaching when we will simply be unable to carry on. You might wonder why the Air Force, the Marines, the Army and the Coast Guard have been summoned along with the Navy for what is obviously a naval matter.

"Well, very bluntly put, the Royal Navy has not been able to produce the results we need and I need a solution *immediately*. Preferably a week ago. You fine officers know strategy and tactics far better than I. Therefore I entreat all of you to openly discuss any strategy or tactics to rid the Atlantic of these extremely dire threats. I ask the Navy, specifically First Sea Lord Robert Stark, to please have patience with your peers. They may not have the answers but hopefully a strategy will come about when such diverse battle tactics are aired. Gentlemen, you know what the goal is. Please proceed."

"Ian, might I start the discussions?" Air Marshal Dowding quietly addressed the First Lord of the Admiralty while looking casually around at the gathered Brass.

"Yes, by all means, let us dig in," First Lord of the Admiralty Ian McLeod replied, grateful that somebody other than the Navy had apparently got the gist of his little speech.

"Let me address the issue with their surface ships first. From the appalling numbers on the board, it is apparent that their two *light* battleships have done an incredible amount of damage in a very short period of time. The essential problem is our lack of intelligence on the whereabouts of *Scharnhorst* and *Gneisenau*. The Luftwaffe's *Condors* can find our convoys, bomb them and at the same time radio back to Kriegsmarine headquarters their position. Once notified, *Scharnhorst* and *Gneisenau* can simply close the gaps with their high speed and have a field day with the merchants as well as our cruiser and destroyer escorts."

The Brass in Whitehall had lost a lot of hair trying to figure out a more effective way to stop the *Condors*. It was imperative that England's war machine deprived the Germans of the shipping intelligence that was costing them such terrible losses of ships. These very ships were bringing in the desperately needed supplies to keep Britain from starvation whilst being able to continue on very much alone in the war.

The long range German four-engine bomber that had been built mainly as a reconnaissance spotter for the surface ships as well as the U-boats had become a very dangerous, deadly and oftentimes fatal weapon.

* * * * *

The Folke-Wulf Fw200 *had started its career in 1937 when it went into service as a long range passenger transport. It was a low wing, all metal aircraft with four nine-cylinder BMW-Bramo 323 R-2 supercharged radial engines that delivered 1,200 horsepower each. Initially a passenger airliner, it immediately grabbed headlines in 1937 when it set numerous records for non-stop flights from Berlin to New York, Brazil and the Far East. The Japanese, who in 1937 were heavily engaged in a serious war effort with China, saw the potential of this superb airplane as a military weapon and, forthwith, ordered a bomber version.*

The Luftwaffe upon hearing of this application ordered a military version for themselves. The first one, designated Fw200C, *was delivered to* Kampfgeschwader 40 *in April of 1940. Once the Luftwaffe saw the huge plane that they now had in the flesh, they immediately called it the* Condor. *With a wingspan of 108 feet and a relatively decent top speed of 360 km/h, it truly resembled a very large bird gently coasting along in the sky. When France fell two very short months later, the* Condor *units were transferred to France where they could cover an enormous area out over the North Atlantic.*

By the late fall of 1940 nearly three dozen Condors *were operating from various airfields in Western France. These great birds of the Luftwaffe could carry more than two tons of bombs and cruise up to an altitude of nearly 20,000 feet lazily coasting aloft for more than fourteen hours covering an amazing 3,560 kilometers or more. The toll on British shipping from their bombing alone was approaching 300,000 tons after barely nine months of operations. Their main duty of spotting and radioing in co-ordinates to Kriegsmarine HQ was even more devastating to merchant marine ships.*

With a convoy pinpointed plus the smoke from some of the burning ships, the U-boats and surface raiders had no difficulty finding what remained of the convoy. After racing to the remains of the convoy and dispatching the cripples and any unlucky vessels that crossed their paths, the German Navy was slowly but inexorably diminishing England's ability to carry on. An angry Churchill soon dubbed the lumbering giant the Scourge of the Atlantic—*and rightfully so.*

The Royal Air Force, under strong and implicit orders from 10 Downing Street, began raids on the airfields in Western France in an effort to convert the Scourge of the Atlantic *into scrap metal. The Royal Air Force had tried bombing the bases but these bases were mostly positioned at the farthest reach of the* Handley Page Halifax *and* Lancaster *long range four-engined bombers. Stretching the bombers to reach the home of the* Condors *proved far too costly in terms of crews and planes which were irretrievably lost over occupied France. The RAF also tried to patrol the skies out near where they knew the* Condors *operated in hopes of catching them shortly after they left France in the early morning. But again the RAF was frustrated by empty skies. Most of the* Spitfires *and* Hurricanes *returned home still full of ammunition.*

The Condor's *success was no big secret or arcane strategy. The big planes simply took off from their partially hidden airfields in Western France south of Brest and North of St. Nazaire and then flew at treetop and wave top heights until they were far beyond the range of any of the British fighters. Then they ascended to observing height and began reporting to Kriegsmarine Headquarters. The simplicity of the* Condor's *magic act was apparently beyond the complex thinking, normally associated with all High Commands.*

*   *   *   *   *

"So, what is *your* brilliant strategy for combating this menace?" The First Sea Lord Robert Stark snapped back with a minor irritation in his slightly elevated voice. Stark instantly regretted his unseemly sarcastic remark when Dowding looked him square in the eyes. Stark's facial expression registered his sincere regret as Dowding went on.

"Gentlemen, I have a two-part plan to eliminate this menace; if I may be permitted to outline this plan without any unnecessary interruptions," Dowding replied softly and evenly with only a slight trace of patronizing irritation on the last few words.

Both men now realized that the score was even for the out-of-character remarks they had both made. All subterranean tension evaporated.

"Very well then, none of us have had any brilliance in the past few months to solve our problems. So let us listen to the Air Ministry and hope that Air Marshal Dowding can give us a direction to take," Ian McLeod sadly commented.

The others also breathed a silent relief that this trite verbal exchange had not escalated into something that would be very counterproductive.

"Thank you for your forbearance First Sea Lord," Dowding replied without even the slightest hint of rancor.

"Gentlemen, I must first ask the Admiralty what the status of our warships in the North Atlantic is versus the Germans," Dowding said, looking directly towards the First Sea Lord Robert Stark.

Without preamble but with normal British courtesy, Stark launched into the status of the Royal Navies warships in the North Atlantic.

"We have a battle group composing of two battleships—*Hood* and *Repulse*—the aircraft carrier *Ark Royal* and seven escort cruisers and destroyers sailing to the Denmark Strait to wait for *Bismarck* and *Prince Eugen*, whose sailing is imminent. Our intelligence reports that they will probably head for this exit into the North Atlantic. With the unusual heavy fog in the Norwegian Sea we have not been able to confirm their whereabouts for over thirty-six hours. So *Bismarck* and *Prince Eugen* could easily have sailed and are headed in that direction or now hugging the east coast of Iceland to get into the open ocean earlier. In addition we have the battle group headed by the battleships *Invincible* and *Renown* cruising off the west coast of the Shetland Islands for the same purpose.

"There is a battle group forming in Scapa Flow to sail shortly to be assigned southward to patrol the sea west of Ireland. This battle group is headed up by *King George V* along with the heavy cruisers *Berwick* and *Cornwall*. They will be accompanied by five destroyers and will work the sea to the southwest of Ireland hopefully maybe getting a crack at *Scharnhorst* and *Gneisenau* as well as protecting the convoys from U-boats and those blasted *Condors*. *Scharnhorst* and *Gneisenau* simply must run into one of these groups soon. Our newest battleship *Prince of Wales* along with the older battleship *Nelson* and the heavy cruiser *Cumberland* accompanied by a half dozen destroyers are cruising the approaches to Gibraltar and thus the Mediterranean to keep shipping flowing to Malta and North Africa in the fray." Stark finished with a flourish trying to gain the confidence of the assembled big brass that it was virtually imminent that *Scharnhorst* and *Gneisenau* would be found and then dispensed with shortly."

Dowding rose and slowly strode over to a very large map of the North Atlantic on the side of the room. The map was nearly eight feet square supported by two rather substantial tripods. Dowding paused a few seconds, then slowly turning, affixed his cold gray steely eyes on Stark and let his intense gaze linger a second or two on each of the gathered men. After his attention-getting pause, Dowding began a dialogue while rapidly scanning over the small group.

"Might I remind all of you that *Scharnhorst* and *Gneisenau* have been at sea for nearly six weeks and have been sighted only by their victims? Then they disappear. Yes gentlemen—disappear. The North Atlantic is a very large body of water that has a rather nasty disposition quite a lot of the time, especially now in early April. Fog and storms make aerial reconnaissance from our aircraft carrier *Ark Royal* difficult at best and surface spotting damn near impossible. Also we know that the *Ugly Sisters* have a penchant for operating in the vast expanse known as *Torpedo Alley* where we simply cannot reach with our land-based aerial reconnaissance. So, at this juncture, we must assume that they are either very, very lucky or have some magic wand that makes them invisible.

"Each time, and I believe there are at least ten occasions, when *Scharnhorst* and *Gneisenau* have raided our convoys that we have gotten a solid fix about where they are. We then immediately dispatch the nearest battle group to the area where we anticipate them to be upon our arrival but they are never where we think they should be. We have had destroyers shadow them during the night with no luck whatsoever, except abominably bad."

It was not lost on any of the men how Dowding had used the plural "we" as though he was part of the Admiralty. However, they all kept silent about this and slowly realized that the Air Marshal was doing his damn level best to blur the lines of rivalry between the services for the good of England.

Stark, unable to countenance the direction the monologue was headed in, literally jumped up out of his chair with obvious agitation and with a barely controlled rage to his voice, broke in and began a defense of the British Royal Navy.

"For the Air Minister to say that we have had 'bad luck' is about as understated a comment as I have ever heard. Air Minister Dowding, the facts are as follows. The *Ugly Sisters* have been pinpointed not ten but fifteen times by merchants in convoy or by themselves. Sometimes we have had destroyers and light cruisers as escorts. During these fifteen encounters we have lost two light cruisers and eight destroyers which I might add we can ill afford to lose if we are to maintain a decent escort service for the convoys.

"The *Sisters* also sank forty-six sorely needed merchants during these incidents. The destroyers we dispatched from the convoys to shadow them at night were either summarily blown out of the water by their nasty little eleven-inch popguns or they just simply outran us during the night. Once they were out of range of our radar they change course and simply disappear for a few days. On four occasions we have dispatched two battle groups on both sides of the destroyers who doggedly kept following on the last heading even long after we lost radar contact. These groups steamed at top speed and should have easily sighted the *Sisters* at first light, or shortly after, but to no avail. It seems inconceivable that they doubled back without our destroyers even getting a glimpse of them. But we have to assume that this is what must have happened.

"Also, if we assume they slow down to a more fuel-conserving speed of twenty to twenty-four knots, there is no way that they could have escaped our spotting them. The simple logistics are quite irrefutable when we and our commanders-at-sea do the plotting of every range they could possibly reach from the last radar contact we have. Yet empty-handed every time and it is agonizing beyond frustration."

Stark finished the last few sentences with a noticeable catch in his voice. His shoulders slouched forward. Then he simply quietly sat down. Dowding and the others were quiet for a moment while they felt the pain that this brilliant and normally energetic optimist was going through. The summation of the naval losses without the Royal Navy even getting a single shot now really sunk in to the assemblage and a palpable pall of doom permeated the room. Dowding was also equally moved by the delivery of these facts but not being a party, until now, of the strategy and tactics to get rid of these voracious predators he snapped out of the universal stupor that had all the men in its grip. With a slight clearing of his throat began again but in a lower softer tone until these men of action shook off the mood.

"Without criticizing our fleet commanders or anyone here at the Admiralty, let me ask a question or two."

At that moment, the door burst open and Churchill strode in. All conversation and most breathing stopped instantly.

"Gentlemen, as I happened to be passing by, I thought a bit of liquid cheer would make for better co-operation between the services; especially at this late hour. I have always believed that a man with a warming liquid coursing through his veins thinks more brilliantly."

With that pronouncement Churchill reached under his bulky overcoat, produced a bottle of his favorite brandy before setting it on the nearest sideboard that was well-equipped with glasses for occasions such as this.

"Now. I shall leave you to your deliberations and solutions. Please keep in mind who the real enemy is and that the essential arithmetic is to rid the Atlantic of German predators or we shall face starvation or even worse—capitulation. Have a drink to invigorate your spirits and clear your minds. Put your animosities in the water closet then bring me a plan that has a high degree of success in reaching our goals."

In an even stronger timbre to his normally commanding voice, Churchill with his eyes piercing into the men stated flatly, "The plan needs to be sooner, much sooner, rather than later." Churchill dropped this verbal bomb on the silent men as he casually strolled out of the room.

The U3200X

The black, uncaring North Atlantic allowed only one tiny belch of oily air from the tanker that now plowed its one-way trip to the perpetual Stygian darkness 9,000 feet below. Her name was *Gay Lily* out of Southampton, but that is just a footnote in passing. She had the dubious distinction of being the forty-seventh vessel that the rampaging *Scharnhorst* and *Gneisenau* had sent on this irreversible last voyage. Few of the skeleton crew had little time to jump overboard where the ice-cold sea would claim them in less than twenty minutes. The *Gay Lily* took seventeen trapped souls to the eternal liquid darkness, while eight oil-soaked merchant marine sailors clung precariously to bits of flotsam hoping for a miracle. The oil fire was almost burned out while the eight lucky survivors pondered what it would be like to die of hypothermia in total darkness. The despair was frightening beyond any they had ever known. The mind-paralyzing fear accelerated by the second.

Abruptly, the sea boiled like an overheated teakettle slightly over two hundred yards due south of their small, huddled group. Then, even in the darkened sea, they saw the shiny prow of a U-boat poking through the surface of the sea slowly surfacing. Brief moments later a brilliant spotlight searched the sea. Very shortly the light fell upon the bobbing sailors clinging to the wreckage. It quickly locked on the seamen. Then a voice came from what was now an invisible source.

"Attention, sailors! Hold on, stay together, and we will pick you up in a few moments. If any of you have weapons on your person please be kind enough to allow them to join your ship in Davey Jones locker," the deep bass voice of Captain Gordon Wittrock, with a slight Teutonic accent to his Oxford English, rumbled across the short distance clearly and distinctly. The eight souls, who had let their minds and bodies accept the grim reality of their hopeless plight, snatched life and hope back from the grave. As one they let out a mighty cheer.

"Ahoy mates. Tighten up on me if you can. Let none even any dead be left behind. The saints, albeit in a strange form, have come to our rescue," the strong bass voice of the giant kitchen worker sang out. He had the good fortune to be on the stern dumping garbage when the ship had been hit.

The U3200X's inflatable dingy quickly closed the short gap and the bedraggled survivors were plucked out of the frigid black rolling sea with typical German dispatch. Two of the survivors had minor burns and a third a broken arm when he had been brutally slammed into a railing. The rather grimy crew of the late *Gay Lily* was quickly undressed, soaped and scrubbed down to remove the nasty, skin-burning oil that coated most of them. The three injured men were cleaned up first, and then taken to the tiny sick bay where they were administered to by the submarine's incredibly young medical attendant.

Real doctors were a luxury that few U-boats had simply because of limited space and limited needs. The Admiralties of most nations assumed that if there were serious injuries on board a submarine requiring a certified doctor, the boat was probably doomed and sinking anyway.

Those land-bound veterans had concluded that submarine doctors were a needless waste of precious talent deemed necessary in the many other theatres of this war.

The remaining English sailors in their clean new German clothes were summarily locked in the aft torpedo room with a guard outside occasionally peering through the small heavy glass inspection port. They did not intend to create mischief, as that was not their instructions from Rear Admiral Hunter.

Rather, Hunter had explicitly made it painfully clear—that if they survived and were picked up by the enemy—they were to be model captives, keeping their eyes and ears open until they garnered the information the British Admiralty desperately sought. After they had learned what they could, they were to attempt an escape, but only if it had a relatively high chance of success.

Chief Petty Officer McKevern was contemplating their fate now that the survivors were securely locked in the entrails of the submarine. No one had spoken for nearly half an hour since they were incarcerated. They all knew that they had lost a great many of their shipmates, including the captain and the first mate. The silence was a tribute to these brave men who knowingly had been willing to sacrifice their lives so that the Admiralty could ascertain the methods and technology the Germans were using to successfully avoid their Navy and the Royal Air Force.

McKevern was a small bull of a man in his prime. He stood a mere five-foot-five inches but tipped the scales at a hefty 220 pounds—not an ounce of it superfluous fat. His head was as bald as the proverbial billiard ball and just about as round. When one looked in his eyes, one could not help but ascertain that a very sharp brain lay nestled behind the bushy-black, beetling eyebrows that had not a speck of gray in them. He also sported a beard that was a perfect match in color and fullness to his eyebrows.

Coupled with his ruddy red complexion, he was a man that you instantly had a lot of respect for; not without a small amount of trepidation. Despite this fearsome countenance, John Peter McKevern was a rather gentle soul and a favorite of all his shipmates. Being the only surviving officer, he had thought for some time about his lost shipmates and the purpose that had landed them here. With a subdued, raspy and very Scottish accent, he broke the silence.

"Men, we all know why we are here. I wish that the captain and the first mate had lived to take my place as your leader. But God did not will it that way. So, be that as it may, I shall assume command of our little group. Seaman Johnston along with two others are in their sick bay but should be returned to us rather shortly since their injuries did not seem too severe. In case the Germans divide us up, I first want to remind everyone again of the orders given to us by the Admiralty. We are to be rather mild prisoners but not too complacent and co-operative as to raise their suspicions. This will not be a hardship on our senses since the Germans consider us to be only ordinary merchant marine sailors. The Admiralty is deeply concerned and rightfully so all the way down to their socks about the Germans ability to elude our magnificent Royal Navy.

"*Scharnhorst* and *Gneisenau* have been the worst scourge on the High Seas since the French Navy gave us so much grief a bit more than a hundred years ago. However, Lord Viscount Horatio Nelson made rather short work of that nasty, thankfully incompetent, lot at Trafalgar."

With the mention of Nelson, the most revered hero of the Royal Navy, the small group of rather downhearted looking sailors once again fell silent. Every Englishman knew the decisive victory Nelson had won for England against numerically superior forces whose purpose was to invade and conquer England for the glory of the megalomaniac—Napoleon. Now, for better or worse, the French were under the heel of the Nazis. Everyone in England knew that this time the threat was even more real especially with the eternal pessimists who knew for certain that the German invasion was imminent. Many English harbored thoughts but did not voice them outside of their closest and similar-minded friends that Hitler and his gang of cronies was the best thing that had happened to the French. These pundits of doom and gloom had a good laugh whenever the subject of the inept French came up. They failed to bring up what would happen to England if she were invaded and subdued. They secretly hoped that the Germans would be benevolent occupiers, as they seemed to be in Denmark—if the worst happened.

After a hanging silence of several minutes McKevern coughed a little and continued, "Men, besides hoping that we can get out of this little spot of bother, our mission must succeed if England is to survive."

McKevern's strong emphasis on the last word imparted to the very heart and soul of the entire small group how important the task ahead was.

"I, for one, do not believe that the Admiralty held back any scrap—no matter how sensitive or trivial it may have been—when they briefed us on the facts of the very bad way the Battle of the Atlantic has been going since the war began. We simply must, repeat MUST, find out their tactics, strategy, weapons and or technology that they're using to achieve the rather one-sided results. *Scharnhorst* and *Gneisenau* are averaging a sinking rate of a nearly ship a day. That means that many hundreds of thousands of tons of critically needed materials and foodstuffs are simply not getting to England. On top of that, they commandeer as many vessels as they can— which means supplies are going to the incorrect place. Moreover, that's not counting the many other ships with their attendant tonnage that their U-boats, pocket battleships and surface raiders are sinking or commandeering as well. It is imperative that this fearsome toll be stopped or at least drastically reduced."

McKevern stopped and let the impact of his little speech sink in before continuing.

"As most of you probably know the French Navy has been interned in French Vichy ports on the Mediterranean and now, for the foreseeable future, will be of no use to us in this hunt. The Americans are escorting the convoys only so far out into the Atlantic from North American ports before their neutrality forces them to turn back. This leaves a very long way through hostile waters for the convoys. Considering our present situation there is a bright spot."

At that pronouncement the men visibly perked up as McKevern went on.

"We do know that on many, many, nay every occasion of a sinking by *Scharnhorst* and/or *Gneisenau* they have always released any survivors of merchant ships. They do not release naval officers or enlisted sailors. We assume that they are taken to P.O.W. camps. So that's the reasoning behind the Admiralties decision to deliberately send us ordinary seamen in harm's way. They are hoping that survivors will be picked up and released. If we can glean any scrap of intelligence, no matter how trivial it may seem, that can lead our fleet to any of their ships, it will prove not only invaluable but of critical importance.

"*Scharnhorst* and *Gneisenau* have always released their captured merchant sailors either in an open boat when they know for sure that they will be picked up rather shortly or at a neutral port if they happen by one. All of the survivors that the Admiralty has interviewed, when returned to England, have unequivocally stated that they were treated with the utmost respect considering they were for all purposes prisoners of war. They also stated that when they were set adrift, if you like, they had ample provisions, proper clothing and protection from the elements. So whatever we may think of the political powers that be in Berlin, let us be grateful that the German Navy seems to be a right honorable bunch."

Then with a light-hearted deep laughter McKevern blurted out, "However, we really don't know how the captain and crew of this metal sausage will treat us. And speaking irreverently of our current mode of travel, did any of you get the impression that this U-boat seemed a tad bit larger than what we were told to look for?"

A crewman with the interesting English name of Fred Fryefish was first to speak up. Fred was a giant bear of a man but despite his size, he was as gentle as a lamb in both actions and voice. Standing six-foot four weighing close to 275 pounds, Fred was a natural to be in charge of the engine room where his size and brawn—which was virtually all muscle—counted for a lot. With his quick and sharp intelligence, working hand in glove with his enormous strength, there was no problem that the cantankerous old machinery in his recently departed vessel that could stump him. Virtually nothing stopped him from making it almost better than new in no time at all.

"Aye Chief, I got a right grand view of her as I was the furthest away when she surfaced and my impression was that she is nearly twice as long as and much fatter than any of the photos the Admiralty showed us. She also has a rounded nose much like a bomb's front end versus the normal sharp prow. The deck was completely clear of any deck gun or railing. Yet there seemed to be some sort of rather long streamlined bulge on the deck behind the conning tower. And the conning tower was rather small in size but quite tall and very sleek in design."

"Well, that's quite an important observation Fred, and I know the Admiralty will treat this information very seriously. Is there anything more you can add?"

Before Fred could reply, the wiry little mechanic, Walter that was Fred's assistant engineer—piped up in a tweedy voice that had a very pronounced Soho accent.

"My mate's spot on with his observations but maybe he didn't see the windlass just forward of the whales' humpback. As I was a mite closer and off to his right a few yards, I got me a corker of a view as well. The light from the searchlight kind of glittered off the stuff and there seemed to be a mechanism with a crank and cable going into the humpback."

"Well now, we seem to have a glimmer of what might just be the Germans' secret weapon. Can anyone venture a guess as to what it might be?" Chief Petty Officer McKevern inquired.

The group fell silent and a couple of the men scratched their heads but nothing came forth for a few minutes until the deep voice of chief engineer Fryefish boomed out again, "Maybe it's a new type of radar device that they raise when they are on the surface that gives them a longer range to see us coming from a far ways off before they can duck down under leaving us none the wiser as to their presence. Perhaps just before they submerge they pop off a quick message in code to *Scharnhorst* and *Gneisenau*."

"Ah, a pretty damn good guess Fred. Now it's truly of vital importance that we get this critical information to the Admiralty."

Mere seconds after Chief Petty Officer McKevern uttered his last sentence, the hatch to their little prison opened and crewman Johnston along with the two others stepped inside. The hatch was again closed and dogged down immediately after the three English men were clear of it. Curiosity took over instantly as chief petty officer McKevern was the first to speak.

"Well now Johnston, you look rather fit except for your arm being in a cast. Please tell us what you have been up to as a guest of our captors."

"Be gosh and begore, Chief, they were a right decent lot. The doctor and his helper, or whatever they are, checked out me arm with gentle care so as not to cause me too much pain and decided that it was broke. Then they gave me a shot of something to ease the pain. After a few minutes one of them grasped the break on each side and popped it back into its rightful place. I'm guessing that without the painkiller I would have swooned dead away but I held fast. Then one after the other they felt around and seemed satisfied that it had snapped back right as rain. Then they looked at me with big grins and said something in their own gibberish. Then they fixed me up with this cast and said 'Gut, sehr gut.' I'm thinking that they were very satisfied with the result and here I am almost as good as new. Do any of you blokes have a clue as to what I'm supposed to do now with this arm?"

Just like it was a stage prompt, all the men instantly sported big grins and spoke all at once, thus rendering any coherent questions null and void. None of the men seemed like they were going to reduce the volume of their questioning until Chief Engineer Fryefish boomed out again characteristically like a Middle Age eighteen-pounder naval cannon."

"Shut your blithering mouths lads and let's get all our questions answered in a civilized and orderly manner. Chief Petty Officer McKevern is in charge here and he gets first go at you."

"Thank you Fred for stilling this motley bunch. My, my, that's some voice you have when even slightly provoked. Now Johnston you say that they treated you right nice and seemed pretty competent. Would you please tell us more about what they were like? How they treated you and most importantly what you saw?"

Scharnhorst

Captain Peter Kastanien still lay reclined on his bunk letting his mind go over the events of the day trying to sort out the circumstances to come up with a plan of action.

Earlier that afternoon the *Condor* had radioed that there were merchant ships to his northwest heading northeast. There did not seem to be many ships or any escort destroyers. Odd on all three counts? The ships were north of the normal beaten paths of the England bound convoys. Odd indeed? Why? Were the English trying a new route or convoy system to avoid his small battle group and the U-boats? Had the ships been separated from a regular convoy because of the bad storm yesterday? On the other hand, maybe the British had cooked up something else entirely?

Then there was the nagging question of why the ship would not stop when it was so obvious that resistance was futile and there could be no doubt of the outcome in what would be a lop-sided battle. But Kastanien partially reasoned that maybe they did not want the precious cargo to fall into German hands. Still, the thoughts persisted.

Kastanien had studied many, many accounts of British Naval tactics over the past two hundred years and concluded that the English mindset was unique. Worst of all for Germany, a few of their commanders could be very creative and unorthodox. He always recalled the seemingly foolhardy tactics of Nelson, especially at Trafalgar. Now that was a battle to be remembered for hundreds of years. Kastanien still marveled at the audacity of Nelson to drive his battleships straight into the combined fleet of France and Spain which decisively outnumbered and outgunned him. But then he would analyze the way the battle had gone and marveled at the result of such seemingly suicidal actions. Peter Kastanien secretly had an almost hero worship of Lord Viscount Horatio Nelson and many a time had to stifle a tear when he thought about the tragic death of this most memorable of naval captains. To die in battle is probably the best way to meet one's maker for a warrior. But to die slowly from a French sharpshooter's bullet positioned high in the rigging just didn't seem to be a proper ending for such a great man. He also realized that on most occasions when he was in command and facing the enemy, he would ponder to himself, *"What would Nelson have done?"*

Speaking softly out loud in a mere whisper to himself, Kastanien went on, "Have I been too reckless again by chasing these anomalies because I was bored with the lack of action for a few days? Attila, what do you think? Have I stretched my luck? Will there be a very nasty surprise tomorrow at dawn? Or will we be able to chalk up another ship or two?" Kastanien whispered in the cat's ear.

Attila raised his head, rotated it slowly to his beloved Peter gazing straight into Kastanien's now open eyes. Kastanien's bright green eyes met the solid gaze of the big Siamese's sky blue, crystal clear orbs. They stared at each other in total silence for several seconds. Attila rubbed his slightly cool and damp nose against Kastanien's cheek and beard. The two old friends nuzzled each other in the cat fashion of love and affection for a pleasant few moments. Then Attila uttered a deep rumbling noise from his chest as he shifted his gaze to the large map of the North Atlantic on the wall behind the desk. Kastanien followed the cat's gaze noting that he was staring at a point due north of where they were currently.

After a few seconds of map gazing the two friends again locked eyes. Kastanien's brain went into overdrive and he suddenly realized what all the odd things about today added up to.

"Thank you again my friend. You have once more given me the answer to my vexing questions."

Kastanien stroked the cat as it resettled into its resting position and closed its eyes. Kastanien did the opposite. He rose up slightly, repositioning the hefty, very solid eighteen pound cat in the pillows thus not really disturbing Attila and gazed at the map again. Continuing to softly speak aloud, Kastanien rose slowly from the bunk. Attila did the cat thing with a slight muttered protest before settling back into a languid semi-curled up position, almost instantly resuming his catnap. Speaking softly out loud to the room he announced, "Yes, I do believe that the Admiralty in London has set a trap for this fox by guiding *Scharnhorst* into a chicken coop where the hungry and impatient British lion awaits."

At that moment came a soft knock on the cabin door.

"Come," was the immediate reply from the captain.

The door opened and Second Officer Mueller entered.

"Here are all of the radio reports from both ships. I have separated them into individual groups and sorted them by time of transmission. The earliest times are on top."

"Thank you Mister Mueller, you may return to your duties."

Kastanien stepped to his desk and sat down. He turned on a simple reading lamp then began reading the messages. He read each stack through once before re-reading and then matching up the two sets of transmissions into chronological order, all the while talking softly to himself. He then rose quickly striding over to the map. Kastanien continued his thinking aloud but not loud enough for the crew to think he was talking to himself.

Unknown to the captain, the crew knew all about the quiet one-sided conversations that went on in his cabin. They knew absolutely that he was brilliant when he and Attila took a few quiet hours together. Silently Kastanien then did a recap of the war so far, mainly to refresh himself about the true role that he and his limited battle group were assigned to carry out. Kastanien once again continued speaking softly out loud. Although he was a proud man his considerable ego was not the monstrous vainglorious ego that clouded his thinking like so many of his peers in every branch of the military of every nation. Rather, he always focused on the strategy necessary to achieve results.

"The English know that they have to stop us sinking their convoys or starve. That is the main mission of the Imperial German Navy—starve the English by denying them materials of war and food stuffs into surrender. The Battle of Britain, directed by Air Marshal Göring, failed to bring the English to their knees so our Führer turned to Dönitz and our Navy giving us much more support than we ever had. Hitler had made it very plain to Dönitz that it was up to him to stop supplies from reaching England. For the English to accomplish their goal they must stop the sinking's by eliminating the cause—our U-boats, our surface warships and our raiders. They know that they have an eight to one surface warship advantage over us, but they have to find and engage us first before they can do any serious damage. Since they have not been able to hunt but a few of us down so far, they are probably attempting to lead us into a trap where their superior force will surely prevail. They probably also know that my character, with its record of impulsive actions, would make it irresistible for me to turn aside such easy targets as they have conveniently provided.

"Therefore they send a few older merchant ships with skeleton crews as bait. They plot a course right at the edge of *Condor* reconnaissance, hopefully preventing being bombed, knowing full well that we would be notified and plunge right into the supposed easy prey. Moreover, they timed it right so we would be led out of *Condor* protective range by dawn and then their Royal Navy would greet us. We know that a large battle group has been waiting for *Bismarck's* group to enter the North Atlantic via the Denmark Strait, and another group is stationed east of Iceland for the same purpose. The Iceland battle group will have had time to steam into the area that we are being led into. Is that their plan of battle?

"But then they still have a fairly large reserve group in Scapa Flow or have they sailed and are on their way to be my welcoming committee? Well we shall let this fox lead them on a merry chase."

Picking up the intercom to the bridge Kastanien spoke into the black funnel, "Mister Gott. How far ahead is that ship and what speed?"

"Twenty kilometers and twelve knots. We are holding station with her," Gott replied immediately.

"Very well Mr. Gott. Reduce speed to ten knots and slowly drop back. Observe what she does and report to me immediately if there is any change," Kastanien ordered.

"Yes, Captain," was the simple reply from the First Officer.

"Attila. Let us rest our eyes for a few precious minutes before any action begins."

Kastanien settled in the leather chair by the desk, put on his boots, then again in a whisper began talking to his beloved cat.

"Attila, we have seen much in our three years together and our actions have made us a legend amongst our crew and the entire Kriegsmarine. I'm sure that you remember your last remarkable service to the Fatherland and our great ship."

Kastanien's mind traveled back to the dock in Brest when *Scharnhorst* had returned from a cruise a couple of months ago in late winter. On the third night, tied up to the dock, an alert sentry on the pier heard a slightly unusual splash near the stern of the ship. After investigating for several minutes and not finding anything untoward, he was about to return to his post when another splash occurred—preceded by a few squeaking noises. This time his senses being attuned to any strange noise directed him to the rear hawser that held the huge ship against the bollards. Turning his powerful flashlight down into the water he immediately spotted a rat desperately attempting to swim to a pier. Rats, although they can swim, only venture into water if there is no other option.

The sentry knowing this shone the flashlight high up the side of the ship and settled the light on the hawser. Then just off-center in the hawsehole that the huge hemp mooring rope ran through, his flashlight ignited two small red orbs that blazed back at him for a few seconds before they turned aside and blinked out. Then he made out a dark brown and dun-white cat calmly sitting astride a close-by, neatly rolled, pile of smaller hemp rope. The sentry did not know that this cat was the famous captain Kastanien's Attila. He became fascinated with the rather large feline that was strangely out of place on a warship. To alleviate the stultifying boredom of night duty, the sentry turned his flashlight off and watched the cat in the sparse lighting of the pier for several minutes. The cat seemed content to just sit there and enjoy the unusually warm, very pleasant night.

Then suddenly the cat visibly tensed and the sentry came to full alertness. The sentry concentrated his sight onto the hawser and was immediately rewarded by seeing a small dark shape quickly scurrying its way up the drooping large strand of hemp towards the ship. The sentry determined immediately that the shape was a rat and it was now only about a meter from the cat. The sentry had also noted the absence of a rat guard on the hawser and queried this break from a very old standard procedure when ships were in port. The cat remained motionless for the short period of time it took the plague of the world to close to within nine inches of his motionless face. At this close range the rat spotted the cat and with a squeak and a vicious snarl launched his attack at his mortal enemy. But against one of nature's premiere predators, the loathsome creature had absolutely no chance whatsoever as the four-legged merchant of death launched a lightning fast, deadly right hook and caught the rat solidly on the shoulder. The rat was knocked sideways, bounced off the rounded metal housing and plummeted to the oily dark water many meters below. The rodent fell loudly squeaking until it hit the oil-slicked black water gently slapping the pier and the ships side.

The sentry shone his flashlight down into the darkness and saw that the rat was still very much alive and struggling to reach the piling closest to him. Then the sentry noticed a glistening dark round object slowly moving into the area that the rodent has just recently vacated. Watching intently for several seconds he quickly surmised that this was a diver of sorts. Realizing that something was dreadfully wrong, the young sentry immediately turned and ran to his sentry box where he vigorously pounded the alarm button. Instantly a shrill siren screamed into life and the main lights of the dock came alive. The entire area was bathed in brilliant light and the ship's night watch scrambled to their intruder alert stations, grabbing their machine pistols as they ran.

The *Scharnhorst's* five high intensity searchlights snapped on only fifteen seconds after the docks, adding much more light to an already brilliant scene—nearly as bright as day. The searchlights were rotated on their mounts to extend over the ship's side and pointed down into the gap between ship and pier. Immediately two additional odd objects were spotted swimming rapidly towards the underside of the dock in a futile effort to escape detection. Machine gun fire from the ship's deck blended noisily with the rifle fire from the sentry. Less than one minute had elapsed since Attila had dispatched the rat before the combined gunfire had stilled the water-born intruders. The three corpses now floated, gently swaying to and fro with the small surges of the water.

Two minutes later a squad of soldiers started a small motor launch moored just behind the stern of *Scharnhorst* and rapidly reached the floating bodies. The three corpses were hauled into the small boat. Then using their own powerful searchlight they spent nearly ten minutes searching the area for signs of further possible saboteurs. None were found. The boat went back to its mooring and unloaded the three bodies onto a waiting truck manned by soldiers in the ominous black uniforms of the SS. The truck left immediately for SS headquarters which was only a mere two blocks away.

After about fifteen minutes, the small boat, being relieved of its nasty cargo, returned to the stern of the battleship with four divers from *Scharnhorst*. Two divers quickly entered the inky black water, turned on their underwater torches and descended.

For nearly an hour the divers moved around the stern, changing their depth with each pass. The diver's first priority was to inspect the paired twin rudders, the triple screws and the general area where the shafts exited the hull. The screws were three-bladed and four-and-a-half meters in diameter. They were made of brass that had taken on a fine patina of discoloration and a relatively thin layer of silt evenly distributed on all of their surfaces since resting for a few days in the polluted confines of the harbor.

The screws were never totally stopped. It had been learned many decades past that even the incredibly strong steel in the shafts would sag a trifle due to their massive weight if left in one position for any length of time. So, like all very large ships with gargantuan drive shafts, the *Scharnhorst's* screws were constantly turning a leisurely seven turns per hour.

This minor degradation of the clean brass meant that it would have been easy to place dirty—looking destructive charges with a better chance of going unnoticed when *Scharnhorst* readied for sea again. The divers spent many long minutes thoroughly inspecting each one. Finding nothing out of order they surfaced. Handing over their torches and other assorted paraphernalia, the now shivering first pair of divers clambered into the boat and stripped off their wet suits. Immediately when they were shed of all the wet clothing, heavy blankets were draped around them to stave off hypothermia. The other two divers also spent an hour re-inspecting the screws, rudders and stern area. Satisfied there was nothing wrong, they surfaced and the first two divers replaced them and began the laborious job of inspecting the entire hull. The *Scharnhorst* had a draft of about eight meters and a length of 235 meters so there was a very large amount of hull to inspect. After two one-hour stints each, the divers were exhausted and the work boat returned to its mooring.

Four hours had now elapsed since the intruders had been first sighted, and the sun well over the horizon. The danger was greatly diminished as the saboteurs were sure to have set any charges to detonate during the night. When the sun rose more above the horizon, with the daylight full, two more fresh teams of divers arrived and began where the night divers left off. The new teams consisted of three divers each. The first team into the water dropped to the bottom which was only six meters beneath the bottom of the hull and began a methodical grid search of the bottom. The bottom was a filthy mess of debris and garbage. The divers were very careful not to let their fins, air hose or any part of their equipment touch the silt. Even the slightest disturbance would create a cloud that would make close inspection impossible for hours.

Luck was with the first team. They found six limpet mines within a small area directly under the screws. These saucer shaped devices packed an enormous explosive punch, and judging where they were found, it was quickly surmised that their target had either been the screws or the rudders. Gently removing them from the silt, they gathered them up and surfaced. The mines were handed to the sailors then handed off again to the shore patrol that had come up in a second boat. The divers went back down to further their search and the second boat headed for shore to dispense with their deadly cargo. Upon reaching the shore the sailors handed the mines over to the omnipresent SS soldiers. The SS men took the mines to a nearby table and thoroughly inspected them. To no one's real surprise, and relief, the timers had never been activated.

The entire day was spent by several dive teams inspecting the great ship and the bottom of the harbor but no more odious weapons of destruction were found. The relentless efficiency of the SS quickly turned up a non-descript decrepit-looking Fiat truck with a tattered tarpaulin cover that had seen much better days. The truck was so sad and forlorn looking, it obviously had been the transport that the saboteurs had used in their attempt to cripple the *Scharnhorst*. Since none of the saboteurs had any identification on them or in the truck, it was assumed they were either British or French commandos working with the French Resistance. What was of great interest were the devices attached to the diver's backs. They seemed to be self-contained underwater breathing units. Very interesting.

The SS officer in charge immediately realized the enormous potential for sabotage that this new concept presented. He rushed to SS headquarters with the important find and burst into the commandant's office without being properly announced. The commandant was seated behind his desk going over his normal paperwork when the junior officer cannoned into his inner sanctum.

Commandant Adolph Reinhardt bolted upright to his feet and with the potent terrifying voice of a senior SS officer barked, "Lieutenant Halder, what is the meaning of this outrageous entrance?"

"I'm very sorry Sir. But I believe what we have just discovered on the divers is of utmost importance to the Reich. I knew that you would want to know immediately."

"Very well Lieutenant, I shall be the judge of the importance. I do hope for your sake it is truly that important."

The lieutenant nodded and silently stepped outside the office door for a moment, then returned carrying a black vest festooned with tubes, valves and hoses. The lieutenant then gently placed the whole device on a utility table off to the right of the commandant's desk. Reinhardt had been closely staring at the captured equipment until it was put on the table. Then he arose quickly from his chair and in two strides was standing directly over this intriguing device. Without speaking a word for several moments, Reinhardt partially picked up the underwater breathing device and began inspecting it very closely.

Straps held a relatively large and heavy cylinder that was connected to a hose and a rather large valve. Reinhardt had a quick and very sharp mind so analyzing the basic workings of this new and intriguing piece of technology was rather simplistic for him. Once he had grasped the working concepts, his mind immediately raced forward quickly realizing the nasty applications that this would have for and against the enemy. He also considered how invaluable this could be to the Kriegsmarine, especially for repairs to ships at sea.

*   *   *   *   *

In 1941 the self-contained underwater breathing apparatus (S.C.U.B.A.) was only in its very early primitive stages of being developed by the French. Up until this time all underwater work was done with the diver's air supplied by a compressor on a ship. These divers were outfitted in heavy, very cumbersome gear which made all work and movement very slow going.

*   *   *   *   *

The junior officer stood slightly behind Reinhardt and stoically suffered the silence of his superior minute after eternal minute. The lieutenant's mind whirled at high speed pondering his fate from the commandant regarding his impertinent entry. Naturally he assumed the worst. He didn't think he'd be shot, but absolutely knew for certain that the retribution would be severe at best. After ten very studious minutes, which seemed like several lifetimes to Halder, the SS Commandant put the breathing apparatus down and turned to the lieutenant with a rather neutral stare.

"Lieutenant Halder, what do you think of this apparatus?"

Reinhardt placed his hand on the shoulder of the obviously very nervous officer, and with a rather disarming grin looked at him straight in the eyes.

"I am not going to eat you or send you to a nasty posting for your rather, shall we say, *refreshing* entrance. What you have brought me is of the utmost and quite likely of paramount importance to our Fatherland. You were absolutely correct in immediately barging into my office with it. Now, tell me what you think of it—holding nothing back. This is of far too much importance for me to stand on ceremony and assess your worthiness. You have already established that."

Lieutenant Halder could hardly believe his own hearing and was momentarily frozen in place. Reinhardt recognized the catatonic state of his junior officer and began laughing. Halder damn near fainted on the spot.

"Come now Halder. I'm not always the fearsome ogre that my staff—you included—would make me out to be. The SS is the elite of the German army and a great many of us have taken on a pompous, self-important attitude. That is not the case with me. Yes, I will uphold the strict and very high standards of our calling, but I can also be quite understanding. Now, your opinion if you please."

Halder breathed a sigh of profound relief and began his narrative.

"Commandant, this device is surely a new invention that will enable humans to go underwater without the bulky suits and very awkward diving tethers we have had to use so far. I cannot estimate to what depth the device is good for or how long the air in the tank will sustain normal breathing. I do believe that it will revolutionize underwater sabotage and repairs which can be used by all sides. That is when our scientists and engineers can develop working units for us. Without the worry of fouling the life lines and air lines we have had to use with our hard helmet underwater suits, repairs to a ship underwater will be dramatically easier, faster—and we will be able to access all parts of any ship. I hope that we can develop this new tool quickly and get it in service. Our U-boat fleet as well as our surface ships will benefit greatly."

Halder had gushed his summary out quite rapidly without taking a breath, which he did now with profound relief. Reinhardt remained silent for a few seconds and then with a very satisfied grin he began his own narrative.

"Very well put Lieutenant. You have summed it up exactly the same way I have. Now let us get this to Berlin as quickly as possible and have our scientific putterers come up with units *we* can use. I want you to personally take this to Grossadmiral Dönitz immediately. I will make the necessary calls and you will receive a first-class reception in Berlin. Before you leave tomorrow, have our photographic department takes shots from every conceivable angle and make ten sets of prints of each shot. Stress to them that the photos must be in my hands by end of day, or failing that first thing in the morning or there will be serious repercussions for them. You will take nine sets to Berlin and one set, along with the negatives will remain here with me."

Then reverting back to his more human demeanor Reinhardt finished with an almost nostalgic comment.

"You know Halder, when we look back at how all this came about, we have that ship's great Siamese cat to thank for this wondrous breakthrough. I want to meet this four-legged champion of the Reich tomorrow. You should still be here when our hero arrives and you too will get to meet him. By the way do you happen to know what this felines name is?"

"Yes Sir! Captain Kastanien named him Attila."

"Attila. That is a wondrous name and I commend the captain for his choice. Attila. Yes that is without any doubt the perfect name. Now, I really cannot wait until we meet."

Like a sudden shift in the wind, Reinhardt reverted to his businesslike command persona.

"Very well Lieutenant Halder. Take our new acquisition to my outer office and get the photographers with all their attendant gear over here immediately, if not sooner. Put a letter together for my signature granting you all the travel permissions necessary to get you to Berlin and back. While you are doing that, I will call the Luftwaffe and get you a plane assigned. On your way out please have my attaché get a call for me through to nearly as quickly as he can. Stress that it is of a most urgent and important nature. Make sure that no mention of what the call is about is brought up. Since all of the saboteurs are dead, we must keep the enemy guessing as to whether we have their new toy or not."

Switching personalities once again, Reinhardt took a step forward to Halder and extending his hand in the universal gesture of a friendly handshake, ended the conversation with a genuine simple comment.

"Well done Lieutenant and just between us, you may barge in here anytime you wish as long as the occasion merits such a grievous breech of protocol."

Halder vigorously shook the outstretched hand and the two SS officers smiled at each other. Then Halder picked up the underwater breathing device and briskly left the office of his superior heading straight to the commandant's attaché. There he relayed his travel instructions. He then procured a guard that seemingly had nothing to do and sternly ordered him to guard the equipment as though his life depended on it. With hardly a pause Halder then went to the far end of the building and informed the photo department of the commandant's order for a vitally important photo session in the outer office. The photographic staff simply blinked at the order they were given. Without a word they proceeded to gather up their lighting equipment, cameras and the entire attendant accoutrements associated with taking indoor pictures—which were considerable.

Halder then returned to the attaché's desk slowly sitting down to wait while the most necessary vital document was typed. The attaché was an older man, probably in his late forties that had no doubt served in the First World War. It was painfully obvious to Halder that the man was woefully unfamiliar with a typewriter because he was very slowly and cautiously pecking away at the keyboard. The document had to be perfect and his progress was so slow that Halder thought to himself that the war might be over before he got to Berlin.

Eventually after nearly a half hour, the old soldier scrolled the paper from the machine and with a proud flourish handed it with pride to the lieutenant. Halder then returned to the closed door of the commandant and lightly knocked. Immediately Halder heard the single word.

"Enter."

Halder marched to the front of Reinhardt's desk, saluted, and then laid the precious paper on the desk. Reinhardt read and then reread the document, very carefully appraising the wording and spelling. After a couple of minutes Reinhardt looked up and pronounced the document perfect. He then signed, put his personal stamp on it and handed the document back to Halder and spoke.

"Lieutenant Halder, this document will see you through any checkpoint you might encounter and allow you immediate access to Grossadmiral Dönitz. I have contacted the admiral's Chief of Staff and they are anxiously awaiting your arrival in Berlin. The Luftwaffe will have a Junkers Ju52/3 here tomorrow morning at 1100 hours to take you direct to Berlin. Let us hope that the photographs are ready by then. Assuming they will be ready, you will take the device which will remain here overnight along with the photographs directly to the admiral. The admiral will then probably issue you orders to return here. However, if he chooses differently, then I require you inform me through proper channels. Do you have any questions or comments at this time?"

"No Sir. Everything is in proper order and I am looking forward to this journey. However Sir, might I ask what the Grossadmiral is like so I can respond correctly?"

Again, Reinhardt let out a raucous laugh and when his composure returned he looked directly at Halder with a slight smile and gave the slightly scared Lieutenant a brief description of Grossadmiral Karl Dönitz.

"You will find the Supreme Commander of our Navy a rather stern-looking individual who stands ramrod straight and will brook no small chit-chat. He is all business with an incredibly quick and razor-sharp mind. He and I have known each other rather well since the last conflict. Since you are coming from my office you will be treated with the utmost respect. If you make any simple errors in protocol, you will find out rather bluntly. He is a forgiving man who will correct you, rightfully assuming that you will never make the same mistake again.

Other than that, you will immediately feel that this man is the perfect choice to lead our Navy. He does like cats very much and if—only if—the opportunity arises you might mention the critical part that Attila played in this chapter of our history. If he warms to the subject of Attila, you will be one of only a few officers who will see his more gentle side. But...

"Do not dwell unnecessarily on the subject. He is incredibly busy thus cannot spare much time in the more reminiscent subject of cats. Speaking of Attila, I have requested Captain Kastanien to be here in my office at 0730 hour tomorrow morning. Please be outside in the waiting area in case I require your attendance then."

The next morning after the aborted sabotage attempt on *Scharnhorst*, Commandant Reinhardt summoned the sentry (who had alerted and stopped the attack) along with Captain Kastanien to his headquarters. Kastanien didn't care much for the SS in general so to tweak their normally pompous, arrogant master-race attitudes, he showed up fifteen minutes late dressed in his very best, immaculately-tailored white dress uniform, replete with a chest full of important medals. After about an hour of going over the details of the attack and its satisfying resolution, the SS commandant rocked back in his chair and then with totally uncharacteristic charm, politely asked Kastanien to bring Attila for a social visit at his earliest convenience. After a short pause he added.

"Captain Kastanien, I do mean Attila's convenience."

The commandant, his two staffers along with the rest of the assembled men burst out into genuine laughter. Kastanien's opinion of the SS rose sharply with this totally unexpected witticism from a high ranking SS officer. Kastanien responded with a sally of his own.

"Commandant Reinhardt, I knew exactly who you meant and upon my immediate return to *Scharnhorst*, I will check with Attila regarding his ' duty schedule and then return at *his* earliest convenience."

The laughter redoubled and with much backslapping coupled with genuine handshaking, Kastanien returned to his ship. Knowing the cat's character along with his habits as best as anyone can, he proceeded to the bridge where he found Attila dozing in his favorite spot for warm sunny days. The sleek feline was spread out on a fuzzy red wool blanket that had been donated by Second Officer Mueller. The blanket lay on the shelf abutting the forward viewing glass at the left center front of the bridge. The cat could see everything that went on in the shipyard as well as checking the coming and goings of the officers in the bridge area. When Kastanien picked up the cat he smiled at the warmth the cat had acquired from the brilliant sunshine streaming through the glass. Cradling the cat on his arm, Kastanien returned to the SS office less than thirty minutes after leaving. At the reception desk manned by an older, rather dour attaché who had not been on duty at the earlier meeting, Kastanien smartly stated.

"Captain of the *Scharnhorst* and crewman Attila to see Commandant Reinhardt. He is expecting us."

The attaché looked mildly surprised, said nothing, and then stood entering the commandant's office after a perfunctory knock. Within seconds Reinhardt almost flew out the door with a grin from ear to ear.

"Come in, come in, come in," Reinhardt spoke rapidly, his speech bubbling over with unbridled enthusiasm.

Kastanien, with Attila still cradled in his left arm, entered and shook hands vigorously with the beaming SS commandant. Commandant Adolph Reinhart looked every millimeter like an SS officer should. He had a close-cropped haircut with not even the slightest hint of gray—even in his sideburns. Kastanien guessed him to be in his late thirties, maybe even forty. When Kastanien had first met Reinhardt less than two hours ago, his facial expression was completely neutral and devoid of any emotion. That was the face of the SS, Kastanien thought to himself. But now a broad grin had transformed one of these normally bloodless, robotic creatures into a most jovial, real human being. His coal-black standard SS issue uniform was the pinnacle of perfection. He, like most of the SS officers, sported only a few but important medals on his chest. Like Kastanien, he did not wear an Iron Cross medal. This medal was sparingly given out to only military personnel who had exhibited outstanding service to the Fatherland. As yet, neither man had attained this most coveted medal.

"Sit down, sit down my friends. Do you or Attila wish anything? A drink? Some food? You name it and if it can be had we will get it," the animated Reinhardt rapidly asked once again with his effervescent enthusiasm.

Kastanien sat in one of the very comfortable black-leather chairs that had replaced the drab standard issue ones earlier that morning and politely said, "Thank you Commandant Reinhardt, we are quite comfortable but a small glass of schnapps for me and a bowl of milk or water for Attila would be much appreciated."

Reinhardt picked up the intercom and ordered the attaché outside to bring the refreshments immediately. Within two minutes a lieutenant entered carrying a beautifully ornate silver platter with three elegant crystal glasses and a fine china bowl with two matching decanters—one filled with a smoky brown liquid and the other obviously filled with milk.

"Excellent Hans, close the door on your way out and ask Lieutenant Halder to join us forthwith," Reinhardt crisply responded.

Kastanien noted the slight lack of politeness to the older man which dropped his opinion of the SS a minor notch or two.

Lieutenant Halder came through the door within seconds, closing the door behind him at a gesture from Reinhardt. When the door closed with a crisp click, Reinhardt's demeanor instantly returned to its good-natured mode. After making simple. Military introductions, Reinhardt motioned for Halder to sit. The SS officer poured three glasses half full with the schnapps; then filled—almost to the brim—the exquisite china bowl with milk.

"Where would Attila prefer to drink?"

Silently Kastanien rose up slightly and Attila soundlessly dropped to the floor. Kastanien then took the bowl of milk placing it gently on the floor just to the left of his chair. Attila immediately began to lap up the delicious white liquid. Milk on board a warship was a luxury that was normally in very short supply. Attila obviously liked milk very much.

Kastanien reseated himself after stoking the cat a few times. Kastanien, Halder and Reinhardt sat silently watching, listening to the cat enjoying his treat. Then Reinhardt raised a silent toast and the three men imbibed of the rather potent fiery-tasting liqueur. After a quiet couple of minutes sipping and appreciating the traditional German liquid delicacy, Kastanien ventured forth.

"Commandant Reinhardt. Does this truly delightful schnapps come from the Oberstaltz winery just south of Cologne?"

"Why yes, it does. You have a very astute palate Captain. I am very fortunate to be able to get it here. But then again, when one's uncle owns the winery it becomes a bit easier. I can get all the French wine and liqueurs that my entire command could consume but the French make their rather lifeless liqueurs without any substance to them. I much prefer the boldness of our own German ones. Maybe the lackluster, incipient quality of French wines and liqueurs are the same traits they applied to their pathetic military."

The three men enjoyed a mirthful chuckle over that condemnation of the French military.

*   *   *   *   *

When the Wehrmacht had invaded France in May of 1940 the French Army had one million men against the German's 300,000. Against this vastly superior force, the German Blitzkrieg, (under very capable commanders such as Heinz Guderian with his armored tank divisions) had rapidly and simply—literally—ran over and around the French Army. The campaign had been so swift and decisive that a rather derisive joke rapidly circulated in Germany.

The joke was a question that even the youngest schoolboys were repeating. "How did our Wehrmacht conquer France?" The answer was. "At fifty kilometers per hour." Propaganda Minister Joseph Goebbels made sure that the English heard of this rather embarrassing joke with its attached humiliation as a prelude to the coming resumption of the Battle of Britain.

*   *   *   *   *

Leaning across the beautiful ornate cherry wood desk with his lightly-manicured hands clasped together stretched out in front, Reinhardt spoke softly.

"Well Attila, it is my distinct pleasure to meet a genuine hero of the Fatherland. I have heard stories about you and I can readily see they were understated. Your uniform is absolute perfection. I can also tell you have a blazing, brilliant intelligence behind those almost unbelievably brilliant blue eyes."

Attila had been sitting like a small Sphinx at Kastanien's side on the chair staring absently at Reinhardt since he had finished with the wondrous treat. Satisfied, with his tummy happy, Attila had gracefully leaped up beside his captain. When Reinhardt uttered his compliments toward him, Attila let out a small noise then stood up. Reinhardt glanced over to Kastanien with a questioning look.

"Would the Commandant like to hold Attila?"

"May I please? And Captain, please call me Adolph from now on, except when state duties are at hand."

"I will only address you by your given name if you return the favor by calling me Peter."

Then Kastanien leaned down to Attila whispering in his ever alert ear.

"Go on Attila, greet your newest admirer. Please Adolph sit still and let him get to know you first."

Attila effortlessly leaped onto Reinhardt's desk and strolled over to his waiting hands. He dropped his head, minutely inspecting Reinhardt's right hand all the while his moist black nose twitched, inhaling the unique odors of this particular human.

The Admiralty
London

Air Marshal Dowding composed himself after he was sure that Churchill was not popping back in with another *suggestion* and continued. Dowding then picked up a rather tired, slightly crooked pointer and slapped the rubber tip sharply on the map and invisibly drew an egg shaped circle.

"Gentlemen, *Scharnhorst* and *Gneisenau* have been operating in this general sector of late."

The pointer slowly rotated around an area due west of Ireland and the northern tip of Spain approximately extending from Latitude 32N to 58N and Longitude 18W to 55W. He then directed his pointer to a semi-circle extending westward from just south of the Brest on the French coast and went on in his controlled soft voice.

"This arc represents the furthest patrol limit of the Luftwaffe's *Condors*." Moving the pointer eastward Dowding continued.

"This arc represents the furthest our fighters can reach with any hope to take down the *Condors*. We have not had much success with this tactic since the *Condors* normally range nearly four hundred miles further out than our boys are able to reach. This smaller arc represents the effective range of our radar and as all of you can see, it covers only a small portion of the *Condors* area of operation. Our *Spitfires* and *Hurricanes* are alerted and dispatched within minutes of reports coming in of *Condor* flights leaving France. Even with a speed advantage of nearly 120 miles per hour, we only have fifteen minutes to find and engage them before petrol pressures force our return to base.

"As I pointed out earlier, our reconnaissance aircraft simply cannot reach this area and our surface ships as well as our submarines have not been able to find them. The two battle groups which you have assigned to keep *Bismarck* and *Prince Eugen* from escaping into the North Atlantic will be too far away from where *Scharnhorst* and *Gneisenau* will probably continue to operate in to have even a ghost of a chance of spotting them."

Dowding knew this was like talking to schoolchildren, and the looks on the assembled men realized they were being patronized—possible mocked. But, when Stark's body moved to protest, a stern look from the First Lord of the Admiralty stilled his actions and he flopped back into the burgundy leather chair slowly stilling his agitated external demeanor.

"*Scharnhorst* and *Gneisenau* will probably continue to operate in this area until we arrive with a sufficient naval force to generate a decisive naval engagement and be done with them both. We simply must concentrate on getting our Navy into a shooting battle with them. We have much more firepower than they do and we would surely prevail."

Dowding paused and slowly, one by one, engaged the eyes of every man at the table for a brief few seconds. Then he started again, but with a much stronger voice, filled with determination.

"Please bear with me with this seemingly non-essential line of questioning. Before I propose my plan, I must know the character and temperament of the main players. For my plan to have a reasonable chance of success, it is critical to know how the two captains think and react. I have, of course, studied the dossiers of Kastanien and Teebolt. However, I would very much appreciate confirmation from the Royal Navy, who no doubt has a far greater understanding of these two men. Please be as specific as you can with any knowledge, almost starting with the day they were born."

Dowding softly put the pointer on the table and seated himself. He thought that this concession to the Royal Navy's knowledge would somewhat soften the obvious resentment he had experienced throughout the entire meeting. Predictably, Stark stood up first and with a slight wriggle and a shrug cleared his throat, started in describing the two German Navy captains.

"I will start with Kastanien first, simply because he is the more complex, and therefore the most dangerous. He was born May twenty-fifth, 1894 in Cologne. His parents, Gertrude and Erwin are celebrating their forty-ninth wedding anniversary next year. His mother has been a housewife and mother for all these years. His father joined the Imperial German Navy quite a while before the First World War when the German Empire was building a seriously challenging naval force. During that war he attained the rank of lieutenant commander. He was awarded two medals for bravery in saving men's lives on two separate ships. When the war ended Erwin Kastanien was retired from the Navy, opened a green grocer shop in Cologne, and has been moderately successful ever since.

"Young Peter, being the oldest child helped his mother with his two younger siblings while the father was at sea. Our young captain was somewhat of an entrepreneur at a very young age. His father had told him that he could achieve anything he wanted if he applied himself to the task. At school he excelled in most subjects, especially mathematics, chemistry and physics. The young Kastanien worked in the basement workshop, where he created lawn ornaments of squirrels and rabbits, which he subsequently sold to raise pin money.

"Two years before the First World War began he joined the Imperial German Navy at age eighteen. There he served aboard several vessels bravely and inspired. He rose very quickly through the ranks and when the war ended he was captain of the light cruiser *Emden*. While the armistice was being hashed out at war's end he had the unfortunate duty of sailing his ship to Scapa Flow and then watching the proud Imperial German Navy be scuttled when the terms of that vile armistice were announced. His command, the light cruiser *Emden*, reportedly brought tears to his eyes when the scuttling charges went off and his proud ship began to settle for all eternity. We strongly believe that he holds a very strong burning resentment towards that insulting, shoddy peace treaty that eventually was put in place and enforced. Don't forget, Gentlemen, that the Imperial German Navy was second only in strength to us during this previous conflict. And that was a close second. He was fortunate to have stayed with their Navy, given the fact that it was reduced to a mere shell of its wartime size. It is believed that his good fortune was attributed to his creative thinking about naval warfare.

"He came to the attention of now Grossadmiral Dönitz in 1935 and was groomed to be an important part of the rapidly building New German Navy. When *Scharnhorst* was commissioned in 1938 he was made captain over the few remaining senior officers from the First World War's High Seas Fleet. Oddly enough, the bulk of the passed-over officers did not resent this blatant break from naval tradition. They all knew him and thought that he was the man to revolutionize naval warfare—the way that Blitzkrieg has done for their ground troops recently in Poland and France.

"His very much unexpected dash down the Atlantic over a year ago really bollixed the fatal trap we had devised for the 'pocket' battleship *Admiral Graf Spee*. As all of you are painfully aware, we had *Graf Spee* buttoned up nicely in Montevideo harbor and were ready to pulverize her after we had pressured the Uruguayan government into forcing her to leave. However, although we knew that *Scharnhorst* and *Gneisenau* had been operating off the north-east coast of Brazil we had no reason to suspect that they would suddenly charge down south steaming at top speed to arrive the same day that *Graf Spee* was to leave. It was a bad stroke of luck for us that they chose to head south at that particular time. Damnable lucky for them as a very cantankerous vicious hurricane cruised into the area that they had just unexpectedly departed. We were so damn intense on watching the mouse hole, our radar and lookouts didn't pick up the two deadly blips closing rapidly from the north.

"Consequently, when we realized it, *Scharnhorst* and *Gneisenau* were upon our four ships from the north and *Graf Spee* from the west. *Scharnhorst* and *Gneisenau* opened fire first with their damnable accurate eleven-inch guns almost immediately making serious hits. Then within minutes we were taking fire from *Graf Spee's* equally accurate eleven-inchers as well. Well, enough of this rather bad chapter in Royal Navy's history. The result of the battle was that *Graf Spee* escaped and sped back to Brest for repairs. *Scharnhorst* and *Gneisenau* broke off the engagement, presumably under orders from the Kriegsmarine High Command, specifically then Grossadmiral Raeder. Repairs to *Graf Spee* were completed rather quickly allowing her to return to the North Atlantic and continue her raiding.

"However, they had inflicted so much damage to *Ajax, Achilles, Exeter* and *Cumberland* that all four of our cruisers had to limp down to the Falklands to be made basically seaworthy before sailing over to Cape Town for extensive repairs. Thank God those two brutish *Ugly Sisters* broke off because with the German's uncannily accurate gunnery and superior firepower, we surely would have lost some, if not all those ships. Well, the upshot of the whole affair was that Hitler became furious that the engagement was called off prematurely before sinking some of our warships, he *retired* Grossadmiral Raeder and replaced him immediately with Dönitz along with Raeder's previous exalted rank of Grossadmiral and commander-in-chief of all naval operations. When *Scharnhorst* and *Gneisenau* pulled into Brest for minor repairs and refit, Hitler himself greeted the two captains."

"Enough of this rather useless history Stark, we need to know the man's character and thinking," The First Lord of the Admiralty interrupted.

"Begging my Lord's pardon, I was about to show how this *history* influenced and solidified Kastanien's mind set," Stark retorted with obvious displeasure at the interruption.

"Shortly after handing over their ships to the repair team in the shipyard for repairs to the rather insignificant damage our ships had inflicted on them, Kastanien and Teebolt were driven in an open Mercedes touring limousine to a large football stadium. Here they were guided up a rear entrance ramp onto a raised podium that had the commanding view of a stadium packed full of all branches of the German military. Slightly shocked to see the assembled throng, they were even more stunned to see Hitler himself stride over to greet them. Well, to save you the boring details, Hitler decorated the two captains along with vigorous handshakes and presented them to the crowd which instantly broke into a deafening, screaming, applauding mass of hero worshippers. The net effect on the captain's characters was to galvanize their belief that they were invincible and could do no wrong. Ergo, they probably have very powerful egos, especially Kastanien," Stark finished with a slight smirk feathered at the corner of his lips.

"Now I have a decent opinion of Kastanien, would anyone like to add to Stark's appraisal?"

Marine Brigadier General Foster Pruitt rose, glanced around the room and began.

"Kastanien has a very passionate love of photography. He takes photos of virtually everything, especially the ships that he has shelled and sunk. Our intelligence moles have brought some of his photos out of occupied Europe. I have seen several of them and I must admit, rather grudgingly, that they are exceptionally good. He dotes on his children to a fault and is totally faithful and very much in love with his bride of about twenty years.

I have also seen portraits of his wife and children that rival the great photographers in the Empire, notably Yoseph Karsh in Ottawa, Canada. It is rumored that he has a small but fully equipped personal darkroom aboard the *Scharnhorst* where he develops his own photographs. Lastly, he is an avid chess player."

"Very good Sir, I thank you. That gives me enough of this man's character for now. Let me hear about his counterpart on *Gneisenau*, a Captain Kris Teebolt."

Again Stark stood and pronounced, "Sorry to hog the conversation, but I believe that I have possibly the most comprehensive file on Captain Teebolt. He and Kastanien are best friends, and as such, can virtually read each other's thoughts. Although they had both grown up in Cologne, the two men first met at the Naval Academy. Since then they have solidly built on their friendship all through their naval careers. It was Kastanien that recommended Teebolt for captain of the *Gneisenau*. Teebolt had been Kastanien's executive officer on his previous command of the light cruiser *Emden*. Teebolt, like Kastanien is a solid family man and a passionate photographer, again much like Kastanien. When they get shore leave, the two men make photographic sojourns into the small towns and forests near their homes.

"Again, I have seen some of these shots. Teebolt is a master of light, and his still-life photographs are simply works of art. I'm quite sure that they discuss naval tactics on these secluded forays, but that is only when they are not engrossed in taking photos. It is in my opinion, that this combination of captains makes a very dangerous situation for the Royal Navy. At present count, these two battleships have sunk or commandeered eighty-six merchants and that in only three forays into the Atlantic. Teebolt is not quite as daring as Kastanien, but rather buttresses Kastanien's unorthodox tactics. Teebolt does not quite have the massive ego of Kastanien; therefore I feel that he is much more predictable and would be the easier of the two to hunt down. But, do not underestimate either of these two gentlemen. They could continue to hurt us very badly."

"Thank you very much Admiral Stark. You have filled in several important gaps in my appraisal of our two adversaries. Let me now outline my plan to get these two marauders in our gun sights and vanquish them," Dowding pronounced with an unmistakable edge of steel to his voice thus ending any further conversation, and then went onward.

"The first part of my plan is to help the Germans locate some of our merchant ships."

The stunned audience was at once galvanized. To a man, they snapped out of their patient stupor and leaned forward onto the impeccably polished conference table. With a slight catch in his almost stuttering voice, the First Lord quietly asked.

"Dowding, are you insane or has my hearing gone defunct?"

"Neither my Lord. And now that I truly have captured your undivided attention, please allow me to continue."

Stark, unable to contain his temper any further burst out. "Enough of this tommyrot. It's bad enough to have the bloody Royal Air Force treating us like kindergarten boys, but now giving us instructions on how to manage the Royal Navy is such utter drivel that it is nothing short of mental illness."

The First Lord of the Admiralty rose quickly and in a commanding voice devoid of political innuendo barked out like a Royal Marine drill sergeant, "Shut up Stark! Let Dowding continue with his plan. We've only heard his opening volley. I have enough confidence in the Air Marshal that this seemingly ridiculous statement has a knockout punch attached to its ending. In addition, while I am still standing, let me remind everyone that we are here to discuss any means, yes, *any* means, to rid the North Atlantic of this deadly duo which we have dubbed with the title of *The Ugly Sisters*. Therefore, gentlemen, stuff your voices in your vest pocket and hear the Air Marshal out. Also keep in mind the directive that Churchill delivered to us just moments ago."

At that sobering outburst, the First Lord of the Admiralty sat down and nodded to Dowding to continue.

Dowding then cleared his throat and with the same level tone as before Stark's outburst asked the high ranking officers a rather simple question, "Who came up with the rather unflattering name *The Ugly Sisters* for these ships? From the photographs I've seen of them they are rather graceful looking."

After a silence of a few seconds when none of the officers uttered a sound, Ian McLeod, realizing Dowding was waiting, spoke up, "Dowding, I have to reluctantly agree with your appraisal of our nemesis regarding their appearance. They are truly graceful but very deadly. The term *The Ugly Sisters* probably originated from rescued seamen, but no one knows for sure the actual soul who coined it.

"However, it would not be in keeping, remembering that they are the enemy, to call them by more flattering names."

"Thank you First Lord." Dowding returned to the map and again slapped the pointer on the same area. Then pausing, some thought for an almost theatrical effect, he slowly laid the pointer down on the rack at the base of the map, turned to face his audience and then with a rather wide grin that those who didn't know him well would have thought him completely incapable of, he simply pronounced, "I believe the Prime Minister suggested that we imbibe of his liqueur. Before I continue, let us do just that. Stark, would you be so kind as to pour?"

"It will be my distinct pleasure," Stark replied and stood also sporting a merry grin.

After dispensing the fabled liqueur, Stark raised his glass in the classic toast and said, "God Bless King George and the Royal Navy."

In complete military unison the assembled heads of the British military stood, downed their tots, smiled and then resumed their seats. The brief interlude notably softened the previous stern countenances. Then Dowding once again picked up the pointer and vigorously slapped it on the map.

"I repeat. We have not been able to find *Scharnhorst* and *Gneisenau* in this area or any other for that matter. As the Royal Navy is painfully aware, this area alone comprises over seventy thousand square miles of very, very empty ocean. Gentlemen, please keep in mind that is an awful lot of territory to cover with only a few surface vessels and no air reconnaissance. Correct me if I am wrong, but even our own submarines are of little reconnaissance value given they are very slow compared to your surface ships. So, we must stake out a sacrificial goat and bring these two bloody big battleships to us."

Dowding paused for effect, looked each man square on for a second or two before continuing, "In advance, I must emphasize that this plan could have very serious consequences for our military and the politicians. It also has a very high probability of casualties. All of this without any guarantee of success."

The Rawalpindi

"What in great blazing hell is going on here? Why are we slowing down?" The very typical loud and angry voice of Captain Kennedy blasted out to his bridge officers as he thundered into the bridge.

First Officer James Cook stood transfixed by the sudden appearance of his very agitated captain who looked quite a bit more upset than he had ever seen him. Quickly regaining his composure, Cook replied, beginning with a halting stammer, then smoothly moved into a much more determined tone that made it clear to Kennedy that this officer had done what he thought was the best solution at the time given the circumstances.

"Captain, it was I who ordered the reduction in speed as the German was dropping back and I believed that I was following the orders given to us by the Admiralty."

"And what, pray tell orders are you referring to?" Kennedy fired back like a blast from one of Nelson's eighteen-pounder cannons.

Standing as erect and proper as he could muster under the blistering glare of Kennedy, Cook went on; still with an unwavering conviction, "Sir, the orders I went by were that we were not to lose the German and to lure him into the trap with the battle groups headed south. As the German was falling further astern of us and our radar was stretched to the limit of its range, I was afraid that if he got more than a mile or two further back we could not track him. I thoroughly weighed the pluses and minuses of my actions beforehand and decided that with this particularly wily bastard, it would be best to make damn sure we still had him in tow. Therefore, I reduced speed to maintain contact."

In the split second between when Cook finished his last sentence and took a breath, Captain Kennedy barreled into the minute opening like an iron wedge into a reluctant log.

"You bloody fool. As I have tried to drill into all of you many times, these German captains are damnable clever and we cannot, *must not*, give them the even the slightest clue as to what we are up to. I fervently hope that whichever captain we are dealing with here doesn't come up with another one of their nasty plans with this blatant blunder on our part. We will continue on at ten knots for another hour and maybe, just maybe, the German will think that we have been having a spot of trouble with our engines overheating or some other bloody stupid thing one of you blokes can conjure up. After an hour or so we will resume our previous speed of twelve knots and we will NOT vary from it one bit. Is that absolutely perfectly crystal clear?"

No one uttered a sound—such was their abject terror regarding the flame-throwing temper of the captain. After an eon of molasses-slow time passed, Kennedy resumed.

"When the dawn comes, if all goes well, we will meet up with our beloved Royal Navy's battleships and whatever else the Admiralty has accompanying them. Then *we* can join in the donnybrook. In the meantime I shall return to my cabin and attempt to grasp a bit of rest. We shall all need to be in top notch mental and physical condition when the battle is joined. As I can see, some of you have been relieved. I trust you will rotate your watches accordingly through the night. I want all officers on the bridge thirty minutes before first light. Without fail!"

Then Kennedy exhaled mightily for the first time in what seemed like an eternity, patted his rapidly thinning hair into a rough semblance of order, and then donned his captain's cap that he had been almost crushing in his left hand since he appeared. All of the officers present had not twitched a muscle and several took deep breaths as the captain visibly relaxed. Captain Kennedy was a veteran of nearly thirty years at sea in merchant ships and his ship had been chosen especially by the Admiralty as one of five merchants for conversion to an armored U-boat and raider killer. The Admiralty had used the term "chosen especially" where in fact it had unequivocally *requisitioned* at the request of Winston himself.

*　　*　　*　　*　　*

The S.S. Rawalpindi *had been built by Harland & Wolff for the P & O line and launched in 1925. She had been one of four R-class ships built especially for the England to India routes. Along with her other three sister ships, the* Ranpura, Rajputana & Ranchi *they had unobtrusively plied the long routes without incident until just a mere week before the outbreak of war. The then First Sea Lord Winston Churchill rather upset the owners with his virtually dictatorial decree that these four ships had been "chosen especially" to be immediately converted into armed merchant cruisers.*

The now HMS Rawalpindi *displaced a touch more than 16,000 tons with a wartime crew of 276. The firm of R&H Green & Silley Weir had done a magnificent job at the Royal Albert Dock in London of refitting her in the almost unheard of short time of only two months. So, the gentle passenger ship that had never caused any notice in the world for the past fifteen years steamed out of her English base in November 1939 to protect shipping between the Faeroe Islands and Iceland.*

*   *   *   *   *

She had been fitted out with (eight) six-inch guns salvaged from a retired WWI cruiser and (two) three-incher's. This armament was the best that could be conjured up on very short notice and the Admiralty truly felt that it would be a sufficient deterrent as well as a decent match for the German raiders disguised as merchants. For a brilliantly good reason that no one could truly comprehend, the shipyard had also removed the aft funnel, refitting the remaining smoke stack to accommodate the double duty when required to move at top speed.

The removal of the funnel instantly made the *Rawalpindi* appear to be a slow single-boiler merchant rather than a faster, more powerful passenger ship. She also had her guns cleverly camouflaged with empty break-away crating that took a well-trained crew less than three minutes to drop before commencing to get off noticeable fire. It was hoped by the Admiralty that this deceptive new look would allow the *Rawalpindi* to blend in with convoys and take out any German raider or unsuspecting U-boats that attacked on the surface. The British had way too much experience for their liking with U-boats but they had learned that most U-boats took nearly four minutes to crash dive to avoid the serious danger of surface gunfire.

With (eight) six-inch guns of which four could come to bear along each side coupled with a single three-incher; for a brief period of about two minutes the *Rawalpindi* had dramatically superior firepower to the U-boats single 8.8 cm SK C/35 naval deck gun. And that gun would be immediately abandoned as the crew rushed to get inside as the U-boat began its dive. The gun crew of the *Rawalpindi* could get off nearly twenty rounds in two minutes. Both sides knew that it only took one decent hit to seriously cripple a submarine. Without watertight integrity, the frail U-boat had no choice but to fight it out on the surface. There had been a few, but rare, instances when the *Rawalpindi* and her sister ships had crippled a U-boat in this manner and the outcome was always the same— one less U-boat.

Within minutes of the first crippling hit by the British six-inch guns, the crews of the U-boats abandoned ship, after setting a scuttling charge. This explosive charge would punch a large gaping hole in the belly of the beast sending it to the bottom within a very short period of time. This frustrated the British High Command since they were desperate to get their hands on an Enigma machine. Without the German decoding device in hand to thoroughly dissect and analyze it, even the most brilliant of the British cryptographers, closeted away in the musky confines of Station "X" up north in Bletchley Park, would not be able to break the German code. They had tried for month upon dreary, stultifying month, working tirelessly around the clock day after day, to solve the riddle of the code to no avail. Regardless of how many messages they pored over, the Enigma decoder remained a baffling puzzle. The Germans were also very much aware that if one of their decoders fell into enemy hands, it would reverberate with deadly and serious consequences, especially if the British got their hands on one without Kriegsmarine having any knowledge of the acquisition.

The British intelligence service had garnered from scattered, but very reliable sources, that the Germans had also equipped eight merchant ships with a variety of very lethal mid-caliber guns and torpedo tubes. Five of these deadly raiders had set sail in early August of 1939, just a couple of weeks before the invasion of Poland—which had started all the fireworks of WWII. British intelligence did not have proof positive that the German raiders had sunk any merchants, but the mysterious disappearance of several vessels off the West coast of Africa made it seem likely that they had been surprised and silenced before they could get off a report. Like the camouflaged British armed merchants, the German's small fleet of raiders would appear rather harmless until they were within range. Unlike the British, whose objective was to sink U-boats and any other enemy ship, the German raiders' only objective was to sink merchants.

The Germans were expert marksmen and always took on the bridge and radio room as their first targets. Even immediate action by the radio operators had yet to be quick enough to get off a signal that had enough information to alert London of the peril.

Rawalpindi had sailed with explicit orders to avoid any engagements with German warships, especially the "pocket" battleship *Deutschland* who had been sighted a few times in the *Rawalpindi's* patrol area. Captain Edwin Coverley Kennedy was notorious for seriously *bending* Royal Navy directives. Because of a shining record of successes previous to this new command, the Royal Navy brass had always turned a blind eye to his indiscretions regarding orders. Kennedy argued very convincingly that he was only invoking a captain's prerogative to appraise the situation and act accordingly.

The real truth behind the Royal Navy's tolerance of his virtual insubordination was rather a different cup of tea altogether. Captain Kennedy was the father of the famous and much loved broadcaster and journalist, Ludovic Kennedy. The Royal Navy absolutely had to avoid a scathing news article by Ludovic that his father had been seriously disciplined, especially after Ludovic had, on many occasions, reported his father's actions with glowing reports that were exaggerated only a tad.

The Royal Navy had been the special pride of every Englishman for several centuries, but the memories of the mindless brutality and severe conditions fostered upon captains and sailors alike in the dark and distant past were lurking just below the conscious surface. The Royal Navy had modernized and adhered to a decent, if overly strenuous code of proper conduct for many decades, and they were determined to continually raise this perception by the general populace of the maritime island, and relegate the rather repugnant past to the history books.

Kennedy's interpretation of Admiralty orders to avoid engaging superior forces was that he was to avoid any pitched battle *only* if he felt that he was going to lose his ship. With an explosive temper akin to the wrath of Zeus, not a single one of his officers or crew was apt to question his judgment when it came to his orders. Consequently, when the deadly *Deutschland* was sighted two hours before nightfall on October 29 of the previous year, Kennedy ordered the ship to action stations. The *Deutschland* was due west of his position, about eighteen miles away driving full tilt towards him. Kennedy knew that he was extremely overmatched, therefore a *strategic withdrawal* was in order.

The sky was heavily overcast with very low ominous gray clouds—heralding that some serious weather was in store for the night. Several dense fog banks could be discerned on the eastern horizon. Kennedy ordered full speed ahead for the cover they offered.

The *Deutschland* had a speed advantage of eleven knots and she was closing the gap between the two ships rather quickly. Ever the scrapper and optimist, Kennedy ordered a ninety degree hard turn to port and orders were sent to the gun crews to be prepared to fire as soon as the *Deutschland* was in range and as rapidly as possible, if not faster. When the converted passenger ship was partway through the turn, the *Deutschland* put a shell across the *Rawalpindi's* bow and flashed a signal. "Heave to."

Kennedy returned the order with a broadside. Although none of the six-inch shells hit their mark, some were disturbingly close. Captain Hoffman of the *Deutschland* was surprised to the point of shock that the obviously decrepit old tub would defy a magnificent warship such as his in what would be a decidedly inequitable battle with the outcome never in doubt.

The *Deutschland* sported (six) eleven-inch guns identical to those of her sister "pocket" battleships *Admiral Sheer* and *Admiral Graf Spee.* However the *Deutschland* and her sisters displaced a mere 14,290 tons and could only support two turrets with such large, heavy guns. Powered by eight diesel engines producing 52,000 horsepower the *Deutschland* could steam at a very respectable twenty-eight knots—matching the top speed of all the British capitol ships except the formidable *Hood* and considerably faster than this truculent tub.

Such defiance from what Hoffman considered a rusty old hulk rattled his sense of propriety and he immediately ordered the forward turret to "shoot to kill." Three eleven-inch missiles were headed for the defiant Englishman within thirty seconds. The gun crew of the *Deutschland* was almost of the same high-caliber as those gun crews of *Scharnhorst* and *Gneisenau.* The first three shots closely bracketed the *Rawalpindi* with towering water geysers that thoroughly drenched the exposed gun crews. *Rawalpindi's* gun crews were made of stern stuff and without missing a beat returned fire rather smartly. *Deutschland's* forward turret belched fire again and the shells from both ships passed each other at the high point of their arcs. Both salvos hit home but with a massive difference. Two six-inch shells from *Rawalpind*i struck *Deutschland* smack on the armor plate just aft of the bridge but did little more than create two rather unsightly scorched dents. The *Rawalpindi* suffered from only one hit at the rear of the forecastle which did enormous damage but fortunately did not penetrate the integrity of the outer hull.

After a few seconds to absorb the disorienting concussion, the *Rawalpindi's* gun crews regained their composure, doggedly continuing to fire. Both ships were maneuvering erratically to throw off the opposition's aim so the next two salvos from both sides missed by a comfortable margin. Quite suddenly, a very dense fog bank enveloped the *Rawalpindi* and all the guns fell silent. Kennedy, who had been watching the German for many minutes, was startled when his vision was abruptly and totally cut off by the dense fog. Never one to appear out of touch with the entire goings on, he let out a belly rollicking laugh and pronounced, "Well, me lads we showed the nasty Nazi's that we're a tough bunch of Brits that will sting when provoked. Now, plot a course for home and tea. We've earned it."

Kennedy stepped back and down a few steps to the radio room and inquired of his radio operator.

"Mr. Kerrwin, you surely did get off the position and bearing of that cheeky German and report our damage? Also, send a message that we are returning to port forthwith for minor repairs."

"Yes, Captain all has been sent and we have a confirming reply."

"Very well then, carry on."

Kennedy returned to the bridge and after a moment or two of obvious thought told his bridge officers, "Gentlemen, with the damage up front we would be at serious risk if we run into heavy seas, therefore we are heading home as you should all know by now; but most important is the course we are taking. For all we know the enemy has deciphered our signals and with their superior speed could easily whiz up ahead of us, lurking and waiting like a cat for a mouse for when we emerge from this nice bit of fog. The Krauts driving those new tubs of theirs are all an arrogant lot. After tweaking their nose a bit, they will no doubt want to repay us in some manner or another."

With that Kennedy stepped over to the central table and with his index finger showed the officers the route he planned to take back to port. The first officer nodded and then issued the command for the turn indicated by Kennedy.

"Now, with night upon us and this fog covering our exit, we can now stand down from action stations. Let us simply resume normal operations. It is also very important that we keep total radio silence with a very keen eye out forward, backward and sideways. Let me repeat. The German, being stung a bit, will want to exact his little revenge. I'm dead certain that he will be cruising around looking for us. We can fervently hope that he does not have that new-fangled device called radar that can 'see' us through this lovely pea soup, thus keeping track of us until he gets a clear shot. We will risk steaming blind at full speed, trusting to the Gods of the Deep that nothing will be in our path until dawn. Knowing the German can easily keep station with us; let us not give him even the slightest advantage. So, please darken ship immediately, letting not one chink of light pierce the night and fog. I shall be in my day cabin and if anything, even the smallest, seemingly irrelevant item pops up, fetch me immediately, and I mean immediately."

With this last statement and orders, sixty year-old Captain Kennedy disappeared down the passageway. This night, regardless of the bigger and more deadly peril that was doggedly stalking him in the almost ink black night, Captain Kennedy nonetheless retired to his cabin feeling rather secure. Upon reaching his lush cabin, the irascible veteran rapidly shed his outer clothing and slipped between the warm, fuzzy flannel sheets that had a wonderfully thick Scottish blanket and an eiderdown stuffed quilt to top off his bunk. Kennedy would never admit it to anyone, but he abhorred the bone-chilling cold of the winter months up here in the North Atlantic. Consequently, the blanket and quilt were his most treasured possession because of the incredible warmth they brought to his aging, arthritic bones when he could scurry into them.

Kennedy lay motionless for a full two minutes as his body warmth became encapsulated in the sheets and he could feel his extremities seem to thaw. During these two minutes his mind processed all the sounds of his ship and then knowing all was well, he relaxed and exhaled mightily. Sleep did not evade him for very long even with the troubling problem of the damnable German at his backside. He was too much of a veteran to let problems that might or might not happen spin around in his brain checking into each contingency creating nothing more than confusing conclusions at best. He considered this the mental anguish the purview of youthful and impetuous fools. He instantly dismissed any further thoughts about tonight or tomorrow morning before quickly dropping off into a dreamless sleep.

The *Rawalpindi* slogged onward at her best speed of fifteen knots through a relatively calm sea for several hours. The entire crew was on pins and needles every minute that passed with agonizing slowness. Their ship was totally blind, blacked out without the help of radar contact. They knew that the *Deutschland* was probably skulking about the neighborhood, just waiting until the porridge-thick fog lifted, before they could simply standoff beyond the range of *Rawalpindi's* smaller guns—speedily blowing the defiant but hopelessly outclassed, converted passenger ship out of the water.

Shortly after the heaven-sent fog had made them invisible, the lookouts caught two dim flashes of light high in the sky, but at a considerable distance off their rear starboard quarter. The captain was informed of the star shells and smiled at the vain attempt by *Deutschland* to illuminate him enough to shoot. He also took great comfort in the fact that the star shells were so far off the mark that it could only mean that *Deutschland* did not have an accursed radar setup to keep track of him. The crotchety old sea dog soon was fast asleep in the knowledge that he again had tempted the fates and survived.

Shortly before dawn the ship went to action stations as a matter of course. When the eastern sky began to show a slight glow, tension amongst the crew reached a high point. The wonderful fog that had saved them many hours before by wrapping itself like a cocoon around them, dissipated as rapidly as it had appeared when the sun broke free of the horizon, shortly basking them in brilliant sunshine. The lookouts strained their young very keen eyes for telltale smoke but the horizons were blessedly empty. There was not a single cloud in the late October sky and the sea was almost dead calm. Most importantly, the German pocket battleship failed to greet them. Kennedy was in a jovial mood this delightful morning. When he realized there was no danger from any quarter, he ordered the feisty little armed merchant to turn starboard and make directly for home the quickest way. He would not break radio silence until he was damnable sure that he would have precious air cover, from some airfield in Scotland, to thwart any attempt by the German to run him to ground. Just before noon a tiny black speck was spotted by a lookout and the entire bridge braved the cold on the flying bridge and focused on the tiny black dot. The dot rapidly grew in size and then the drone of a multi-engined aircraft made its way through the insulating scarves and various headgears into their ears. And a sweet sound it was to Kennedy. He bellowed out a cheer.

"Hooray, me fine lads. That's the unmistakable song of one our *Sunderland* flying boats. Tonight we'll all have a round on me at the Horse and Unicorn pub that always has a warm fire to keep us cozy. Mr. Cook, signal the plane that all is well with us and we are appreciative of the escort home. Ask him to make a sweep to the west and south to see if our friend, the *Deutschland,* is in the neighborhood."

The lumbering, rather pudgy-looking, quite large four-engined seaplane was a welcome sight for the red-rimmed eyes of the *Rawalpindi's* officers and crew alike. This heavily armed flying boat could hold its own against enemy aircraft. Many were the Luftwaffe pilots of deadly ME 109's who turned away rather than risk attacking this formidable beast. The Luftwaffe had dubbed the big craft as the *Flying Porcupine.* The eighty-five foot long ship bristled with eight .303 Browning machine guns in turrets, four fixed .303's in the nose and two .5 inch machine guns in beam positions. Small wonder where the name came from with all this firepower. U-boats commanders also flinched when these long range guardians of merchant marine vessels came in sight. From last second radio flashes, they had learned from their former comrades that this British seaplane could take them out rather handily with her carrying capacity of nearly two and a half tons of bombs and/or depth charges. U-boat crash dive drills became commonplace almost daily as commanders harangued their crews to faster and faster times. Those U-boats that survived an attack by a *Porcupine* lent authentic testimony to the deadly killing efficiency the lumbering giant possessed.

Even with four Pratt & Whitney R-1830 Wasp fourteen cylinder engines turning out 1,200 hp. each, the Sunderland could barely manage a top speed of 213 mph. On only a couple of occasions had this British weapon of air and sea war encountered its opposite number in the Luftwaffe, the equally formidable *Focke-Wulf Fw 200.* The *Sunderland* slightly outgunned its comparable large German counterpart but was a critical eleven miles an hour slower so any chasing after the more vulnerable *Fw 200* was out of the question. On those scarce occasions when they occupied a close piece of the sky, the crews of both aircrafts simply waggled their wings at each other and went their separate ways without firing a shot.

Several minutes passed in silence on the bridge while the binoculars slowly traversed the sky with the *Sunderland* as it made its leisurely scan of the ocean for any sign of danger. Suddenly the bridge speakers came alive with the most welcome news.

"Right-o me brave sailors. The seas are yours for as far as we can see which is at least eighty miles in every direction. You'll be quite alright from here to home although that hole you have up front might make it a bit drafty for those below decks. Right. Now we're off to find a U-boat or two that forgot to duck under during the day. Signing off."

With that bit of British cavalier attitude, the *Sunderland* made a slow bank and headed due west. With the sun at her back any U-boat in her path foolish enough to be surfaced would not spot the deadly *Porcupine* until it was too late.

"Well, lads, we're home free. Make best speed to port. Mr. Cook, you have the ship. I am off to my cabin to finish up the log.

"This little episode should make rather quite interesting reading for their Lordships," Kennedy silently mused to himself.

With this final pronouncement, Captain Kennedy retreated to his rather sumptuous cabin; a leftover from the bygone days of being a luxury passenger ship. Kennedy had insisted that the shipyard leave his cabin alone as there was precious little point in wasting money to redo something that was perfectly serviceable the way it was. Once there, he proceeded to write a rather lengthy tale of battle on the high seas, where his little cobbled together almost-warship had taken on the best the Germans could throw at him and came away a victor. The Admiralty did have a much welcomed hearty laugh at their crusty captain's humorous tale that read like an excerpt from King Arthur's Court.

Gneisenau

At the same time that Kastanien was writing in his log, five hundred kilometers to the southwest his dear friend and fellow captain, Kris Teebolt, had just finished entering his most productive day's work in his log. The *Gneisenau* had chanced upon a large convoy shortly after *Scharnhorst* had steamed to catch the stragglers reported by the *Condor*. *Gneisenau's* Captain Teebolt and *Scharnhorst's* Captain Kastanien, upon hearing the report from the *Condor* about the few seemingly stragglers had closed to within three hundred meters of each other and began a lengthy battle strategy over very short-range radios. When they were finished with the strategy and planning, *Gneisenau* headed west-north-west while *Scharnhorst* steamed almost due north. Only three hours after parting company with *Scharnhorst*, *Gneisenau* spotted smudges of smoke a few degrees off her port bow.

Signals were flashed to the two accompanying German destroyers *Schmelling* and *Schwartzadler*. The destroyers replied immediately and the small battle group altered course ten degrees to port from 285 degrees to 275 degrees increasing speed to twenty-six knots—the maximum speed the aging destroyers could muster. Although the two destroyers were nearly twenty-five years old, they had been updated to the standards of the newer ships, with better guns, radar control and they had been refitted with superior torpedo launchers. These two veterans of World War I were part of the precious few warships of the proud Imperial German Navy that survived the humiliating scuttling when the previous war ended.

The slower speed of the two old warriors was a part of the plan hatched up by Kastanien with Grossadmiral Dönitz before the *Scharnhorst* and *Gneisenau* had set sail on their first Atlantic foray. The two sleek and graceful battleships were capable of thirty-two knots, a dramatic two to six knots faster than any of the Royal Navy's capitol ships. This was a fact that no one, save a few in the High Command of the Kriegsmarine knew. Dönitz, after listening to Kastanien's intriguing strategy wholly concurred that it was best kept as a top secret. Kastanien's thinking was that this superior speed would only be used to escape from a superior Royal Navy force or to overtake a smaller enemy naval force. Only a few officers of the *Scharnhorst* and *Gneisenau* knew of this decidedly major advantage. They had been sternly warned by Kastanien to divulge this fact to no one, crew and shore personnel alike.

Knowing full well the submerged, scalding temper of Kastanien, backed up by the even more formidable temperament of Grossadmiral Dönitz, the knowledgeable few kept this secret closer than their own skin. Since the two battleships had not taken their first serious sea trials until after the outbreak of war on September 1, 1939, no one outside of Kriegsmarine High Command was privy to the astounding results. The first sea trials of the sister ships had been the *Scharnhorst* and she had attained the almost miraculous speed of thirty-three and a half knots. Alas, the sea trial had revealed some rather serious design flaws and *Scharnhorst* underwent some interesting changes.

It had been discovered in the relatively quiet waters of the Baltic Sea (quiet only when compared to the brutality that the North Atlantic could conjure up) that *Scharnhorst* needed to be refitted with a clipper, or more commonly called, an Atlantic bow. The freeboard was also considered to be too low and had to be raised up to prevent the much heavier Atlantic seas from cascading onboard. The Atlantic bow was a handsome, high and flaring addition that would enable the great ship to plow forward at speed in wickedly heavy seas without the worry of the bow going under the waves to an extreme and dangerous depth. When *Scharnhorst* left the refitting dock and headed down the estuary from Kiel, the populace of this major German port was spellbound by the beauty of the *new* ship. The graceful tumblehome of the Atlantic bow simply added that indefinable extra touch of majesty.

Gneisenau rapidly closed on the smoke. At a range of about twenty-five kilometers a very large convoy was spotted. The convoy was spread out in the classic square pattern deemed the safest by the British Admiralty. As the gap closed, twenty-eight merchants were spotted with two destroyers on the nearest side, with one leading the convoy and one trailing. It was presumed that the yet indiscernible far side of the mixed bag collection of ships had two additional guardian sheep dog destroyers.

Gneisenau opened fire at a range of seventeen kilometers. Her targets were the near escort destroyers. Being well beyond the range of the British escorts' 4.7 inch guns, *Gneisenau's* fire went unanswered for several minutes. On the third salvo from "Anton", the forward eleven-inch turret, one of the three 337 kilogram shells slammed into the leading destroyer just aft of the single smoke stack. The lightly armored ship hadn't a chance against such an awesome missile—blowing apart in a wild display of flaming, flying metal that was swallowed by the sea in mere minutes. Even before the high flying shrapnel of the devastated destroyer had returned to the surface of the sea, *Gneisenau* had trained her deadly eleven-inch guns on a now wildly maneuvering fresh target. The trailing destroyer's captain, knowing he was hopelessly outclassed, was making smoke but still began firing back.

He had watched with stunned shock at the virtually instant demise of his fellow destroyer. Never having tasted real battle until now, the full impact of what he had just witnessed, the enormity of his responsibility thudded into his brain like a twelve-pound sledgehammer. He would give everything he had to keep his ship and crew along with his helpless merchant charges out of this imminent danger. In reality, he knew that his ship was almost certainly doomed, but he would use his entire arsenal of weaponry to inflict as much damage as possible upon the German and hope that she would break off, hopefully limping a bit.

The range had shortened to thirteen kilometers but was still just a bit long for the destroyers' 4.7 inch guns and her shells still fell frustratingly short. *Gneisenau* opted to turn broadside to the enemy destroyer thus keeping herself just out of range while shooting for a kill. The destroyer's captain knew his shells would fall short but hoped that they would create enough of a distraction to prevent the enemy ship from noticing the four high-speed torpedoes that he had launched only a few seconds after his rather puny 4.7 inch main armament had opened fire. The *Gneisenau's* maneuver to run parallel to the enemy lasted only a couple of minutes before the second escort destroyer felt the stunning shock of a hit by one of the enormous eleven-inch shells. This shell hit her at the waterline and penetrated the relatively paper-thin hull before slamming into the engine room and exploding.

The volcanic detonation virtually vaporized the engine and blew a giant hole through the bottom of the ship. The destroyer died instantly and once again, within precious few minutes, the destroyer was gone from the surface of the sea with all hands lost. Mercifully most of the crew died from the titanic blast and shock wave that slammed them like rag dolls into unforgiving cold steel. The precious few that were not smashed instantly were either sucked under to drown when the destroyer did her final death dive or they perished slowly and miserably within minutes from hypothermia.

"Captain, Captain. Torpedoes in the water. Approximately 10,000 meters and closing fast heading just forward of our position," the high shrill and very excited voice of Gren Schultz the radar/sonar operator broke the silence on the bridge.

Executive Officer Karl Erhlich grabbed the intercom, loudly demanding, "How many torpedoes are in the water, what speed and how wide a spread?"

"I detect four torpedoes traveling about fifty kilometers per hour without much spread. They are less than half a kilometer apart," Gren Schultz replied, his voice had lost its near panic timbre and sounded far more mature than his tender young age of nineteen.

Teebolt responded instantly, "Starboard and center engines maximum revolutions. Port engine full reverse. Turn ninety degrees to port immediately."

The order was repeated and within a few short seconds the ship shivered and shook with the reversing of one huge propeller and the increased turns of the other two. The steering officer spun the large dark oak wheel and the 38,100 ton warship heeled into a turn sharper than anyone expected. Again, this was the genius of Dönitz. He had learned the lesson of too small a rudder from the fate of the "unsinkable" Titanic. Titanic simply couldn't turn fast enough to avoid the iceberg because her rudder was undersized for her bulk.

In the early spring of 1935, Dönitz began planning ahead to the day when war came, as he knew it surely would. He knew that submarines would play a big part of the war at sea and the enemy would like to sink his surface ships from the unseen depths of the ocean. There was little argument from the builders when he insisted and ordered that the rudders be made twenty percent larger. When the chief engineer started to protest that this enlargement would require re-engineering the entire power structure and connections to the rudders, Dönitz simply stared at the man and it was over and done with after only a tight two word command.

"Do it."

Gneisenau made the ninety degree turn and straightened up as the four deadly sharks of steel with their PBX explosive warheads continued their relentless path towards them. Orders were given and the port Deschimag geared turbine returned to its forward direction. *Gneisenau* resumed steaming at twenty-six knots towards the center of the convoy. With a closing rate of nearly eighty kilometers per hour it took only mere minutes before the torpedoes screamed past the *Gneisenau*, the closest one half a kilometer off the starboard side.

The one-sided battle had been underway only about fifteen minutes, but standing British Admiralty orders for scattering under this situation were very explicit so the relatively tight box formation of the convoy was disintegrating as rapidly as the slow merchants could go. Most could only manage ten knots, a few more twelve and three could make nearly fifteen knots. The two far side, rear guard and vanguard destroyers had managed to steam slightly ahead to the starboard side of the convoy and were belching as much black smoke as possible to thwart the all too precise range finding of the German.

While the two ill-fated destroyers tangled with *Gneisenau*, the two German destroyers had dropped back behind the convoy without firing a single shot. Aboard the British destroyers the captains were doing all they could to disrupt the accuracy of the German guns that would in all probability soon come to bear on them. As the *Gneisenau* bore down on them, the closest two British destroyer captains loosed a dozen torpedoes at the impending doom. No sooner had the torpedoes hit the sea and began their high speed runs in the general direction of *Gneisenau* than once again the shrill voice of the still very agitated sonar operator pierced the calm of the battleship's bridge.

"Many more torpedoes coming at us, I cannot discern how many but it at least eight, maybe ten or twelve."

Captain Teebolt calmly stepped a few paces to the radar/sonar room and asked Gren Schultz the distance to the enemy.

"Captain, the nearest torpedoes are ten kilometers from us; a second batch is eleven and the others about twelve kilometers away," The almost breathless young seaman replied.

"Thank you Schultz and calm yourself. We are not in very much danger as their torpedoes only have a range of barely ten or less kilometers before they run out of battery power and sink harmlessly to the bottom. However, the British may have improved their underwater bullets as we noted by the recent passing of their little *fish*. I rather think that those British captains are desperate and not thinking too clearly. They are also hoping that we will be distracted and break off this engagement."

Then Teebolt, knowing his ship was reasonably safe for a moment or two, softened his tone and spoke rather kindly to his trusted eyes and ears, "Seaman Schultz, it is my understanding that you are quite good friends with your counterpart Seaman Marvin Molter on our sister ship, the *Scharnhorst*. I also hear that you have a unique nickname just like he does. I know his is 'Merlin' and I have heard some of our own officers refer to you as 'Genie'. Is this true?"

Schultz was equally stunned as Molter had been to hear a captain use such a familiar reference to an ordinary seaman. He swallowed a couple of times before he stammered out, "Captain that is what I have been called on occasion and begging the Captain's pardon the name gives me pride in my job. Regardless of what I am called, I will always give my utmost to earn your confidence."

Teebolt let a big knowing grin transform his face before he reached down and squeezed the apprehensive operator on the shoulder and then returning to his normal captain's tone of voice he said, "A 'Genie' is what you are with this strange new device that makes our dangerous jobs just a bit safer. The nickname stands well with me. Now back to the business we are here for. How much closer are those torpedoes since we've been chatting and can you give me their headings?"

Schultz had been watching the bouncing green bars all the time with one earphone still glued tightly to the ear opposite the captain. His response was instantaneous and said with a solid conviction that he had not had before his little "chat" with the captain.

"Captain, the closest group consists of a narrow spread of four torpedoes heading very much to our port side at a range to us of about seven kilometers. I can now clearly make out the second grouping of four more torpedoes approximately one kilometer behind the first group heading almost in the same direction as the first, still a ways off our port bow but running inside the first group. The third signal is still too weak to give an accurate heading and distance. I will be able to ascertain the number, direction and distance within one to two minutes."

Teebolt smiled inwardly to himself with the pleasure of knowing that this seaman was officer material.

"Very well Schultz, I will be back in two minutes."

Gren Schultz was as shocked as Marvin "Merlin" Molter with the use of his nickname. He had never, never thought in his wildest dreams that the lofty captain Teebolt would ever use such familiarity with a junior seaman. Unbeknownst to both "Merlin" and "Genie", Kastanien and Teebolt had chatted about these two brilliant youngsters during a leisurely dinner before they had steamed out of Brest a few weeks earlier. The two captains, being realists, knew that they had to utilize to the maximum every tool and device at their disposal if they were to have a fighting chance against the formidable British Royal Navy. So, they concluded that radar and sonar could be of definite advantage. Chief of German intelligence Admiral Wilhelm Canaris had informed them that the British radar and sonar was inferior to that of Germany. Kastanien and Teebolt were rather thick-skinned and secretly skeptical when it came to another proclamation of *superior* German technology. They had to live and die in the real world, not pushing a stack of papers around, all the while spouting armchair expertise.

They both thought that Canaris was a rather incompetent officer who had blathered away in the high political circles of the early Nazi party. He had convinced Joseph Goebbels that he was a loyal and devoted party member as well as an intimate friend of the Führer. Goebbels was a very sharp propagandist but a bit weak on judging the human race. Minister of propaganda Goebbels did check up on the friendship that Canaris professed and found it to be true to a reasonable degree. Thus did Admiral Canaris attain this rather important post within the Nazi Party. However, Kastanien and Teebolt had nothing to lose and much to gain by at least giving this tidbit of information about the superiority of German radar and sonar a credible chance to be proven.

Teebolt strode back to the bridge and ordered a change in course of ninety degrees to starboard at full speed. Again the nimble leviathan heeled while churning up the North Atlantic's choppy waters. The order reverberated throughout the bridge and brief moments later the crisp reply from First Officer Adolph Kleinst replied, "Course steady on oh-two-five Sir. Making twenty-eight knots."

"Very well Mr. Kleinst, hold your course."

Teebolt took the few steps back to the radar/sonar room and inquired of the "Genie".

"Captain, all twelve torpedoes are traveling at about forty-five knots. The first group is now four kilometers behind and heading two kilometers off our port side. The second group is six kilometers and about one kilometer off the port side as well. The third and last group is eight kilometers behind and three kilometers off our port side."

"Very well, keep a keen eye on them and inform me immediately if these bearings change."

That was all Teebolt said before striding back to the bridge and issuing new orders, "All ahead maximum speed. Come to course one-five-five."

Immediately that the orders were telegraphed to the engine room, a slight shudder went through the ship as she sped up to her maximum speed of thirty-two knots. At this speed, even the North Atlantic seemed no match for the formidable power of 165,000 horsepower driving the three tripled-bladed, four-and-a-half meter diameter hardened-brass screws.

Teebolt again stepped back into the radar/sonar room quietly inquiring, "Mr. Schultz, give me the dispositions of all the torpedoes relative to our newest course."

"Captain Sir, all of the torpedoes will pass us a kilometer or more off our port quarter."

Teebolt nodded and stepped across the passageway into the radio room.

"Mr. Staffen. What radio transmissions from the enemy destroyers have you picked up?"

"Sir, the enemy destroyers have been transmitting regularly keeping the British Admiralty and probably all their warships at sea up to date on our position. They have been in my opinion also desperately requesting that their Battle Group "C" steam at top speed to relieve them from our devastating attack."

"Have they been sending these reports in the clear or in code?"
"Sir, they have been using their standard code which I can decipher almost perfectly and very quickly."

"Very well Mr. Staffen. If they add any new requests, please inform me at once."

"Yes Captain."

Teebolt returned to the bridge and in his unorthodox, admirable fashion of keeping his crew pretty much up to date he told the officers what was happening and his battle plan.

"We're not running from the battle, rather we're evading some rather nasty little presents that the Royal Navy has sent our way. The nearest little fishies are about four kilometers away and running behind us about a kilometer or two. The other two groups are further behind with one group a kilometer closer and the other one about the same. As you all know our sonar is not entirely perfect, so to be prudent, we have to assume that we could still be hit. We will maintain this course until sonar tells us the torpedoes have spent their batteries, stopped and sunk to the bottom. With our ship running at thirty-two knots and the torpedoes at forty-five we should still be well ahead of them when they have exhausted their propulsion systems. I have sent our destroyers to pick off a few of the trailing ships. They will engage these stragglers and keep the Royal Navy scrambling for a while. Our destroyers will break off their engagement after thirty minutes before turning to join up with us. This rear attack will no doubt draw the remaining Royal Navy's destroyers back to do battle with our destroyers. By the time they arrive our destroyers will have broken off and heading our way. I am hoping that the British will think that we're retiring from battle rather than face their dangerous little stingers.

"That is not to be the case. When the torpedo danger has passed we are going to turn and run parallel to the course that the convoy was on before we arrived to spoil their little party. The merchants will by now have no doubt scattered to the four winds since our attack began. But when the lead ships and the remaining destroyers, if any, assume that we are gone they should regroup resuming their earlier course. When we turn parallel, we will run at top speed for two hours. With our speed advantage of close to twenty knots this will position us about forty-five kilometers ahead of them on their starboard side. We will turn then sixty degrees to port and steam at maximum speed until we are directly ahead of them. Long before then, night will have enveloped the sea and our smoke will have not been visible to them for quite some time. Then we turn again and charge directly into the center of their group.

"At the time we commence the run into their center, our destroyers will have taken up a position thirty kilometers to the east of the convoy and running parallel to it at fifteen knots. When we begin the run I will signal our destroyers to turn west to intercept the merchants. Unless their radar is very long ranged we, along with our destroyers, will be almost on top of them thus giving them precious little time to scatter. No doubt that many of them will break to the west and will be unguarded by any British destroyers. The British destroyers, if any are left, will again take us on hoping once more to inflict damage with their torpedoes. We will use our main armament to fight the destroyers. With our superior range we should be able to at least knock some of them out of action before their tiny guns can reach us and before they can launch torpedoes with any hope of success. We will make the assault at twenty-eight knots. The destroyers will undoubtedly speed up to intercept. Their speed should be approximately twenty-eight to thirty knots, therefore the closure rate will be at or more than fifty-six knots per hour. Gunnery Officer Jorgen, maybe now you will understand why I have chosen in the past to fire at long range instead of closing in and making your job easier. Your gun crews, working with the rangefinders, have done an exemplary job of making difficult shooting look easy. However, this will be a bit more difficult as we will be attacking at night. Do you have any questions or suggestions?"

"No Captain, my gun crews accept the challenge gladly. We will do you and our ship proud."

"Very well then. Now, there has been a lot of radio traffic coming from the British destroyers since they first spotted us. As you know the British are unaware that we are deciphering their code almost as fast as London is. We have ascertained that our actions along with the *Scharnhorst's* have prompted the British Admiralty, within the past hour, to dispatch the battle group that has been watching the Denmark Strait for *Bismarck* to steam at full speed to engage us or *Scharnhorst*. I'm quite sure that they are hoping to engage both of us. It's rather a shame for them, but once again we simply will not be where they expect us to be when they arrive. First Officer Kleinst, please order our chief radar operator Schultz to get some sleep right now. I want him alert and at his best when the action begins. Make sure that his replacement reports any blips on his machine once we are clear of the convoy and until we begin our attack. Now, my good officers, do any of you have any questions regarding our plan of attack?"

Not a man on the bridge spoke. Several glanced at the others with a quizzical look but remained silent when no response was forthcoming.

Then Executive Officer Karl Erhlich broke the silence, "Come on now mates, you know that our Captain wants nothing held back. If you have any questions or modifications to his plan, then speak up right now."

Still no response.

The silence dragged on for nearly a full minute before the gunnery operator spoke again, "Begging the Captain's pardon Sir, I was wondering if we can use our secondary guns against the merchant ships while my little darling's Anton, Bruno and Caesar work on the destroyers? That is if the opportunity presents itself?"

The entire assemblage simultaneously chuckled. Even though the entire German Navy's big guns on battleships and "pocket" battleships had names, they were rarely used in everyday communications on the bridge. Only the *Bismarck* and *Tirpitz* had a second aft turret which was called Dora. Then Teebolt with an impish grin responded, "Mr. Jorgen, always the opportunist. Of course you may use your secondary guns anytime against targets of opportunity. But I must caution you that I will not have the concentration on taking out their destroyers with your 'little darling' eleven-inch guns compromised in the slightest."

"Absolutely Sir. The destroyers will be rapidly destroyed. When we have gotten in range I assume we can light up the scene with star shells?"

"Yes, of course you may use star shells, but in addition I expect you to find your own ranges by setting some vessels on fire."

"Absolutely, my Captain. There will be several fires in rapid order. And even the ships that might be a bit hard to spot, I have every confidence that with the 'Genie' giving us his always accurate radar information, we can handle multiple targets with ease."

The rest of the officer's faces took on an odd look at Jorgen's use of their chief radar operator's nickname. Teebolt instantly caught the high flush of red in his chief radar operator's cheeks coupled with the odd looks on all of the assemblage, quickly deduced the reason. Visibly relaxing his stance he quietly made a proclamation that would have a profound effect on his crew forever.

"Gentlemen, it is my strong belief that such camaraderie as the use of nicknames implies is a very important part of building and maintaining a strong sense of teamwork amongst us all. While we must maintain proper respect for superiors at all times, it is the duty of all officers and senior crewmembers to remember that those in lesser rank are nonetheless human beings like ourselves. As such, they are to totally respect all of our 1,669 fellow shipmates. Each and every one of these men is special and every job is vital to this ship. I might add that our 'Genie' has an equally talented counterpart aboard the *Scharnhorst*. Also a very young man, *Scharnhorst's* chief radar operator has a similar nickname and that is 'Merlin.' Captain Kastanien and I are the ones who gave them these nicknames and we did so because of their almost magical interpretations of the squiggly bouncing green bars on their machines."

Then Teebolt turned his full attention on Gren "Genie" Schultz and continued, "Mr. Schultz, I would be pleased if you would allow *me* to address you as 'Genie' on occasion."

Stunned at the import of the captain's little speech the youthful radar operator was momentarily at a loss for words, then he regained a semblance of composure and stammered out, "Or course you may call me 'Genie' anytime my Captain." And then in a flash of youthful exuberance he vigorously shouted out, "God bless our Captain, he is the best captain in the world."

The officers immediately repeated the words of praise but with much more gusto. Now it was Teebolt's turn to be slightly embarrassed. He turned away momentarily to hide any trace of the emotions that his countenance might betray. Teebolt slowly turned back to the group and resumed, "Mr. Schultz, can you provide our gun control with simultaneous information regarding multiple distances and bearings as he has requested?"

"Yes Captain, it's no problem as our radar system *sees* every vessel within its range at the same time, and each blip on my screen represents a different ship with different distance and bearing readings. The only shortcoming is that the readings are not quite as precise as our rangefinders but after the first star shell lights up some of the convoy I can refine my readings and with the information from the rangefinders, we will be able to pinpoint the multiple targets and give gun control the corrections within seconds."

"Very well Mr. Schultz. We'll all be counting on you to co-ordinate the exact positions of their destroyers as rapidly as possible. With them out of our hair, we should be able to commandeer a goodly number of merchants or blow any stubborn ones out of the water. Hopefully the

British will not darken their ships and our rangefinders can assist you before the star shells are effective."

Teebolt then addressed all the officers, "Gentlemen, are there any other questions or suggestions?"

When a full minute went by and no one had spoken Teebolt ended the conversation, "Very well, I am going to my cabin. Please inform me at once if there is any new development. The British are not always as co-operative as they might be in following *our* order of battle."

Again the group of men on the bridge chuckled and laughed quietly. Feeling very confident in his crew and their abilities, Teebolt was especially pleased that they all were self-assured in their own abilities. Teebolt turned and disappeared down the passageway.

Scharnhorst

Scharnhorst was far over the horizon when the *Gay Lily* finished her last voyage to the bottom of the cruel, ageless Atlantic. Captain Kastanien fully realized that breaking formation with *Gneisenau* earlier that day to pursue a lone straggler or two was somewhat foolhardy, but they were too tempting to ignore. Kastanien knew that the Royal Navy was not close enough to endanger his pride and joy before he could dispatch the merchants and return to the small battle group now headed by *Gneisenau*. The *Condor* had spotted the *Gay Lily* and possibly more vessels on the far horizon as it was banking to start its return to base in France. "*God, how the British must hate the* Condors," thought Kastanien.

The big, slow four-engined, lumbering reconnaissance bombers were ideal for this duty. With formidable guns and armor to protect them, rare was the occasion that a British fighter even saw them, let alone down one. There had been a few clashes in the war between the Royal Air Force and the *Condors*. The results were mixed. The Royal Air Force had downed three *Condors* but had lost two precious *Spitfires* to the heavily armed big birds, which could take seemingly brutal punishment and remain airborne. The *Condors* did double duty, acting mainly as reconnaissance for the Kriegsmarine and because they also had the opportunity, they preyed upon convoy stragglers that were out of range of the escort's anti-aircraft batteries. Because they had sunk many vessels with their own bombs, they had gained a healthy respect from the Royal Navy and even more respect from the Luftwaffe High Command. Since the *Scharnhorst* and *Gneisenau* were relatively close by, the *Condor* decided to let the big ships claim these prizes. The *Condor* had already sunk an errant merchant today and was down to a single bomb. The Condor's crew cherished the hope that they could find and sink another straggler on the way home. The radioman opened the proper channel and began transmitting in code.

"Attention, Attention, this is Big Buzzard Three. We have spotted one, possibly two or more merchant marines heading approximately north-east at maybe ten to twelve knots in grid KZ 15. There are no naval escorts in sight. However, we do not have enough fuel to do a larger fly over and verify the presence or lack of enemy warships to the west. Big Buzzard Three returning to base immediately. Over and out."

"Captain, Captain the ship has decreased speed." The intercom from the bridge to Kastanien's cabin barked a mere ten minutes after he closed his eyes.

Kastanien, not really being asleep, reached to the hand microphone and responded softly, "Very well, I shall be on the bridge shortly."

Kastanien put his boots on, donned his jacket, checked his appearance in the mirror and walked the few steps to the cabin door.

"Come Attila, we're off to the bridge to play your favorite game of cat and mouse."

Attila snapped his head up, stood up and stretched, then jumped to the floor making only an almost soundless ka-thud. Kastanien, with Attila running ahead, strode with deliberation to the bridge. When Kastanien entered the bridge, Attila was already perched on his blanket high up on the shelf staring out the forward-facing window at the almost total blackness. Kastanien walked back to the radar operator and asked, "How long after we reduced speed did our friend do the same?"

"Less than five minutes Captain," came the immediate response from Seaman Molter.

"Very well, keep a very sharp watch on her, especially if she changes course," Kastanien said.

Turning his attention to the silent bridge officers who waited his next pronouncement Kastanien softly asked, "Gentlemen, what do you think of this? A ship that knows its being closely followed by an unfriendly heavy warship reduces speed coincident with us and even more strange it has made no effort to deviate from its original course. That makes no conventional sense," Kastanien inquired while scanning all of the silent faces that stared back at him.

First Officer Gott was the first to reply, "Captain, they are either experiencing engine overheating with their previous twelve knot speed and have reduced revolutions to let the engines cool somewhat or they want to make very sure we don't lose them. In addition, if the latter is the case, that brings up your question. Why? I believe they are leading us into a trap when the dawn will greet us with the Royal Navy's reception committee on the horizon."

"Excellent thinking Mr. Gott. That is my appraisal of the situation exactly," Kastanien replied. "Now, gentlemen may I have your suggestions as to a plan of action. We have nine hours of darkness before dawn."

Executive Officer Schmidt spoke a fraction of a second before Second Officer Mueller.

"I agree with Mr. Gott's appraisal of their actions and I suggest we change course and rejoin *Gneisenau* immediately just in case the Royal Navy was after her in the first place, and they decoyed us into following these few stragglers or decoys, whichever the case may be."

Second Officer Mueller seeing a minute gap in the conversations spoke up in a firm voice with a conviction that he didn't necessarily feel inside, "I agree with the Captain and Mr. Gott's assessment of the situation but why not sink the vessel now and then change course to rejoin *Gneisenau?*"

Kastanien eyed his Second Officer and let a small smile traverse his lips.

"An excellent idea Mr. Mueller," Kastanien cheerily responded to his Second Officer.

Taking a few steps backward to the small enclosure where radar operator Molter plied the very new, mystical art of interpreting wiggly green lines and bars, *Scharnhorst's* Captain Kastanien entered the radar room and looked rather fatherly at the chief radar operator Marvin "Merlin" Molter. He then asked in a quiet voice keeping with the tomblike atmosphere of this tiny cubbyhole, "Mr. Molter. Am I correct in thinking that our radar can only 'see' about forty kilometers?"

"Yes, Captain, that is very accurate. Our radar can see slightly further, maybe forty-five kilometers in very calm seas but it is reduced to only thirty-five kilometers in heavier seas. Moreover, in very heavy seas the signal is interrupted by the rising and falling of both our ship and the one we are watching. We'd be lucky to 'see', with any real consistency, more than twenty to twenty-five kilometers. With the relatively quiet seas we have right now, I would say we can see most anything accurately up to about thirty-five to forty kilometers."

"And what do you think the British radar system can do?"

The young boy's heart skipped and his innards roiled with the importance of the seemingly simple question. He realized instantly the peril to his captain and the ship if the answer was too far off base either way. He also knew that Kastanien would want the truth, regardless of whether it was good or bad.

"Captain, from what I have been told, and what I have learned from limited experience, heavily laced with a strong dose of guesswork, I believe that the British radar is about on a par with ours."

Kastanien placed a reassuring hand on the boy's shoulder and almost whispering in his ear softly asked, "Merlin, please tell me the part that you left out. I promise that it will be treated with respect and your stature will not be diminished in my eyes or anyone else's. Remember that it is I, and I alone, who makes the final decisions which governs our fate."

"Thank you very much for your confidence and insight Captain. What I said before was truly my honest opinion. However, the British system operates on a completely different principle, therefore they are getting different results than we are. What the differences are I truly do not know and any speculation on my part would possibly only confuse the issue. My only belief is that our system needs to be improved upon rapidly or we may be at a serious disadvantage soon," Molter finished and stared apprehensively at Kastanien.

"An excellent report and conclusion. If there is anything else you come up with regarding the use of our invisible 'eyes' inform me at once. Now, back to the business of war. How far behind this ship are we and what is her approximate speed?"

"Twenty kilometers and about ten knots, Captain," Molter replied quietly and firmly. He was still in a euphoric stage of shock at being treated so well by the great captain Kastanien.

"Very good Merlin, please keep me informed of even the slightest change," Kastanien replied in the same quiet voice, and with a conspiratorial knowing wink, departed the small room, returning smartly to the bridge.

Molter, a very quick minded twenty year old, had studied the new technology of radar and taken it to heart back even in high school. He was a stellar student who quickly came to the attention of then Admiral Dönitz.

Dönitz had visited the boy's high school in Düsseldorf and was immediately impressed with this youngster's grasp of radar's importance and its operation. With Molter graduating in two months, the timing could not have been more opportune.

"Have you been drafted by the Army yet?" Dönitz inquired of the boy.

"No, Admiral. They approached me but I told them that I would be of far greater service to the Fatherland at sea operating a radar station aboard a great warship," The youngster replied.

"And the Army actually believed that story?" Dönitz replied rather incredulously.

"Yes Sir, they told me that no one had ever seemed as sure of themselves as I did that day so they left. As they were leaving, they turned and the senior one said in a very stern voice.

"Report to the Kriegsmarine office tomorrow after school and get signed up with them. We'll be back to check."

Five months later, this high school youngster held a very new and very important position aboard one of Germany's newest and best warships. Molter had been tested during some sea trials aboard *Scharnhorst* immediately leaving school. His uncanny accuracy impressed all who watched and heard his analysis. During a friendly visit with Captain Teebolt, who commanded *Gneisenau*, Kastanien had tabbed him with the nickname "Merlin". When Teebolt had asked why he had chosen an English magician, Kastanien had simply replied," I don't know of any German magicians who were as famous as Merlin. And I firmly believe that this boy will change the thinking of many of us as the mythical Merlin did many centuries ago."

Molter's spirit was never as joyous as now. The great captain Kastanien had called him by his nickname. Molter did not think that captains even knew nicknames existed, let alone use one to address a very junior crew member.

"I will never let our captain down," the youngster thought to himself.

Upon returning to the bridge Kastanien firmly ordered, "Mr. Gott, signal U-3200X to surface alongside of us immediately"

"Right away Captain."

Gott then went to the radio room and had the signal sent through the underwater sonar dome. The signal was a very simple series of pings but spaced at specified intervals. Kastanien and the U-boat's captain Gordon Wittrock had worked out a very simple but effective method of communications when the U-boat was submerged. Even if the British could hear the pinging, there was no way they could ever decipher what the signals meant unless they witnessed the actions taken as a result. Aboard the U-boat the sonar/radar operator received the signal and immediately shouted for the captain. Captain Wittrock sprinted the seven meters to the sonar/radar station and sharply asked the young operator, "What instructions from *Scharnhorst*?"

"We are to surface immediately and pull up alongside *Scharnhorst*," came the instant reply.

"Very well, execute now."

The fearsome, dark-gray predator of the North Atlantic blew her ballast tanks and began a rapid rise to the surface. It was not a very long trip as the U-boat had been running less than thirty meters below the surface. As when she had surfaced to rescue the survivors from the *Gay Lily*, the sea boiled and phosphoresced in the brilliance of the powerful searchlights from the *Scharnhorst*. The radar/sonar operators of the two ships had kept the vessels within a quarter mile of each other for several hours at an earlier command from Kastanien. The U-3200X had no trouble keeping pace at twelve knots with the mammoth battleship.

She was an entirely new type of submarine that Grossadmiral Dönitz himself had designed. Dönitz had been a submariner for most of his Navy life and was respected for his inspired grasp of submarine warfare, its strategies and tactics. He had over the past few years contemplated the mentality that had created the modern submarine in the first place and how it played its part in the current art of war far out in the open ocean. Shortly after the war began a dramatically different concept from the traditional design of submarines gelled in the mind of then Admiral Dönitz. With the amazing speed and urgency that only a state of war can create, Dönitz worked tirelessly with his designers and engineers for just a brief three weeks before the U-3200X had been conceived and put to paper.

The concept was no doubt years ahead of its time and maybe too radical to be accepted by the Führer. So, Dönitz with a tube of plans and a brilliant scale model of his newest brainchild strode confidently through the beautifully appointed halls of the sparkling new Reichstag. He had deliberately chosen mid-morning since that's when the Führer was noted to be in the best frame of mind and receptive to new ideas. Like all canny politicians Adolph Hitler never saw anyone without letting them cool their heels for at least fifteen minutes, but for this visit from one of his favorites, he broke the unspoken rule and had Dönitz ushered into his rather Spartan but huge office after a wait of only five minutes.

"Well Karl, what is this new idea and design you have for the Fatherland's Navy?" was the Führer's simple greeting. No courtesies or idle chat issued forth from the leader of the new Germany.

"My Führer let me explain my theory and strategy first. Then I will show you how I have planned to implement it."

After listening for ten minutes, Adolph Hitler spoke with genuine enthusiasm, "Admiral Dönitz, I believe that you have captured the essence of submarine warfare and your plans to make this splendid model into reality might, no, *will* revolutionize our undersea fleet. However, as you know, we must get as many U-boats out on patrol as quickly as the yards can turn them out. I only question how much time and resources your new ship will take."

"My Führer, I too know the need to get the maximum numbers of U-boats out hunting the merchants that keep England in the war, but we must also contend with the attending warships, and the toll they can take on our present fleet. This new submarine will give the British cause to use more caution and thus reduce their effectiveness against us. I do not propose switching our shipyards to this new type until one or two have been built and sent to sea. Only then will we be able to properly evaluate their strategic effect," Dönitz finished his short speech and waited.

"Karl, you understand me only too well. Yes, you have my strongest approval and backing for the immediate production of *three* new boats. Three should not reduce production of our present Type VII submarines enough to matter, and the results could very well be significantly better than we imagined. If they work out the way you have presented them, we will commit many more resources to creating a dynamically new underwater fleet. Now, my old friend, tell me about your family, especially that beautiful wife and headstrong son of yours," Hitler closed with genuine warmth in his voice.

After a pleasant chat of less than ten minutes, Hitler reached into a drawer, produced a single sheet of heavily embossed official Führer stationery, rapidly scribbled a simple note, signed it then handed it to Dönitz.

"Admiral Karl Dönitz, here is all the authorization you need to proceed with utmost speed to get our new killer submarines into action as quickly as possible."

Without realizing it at the time, Hitler handed Dönitz the single sheet of paper that would revolutionize the role of the submarine and its effectiveness beyond even Donitz's wildest dreams.

It was not lost on Dönitz how in the span of less than an hour "his" submarine concept had become "our" submarine. He inwardly smiled to himself about how all politicians were quick to take the credit. He thanked Hitler and snapped off a smart salute. Hitler returned the salute, but it was a rather poor excuse for a former soldier. Turning smartly on his heels, Dönitz strode towards the massive oak doors that were the guardians of the most powerful office in Germany. He was a little taller and straighter as he exited the office. Upon walking down the marble steps of the Reichstag, Dönitz got into his waiting Mercedes and told his driver to get him to Templehof airport as quickly as was prudent, given the amount of traffic in this very festive and bustling city at lunchtime. Inwardly he was overjoyed at how well the meeting had gone, but the secret apprehension he had been harboring about the viability and true effectiveness of this dramatic new concept in naval warfare still nagged a tiny bit in the back of his mind. Realizing this as an unworthy thought, he dismissed it out of hand after looking once more at the real possibilities which buoyed up his spirits even more.

The Admiralty
Present Time

Gathered once more in the great room on the second floor of the Admiralty building the five most senior officers of the British military were all stoically seated in the same placement around the conference table. This was the first time since that momentous gathering nearly a month previous that these illustrious officers were all assembled together again.

"Gentlemen, I believe that we have some quite portentous news that we need to discuss," The First Lord of the Admiralty Ian McLeod began.

Every one sat ramrod straight in his chair, rather calmly waiting for McLeod to continue. After a short pause, mainly for dramatic effect, Ian McLeod continued, "Without being overly optimistic, it appears that Air Marshal Dowding's rather chancy and audacious plan is coming together pretty much the way he anticipated it would. However, before you get all excited and rambunctious on me, let me caution you that the German driving the *Scharnhorst* is damnable devious. The folders in front of each of you are a summation of the situation as it has been developing over the past few hours. Our Station X at Bletchley Park has done an outstanding job on this situation and even the German intercepts from both the *Scharnhorst* and Kriegsmarine are considered fairly accurate and most importantly very current. Now, before my political rhetoric gets too good a start and I bore you with Parliamentary bombast, I will cease babbling on and ask all of you to please take a few moments with me to read the contents in the folders and then when all are done, we will then discuss any changes that need to be made to the plans we have implemented to date. I myself have only given the contents a quick cursory glance as they were delivered to me less then fifteen minutes ago."

The sudden silence in the room when the First Lord ceased talking lasted less than a second before the folders were noisily snapped open and the wise old eyes of these battle-hardened military men quietly read the first summary sheet. Virtually simultaneously the six men turned the first page together and began in earnest reading the detailed body of the folder. No one spoke for nearly half an hour but all during that time the silent probing and appraising eyes of Ian McLeod were constantly raising up from the folder and with his finely-tuned political acumen cataloged the facial expressions of each man. Ian McLeod was the grand master of people-reading. Many had been the time when after studying a particularly troublesome parliamentary opponent he came back with such an insightful and deadly accurate reply that his opponent blanched knowing that his real politically charged subterranean truth and agenda had come out. McLeod had the luxury of studying the gathering because he simply read and absorbed documents like this incredibly faster than all but Churchill himself. He mentally noted who backtracked a lot to previous sections and who read methodically and pedantically each page thoroughly. He knew, as all astute politicians knew, that the information would probably create a minor if not major firestorm when the discussion began in a short while.

Meanwhile, he waited in contemplative silence while the crackle and snap of the paper sheets went on. Those who finished first simply and without much ado closed their folder, eased back into their chair and closed their eyes. McLeod could visualize the machinations going on in their military minds. When the last folder was rather noisily closed, the reposing men snapped back to reality, sat up straighter and placed their hands on their folder and waited.

As everyone expected and secretly dreaded, the First Sea Lord Robert Stark was the first to break the silence and get the discussion into high gear.

"Gentlemen, this is rather an incredible amount of extremely interesting intelligence. Since I'm the one who rather discourteously dominated the conversations at our first meeting I am going to hold my comments until we hear from all of you. I do this mainly because when all is said and done it is I alone, along with Winston of course, who bears the burden of making the final call as to our future actions in the North Atlantic. With that said who wants to take the preverbal first shot?"

"Gentlemen, as this was my brainchild in the first place, I too would prefer to hold my comments until I have heard from the rest of you," Air Marshal Dowding quietly responded.

Ian McLeod was a bit perturbed at these two opening comments but to keep the senior British lions on track he jumped right in with a soothing comment, "The First Sea Lord and the Air Marshal have stated their positions on this weighty matter quite succinctly and I agree with their thinking. Now, let us hear from Field Marshal Montgomery if you don't mind Sir."

Like an actor taking his cue, Field Marshal Bernard Law Montgomery slid back his chair and stood up. Before speaking, he straightened his jacket and clasped his hands behind his back. All the men knew that this characteristic stance of his was to be expected but with trepidations. Montgomery was notorious for always wanting to be the absolute center of attention and, to a man, the others groaned internally knowing what was coming. Holding true to his mannerisms, Montgomery began striding back and forth the length of the table twice before he began.

"Just like the damn bantam rooster peacock that he is. Always the bloody boring dramatic effects before his pathetic theatrics," thought Ian McLeod wondering if the others had the same rather deprecating thoughts about their peer.

"Gentlemen, at first glance it appears that our illustrious opponent has moved in exact accordance with the Air Marshal's scheme. But the very odd actions of the *Scharnhorst* make me wonder who is being led to the slaughter?"

Stark immediately plunged in. "To answer your question Field Marshal, as the senior representative of the Royal Navy, I did note, as I'm sure you and the rest did, that their shooting was rather subpar, *or* simply incredibly accurate for their purposes. Also, we must consider the possibility that she was rather short on ammunition given as she has no doubt expended a great deal of her supplies during this sojourn in laying to waste many of our own precious vessels, both warships and merchants."

Stark then nodded at McLeod giving him the message that he was done for now and someone else needed to pick up where he left off. McLeod looked inquiringly at the Royal Marine General and motioned for him to give his Threpp'nybit worth. Somewhat reluctantly Royal Marine Brigadier General Foster Pruitt stood up, opened his folder, and after finding the right page he slowly began.

"Gentlemen, as you all know I am a silent thinker until I can fully understand the tactical situation before I can hatch up a plan to solve the problem. Then I act, rather decisively, if I might say so myself. The strange actions of *Scharnhorst* still have me slightly baffled, but since I have been asked for my humble opinion, I will respond only with a question first."

"Humble opinion, now that's what I call the pinnacle of British understatement," The First Lord of the Admiralty interjected quickly laughing at his own witticism. The other four men immediately burst out laughing at the blatant truth of the jibe. Pruitt took it in stride and smiled a rare, knowing smile which threatened to crack his jaw. Quickly the humor passed and he continued.

"Now that you blokes have had a good laugh on me, let us continue. But first I am going to check the cabinet behind me to see if the excellent bottle of brandy that Winston persuaded us with last time still has enough left to cheer us up a trifle."

General Pruitt quickly found the spirits and poured a short snifter for everyone and when the glasses were distributed, he proposed a toast. Everyone stood immediately.

"Here's to the impending and rapid demise of *Scharnhorst* and/or *Gneisenau*."

"Hear, hear" came an instantaneous, cacophonous and hearty reply. Everyone touched their glasses, took a small sip and then reseated themselves and waited for Pruitt to continue.

"Gentlemen, especially you Admiral Stark, I need to clarify a disturbing point. Why would *Scharnhorst* drop back behind *Rawalpindi* and continue to stalk her if she herself is toothless? This disturbs me and I think that it does some of us here as well. I have an opinion, but I defer to the naval tacticians on this one. I sure as damnation would do a rapid retreat if my men were out of bullets."

Before Stark could answer, the heretofore silent Commander-in-Chief of the Atlantic Fleet, Rear Admiral Max Horton jumped in. Horton was known by every Royal Navy person of substance as a brilliant strategist, who thought far in advance of the daily operation of his charges. His closest associates also knew that when it came down to pushing and shoving, he never hesitated to plunge right in. The only irritating side to him was his penchant for mind-numbing bombast circling about the issues at hand. The five other men mentally steeled themselves and silently prayed he would not go on one of his notorious interminable boring diatribes.

"To answer your question Brigadier is a trifle complex but I shall give it the old Sandhurst try. First, as to their gunfire being uncharacteristically subpar, it is my theory that they probably had some minor, but repairable malfunction and are shadowing *Rawalpindi* for a few more hours while they effect the necessary repairs. Then at dawn or shortly thereafter they will pull up into convenient gun range for themselves and deal our beloved *Rawalpindi* a death blow. If the guns required shipyard help, she would definitely not be shadowing a single vessel into dangerous waters. Secondly, if she was short on ammunition, she definitely would not have even considered going after our string of lone stragglers in the first place. My third and last point is one of character, or should I say ego. With the detailed description of Captain Kastanien's character Admiral Stark gave us at the last meeting, it's most probable that our vainglorious Captain Kastanien didn't like it one iota that we had the audacity and reckless temerity to shoot back and score a hit, however minor, and now he is out for retribution. However, still none of these points makes any truly coherent conventional sense and that is why I need to eschew some more of my rather limited brain power to sort out this conundrum. I thank you gentlemen for your indulgence."

Air Marshal Dowding mentally debated for a split second on whether he should come back with a retort that only a few scholars of the English language could understand but threw that idea out because of the useless squabbling that would surely come of it. He simply stepped into the discussion that had to this point been surprisingly polite and courteous.

"My fellow officers, might I be as bold as to simply get to the real issue. It really matters not what the German is up to. All that really matters is that we hopefully are going to get a crack at him. It is now about 2100 local time where *Scharnhorst* is located. At present speed of ten to twelve knots she will have traveled somewhere between a 120 to 150 miles when first light comes on the scene. Battle Group "C" spearheaded by *King George V* will be waiting with open arms. About an hour later the larger Battle Group "A" with battleships *Hood* and *Repulse* accompanied by the aircraft carrier *Ark Royal* will show up on the scene. As soon as it is light enough *Ark Royal* will launch all her planes. If the favorable weather conditions hold, they should arrive just as the shooting match from Battle Group "C" commences. *Scharnhorst* is damnable fast. If she opts not to engage us and runs for France all we can do at this juncture is to follow along doggedly and hopefully inflict some damage from *Ark Royal's* aircraft to slow her down. Then wait until our battle group can catch up and finish her off. We might even get lucky with some long range shells from *King George V* and that would be the end of one nasty menace. *Gneisenau,* after severely mauling Convoy PK 17, and sinking three of our destroyers and several merchants, broke off the engagement at dark and was last tracked by radar heading north-east.

"Putting these facts together it would appear the *Ugly Sisters* are planning to reunite later tomorrow to the west of *Scharnhorst's* location—after she deals with *Rawalpindi.* We should fervently hope that this is the case, for then we just might get the two of them ensuring our convoys will at least be safe from these dangerous and damnable efficient surface raiders.

"In summary, let me just simply state again that our only true objective is to sink the *Sisters.* What either of them is up to now matters not a fiddler's damn if we get them under our guns."

"Well put Air Marshal, I know that you gentlemen would like to finish your brandies before we adjourn so if there is any other salient points about how the plan is progressing, please air them now. However, I caution you not to get into any heated arguments, as now is not the time. We will meet again in the morning at 8:00AM and then we shall see what we shall see."

Oddly enough it was Montgomery who brought up the next point.

"Gentlemen, and although I address this question to all, it mainly is aimed at Admiral's Stark and Horton. If *Scharnhorst's* gunfire is truly a bit out of whack and they are affecting repairs through the night, then why can we not see any light from her since she is following us only a dozen miles or so back? The weather is clear and the seas are relatively calm. Surely they cannot affect repairs in the dark. It is my fervent belief that there's much more to this cagy captain Kastanien than we are giving him credit for. Tomorrow morning should be interesting, yes, very interesting. That's all I have to say except I shall bid you good night after I quaff down the truly exquisite brandy. Bye the bye, does anyone know how Churchill gets this Armenian Brandy?"

Silence reigned for a brief moment before Ian McLeod spoke up, "As I seem to be the only one to answer Monty's question, here is the rather *interesting* answer. Although Germany and the Soviet Union are partners in crime right now, the Armenian Brandy comes to Winston courtesy of dear old 'Uncle' Joe Stalin. And if you're wondering how much, which I did not know until enlightened, it amounts to slightly over 400 bottles a year. It seems to me that good old Joe is hedging his bet by keeping Winston on his good side. I shan't get into the politics of this enigma right now as it will probably clear itself up down the road."

With the critical intelligence report delivered and a rather smooth, partially productive meeting behind him, The First Lord of the Admiralty decided that there was really nothing more to be gained except to finish their brandies. Standing quite smartly after the Field Marshal had finished, he adjourned the meeting with a few short sentences.

"The contraband brandy is an excellent closing to an excellent meeting. Thank you 'Monty' and thank you gentlemen for all your valuable input. We shall meet again on the morrow at eight in the morning. That will be about an hour before first light in the battle zone. Let us hope that it will be a jovial occasion. Good night."

Scharnhorst

The glossy black metal shark smartly cruised up alongside *Scharnhorst* and the signal lamp chattered rapid blinking instructions directed by Kastanien. U-3200X responded and the exchange of new battle strategies was over in less than five minutes. The signals being finished, the U-boat moved to a position two kilometers from the starboard side of *Scharnhorst* and maintained her station there.

"Mr. Schmidt, we are about twenty kilometers behind the vessel. How long will it take to close to five thousand meters at twenty-five knots?" Kastanien asked his Executive Officer.

"Give or take a few minutes, about an hour and fifteen minutes Captain."

"Very well Mr. Schmidt. We will maintain our present speed for now. I am returning to my cabin. Remember also that they can drop mines into the water so keep us well off their starboard side, preferably not less than three kilometers. And again, most importantly, inform me if the ship makes any change in speed, direction or does anything other than maintaining her present course and speed."

Kastanien, with Attila tucked in the crook of his left arm, walked the short distance to his cabin, and entered, quietly closing the door.

"Well Attila, we are about to test our theories about our strange ship."

The big Siamese raised his head, stared at the captain, and then sprang gracefully to the bunk. Kastanien once more put his jacket in the closet, removed his boots, with a slight nudge moved his friend, and sat on the edge of the bunk proceeding to methodically massage his feet. After a few minutes of this therapy, Kastanien shifted his body into a reclining position on the bunk and tucked his stocking feet under a soft gray woolen blanket that his beloved Andrea sent with him every time he went to sea. Attila didn't twitch his ears or open his eyes at his companion's movements. The cat was so accustomed to his human's habits that nothing commonplace would disturb his beauty rest.

Picking up the direct intercom to the radar room that hung on a convenient hook, Kastanien spoke quietly, "Molter, are you still there?"

"Yes Captain. What can I do for you?" The young boy responded.

"The U3200X is two kilometers directly on our starboard. Can your radar 'see' her?"

"Yes Captain. I can see her but her low profile causes the blips to be slight and intermittent."

"Please answer the next question as truthfully as you can. It is very important. Given the sea conditions do not change for better or worse, how far away would she need to be before our radar would not get even the slightest indication that she was there?"

Again Molter felt the pangs of anxiety with the import of his Captain's question. He took a deep breath and ventured his opinion. Since the captain had been so truthful with him, he decided to give the question his most honest opinion.

"Captain, I believe we might have the odd very slight indication of a vessel with such a low profile at a range of five kilometers. But even if a skilled operator was looking intently at his screen, there would be no signal whatsoever much further away than that."

"Very well Molter. Continue to monitor the U3200X as she will start moving further away from us shortly. Report to me every two minutes until she is eight kilometers off our starboard side, or when you lose any radar contact, and I mean absolutely no contact whatsoever."

"Yes Sir, Captain."

Kastanien had ordered the U3200X to move gradually away from *Scharnhorst* starting five minutes after the signals had been completed. This exercise was part of a plan that had been conceived by Grossadmiral Dönitz and himself many months ago. Molter dutifully reported to Kastanien precisely every two minutes. Every two minutes the reports stated that the signal was becoming progressively weaker as the distance the radar had to "see" increased. When the range opened to five kilometers, Molter reported that there was no signal whatsoever. Kastanien smiled to himself at the genius of the strategy that Dönitz had confided in him just before this sortie. Kastanien spoke once again into the intercom, "Molter; I want you to keep your eyes glued to that screen and let me know when you 'see' the U3200X again and tell me the range and position relative to us."

"Yes Captain."

Captain Kastanien then closed his eyes and tried to relax a bit knowing that he needed to be very sharp and alert come first light. The pulsing throb of the powerful engines coupled with the soothing rhythm of Attila gave the captain a sense of relative peace and his hitherto tension relaxed noticeably. Twenty minutes passed in relative silence before the excited voice of radar operator Molter broke through the intercom and announced, "Captain, Captain, I have picked up a very minor blip five kilometers directly behind us and maintaining her station with us. I know that it's U3200X."

"Very well Molter, stay with her and keep me informed. I am returning to the bridge so direct your reports there."

Kastanien then quickly rotated off the bunk and proceeded to put on his boots. Retrieving his jacket and after donning it, he carefully checked his appearance in the mirror. Satisfied that he looked every bit the part of the guiding force of a very serious warship, he left the cabin with Attila jauntily bouncing along at his side, and returned to the bridge. Navigating the short trip to the command center, he settled into his comfortable captain's chair and remained silent. Attila, sensing that his human was going to remain seated for some time floated up to the special place that he commanded and began the exercises that all cats do when they arise from even a short catnap. He stretched his back legs one at a time, then the fore paws, yawned a yawn so wide that it seemed impossible that such a tiny mouth could open that wide.

Then he gracefully leaped from the bridge shelf onto Kastanien's lap and nuzzled his beloved Peter under his chin. Kastanien relaxed under the soothing music that emanated from the sleek feline and unconsciously began rubbing the cat's ears. Attila responded with an increase in volume that could be heard throughout the entire bridge. Many minutes passed with only the sounds of the ship speeding through the North Atlantic, the pulse of the engines and the melodic purring. Then Kastanien rose from the chair, placed Attila back on his blanket and strode back to the radar room.

"We've done well so far Molter. Continue watching her and let me know when she is directly opposite our port side."

"Yes Captain."

Kastanien returned to the bridge and remained standing staring out the front window pane. None of the bridge officers spoke to him or to each other. They had learned that the captain had his mind very busy planning his next move and preferred total silence.

Less than fifteen minutes later Molter's voice, this time less excited, announced through the intercom, "U3200X is now holding station four kilometers directly off our port side. Signal is weak but there is no interruption or variance in the signal."

Kastanien made a small positive nod mainly to himself and again returned to the radar room.

"Well done 'Merlin.' That exercise is now over. Your earlier appraisal of our radar's eyes was very accurate. The next exercise is most important. I will stay here with you as it progresses and we shall see or not see."

Molter looked questionably at his hero but kept his normally inquisitive tongue still. As the veteran captain and the young man watched the bouncing green bar that was U3200X moved slowly closer to the larger blip that was the mystery vessel they were shadowing. After fifteen minutes the small weak blip of the U-boat blended with the larger one and the two signals became one.

"Well, Molter what do you surmise from this?"

Once more Molter's stomach churned a trifle at his responsibility to the importance of Kastanien's question. But, as his entire appraisal to date had been accurate, the captain's quiet assurances had bolstered his confidence. The stomach spasm passed almost before he responded, "Captain, it seems to me that when two ships are aligned the signals become one, and one ship cannot be distinguished from the other. Even though the two ships right now are twenty and four kilometers from us, the signal from U3200X is completely hidden from our sight. All that we can 'see' is the larger vessel we're following and it shows that it's twenty kilometers away. There is no trace of our U-boat whatsoever even though she is relatively close. On radar the U3200X does not exist."

Kastanien stood for nearly a minute in deep thought then put Molter on the spot once more.

"Merlin, assuming British radar is twice as good as ours and they can 'see' the very low profile of U3200X at a range of ten kilometers, would they be able to distinguish our signal from the U-boat if we were much closer and aligned as we are now?"

Molter, inwardly beaming at Kastanien's use of his nickname again, gave him even more confidence to his reply.

"Captain, first of all I don't believe that British radar is twice as good as ours and this vessel is a merchant ship, which, if she carries radar at all, it would not be the best that they have. They surely would save that for their top of the line warships. Begging the Captains pardon but before I answer your question let me explain how radar works."

Molter immediately stiffened when he realized that he was almost lecturing his hero and his apprehension was palpable. Kastanien noted the boy's bodily reaction, immediately realizing what he had said and how it could have affected him. He instantly broke in before his radar operator blundered into much deeper water trying to appease his slight impertinence, "Merlin, unfortunately I have not had the time to grasp but only a rudimentary understanding of this invisible electric witchcraft. I welcome your teaching and right now would be the most perfect time. Please continue. I shall only interrupt if there is a point I do not fully comprehend."

Molter inwardly felt an enormous relief and being very insightful, especially for his age, he realized that his beloved captain had salvaged what could have been a very awkward situation. He had done it so skillfully that both parties came away relieved of tension. Best of all, further rapid progress in the infant technology of radar was definitely going to happen, now that the captain had laid out the ground rules. He knew without question, that when there was a quiet time away from action stations he could approach his captain and explain his theories on how to dramatically improve Germany's radar effectiveness.

Kastanien moved up another notch in the boy's hero worship even though he already felt that Kastanien was the most wonderful person on Earth, and could not be improved even one iota. He was pleased to think that he was wrong on this point, and looked forward to his bright future with a captain that was going to be noticed by the entire world. Kastanien, long a student of body language, sensed the boy's train of thought and immediately knew that their relationship, both personal and militarily, would be very satisfying. Kastanien's wily brain decided that a short break before the lesson began would make things even easier, so he ventured forth knowing what he was about to do would endear Molter to him and he would be able to glean every speck of important information regarding radar much sooner.

"Merlin, I shall be back in a moment."

Kastanien strode the few paces to the bridge, paused by his captain's chair and inquired of the bridge officers if there was anything he needed to know. All the officers replied that all was well and running smoothly. Kastanien then walked over to Attila, picked him up and returned to the radar room. Cradling the now ever-curious feline on his left arm, Kastanien with an obvious mirthful grin very quietly said to Molter, "Merlin, would you like to hold Attila for a bit and maybe he will impart some of his infinite wisdom to your appraisal?"

Molter's heart almost burst with joy. It was the highest compliment possible on the ship to be blessed with Attila's close presence—let alone to hold him. With a euphoric electric charge coursing through every artery, vein and brain cell, Molter reverently and silently reached up for the cat. Attila, sensing that this human revered him, made a small hop and gracefully landed in the radar operator's lap. Almost stunned by the cat's actions and obvious acceptance, Molter gently grasped the cat by his shoulders and began to gently rub under the cat's chin. Attila responded by raising his head so the boy could reach his favorite spot easier and started a strong, loud purring. Molter was almost beside himself with boundless joy but managed to control himself in front of Kastanien.

"Merlin, I can see that you two have become instant friends. That is wonderful. Now Attila will give you his very best advice. You must understand that it will be mostly silent, but if you listen with your hands, you will get his very sage advice. "

"Captain, I have adored Attila ever since we became shipmates but this is the very first time that I have actually held him. I cannot thank you enough for this wondrous moment."

"You are quite welcome. Now, before my duties take me away, let the lesson continue."

"Sir, the concept of radar is quite simple. We send out a signal on a certain frequency that goes a very long way until it fades and is absorbed by the atmosphere. However, if the frequency wave encounters a metallic or otherwise solid object, it bounces off and redirects a portion of the wave in the reverse direction. Overlapping outgoing waves burst out approximately thirty degrees a second until they have covered a full circle which is called a sweep. Then they continue on their next revolution and continue to complete each three hundred and sixty degree sweep about every three seconds. The outgoing pulses overlap each other by five degrees. So, there are fourteen segments to the sweep, which are shown here as fourteen bars that pulsate vertically ever so slightly. If the pulses encounter nothing they will only go so high. But when a pulse reflects a metallic object that it has encountered, that particular bar jumps up higher. The higher the bar goes the larger and closer the object is. The object of the overlapping causes the adjacent bars to pulse higher as well. But they do not rise as high. It is my job to analyze the height of all three bars to determine the distance to the object. It took quite a bit of training and an awful lot of just staring at the screen to become accurate.

I had a lot of help from the men manning the rangefinders to gain the knowledge needed to give you answers as accurate as possible. I think that I learned the most about accuracy when we were engaging the British at the River Platte. The bars were jumping all over the place with our three ships engaging the four British cruisers. I watched the screen all the while, listening intently to the rangefinders calling out the range and direction."

"Merlin, please excuse the interruption but I can see the larger rise on one of your bars. Is that the U3200X or our mystery vessel?" Kastanien pointed to a particular spot on the screen.

"Yes Captain that is the mystery vessel. If you look closely, you can see the bar to the left also bumps a trifle as well. That is caused by the overlap of the pulses. The tiny jump from the bar on the left in relation to the larger one is how we determine the range. The largest jump gives us the direction. My interpretation of these pulses tells me that the ship is about twenty kilometers away from us and that the bar you pointed out means that she is ahead of us, four kilometers on our port bow. Because the U3200X is so low in the water compared to the other much taller vessel, the U-boat's signal has been overridden by the stronger return pulses of the larger vessels."

"Merlin, do you think that the British system, which is different from ours, particularly the one aboard our mystery vessel can distinguish the U3200X from us?"

"No Sir. Their system can't because the theory of radar is universal. Only the technology that they use to interpret the return signals is different," Molter replied with complete conviction in his voice.

Just then Attila, who sensed he was no longer the center of attention that he felt was always warranted, rose up on Molter's lap and stepped onto the radar console. The cat delicately sniffed at the bouncing green bars, and then proceeded to minutely inspect every switch, knob and screw on the entire console.

Molter and Kastanien paused silently enjoying watching the very graceful feline do his inspection. Attila satisfied that he now knew everything about radar returned to Molter's lap for a moment. Then he looked up at Kastanien. Kastanien, finely attuned to the cat's subtle looks and body language, picked Attila up and returned him to the cradle in his left arm. Molter felt a bit crushed that the cat had left him but he rose to the occasion and said.

"Thank you Attila for imparting your blessing on my machine. I know now for certain that the machine and I will perform much better."

Kastanien smiled and reading this incredible boy's body motions quietly said, "Mr. Molter, you have now attained a special status with our guiding star. You may ask me anytime, particularly when you are off duty, to visit with Attila."

"Oh, thank you so much Captain. I shall treasure those moments with him."

Kastanien knew that with this simple gesture that his beloved cat had cemented a powerful relationship with his young head radar operator. He knew positively that he could count on risking his wondrous battleship on the interpretations of wiggly green lines by a mere youth. He was remembering how sure of himself he was at that age, and his faith was solidified in Marvin "Merlin" Molter.

Reaching across with his right hand, Kastanien grasped Attila's front right paw then leaned forward and touched the paw to Molter's cheek.

"Now, Mr. Molter you have our official blessings, and now I must return to my duties. Your explanation of the intricacies of our new tool of warfare was very enlightening and concise. I thank you for your valued help and please continue to keep us so well informed."

Kastanien, with Attila still cradled in his arm returned to the bridge. Upon his arrival in the center of the massive ship's decision-making room, he ordered, "Mr. Gott. Signal U3200X to come alongside our port beam immediately."

The underwater signal was instantly sent. Kastanien then turned to his officers and informed them to prepare to transfer all prisoners from the U3200X on board. The officers immediately sprang to the ship's various intercom systems to relay the order to receive prisoners. From several internal body parts of the steel leviathan, twenty able bodied seamen with their ever present chief petty officer, scurried about donning their cold weather gear. Twenty minutes later Executive Officer Schmidt informed the captain that U3200X was two hundred meters off the port beam. Kastanien with the signal man and First Officer Gott went out into the relatively calm but cold ink-black night through the bridge wing door. All three men had donned their long greatcoats in anticipation of the cold which would be magnified considerably by the forward movement of the ship and the wind. The wind had died to a mere breeze, but the temperature had dropped to a nippy 16F which didn't seem all that cold as the humidity was fairly low, mainly because of the lack of cloud cover.

However, their breaths immediately became visible. The sea had reduced itself to lackadaisical smooth swells, not much more than a meter high, but elicited a short quick intake of air from the signal man. Kastanien then gave instructions to the signal man who immediately started sending new orders with amazing speed on his signal lamp. The message was relatively brief. It simply told U3200X to come alongside and prepare to transfer all the prisoners.

After a very short interval the U3200X began closing to about a hundred meters from *Scharnhorst* easily keeping station with her. The twenty seamen from the innards of *Scharnhorst* had already reached the main deck. This was where the eight-meter long open wooden tender was stored. The storage area was just a few meters in front of a 5.9 inch SK C/28 naval gun and directly below the open flying bridge. Each seaman had done this exercise many times and knew exactly what his duty was to prepare the tender for launching. Within a minute, the tender was swung outboard on its davits and was lowered almost to the water. Kastanien had opted to transfer prisoners on his port side because of the slight easterly wind. Eight sailors, each equipped with a sidearm, scrambled down the rope netting and settled in their respective places. Chief Petty Officer Günter Teaset, carrying the standard issue Spatz machine pistol, dropped the half meter from the net into the tender immediately barking the order to cast off. Knowing the exercise so well and exactly what and when Teasel would order, the tender was severed from the mother ship, almost before his last words were uttered.

On the deck of the U3200X the eight survivors of the *Gay Lily* were coming up the forward hatch. The searchlights of the *Scharnhorst* blazed down with an almost blinding brilliance. The prisoners and their guards all had to shield their eyes by looking down at their feet and the deck to avoid serious injury to their optic nerves. The U-boat's crew, although they had done this same exercise several times, were still shocked at the ferocious candlepower of the *Scharnhorst's* lamps. When one of the submarine's crew had suggested that they really didn't need all the lights at full power he was slightly criticized by the executive officer who patiently explained the very sound reasoning behind the intentional use of blinding light. The transfers were always done at night with maximum lights from the *Scharnhorst* to deliberately ruin any night vision the prisoners might have had. Since the U3200X was so new and revolutionary, the top priority of the High Command, as well as the respective captains and crew members, was to prevent any enemy from getting a good look at the U3200X.

It was felt that if any rescued merchant marine sailors could have seen the apparatus behind the conning tower, they might have deduced what it was. Even if they didn't grasp the enormous significance, they were bound to report their observations to the Royal Navy, and those clever, razor-sharp minds would no doubt figure out what the hump did, or at least let it fester until the answer was forthcoming. They would probably string together any and all unexplained phenomenon and occurrences to make a very educated guess. So, to keep the stellar reputation of the German High Seas Fleet, all the non-combatant rescued persons were always released and none the wiser about the special features of the U3200X. While the transfer was taking place, Kastanien, with Gott and the signal man started fresh orders to U3200X.

This time the orders took more time as they were lengthy and complex. After nearly ten minutes in the biting cold damp weather the three men returned to the warm comfort of the bridge. Even the heavy winter coats could not keep the bone chilling damp cold from penetrating seemingly right into their bones. All three men huddled close to the radiators that kept the silent devils of winter weather at bay. Kastanien removed his gloves proceeding to massage his hands and cheeks for a few moments. Then he ascertained that the prisoner transfer was complete. With the transfer attended to, Kastanien crisply issued his new orders, "Ring up twenty-five knots and close the gap. Plot a course to put our friend directly on our port side at a distance of three kilometers. Please inform me when we are within a few minutes of this position. Maintain our normal night lighting."

The order was repeated through the bridge and within less than thirty seconds, the ship began throbbing slightly as the huge diesels came up to the needed revolutions. The battleship's engines reverberated throughout the ship settling her far more comfortably in the sea and she sped towards the mysterious vessel.

"Gentlemen, we are going to close on the vessel we have been following. We should be in position in about an hour. Go to battle stations in forty-five minutes. Have all guns ready but we will be only using the 105mm forward turret in the beginning. There have been too many strange things about this ship so we are about to do some strange things ourselves. Maybe then the mysteries will unfold, and we will have some answers. I intend that the answers are to be decidedly in our favor. When we are in position almost directly beside the vessel at three thousand meters, fire a star shell over her. We will open fire with one of the 105mm forward turrets only. Now, Mr. Gott, please inform your gun crew manning the 105 that they are to deliberately miss any vital part with their shooting. I do not want this vessel badly crippled or worse yet, sunk. I want only to score a few hits that will do little damage. When we have accomplished this goal, we will continue at full speed past her for two hours and see if there are any more 'floating ducks' to this apparent string of ships the British have so conveniently presented to us.

"Regardless whether we spot any new contacts or not, we will reverse our course and come back on her opposite quarter. We will then simply return to our present position 20,000 meters behind her. When we are back in that position, we are going follow for a short while and then disappear.

"However, if our mysterious friend up ahead turns out to be something other than an innocuous merchant, then we will begin the high speed turn sooner, and deal with her accordingly as the situation presents itself. Have the radar room keep me informed of any change, regardless of how minor, in our prey's actions. Have the radio room monitor any signals coming from the vessel and relay them to me immediately upon their being deciphered. I will be in my cabin for the next thirty minutes. I will leave Attila here to answer any of your questions. I'm sure that all of you have some that need answering before we begin our rather *bad* shooting run."

Kastanien and all the bridge officers' faces broke into knowing grins with a few chuckles all around at the captain's rather humorous and sarcastic last remarks.

Attila came to attention at the mention of his name and turned his head toward his closest human friend. Peter Kastanien returned Attila's questioning look and gave a sign back to the cat to stay on his blanket.

Attila shnurgled his head the way only cats can do and turned back to stare out the window at the endless black of the clear, calm moonless night. Kastanien disappeared down the short hallway and entered his quarters. He only unbuttoned his jacket before seating himself at the desk. Opening the top right hand drawer, he took out the rather large log book and began his entries for the day so far. He wrote nearly an entire page in his rather fine handwriting—the bulk of which were his conclusions regarding the mystery vessel and its unorthodox actions. Then he finished by stating what his battle plan would be commencing in an hour. When he finished writing he reread the entire page twice. Leaning back in the chair, he silently pondered to himself, *"Well, I have cast the die. I hope on one hand that I am correct and then on the other hand I don't. Regardless of what the next twelve hours bring, I cannot turn aside now."*

Suddenly, he stiffened with a look of amazement on his rather handsome face and spoke out loud, "Shoot without shells!"

Kastanien immediately picked up the intercom to the bridge and spoke, "Mr. Schmidt, please have Gunnery Officer Rost, First Officer Gott, along with yourself join me in my cabin as soon as possible."

The Gunnery Officer was in the galley chattering away in his usual quite loud voice when the order was announced over the loudspeaker. Since it was only a short distance up two decks, he arrived less than a minute after the other two officers who had been stationed on the bridge. The three officers were waved to the small conference table where they quickly sat down. Kastanien was clearly a bit livelier than his usual reserved self so he did not sit immediately, but paced silently for a minute or two.

The three officers had seen their captain in this state more than a few times in the past so they simply waited patiently. Kastanien paused near the cabin door for a moment, then quickly strode back to the table and seated himself. He stared over the head of the gunnery officer who was seated directly opposite him for only a brief moment before he affixed the gunnery officer with a questioning look and spoke, "Mr. Rost, gentlemen, I have been pondering our mysterious friend out front, and the strange way she has been behaving has gnawed at the back of my mind ever since we started following her. I just finished putting my thoughts and conclusions in our log book and then an idea struck me. First let me review her actions for all of us to consider.

"When we sunk the first ship, our friend up ahead made no evasive maneuvers; which merchants always do when threatened by any type of warship. She did not darken herself, which would be the natural thing to do since it was very near totally dark. We could not get a real good look at her because of the darkness and distance. All we have to go on as to her identity and type is her lighting. It appears to be about the normal configuration for a merchant ship but the wily British could very well have disguised a small warship to throw us off and get us in close, where their smaller armament might inflict some crippling damage. The glaring, rather stupid action she took was to reduce speed when we did. She probably realized this blunder too late and is maintaining a slower than possible speed hoping we will come to the conclusion that she has tired engines after the supposed long trip from the Western Hemisphere.

"Our radar had not had even the smallest blip of other ships that should have been in relatively close proximity after our first strike. These things are just too odd for me to take at face value and go charging in to sink her. Parts of my deductions are based on reading the radio intercepts from both ships. The Admiralty has been strangely silent. We have not intercepted a single message coming from England advising the ship what to do. Now, before I surprise you with my interesting idea, please give me any thoughts you might have regarding what I have said or what you may have surmised or concluded."

At that Kastanien leaned back in his chair and waited. There was a brief silence before the first officer cleared his throat, leaned forward and began, "My Captain, I believe that I speak for all of the officers on the bridge. We have gone over all the ship's actions and we reached the same conclusion as you. And that is that this ship and her actions are definitely out of the normal way of merchant ships, therefore we must be very wary."

Sensing that the first officer was finished, the gunnery officer quickly jumped in with his usual loud voice. Erwin Rost was in his mid-forties, but would not admit it to any of the crew of mainly youngsters in their mid-twenties, which he considered rather green pups. He had served on Kastanien's last ship in the First World War as a gunner. He had shown a singularly, almost mystic touch, when it came to aiming his guns, but like most of the Imperial German Navy he had been mustered out at war's end. Kastanien had kept in touch with him through the bleak years until the new *Scharnhorst* was near completion and then had asked him if he would serve again, but this time as gunnery officer of a battleship. Rost was a very proud man and the golden opportunity to hold his head up high in the new Navy was irresistible.

Back in his old ship, devices such as ear plugs and ear phones were relatively ineffective against the repeated fearsome blasts of large-caliber naval guns. Consequently, his hearing was badly impaired. The entire crew knew that to bring it to his attention would not only be rather impolite, but would elicit a ferocious denial. So, the small gathering of officers politely ignored what almost amounted to shouting and listened to the rough, tough but very talented man.

"Captain, you have stated that we are definitely not to sink our friend, but just shoot good enough to wound her. I for one would like to know your reasoning."

The slight impertinence passed without even a raised eyebrow, such was the respect everyone had for this incredibly talented Officer.

"Yes, Mr. Rost you may ask, but right now, until we can all least see who and what we are going against, I will keep my future plan to myself, as I feel we will have to modify it very shortly.

"Now, this next question is for you Mr. Rost. I would like for you to answer honestly and then I shall outline our plan to all of you. What would the visual and acoustic effect of shooting our main guns without shells— just the powder bags?"

The two other officers sat straighter in their chairs and waited for Rost's answer.

"Captain, before I answer could I inquire what effect you would like to achieve as there are a few different ways to shoot without shells, each method producing a different effect."

"Excellent question Rost, I wish to send a message to the ship ahead which hopefully they will interpret as a serious malfunction of our main armament and report this conclusion to the Admiralty in London."

"Right, Captain, the best way to create the biggest flash that would appear to be a gun blowing apart would be to simply use the normal powder load with a little concoction of mine in the front of it that would light up the night sky like the biggest Chinese fireworks you've ever seen. My little concoction is mainly comprised of magnesium which burns exceedingly hot and bright. The blast noise would be about the same. Would this be what the Captain wants?"

"Absolutely Mr. Rost, you have again delivered to us a perfect solution to the subterfuge I intend to impart on our British adversaries. I will only require one round from each gun in the forward eleven-inch turret if we are to hoodwink the British into thinking our big guns are inoperable. More than one shooting would be improbable anyway. Now, before I continue do any of you gentlemen have any comments?"

Curiosity won out over conversation and the men waited impatiently for Kastanien to continue.

"Very well then. Here is my plan of action. We will follow the previous plan by commencing fire with the forward 105 turret only. These will be our normal shells and please Mr. Rost, don't let any of them hit causing any serious damage. At the short range you will be challenged to shoot very close. I want them close so as not to raise questions since we have a reputation to uphold for superb gunnery amongst the British Navy. After it has been determined by the prey and ourselves that we have missed, that is when you will fire turret Anton with your fireworks display.

To prevent the watchers from being able to see what effect this 'accident' had on our ship, we will be approaching with all of our searchlights on and pointed toward them. This will effectively blind them. That will be all of our shooting for the time being. We will then continue at high speed until we are fifteen kilometers ahead of them. At that point we will turn off all of our lights and turn 180 degrees back towards them. We'll be relying on our young radar operator 'Merlin' to keep us informed of their relative position. We'll approach at high speed until we are three kilometers directly off their port side. Then we will turn on our searchlights again and commence firing with only the forward 105 gun again. Now, Mr. Rost you can once again show us how accurate you can be by scoring a few hits that are not fatal, nor will slow them down. We want them to continue on their course as though they had not been harmed. When we have gone past effective gun range, we'll douse our lights again.

"Now, that is the basic plan which could very well be revised when we determine what we have to deal with. If all goes close to this plan, we'll steam back to twenty kilometers behind our now wounded, but not crippled friend and continue to shadow her as before. She definitely had radar on board because I don't believe for one brief moment that her slowing down to match our speed was a mere coincidence. Being as the British have precious few radar units in operation, this is another strange thing that we'll be very wary about. It could well be that this plodding merchant is anything but harmless. Well, that's our plan of battle gentlemen. Do any of you have further comments?"

His small audience had sat transfixed during Kastanien's dissertation outlining his rather interesting if not outrageous plan No one even realized for a brief moment that they had been asked to join in the conversation. Executive Officer Schmidt shattered the mesmerized silence like a hammer breaking a pane of glass.

"Captain, I can speak only for myself regarding your plan. It is so different from anything I was taught at the Naval Academy I will need a few moments to digest the many facets of this rather clever plan that we will accomplish—should all go as planned. I mean no disrespect Sir, but what will we do if the ship is armed and presents a danger?"

"If this ship is armed and she fires on us with deck guns or torpedoes, what shall we do at such close range?" Rost loudly chirped in.

Kastanien let a somewhat mirthful grin flow over his face and then looked over at the gunnery officer.

"Mr. Rost, I believe that you now have your targets laid before you, assuming that they will exist. And if, or should I say when, they open fire we will scuttle away as quickly as we can so as to maintain the illusion that our main guns are not functional and our shooting is rather below par referring to our previous stellar reputation. Let's decipher all incoming and outgoing messages to the ship when the fireworks start. That should give us a very good insight into the British mindset. My secondary intention, regarding this ruse, is to let the British determine that our rangefinders and radar combination has also been damaged, resulting in our poor accuracy."

Noting that the proud gunnery officer's rather dour face, Kastanien started to placate the man's wounded pride in having to deliberately miss with a gentle word or two—then remembered that he needed to talk a bit louder than normal so this key man could hear with his gun-blast damaged hearing.

"Mr. Rost, do not despair in having to shoot rather poorly. I will consider your ability to knock out any of their troublesome armament as a confirmation that your shooting will be as good if not better than we have witnessed in our previous encounters. I recall, as all of our crew no doubt does, your incredible shooting when we aided *Graf Spee*. Hitting the cruiser *Ajax* at a range of nearly thirty kilometers was nothing short of art."

Rost, along with the others grinned broadly at the compliment and returned to his normal demeanor, now that his character had met with official and public approval. No one spoke for nearly a minute so Kastanien stepped in, "If no one has anything further to offer up for discussion, this meeting is now over. We will go to battle stations fifteen minutes before we are broadside to the ship. Be sure to pass on our plan of attack to all the other officers, and especially the gun crews. They must, absolutely must, understand that the orders are not to inflict any serious damage. Lastly, let everyone here understand that all battle plans usually change significantly when the fight is joined. Be prepared for instant changes in orders. That is all."

The three officers stood immediately, saluted, and filed from the cabin. Kastanien reflected for a moment, and then went to the bridge. On his arrival, Attila bounced down from the second officers arms prancing over to his beloved Peter. Kastanien reached down and picked up the happily purring cat. Kastanien then proceeded to settle comfortably in his captain's chair with Attila who quickly made a few circular turns in his lap before settling down—making himself at home. Kastanien was leaning slightly forward signaling to the cat that he was on alert. Attila had sensed this in Kastanien several times and knew what it presaged. Although the feline maintained the unwritten code of all cats by seeming to be unconnected with the rest of the world, nonetheless his ears, eyes and nose were also on high alert anticipating some new adventure.

"Mr. Mueller, what distance to the quarry and your estimate when we'll be broadside of her?"

"Captain, we have a closure rate of eighteen knots and are now eight kilometers behind her and three kilometers off her starboard side. I estimate we will be broadside of her in twenty-six minutes."

"Very well, Mr. Mueller. Please fetch me all the recent intercepts from the radio room."

Mueller dashed the short distance to the radio room returning within thirty seconds. He simply handed three slips of paper to the captain before returning to his post. Kastanien first checked to assure himself that the messages were in proper sequence and slowly read them through, and then read them again. He then let his head rest on the high back of the chair, closed his eyes, and let out a deep but quiet breath. Even on the darkened bridge, the expression on his face telegraphed, to every one of his superb officers, that he was in very deep and analyzing thought. They had all witnessed this thoughtful characteristic mood of the ingenious and daring man that had preceded him before leading them into battle. To a man, they recalled that his unorthodox battle tactics had always resulted in spectacular victories—sometimes against quite bad odds.

After a few moments Kastanien opened his eyes and leaning forward silently glanced over the bridge officers stopping on no one— seemingly still in his thoughtful frame of mind. All the while he unconsciously stroked Attila. Attila, of course wiggled his head slightly, so that the stroking would include his favorite rubbing spot under the chin. Then Kastanien blinked back to the present, cradled Attila and stood up. He deposited Attila on his favorite red blanket and then began to slowly pace the width of the bridge. He clasped his hands behind his back, and with his head bowed a trifle, returned to his silent private deliberations. After four transits of the bridge he turned and went directly to the radar room.

"Mr. Molter, what distance are we from the ship?"

"Captain, we are six kilometers behind and three kilometers off her starboard side."

"Thank you."

Returning to the bridge, his reverie over, Captain Kastanien walked over to his Executive Officer Hans Schmidt and asked, "Mr. Schmidt, your best estimate when we will be alongside the ship. Be as accurate as you can."

"Captain, we will come parallel to her in fifteen minutes."

"Thank you Mr. Schmidt."

Kastanien then strode over to the red blanket and after stoking Attila for a moment, whispered in the cat's ear, "Battle stations, my friend."

At the mention of those two very dangerous words directly into his ear, the languishing feline instantly sprang to his feet and stared intently into the captains' eyes. Many say that cats cannot be easily trained to do anything on command—Attila being no exception. However, Attila had learned from painful past experience exactly what "battle stations" meant. When the captain returned his stare and nodded his head, Attila knew that this was for real and precisely what he needed to do for himself and the ship's company. With a grace that only cats can have, he launched himself forward several feet to the deck taking off like a brown and white projectile. He knew the route to his "battle station" and was virtually flying down the corridors to get there before the hated sirens, bells and thundering commotion that the ship and crewmembers always made began.

He was headed at breakneck speed to the galley, located two decks below and fifty feet aft of the bridge. A seaman coming up the first flight of stairs barely saw the hurtling brownish bullet barrel past him. The seaman knew exactly what was about to happen. The crew spent much of their off duty time, and some while on light duty, talking about Attila and his actions. The sighting of the special sailor rocketing down the stairs was immediately affixed to the ship's grapevine. Almost before Attila reached his destination, the entire ship's compliment was mentally preparing for the call to battle stations.

Reaching the galley in his usual record time, Attila slowed to a fast walk and sought out his special friend here in the warm and cozy section of *his* great ship. After a brief few seconds he spotted chief cook Manfried Strass at the opposite end of the galley. He quickly broke into a loping run towards him. Strass had already been pre-warned from the bridge that battle stations were imminent and Attila was on the way. It was one of the chief cook's primary duties to ensure that the pride and joy of *Scharnhorst* was properly ensconced when the ship was employed in the business she was designed for. For chief cook Manfried Strass, he took this duty as his primary function and never would he allow anyone else to make sure that Attila was protected as best as could be done for him. Strass had a very special fondness for his feline friend.

Once more he recalled his first encounter with Attila. During the first Atlantic deployment of *Scharnhorst*, Attila had quickly discovered the galley, immediately deciding that this was a wondrous second home for him. With the sudden arrival of the captain's cat, the galley crew stopped what they were doing and silently watched their most interesting fellow crew member as he began methodically checking out everything with his nose, ears and eyes. After nearly five minutes of close inspection at floor level, Attila made a perfect leap onto an empty stainless steel preparation table and slowly walked down its four meter length. With the cat now at waist level, the chief cook unhurriedly advanced towards the cat, slowly reaching out to pet him. Attila did not have the typical shyness to strangers that most felines do, so when Manfried Strass extended his right hand he turned towards it. As Manfried began stroking him, Attila started to purr and nuzzle the hand with wondrous scents attached to it. The strong and rather loud purr immediately generated ear to ear grins on the entire galley crew. Attila soon stretched up with both front paws laying them on the cook's chest and began to minutely inspect this human's face.

Attila had never seen a completely bald human before in his life so this was an interesting first for him. The cook responded with quiet words of affection that seemed to please the cat immensely. After the inspection was complete, Attila sauntered to the end of the table, and then made the short leap to the adjacent preparation table, whose delicious scents had drifted over to him. The table was half covered with sliced cooked ham that was of very serious interest. He had his nose a mere five millimeters away as he sized up how he could handle the half inch thick and five inches round morsel. The chief cook sized up the situation instantly and produced a wooden cutting board. He quickly began chopping off cat-size chunks of the delicacy. Attila looked up at the man, then settled on his four feet and began to feast on this treat. The cook and crew were mesmerized by this break in the monotony. Everyone simply watched in silence as the cat downed a dozen or more morsels. Cats never eat more than they want or need to at a sitting so when he had eaten his fill, he stood erect on his front paws and began licking his mouth.

Sensing that the time was right, the cook reached out and picked Attila up. To his pleasant surprise, the cat once more started up his melodic engine after settling comfortably into the cook's arms. The crew thought that the chief cook's face would crack—such was the expanse of his grin. After a few moments letting his luncheon meal digest a bit, Attila leaped down and proceeded to stroll into the open stores locker. The chief cook followed him, keeping a respectful distance back. When the cat vanished into the piles of boxes, the cook brought himself back to reality and proceeded to continue what he was doing. When Attila had first appeared, Manfried had been entering this very store room to obtain the supplies for the next meal setting.

Manfried knelt down to pull out a package wrapped in brown paper from the stack of similar items halfway back under the lower shelf and froze. Staring back at him from less than two feet away, perched on the package adjacent to the one that he wanted, were two tiny, fiery red eyes. Manfried knew instantly that this was one of the ship's most unwelcome guests—a big, ugly wharf rat. Rats were the ever-present bane of every vessel. There were just too many nooks and crannies aboard all large vessels for them to be completely exterminated. No matter how many rats, and their junior cousins, the mice, that could be eliminated, they just kept on coming and coming back. Although the galley was always manned and lighted, no amount of effort could ever seem to rid the galley of these obnoxious, greedy and unsanitary pests.

The rat had his back to the wall of the shelf with nowhere to go when the intruder appeared. Both rat and man stared at each other for a split second before the rat acted first. The rather large rodent launched himself directly at Manfried's eyes and Manfried realized too late that he could not avoid this nasty creature in time to avoid serious facial injury. The rat extended his front claws and barred his teeth which turned his face into a hideous snarling beast from the underworld. When the flying rodent was a mere six inches from Manfried's vulnerable face, his vision of impending disaster was cut off by a side view of a much larger, snarling set of barred teeth. Neither the rat, nor Manfried had seen Attila until his teeth slammed into and locked on the rat's neck. Both cat and rat caromed into the other piles of foodstuffs. Although the rodent struggled mightily while screeching an ear-piecing scream, it was no contest whatsoever. Almost before Manfried could extricate himself from the lower shelf the battle was over.

Shaken by the close encounter with the rat, Chief Cook Manfried Strass stood up resting his shaking hands on the top of the shelf. Not so silently he inhaled and exhaled several deep breaths. While the cook was struggling to regain his composure, Attila, with his now quite dead victim, hanging by its neck from his mouth, reappeared on the shelf top. Attila dropped his latest victim and began to rub his head against Manfried's quite hairy forearm. Manfried looked slightly downward at what had now become his hero and gasped out, "Oh my God Attila, thank you, thank you, thank you. That would have been very ugly indeed if that slimy creature had gotten to my face. You will always be the guest of honor here in my galley and your every wish will be my command. Let's return to the main galley and herald your exploit."

Manfried reached for the dead rat, but Attila intervened and picked the corpse. Holding the dead rat again by the neck he dropped to the deck; quite a bit louder than normal. The cook had pretty much regained his composure when he stepped out of the storeroom back into the galley but not enough so that the closest crew members stared at his ashen complexion. The youngest cook's helper, who was the closest exclaimed, "Good Heavens Mr. Strass, what has happened to you?"

As the last words escaped the boy's lips, Attila gracefully alighted on the table carrying his trophy. Everyone's eyes were transfixed at the sight of the cat with his dark-gray burden. Most of the crew was in awe of the nonchalant demeanor of the cat and his ability to sail up to the tabletop carrying a dead weight which appeared to be fully half his size. Although everyone had a burning curiosity to find out what had transpired, no one spoke for nearly a minute before Strass began his explanation of the incident. The galley crew gathered around and like small children listening to a fairy tale moved not a twitch, except for their eyes which traversed between Attila, the rat, and the cook. When Strass finished, a stunned silence fell over all until as their leader, Strass reached down and placed his rather large beefy hand on Attila's shoulders and proclaimed, "Gentlemen, we have no schnapps to properly give a well-deserved toast to our shipmate but at least raise your imaginary glasses in tribute."

As every man raised his cupped empty hand, the cook uttered a sincere and prophetic toast, all the while smiling and looking very gratefully at the proud hunter regally sitting on the worktable, "To Attila, although he might be the smallest crew member of *Scharnhorst*, I hereby bestow upon you the rank of Seaman First Class. Your instant grasp of an ugly situation with your lightning quick resolution will go down in the log book for all to behold. Your bravery is second to none and your legendary namesake from history would surely regale you as much as we do."

With that, the crew exploded into cheering for their new hero. Attila had been sitting on his haunches throughout the speech methodically washing the blood and small bits of fleshy fur off his face. When the cheering died down, he arose and again went over to Strass. After looking him square in the eyes, leaped down quickly disappearing into the other nether regions of the ship that still remained unexplored. He had obviously lost interest in the dead rat and was probably on the prowl for one of its relatives.

Strass had pretty much regained his composure and the color had long since returned to his normally ruddy complexion when the thought occurred to him that he must inform the captain. He also needed to find out if it was with the captain's permission that Attila seemed to be on the loose. With these thoughts in mind he went over to an intercom and switching it on to the bridge requested to speak to the captain.

Within a few seconds, Captain Kastanien replied, "Captain here, what is it you wish Mr. Strass?"

"Begging the Captain's pardon Sir, but might I have a few minutes of your time to inform you of an incident that has just happened here in the galley?"

Kastanien's curiosity was piqued by the thought of what could possibly have transpired in the galley that required him to be informed, "Of course Mr. Strass, come to the bridge immediately with your news."

Manfried Strass hurried very quickly to a part of the ship that he had only been to on three previous occasions. He entered the bridge with his emotions running high as he thought of the power and how life-giving and taking decisions were made here. Sensing his presence, Kastanien turned in his chair smoothly ordering his chief cook to come forward and tell his story. Since the ship was cruising along with nothing pressing happening, Manfried Strass began at the very beginning, stretching the story out a bit longer than necessary. As the tale was being rather well told, most of the bridge crew began to listen intently as the drama unfolded. When he was finished telling the incident, Strass, looking a bit embarrassed, continued, "I hope the Captain will excuse my impertinence for giving Attila a rating."

Kastanien was duly impressed with the manner in which his cat had attained such a high standing with some of his crew. Being thoughtful for a moment he came up with ideas of his own.

"Mr. Strass, your storytelling has been a wonderful relief to the rather boring chores that we on the bridge endure most of the time. Giving a rating to your obvious hero is most welcome and has offended me not in the least. I have a suggestion, that, with your permission, we will upgrade Seaman First Class Attila to Honorary Sergeant-at-Arms."

Strass visibly relaxed, now that he knew that he had not overstepped his boundaries with what was normally only a privilege given to high-ranking officers. He had met the captain only twice before, therefore he only had his shipmate's appraisal of the master of the ship as a guide to conduct himself. Now, he knew what they had told him about the captain was inadequate to describe his superb interaction and thoughtfulness with the ordinary crew members.

"Thank you very much Captain. Shall I pass the promotion on to the crew, or is it a promotion you would like to announce? Sir, there is one more thing that I would like to know. Is Attila allowed to wander throughout the entire ship? There are some places that could be very dangerous to him. None of us would ever forgive ourselves if any harm came to him."

"You are most welcome to pass along Attila's promotion with my blessing. As to Attila running loose in the ship, that was my decision knowing the nature of cats. Cats, most notably male cats, stake out their own territory and Attila is no exception. He does have a rather larger territory than most and you are correct in stating that there are many dangerous places for him. However, Attila is a most extraordinary cat as you have found out and I believe the risk is minimal. I would appreciate it very much if you would make sure that the entire crew looks out for him during his travels. Once he has checked out most of the ship he will probably restrict himself to those areas that he likes and avoid the unpleasant ones. He will no doubt avoid the engine room as it will be far too noisy for him and that is probably the most dangerous area of all. Please pass along my order that Attila is forbidden to be in the engine room, and most importantly, he is never, never to go outside when we are at sea. He probably will not do either of his own accord, but like all cats, he is very curious about things and places he can't personally inspect.

"Now, I have a task for you and your staff to perform. To this point in time Attila has been restricted to my cabin during battle stations and it has worked rather well with a few minor exceptions. The position my cabin occupies in the ship makes it a prime target for the enemy and it is rather a loud place when our main guns fire. As you know, cats have an acute sense of hearing and I personally have witnessed his discomfort with the thunderous noise. I would like you to create a more appropriate 'battle station' to confine Attila in when we are at battle stations. Please make sure it is comfortable and with as much soundproofing as possible, but make sure he can breathe easily. Also make sure he is ensconced in it as soon as possible when we go the battle stations.

"When the compartment hatches are closed up for battle stations we do not want him underfoot and in serious personal danger, looking for a place to hide and weather the storm. As you know, you normally receive orders for battle stations fifteen minutes before we sound off for battle. Together, we will attempt to train him to head for his 'battle station' as soon as possible. Until then, when I inform you of impending battle stations, I expect you to come and fetch him from wherever he might be. Most of the day he spends on the bridge, so he should be relatively easy to track down. I expect you to make sure he is secure and report to myself or a bridge officer that fact as soon as it is accomplished. Any questions?"

"No Sir, it will be our most pleasant duty to see that our most Honorary Sergeant-at-Arms is perfectly taken care of during all battle engagements."

"Very well Mr. Strass, please inform me when you have his battle station ready for occupancy. I would like to inspect it when it is finished."

"Yes Sir Captain, it will be done immediately and to your specifications."

At that Manfried Strass smartly saluted and quickly vanished back to the central innards of the ship. Strass quickly arrived in the galley where his staff had been continuously gossiping as to the fate that would befall him topside in officer's territory. The staff knew his moods and demeanor extremely well, considering they all had to work like a very well-coordinated orchestra to keep the almost non-stop flow of nutritious and delicious meals streaming into the mess halls for a crew of nearly 1,700 hungry seamen. Manfried was obviously in an elevated state of euphoria. He motioned for all the men to gather around him. The men quickly, without too much whispering, assembled around the nearest work table. Manfried slightly calmed his nervousness and like a machine gun's stuttering action rapidly told the men everything that transpired on the bridge, with a touch of his own embellishments thrown in for good measure.

The men let out a thunderous cheer when they heard that their humble galley had been chosen by the great captain Kastanien to be the permanent "battle station" home for *their* hero. A couple of seamen from the adjacent mess hall poked their heads into the galley to discover the source of what seemed to be a party going on. They were quickly shooed out by two sprightly junior cooks and the bulkhead hatches were summarily closed to all outsiders.

Barely keeping watch over some simmering pots of stew and soup, the galley staff proceeded to discuss where the "battle station" should go and its construction. There were some decidedly heated arguments, but they were quickly quelled by Strass. Strass was a solid beefy man, weighing two hundred and forty pounds, very little of which was superfluous fat. When he barked an order, it was obeyed. No one was willing to find out the hard way if his bite was as ferocious as his bark. In forty-five minutes the essentials of the "battle station" were agreed upon. The serious business of the "battle station" resolved, the staff returned to preparing for an invasion by another relieved watch crew.

Miraculously only one soup pot had boiled over and had done no damage at all. With some rough sketches tightly clutched in his hand Strass headed out the aft hatch to find the ship's carpenter. When the chief cook had passed through the mess, the same two curious seamen returned to the hatch and looked in. They were again shooed away, but this time the hatch doors were left open.

It simply gets almost unbearably hot in any ship's galley when the circulation is cut off, so rare is the occasion when the ship is standing down from battle stations that the galley hatches are closed. The sailors that had begun to invade the mess hall by the dozens were grilled by those present earlier to find out any source for the commotion that had just concluded in the galley. There were several truly outrageous suggestions, but like the vast majority of grapevine gossip, all theories were dismissed and the sailors knew that they must wait impatiently for the truth to surface.

Strass arrived in the ship's very well-equipped machine shop and quickly found the ship's carpenter working at repairing a shattered locker box. The carpenter was a stringy man, probably not weighing more than one hundred and fifty pounds. He wore only a filthy tattered undershirt and long work pants that were riddled with holes from the arc welding that seemed to never end on board the ship. "Willy" Schultz was a taciturn individual who had also served with Captain Kastanien during the conflict twenty some odd years previous. Virtually all of the crew avoided him and only went to his shop when they couldn't order or send some other poor soul to inevitably listen his perennial vituperations. Strass was one of the few exceptions that "Willy" genuinely warmed to. The burly cook had also served with Kastanien and "Willy". Strass had tried on numerous occasions to convince the sour carpenter to change his attitude and simply accept the past and move on to the present, but to no avail. "Willy's" miserable outlook on life had no individual personal basis.

He harbored intense hatred for the accursed treaty that had forced the Fatherland to shamefully scuttle the bulk of the Imperial German Navy. In his late forties, he was a bit old to be an ordinary sailor. His genius at repairing, modifying, and creating was his one legendary saving grace. However, any praise delivered by any grateful individual would always be accepted without a single word in reply. If anyone failed to thank him and offer praise for a superb job well done, he would be the unfortunate target of a vicious tirade. Several officers had brought his vile temperament and virtual insubordination to the captain's attention.

Kastanien would patiently explain to the officer that "Willy" Schultz had his share of grief to live with and to just ignore his nasty but harmless tongue. On a few occasions of perceived grievous outbursts, Kastanien would quietly visit the carpentry shop and have a few kind words with his old friend and things would go considerably more pleasant for a few days, sometimes even a couple of weeks.

Willy did not look up when he heard approaching footsteps. He finished tightening the last bolt on the locker's lid and then with a satisfied sigh leaned back from his workbench. Only then did he turn to see who had come into his inner sanctum. Seeing his old shipmate, his craggy cadaverous face suddenly broke into a mild grin.

"Manny, what brings my old friend down to my humble little abode?"

"Willy, you crotchety old reprobate, it's a superb pleasure to once again visit the reigning Duke of the Carpentry and Machinery world and listen to his kind and melodic soothing voice."

At the sarcastic jibe, both men burst into raucous laughter that went on for a full minute before Willy calmed his laughter and enquired, "So, Manny what does our illustrious Chief Cook need of my humble services today?"

"Willy, I am here on a direct order from our captain with a project of incredible importance that must be a work of art as well as perfectly created and functional. You are hereby charged with producing a "battle station" for our beloved Honorary Sergeant-at-Arms, Attila. I have brought you some rather crude sketches that we mere mortals in the galley have cobbled together. We implore upon your grace to analyze and improve upon. The basic dimensions are firm in that they reflect the space that we have determined will be the safest and most convenient for him during battle stations. Other than that we trust implicitly in your unsurpassed craftsmanship and creative genius to produce a proper second home for who will probably be our personal future on board Admiral."

"Your Most Honorable Count of Culinary Opulence, I am honored beyond words to accept this incredibly important task. Only yesterday Attila wandered into my shop. We spent quite some time together as he inspected everything without getting into any trouble. After he knew all that was worth noting, he hopped up on my bench where we *chatted* for quite a while. As you well know, I am a fervent cat lover so it was most enjoyable for me getting to know him. I think it is just wonderful to have a cat on board—especially one who is obviously of royal descent. I did hear of his exploit in saving you from what surely would have been a nasty scarring.

"I assure you that your rudimentary sketches, although they remind me of rather childish scribbling will be analyzed and I will be back in touch with you when I have produced some proper architectural views."

Again both men burst into a loud and long laughing bout at the absurdity of their eloquent, rather flowery compliments to each other. When they finally quieted down, Willy slightly broke the mood.

"Manny, first let's go to the galley right now where you can show me where this palace will be situated."

"Excellent thought Willy. Let's go"

The two old friends were soon kneeling down and measuring the allocated space all the while jabbering back and forth. The galley staff for the most part had never met the infamously nasty-dispositioned head carpenter. They were staring in total silence as the two men worked and conversed in very pleasant terms. There were a few differences of opinion on several points, but they quickly resolved them, and within twenty minutes the carpenter vanished. Strass turned to his men and ordered them to get back to work.

Later that night when Willy knew that his friend Manny would be off duty, he summoned him to the sailors ward room. The ward room was deserted except for two sailors playing chess off in one corner. The sailors glanced up and when Manfried shook his head warding them off, they just went back to their game making themselves part of the furniture. Willy, seeing that there were to be no intruders, carefully spread out his plans. He then looked up at Manny trying to read his friends expression for approval. Manny did not speak for several minutes while his eyes and fingers deliberately wandered over every line and detail on the proposed "battle station". Finally Manny stood erect, looked fiercely at Willy and grinned. Willy knew that grin and returned it in silence so the sailors would never know what was going on. Willy and Manfried departed the ward room and when they were alone in a passageway, Manfried put his hand on Willy's shoulder and gently urged the carpenter to stop. Willy stopped and turned to face Manny. When Willy looked at his friend, he did not see the happy grin of a few minutes ago, but a very serious look on the chief cook's face. Apprehensively, he waited.

"Willy, I knew you were extraordinarily gifted when it came to special projects, but this, this is truly magnificent. It is a magnificent palace that is built like a fortress. We must show this to the captain immediately."

Totally out of character, Willy slightly lowered his head with embarrassment. He did not blush as his wrinkled, flame-tanned face wouldn't show even the slightest signs of a flushing.

"Do you really mean that Manny?"

"By mighty Apollo and Zeus, I do. We're headed that way right now."

"Wait, maybe the captain is busy. Let's check with the bridge first."

"Excellent idea."

Manfried took a few steps to the nearest intercom and called the bridge, "Bridge, Chief Cook Strass here, could I trouble you to tell me where the Captain is?"

"The Captain is right here Mr. Strass, what can I do for you?"

"Begging the Captain's pardon Sir, but Head Carpenter Schultz and I would like to show you his plans for the project you gave me earlier today."

Kastanien inwardly smiled at the way his old shipmates phrased the obvious. But he realized that there was very little creativity in their duties aboard a warship so he would unselfishly use this clandestine project to improve moral and create new harmless gossip for the insatiable appetite of the grapevine.

"Very Well, Mr. Strass. I will be waiting for you and Willy in my main cabin as soon as you can get here."

Willy and Manny looked at each other and simultaneously their faces returned to the earlier joyous grins. They both took off at a fast jog to the captain's cabin. Breathless with anticipation and the unaccustomed exercise, they arrived at Kastanien's cabin and found the door being held open by the captain. Kastanien smiled at his two old friends and motioned them in. The two sailors stepped inside and Strass gently closed the door. Standing side-by-side the two sailors, replete with their outrageous grins attempted a smart military salute. Although the salute was a bit sloppy, Kastanien let it go and returned the salute with a slight grin on his face.

"Gentlemen, please take a seat and spread out your plans. Would you join me in a glass of fine German schnapps?"

Manfried and Willy looked at each other rather dumbfounded but they recovered in a flash and in unison blurted out, "Yes Sir. Thank you very much."

Peter Kastanien took two quick strides over to his desk and opened the bottom left drawer. With a bit of theatrical flair he produced a bottle of good quality schnapps and three simple glasses. Unknown to all but a few prior high-ranking guests, the bottom drawer on the right side was home to two bottles of truly superb schnapps with appropriate Bavarian crystal glasses. Kastanien knew that the two men he now entertained would be quite uncomfortable if he served his top notch alcohol in fancy glasses, the likes of which they had probably never seen before. Returning to the small conference table, the captain proceeded to fill the three glasses about two-thirds full. Capping the bottle he took his seat and turned to the two men sitting rather close together on the opposite side of the table. He rightly assumed that they felt a bit uneasy here in his cabin, and sat close together to gain a bit of confidence from each other. With a laughing grin, Kastanien opened the discussion.

"Gentlemen, a toast in honor of our shipmate. The Right Honorable Sergeant-at-Arms, Attila."

The three men then gently tapped their glasses together and then took a rather healthy shot of the fiery liquid. The three glasses returned to the table almost in unison. The two sailors were sporting huge grins at their special treatment. This was for them a very, very special occasion.

"Now, Gentlemen show me what you have conjured up and let us finalize Attila's battle station."

Willy, who had been guarding the rolls of paper like his life depended on them rose to the occasion and standing up began to unfurl the plans. Strass and Kastanien scooped up the schnapps glasses and then placed them on the corners of the plans to hold them in place. To hold the fourth corner down, Schultz pulled a small wrench from his work pants making the plans secure to the table. Willy had diplomatically positioned the plans so they were facing Kastanien correctly. No one spoke as Kastanien pored over the very detailed and beautifully executed plans. After several minutes, with the internal tension building in the sailors, Kastanien leaned back a bit and looked over at his two men, who definitely had an apprehensive air about them.

"Willy, these plans are magnificent. I've not seen plans from Germany's best architects, even the exalted Albert Speer, which are any better. Now, please explain a few items to me."

The captain and the two seamen spent nearly an hour going back and forth refining some small details. Suddenly all three realized that they had the project design and implementation done. With this realization, the three also simultaneously remembered the schnapps' glasses that were only half consumed. Taking the lead naturally as expected by Willy and Manfried,

Kastanien lifted his glass and nodded to the others to do the same. Willy shoved the wrench off the plans, picked up his glass and captured the plans as they were about to take off now that their shackles were gone. Feeling more joy than he had known for a couple of decades, Willy Schultz raised his glass and beckoned to be joined. The other quickly raised their glasses and a second later Willy burst out, "To Attila and our Captain. May God bestow his blessings on them."

The men quickly downed the remains of the liquor and smiled the smile of men that have successfully accomplished a major project. After an appropriate passage of time in silence, Kastanien rose quickly followed by Willy and Manfried.

"Thank you Gentlemen, now let us proceed with bringing this design to reality. I won't ask you how long it will take as that could be counterproductive on several fronts. I also know that you will proceed with dispatch that is tempered with prudence. If you have any improvements or revisions as the project progresses, you may use your own judgment. However, if you would feel more comfortable in bringing any changes to me, I will be at your disposal unless the exigencies of war demand my attention."

Knowing the meeting was over, the two men requested permission to leave. Permission was instantly granted. Willy and Manfried snapped a very smart, very military salute which was returned immediately. Smiling like a couple of mischievous little boys, Willy and Manny exited the cabin heading for the galley. Neither spoke a word down the passageways. They did not want to break the spell that had clutched their emotions. Reaching the galley, Willy let his friend Manny guide him to a small room just off the main room. This cubicle was what passed for an office that the chief cook used to manage his foodstuffs. Motioning Willy to take a seat on some boxes, Manny then repeated the drink ceremony of an hour ago in the captain's cabin. However, this time the drink was not the delicious schnapps but rather a very dark, almost syrupy beer. The glasses were a bit on the chipped side but they were reminiscent of several happy times from Manny's past.

This highly illegal liquid on board a warship was only dispensed by the chief cook on very, very special occasions that occurred maybe once or twice during a deployment. Manny had kept this secret cache of a couple of cases of beer a secret from all but the few crewmembers that he shared it with. Kastanien had heard a rumor about the contraband beer, but had opted not to investigate. Peter Kastanien had always felt that the Royal Navy was far more intelligent about alcohol than the Navies of other countries. He thought that the small "tot" of rum the British dispensed was good for moral and voided all reasons for sailors to sneak alcohol aboard and risk serious discipline.

"Well, Willy what do you think of our captain?"

Willy's face and posture emanated a glowing radiance that his friend had not seen in many a year. He also seemed to have grown taller and straighter in the past hour. Even his normally rather dull-gray skin pallor had taken on a low-grade glow.

"Manny, my good friend; our Captain has rekindled my faith in mankind. Although I have heard many glowing reports of his wisdom and kind treatment of us in lower ranks, I must admit that I was skeptical and tried my best to countermand the claims. But now I know I was dead wrong, and you know it is not my normal personality to ever admit that I might be mistaken. He is not one of those stuck-up upper-class Prussian snobs. He is just like one of us who has stuck to his guns and made something of himself. And his record of keeping us safe while in deadly peril is nothing short of amazing. Yes, Manny we have a Captain that we can all be proud of. We must all give him nothing short of our best—and then some. Now, my good friend, leave me to my craft and I shall put our plans into a work of art for our Attila."

Noting that Manny seemed to be getting a bit anxious, Willy interjected before his friend could utter a complaint or objection.

"Manny, fear not about this project, I shall keep you up to date on my progress, and please feel free to visit my workshop anytime to check up on my progress. And I would like some company from time to time just to have some friendly conversation and maybe solve the mysteries that abound through our grapevine."

The two old friends guffawed at that and in mock seriousness Manny replied, "Thank you Willy, I shall do just that. And now, back to my pots and pans. We mustn't let our captain's crew faint from lack of my excellent cuisine."

With a roaring laugh, Willy countered with his own deprecatory comment about his friend's culinary skills, "Manny, you serve good nourishing food, but no one, least of all I, would consider what you serve as *cuisine*."

"Now, you listen to me Willy, just for that I'm going to come back here in a couple of hours with a bowl of Kartoffel soup just for you. Then we shall see what you think of my *cuisine*."

"Manny, is that that wonderful creamy potato soup flavored with marjoram and slices of pork sausage that I have heard about but never tasted?"

"Yes, my skeptical friend. It is a dish fit for those 'upper-class Prussian snobs' as you call them. Also, our captain is most definitely not from Prussia, he is from the heartland of our Germany, Cologne. On second thought, I will make enough of this special delicacy to also feed our captain a snack—if he's a bit hungry. After he has tasted my creation and given me his opinion, I will bring you your bowl along with what I am absolutely sure will be his glowing praise."

Willy looked askance for a moment, lowered his head a shade and then rather sheepishly, but with pride and conviction responded with solidity to his voice that had been lacking since the First World War ended, "Manny, my very good friend, please accept my apology for deriding you. The nasty mean-spirited habits of my recent past are a bit hard to toss overboard in a moment in time. You truly do wonders in your galley. I have never heard a single nasty comment about the quality and variety of your culinary fare. I'm honestly looking forward to your exquisite soup on your return."

Manny knew that this was a bit of a white lie, but opted not to correct his new-found optimistic friend. He knew that after the spectacular victory over the British off the River Platte, Dönitz himself had ordered unequivocally that the food for the *Scharnhorst* and *Gneisenau* be the best that could be obtained as a small reward for saving the great warship *Admiral Graf Spee* from probable demise by the Royal Navy. On this new deployment, the captain, all the officers and the entire crew had passed along many strong accolades about the quality of the food. The captain, in one memorable dinner that Strass had served the food himself to the officers in their private mess, had raised his glass in a salute to Strass calling him an extraordinary chef. The other officers seated around the table all stood up instantly and gave a rousing and very noisy cheer for their extraordinary chef. Strass still basked in the glory about his new status and remained uncharacteristically magnanimous in his praise of his captain and officers ever since.

Gneisenau
20:10 Local time

The slightly excited voice of radar operator Gren Schultz reverberated throughout the bridge which had been rather quiet for the preceding hour or so, "Captain, I have the lead convoy ship on my radar at a range of thirty kilometers. She is about two kilometers off our starboard and heading directly for us."

"Very well, Mr. Schultz, please inform me every time you pick up a new contact with their position relative to the leader and especially quickly if our lead target makes any turns."

"Yes Captain. I will keep you informed of all new contacts and their positions immediately."

"Mr. Ehrlich. Inform 'Guns' Jorgen that we will be well within twelve kilometers in fifteen minutes. Be prepared to commence shooting immediately with Anton and Bruno at that time. As the range shortens he may open up with his secondary guns but once again remind him that we are primarily only interested in the destroyers until they are taken out of the action. Also please send fresh lookouts that are very keen-eyed as we should be able to see their lights soon enough if they have been so gracious to continue sailing with them on. Instruct the lookouts that I am to be notified immediately upon their sighting. And remind them that although the British are dead ahead of us, it is very possible that there may be other unfriendly vessels in other quadrants. We do not want surprises popping up to distract us. Bring the ship to battle stations."

Immediately the executive officer sprang into action. The orders were implemented almost before the captain's echo faded.

*   *   *   *   *

Karl Erhlich had been rescued by Teebolt from his miserable posting of the past few years. He had been the very proud captain of a World War I German battle cruiser; the *SMS Derfflinger*. Being a patriotic, excellent and competent naval officer, Erhlich chafed when his proud ship had been scuttled in Scapa Flow at the end of the war. Teebolt had known Erhlich during that great conflict that was to be the war to end all wars. Because of his outstanding record with the Kaiserliche Marine, he stayed in the German Navy but remained ashore for many years at a boring desk job. Finally in 1929 as the German merchant fleet was launching more commercial ships, Erhlich was given command of a new bulk carrier to ply the waters between South America and the Fatherland. He was happy to be at sea but driving an unarmed ship with a cargo of bananas was vastly different from commanding a battle cruiser with twelve-inch guns at double the speed of his current assignment—but still a whole lot better than sitting at a desk.

When the National Socialists came to power in 1933, Erhlich made the career-crushing mistake of publicly criticizing the new regime. Early in 1934 when he docked in Kiel with his load of sulfur from a Caribbean port, he was commanded to appear before the governing body of the merchant marine—immediately. Handing over the task of supervising the unloading to his first officer, he proceeded to merchant headquarters. After checking in with the secretary, he was kept waiting for over two hours in a rather drab waiting room. By now he knew that his summons was going to be an unpleasant meeting. When he was finally ushered into the office, it only took a cursory glance to know he was correct.

The meeting was a complete sham. Erhlich sat in a very uncomfortable chair for several minutes listening to a string of derogatory charges deriding his ability to properly command. The end result was not as severe as he feared it would be. They did not strip him of his master's papers, but re-assigned him to probably the worst merchant ship Germany had. To finish him off the kangaroo court laid out in minute detail the paths he was to sail.

For five long years Erhlich slogged his new command, the ancient tramp steamer, *Ergentratt* from Asian ports to Germany. A few days before war broke out on September 1, 1939, he along with every German merchant received the order to proceed home as quickly as possible. Karl Erhlich was in Yokohama when he received the order. Within six hours the rust-stained hulk of the *Ergentratt* departed the Japanese port for the over 14,000 mile trip home. Erhlich was not optimistic as to his chances to reach a German port. The trip would take nearly two months along with a few days in neutral ports for resupply.

With incredible seamanship and blessed with a healthy dose of good fortune, Karl Erhlich finally dropped anchor in Kiel. His arrival was a complete surprise to everyone. His radio had died shortly after rounding the tip of South America. Consequently, he and the *Ergentratt* had vanished from any contact with Germany. Erhlich was actually pleased that he could not contact anyone, as any radio transmission would have alerted the omnipresent Royal Navy as to his existence which would no doubt have very repugnant results. Luck was with him all the way up the Atlantic. Fair weather with gentle seas devoid of any shipping persisted until he was in the temperamental North Atlantic. Then foul weather became his friend. The seas became quite rough, but not enough to slow his progress very much. Then when he was navigating through the most dangerous passages, Mother Nature blessed him with a thick fog for several days until he entered the Baltic Sea. With the weather now clear and cold, the intrepid Karl Erhlich soon reached Kiel. His arrival was spectacularly uneventful until he reported in to the powers at hand. In the course of relating his epic voyage it soon came out that he had been literally written off as lost at sea. To maintain the mystery of where he was, Erhlich had refueled at a very minor port in southern Argentina. Neither he nor the lackadaisical, totally disinterested port authorities had broadcast his presence.

Fortuitously *Gneisenau* had been in port when he arrived. The news of his arrival travelled at lightning speed throughout the busy port, quickly reaching the ears of Admiral Dönitz. Dönitz had been conferring with Captain Teebolt when an excited lieutenant had entered the room informing the two men of the miraculous arrival of a missing-presumed-lost-at-sea vessel. Dönitz immediately ordered the lieutenant to fetch Erhlich to his meeting. While the lieutenant ran the errand, Dönitz and Teebolt discussed what they should do with Erhlich.

Gneisenau was due to sail in two days to join up with *Scharnhorst* where they were to sail to the Caribbean on a hunting expedition. Teebolt and Dönitz shortly came to the conclusion that Erhlich had served his punishment long enough. Being unsure as to how to handle the delicate political miasma with Erhlich, Dönitz put in an urgent call to Minister of Propaganda, Joseph Goebbels in Berlin. Goebbels listened carefully to the relating of the incredible journey before he spoke, "Admiral Dönitz, Karl Erhlich has delivered to us a magnificent tool to humiliate the British. Just think of it. That old piece of sea flotsam managed to elude the mighty Royal Navy for two months from half way around the world—much of the passage through very perilous waters. I will make sure the Lord Haw-Haw shoves this *embarrassment* down their pompous, egotistical throats.

"Now, to award Erhlich some justly due recognition, I suggest that you confer upon him a posting in our Navy. I know of his outstanding achievements in the last war and the demoralizing penalty that he has suffered through for these past many years. I will let you decide the nature of his new assignment with these two conditions. The posting has to be high enough to show our people the respect that he deserves because of this singularly spectacular feat of seamanship—which I still find rather hard to believe.

"Karl Erhlich was *demoted* to the command of a piece of floating junk simply because he spoke derogatorily about our new Germany's politics. Enough time has passed for this unpleasant lapse of judgment to have faded from the forefront of common knowledge. The second condition is very, very important and strict adherence to my terms is absolutely essential. Erhlich *must never* utter a single disparaging word regarding our new government, most especially our beloved Führer. Do I make myself crystal clear?"

Dönitz had been listening stone-faced to the much-feared propaganda minister—expecting the worst, but hoping for a reprieve. When he heard the parameters for releasing Erhlich from his version of purgatory, a thin smile slowly creased his face.

"Yes, Minister you have outlined the course of action perfectly. I will personally guarantee you that they will be carried out to the letter. Thank you very much Minister and I am very much looking forward to hearing Lord Haw-Haw relate this misadventure of the Royal Navy. Is there anything else I should know regarding this issue?"

Hearing nothing but the click of disconnection, Dönitz softly replaced the handset. Teebolt had been silently sitting in a sumptuous Moroccan leather chair until Dönitz was finished. Reading the silent anger in the face of his commanding officer, Teebolt rose from the chair and waited expectantly. Dönitz turned to Teebolt, suppressing his anger at the blunt rudeness of Goebbels, and grinned. Dönitz relayed the good news to the relief of his nervously expectant captain.

"Now Captain Teebolt, we must devise a plan for our comrade before he gets here. I have some ideas but I will withhold them from you so as not to jade your suggestions."

Teebolt, like his friend Peter Kastanien of the sister ship *Scharnhorst*, had always had an easy but strictly professional relationship with the head of the Kriegsmarine. He knew from the many years of serving together that Dönitz was not an egomaniac that required politically charged answers. Dönitz simply wanted the simple truth.

"Admiral Dönitz. Might I suggest that Karl become an officer on my ship? Although my executive officer is quite competent, he lacks imagination and creativity. Karl has shown us that he is quite good at this especially with his latest exploit. I am very familiar with his record in the previous conflict where he showed ingenuity and daring—resulting in unexpected victories against the English."

Dönitz pondered this for only a moment before responding.

"Captain, may I call you by your first name when we are alone or amongst friends? I must be formal so much of the time, it would be a very welcome relief. After all, twenty some-odd years ago we were not much more than simple sailors who could relax in each other's company. And with the same restrictions I would deem it a personal favor if you would address me as just Karl. When our newly released *prisoner* arrives we will resort to normal protocol."

"That is very generous of you Ad----Karl. Thank you very much."

"Now Kris, about your suggestion. I had exactly the same thought. So Karl Erhlich will now report to *Gneisenau* immediately if you deem the time is right, which should be rather soon since you are scheduled to sail in two days. When our Karl arrives, I will outline the rules to him before telling him of his new assignment. If he balks, no mention of his change in status will be said. I seriously doubt there will be any reluctance when he is informed that these guidelines came from Goebbels himself."

Only a moment or two passed before Karl Erhlich was ushered into the presence of Dönitz and Teebolt. Standing perfectly erect Dönitz greeted Erhlich with his outstretched hand, which was handily grasped. Then his old friend Kris shook his hand strongly. When Dönitz told him of his new posting and the firm terms of his future behavior, Karl Erhlich's face showed no emotion. With an enigmatic smile, Erhlich immediately took a step forward and solidly shook hands with the two men again. Now with his emotions running in high gear, Captain Karl Erhlich spoke, "Admiral Dönitz and my friend Kris—words to express my gratitude are inadequate. All I can say is I thank you with all my being. To be back at sea on the magnificent *Gneisenau* is a dream that I never imagined could come true. You can fear nothing will issue forth from me that is uncomplimentary to the current government."

Fighting back his tears, Erhlich quickly ended his short speech, "Thank you again very much, I will do my absolute best to earn this wonderful posting—and then some."

Dönitz realized that this superb naval officer was close to an "unmanly" show of high emotion, so he took the step forward and grasped Erhlich's shoulders with both hands.

"Karl, welcome back. You have been truly missed."

This simple, genuine gesture snapped the emotional tension. Dönitz turned away, quickly striding over to the door, motioning to his aide.

"Corporal Schmidt, please fetch a bottle of our best schnapps and three crystal glasses. We have a celebration to toast."

*   *   *   *   *

The teeth jarring blare of the battle station horns created a whirlwind of activity as it always did and nearly 1,700 men performed each of the tasks he was assigned to with the highly efficient competence and speed that constant drilling created. Within three minutes the calls to the bridge confirmed each section of the ship was in proper battle condition. Teebolt relaxed back in his comfortable captain's chair and mulled over the impending rendezvous with the enemy. Minutes after battle stations were given and the ship secured, the radar room came back over the bridge speaker.

"Captain, I have three more ships on the screen. They are all abreast of each other and approximately two kilometers behind the lead ship. All four ships are maintaining the same course directly towards us."

Teebolt silently pondered this new information and was satisfied that there was nothing untoward about the sightings and that the convoy was formed into the normal box formation. He then told the second officer to check with the lookouts as to whether they had seen any lights yet. After a brief exchange over the intercom to the lookouts on the forecastle and in the crow's nest the second officer reported that nothing had been sighted yet.

"A minor inconvenience, but nothing we cannot handle. Mr. Erhlich, continue to check in with the lookouts every minute. With this waxing gibbous moon we should be able to spot them soon enough as I'm sure that they have doused all lighting and are using this moonlight to prevent blundering into each other."

"Captain, radar operator Schultz here. I'm picking up what appears to be destroyer escorts moving up very much faster than the four previous vessels. I estimate their speed at thirty-two knots each. They are now ahead of the slower vessels and on each side. The distance to the ship on the port side is thirty kilometers. The starboard destroyer is slightly closer at twenty-nine kilometers. The distance to the merchants is thirty-one to thirty-three kilometers."

"Very well Mr. Schultz. Continue to monitor your machine very closely. I need to know when the range to the closest destroyer shortens to twenty."

Turning from the intercom and addressing the bridge staff in general Teebolt issued his orders for the impending battle.

"Mr. Ehrlich. Begin a fifteen degree zigzag pattern right away. I only want to hold each new heading until we get off two salvos each from Anton and Bruno before reversing. Maintain our speed at twenty-eight knots. Order Mr. Jorgen to target both destroyers at the same time. Have him be prepared to fire immediately on my order. We will open fire at twenty kilometers. With our closure rate of nearly sixty knots on the destroyers it will not be but a few moments until then. Make very sure that 'Guns' Jorgen fully understands our zigzagging maneuver. We will never hear the end of it if he misses too often because we are driving like drunken maniacs."

The light hearted comment about the proud gunnery officer slightly reduced the adrenalin overload that was pumping full throttle through every officer on the bridge.

"Captain, I'm picking up multiple contacts behind the front row of four. It appears that this is the next row in the convoy box formation. I'm also picking up one more destroyer coming up fast outside the box on our port side. She appears to be traveling about thirty knots."

Seconds later First Officer Kleinst piped up, "Captain, lookouts have spotted the destroyers charging up on our front quarters. They are steaming without lights but their bows are throwing up a phosphorescent wave that our sharp eyes have spotted."

"Captain, the two lead destroyers have altered course and are heading directly for us," the now very excited voice of "Genie" Schultz blurted out of the intercom.

"Mr. Schultz, thank you for the information. Please calm yourself as we are about to get a lot busier."

"Yes Captain. I'm sorry for my outburst. I will stick to my machine and give you all new developments immediately. Range to starboard destroyer now twenty-two kilometers. Range to port destroyer now twenty-one kilometers."

"Mr. Ehrlich. Have the rangefinders been able to get us accurate positions on the destroyers yet?"

"Yes Captain. Just this very minute."

Teebolt hesitated only a split second and then calmly gave the anxiously awaited simple two word command, "Open fire."

"Guns" Jorgen enjoyed the light teasing that Teebolt and some of the other officers gave him occasionally about his darling guns. He always just inwardly smiled as he knew the true respect they all had for his gunnery proficiency. This order was not going to be any exception to his reputation. Rather he thought, I can enhance the reputation and knock out those two little pesky destroyers at the same time and do it by moonlight. Happy with himself and the targeting information from the rangefinders and radar to a lesser degree, he let loose both turrets simultaneously at their respective targets. His gun crews could reload and fire each of these magnificent eleven-inch guns at a rate of three-plus rounds per minute which was amazingly quick given that each shell weighed 337 kilograms.

At a range of twenty kilometers a second salvo was capable of being on its journey before the first one arrived. The guns were ready to shoot a second time but Jorgen held off giving the order. Knowing there was only a three second wait until the first shots arrived he wanted to see if he could get them on his first shot. In seconds he saw that all the shells had overshot by a shade under a hundred meters. Quickly adjusting the range, with due compensation for the rapid closure rate, he fired again. And once more he waited with readied guns for the shots to strike.

This time was considerably different. Both the aged destroyers of the Royal Navy were ripped asunder as two highly-explosive shells struck each one only a second apart. One eleven-inch shell is more than enough to finish off any destroyer as they are notoriously lightly armored and two hits by these quite large missiles left nothing of consequence except a lot of sinking steel to litter the ocean's floor.

Destroyers are not made to do pitched battles with serious capitol ships. Their main defense is their speed and maneuverability. Unfortunately, neither of these defenses was of any help this night and now the convoy defense was left in the hands of the sole surviving destroyer that was bravely charging into the fray hoping to stop the enemy capitol ship from scuppering the convoy ships. The destroyer captain did hear a last second radio message from one of his fallen comrade ships to London and now knew that he was on his own. He quickly ascertained that there was no way that he would have any chance whatsoever charging directly at a heavy enemy ship that obviously had frightfully good shooters.

His was a destroyer that had a very early version of radar, reasonably functional but not too terribly reliable, let alone accurate. Right now the rudimentary radar unit was in one of its reliable moods and he could "see" the large German warship charging into his defenseless flock.

Captain Herbert MacDonald was a feisty Scottish destroyer veteran recalled from retirement. He had served the Royal Navy tirelessly and with distinction during the first conflict with the German Imperial High Seas Fleet. His Scottish temper was up and in an excellent fettle. He was not about to let the "Heiney" get the best of him without some accounting. He knew that his fine destroyer was not much better than a sardine can against the big guns. He had very little doubt that he was doomed but he would make the German pay regardless of his own imminent peril. He calculated that his chances were at best damn near zero, unless of course divine providence stepped in and lent a hand. During his twenty year retirement, which he passed as a sheepherder in the Highlands, he rarely let a day go by that he didn't play out battle tactics in his mind. He had conjured up this very scenario many times and he was about to put his best plan into action.

"Helm, tuck us right up under the big tankers fat arse so that the Hun cannae 'see' us with his radar. I want to be less than two hundred yards behind her and only one hundred yards from her starboard side. When you get there maintain station with her and none of you gents give me any lip about toddling along at ten knots or so. I am not about to suffer our other destroyers miserable fate. The German will probably best us in the end but he will never forget the H.M.S. *Orkney*. Now, me fine little laddies, let this old curmudgeon show you a trick or two. I will nae spin ye a fairy tale about our chances for survival but we will go down fighting the good fight. And if the Gods be with us, we will drop kick the German in his nether regions."

It took only a few minutes for the nimble destroyer to hide behind the large ponderous tanker and following orders to the letter, the deft management by the capable first officer of the *Orkney* had her positioned so close that the tanker's backwash tossed and twisted the little greyhound of the ocean quite noticeably.

"Well done me boys. Now we wait here until she pops her snout out where we can spot her. She is traveling in the dead centre of our little sheep and should arrive for our little surprise party soon enough."

*   *   *   *   *

Even amid the constant thunder of the guns, the strident scream from the radar operator Gren "Genie" Schultz garnered everyone's attention, "The British destroyer has vanished from my machine. I don't know where she is. All I have left on the screen are the multiple targets that were there before."

Teebolt reacted instantly.

"Mr. Ehrlich, go and calm the boy down and see if you can make any sense of the situation. We absolutely need to know where that destroyer is. She might be small but her torpedoes are nasty little fish with a real bite. Make haste and report instantly."

Executive Officer Karl Ehrlich ran at full tilt the short distance to the radar room and was back at the captain's side in what seemed like an eternity but in fact was less than thirty seconds.

"Captain, the boy is right. There's no sign of the destroyer."

"Thank you Mr. Erhlich. It seems our British adversary does not want to duel it out with us and has no doubt hidden himself behind a merchant so we cannot 'see' him with our radar let alone our own eyes. Light up the nearest ships with star shells and warn the lookouts to scan every ship very carefully. Maybe we can spot him before he gets rambunctious and shoots some of his little fish at us."

Within forty-five seconds the North Atlantic was lit up like a Hollywood movie set. It only took the lookout in the crow's nest fifteen seconds to spot the destroyer hugging the rear starboard quarter of the big tanker. *Gneisenau* was only six kilometers away from the tanker and already had the fearsome eleven-inch triple guns of Bruno's turret ready to fire at this prized target when the order came from the bridge to slightly overshoot the stern of the tanker to where the destroyer was masked from direct view. Eleven-inch turret Anton was also trained on the merchant six kilometers off the starboard bow of *Gneisenau* searching for the destroyer as well. "Guns" Jorgen held off firing at this merchant until Bruno had fired. He did not want the normal recoil that would slightly heel the ship and spoil his delicate aim on the little, but very dangerous destroyer.

*   *   *   *   *

"Right lads, the blasphemous Bosch bastard probably has got us in his sights now. Let's bloody up his nose. Helm, port twenty degrees, flank speed and then some if you can get that Irish bugger down in the engine room to give us all this old girl's got. Pull out around our tanker friend and as soon as you can get a decent bead on the German, get off the torpedoes. Make them count and continue to reload and shoot at record rate. We might just get our licks in before one of those small trains they call shells does us in and we get to meet a fine Scotsman called St. Peter MacClenny at the Pearly Gates. Lively now, all of our lives depend on a quick action and surprise."

Within seconds the spritely lightweight warship heeled into the turn, rapidly accelerating. Fifteen seconds after the destroyer's screws bit deeply into the now shimmering silver water, Bruno unleashed her thunderous broadside. Jorgen had fired the three big guns with slightly varied elevations as this was a tricky shot. One shell didn't clear the tanker and smashed into the tankers stern quarter creating a massive hole in her but no explosion or fire was forthcoming. The remaining two shells barely skimmed over the fantail striking the destroyers stern. The hits were high on the aft section of the destroyer and although they struck the small warship with blows as heavy as using a sledgehammer to swat a fly, they did little damage as David charged forward to meet Goliath with her speed unchecked. The impact of the two shells did skew the destroyer a bit off course dangerously close to the tanker.

The engine room had put the steam turbines past the maximum safety limit and the lithe greyhound responded instantly to a quick course change from the bridge. She missed the stern of the tanker by a mere twenty feet and then she was in direct visual contact with the shockingly monstrous battleship.

*   *   *   *   *

"Open fire with all guns. Shoot all torpedoes and reload and fire as fast as you can. Train the searchlights on the rangefinders which hopefully will temporarily blind them and give us a wee few precious moments before she opens up again."

$*$ $*$ $*$ $*$ $*$

"Guns" Jorgen had trained his crews well and they could let loose full broadsides at the incredulous rate of a broadside every seventeen or eighteen seconds. Most large caliber naval guns struggled to get off two salvos a minute so a mere fraction of a minute in time went by after the H.M.S. *Orkney* had been slightly injured before that Bruno shot again. The searchlights had blinded the *Gneisenau's* rangefinders a bit to the degree that the second volley of missiles, which meant virtually certain doom splashed harmlessly into the ocean except for one which pounded into a non-critical area of the destroyer, causing only minor damage to the aft superstructure and well deck of *Orkney*.

$*$ $*$ $*$ $*$ $*$

"Helm, steer straight at her like we're going to ram and maybe they will turn off before they do us in," Captain MacDonald ordered.

Orkney was now slicing through the North Atlantic at nearly thirty-five knots and still the engines were striving to give a little more. The closure rate was now sixty-plus knots and it would take less than four minutes to collision. The three torpedoes loosed minutes ago screamed through the water at forty-five knots.

$*$ $*$ $*$ $*$ $*$

"Captain, torpedoes in the water headed straight at us. Range four kilometers."

Although the star shells were almost spent, there was still enough illumination from the slowly descending remaining one for all on the bridge of *Gneisenau* to see that the Lilliputian destroyer was now headed directly for them and closing very fast.

"All eleven and 5.9-inch guns target the bow of the enemy. Four-inch and flak guns target the bridge. Maximum fire rate on all guns until further orders or she blows up. Helm, starboard fifteen degrees, maximum speed."

Time seemed to crawl by on the bridge of both warships as their meeting with destiny beckoned. *Gneisenau* responded with her nimble turn that allowed the aft guns to bear on the charging destroyer. All the gun crews knew the imminent danger of collision or torpedoes, so with their superb training every gun pounded away mercilessly at phenomenal rates of fire that far exceeded any captain's fondest wish. Even the nine guns of Anton, Bruno and Caesar were each sending nearly four rounds a minute screaming across the rapidly shortening distance. "Guns" Jorgen was caught just bit off guard with the sudden turn and increased speed but instantly regained range and fire direction. The first rounds from the three big turrets missed entirely. However, the second shooting from Anton, Bruno and Caesar all hit the bow within seconds of each other and the knife-edged destroyer's bow simply disintegrated and peeled back on the port side of the destroyer before being ripped away by the sea rushing by at well over thirty knots.

The onrushing open bow immediately drooped into the sea, swallowing thousands of gallons of sea water every second. The engines had not been damaged but the engine room seamen had been roughly bounced around by the onslaught forward and many were wounded or knocked unconscious by the reverberating battering ram effect the big shells inflicted throughout every square foot of the now smashed and doomed destroyer. The engines had now reversed their roles—becoming enemies as they relentlessly drove the hapless *Orkney* downwards into the endless black, icy, fathomless depths of the North Atlantic.

Seemingly calm throughout the battle so far, Teebolt almost barked the next orders, "Helm, port twenty, cease firing. Prepare for torpedo collision."

The grand battleship again skewered her way through a quick turn as the deafening alarms continued to blast throughout the ship. Every seaman that could made very sure that he held onto a substantial metal or oak structure of some sort to prepare for the impending shock. Within seconds a bone and teeth rattling explosion shuddered throughout the 235 meter long warship. A few seamen had underestimated the shock and were wrenched from their handholds, bouncing into some unforgiving machinery but without any serious injury. None would report to medical office out of pride and slight humiliation.

The huge warship lurched a meter or two to starboard when a torpedo slammed into the port side at forty-degree angle just slightly forward of the magazines for Anton and Bruno. A few meters further back and the results would have been disastrous. It was the thick armor belt that absorbed the bulk of the explosion, but even with the partial glancing blow, the several hundred pounds of high explosive punched a three-meter wide gaping hole through the hull and *Gneisenau* immediately began taking on water. The other two torpedoes that *Orkney* had unleashed with a wide spread screamed harmlessly past *Gneisenau* to spend themselves on the empty ocean before dying and joining their mother ship on the sea floor. Even before Teebolt could call for an assessment of the damage the always excitable voice of the damage control officer Frederick Mansel blared through the communication speakers, "Captain, we are taking on water just forward of the magazines in the crews quarters. We have a quite large hole in our side but no fires thanks to the water. I have sealed the flooding compartments off and any real danger to the ship is past."

"Casualties, Mr. Mansel?"

"The crew's quarters were empty Sir so there was no one killed but I have seven injured, one rather severely with two broken legs. The other six only have minor cuts and bruises. They will be fine after the doctors patch them up a bit."

"Very well Mr. Mansel. Can you give me an estimate for repairs?"

"Not yet Sir, but I will get back to you in a few minutes when we have come up with a way and schedule to affect repairs."

"Thank you Mr. Mansel, carry on."

Teebolt who had been gripping the handrail on the front left side of the bridge visibly relaxed now that the battle was over and his ship was safe. After a moment of reflection he calmly announced, "Gentlemen that was one of the most audaciously clever and extremely brave things we shall probably ever see. We must make an effort to rescue any survivors before they perish in the cold sea."

Teebolt reached for the intercom and made a quick request, "Mr. Mansel, are you ready to make repairs yet?"

"Yes Sir, but I need the ship to slow down a bit or we will not be able to stem the onrush of the water."

"How slow do you need us to be going?"

"Any speed under ten knots will reduce the incoming pressure sufficient to make repairs."

"How long will it take to get us back in decent condition?"

"About two hours Sir."

"Very well Mr. Mansel We shall slow down shortly."

Turning to his bridge officers Teebolt gave several quick orders, "Light up the ocean with star shells, reduce speed to eight knots. Launch two rescue tenders when we have slowed down enough for safety and have the lookouts determine where any survivors might be clinging to a piece of flotsam and then go and get them quickly. Mr. Erhlich, radio our destroyers to round up as many surviving merchants as possible, especially the tankers and escort them to the nearest French port. Have them follow standard procedures when commandeering enemy vessels. Especially guard the radio room. I do not want the British Navy to intercept our prizes and retake them. Radio the *Max Schultz*. I want her to assist in the rescue by circling around us while we affect repairs and fish some damn brave dripping-wet Englishmen out of the ocean. When we have affected repairs, she is to accompany us to the rendezvous. If all that is crystal clear, let us get on with it. Immediately send our status to Kriegsmarine headquarters."

Always one to speak up, Second Officer Joseph Spatz addressed the captain, "Captain, Sir. We should not be breaking radio silence."

With a quick chuckle Teebolt glared at his youngest officer and in a conspiring whisper that all the officers could nonetheless still hear, asked the young boy standing but a few feet away, "Mr. Spatz, don't you think the British know where we are by now?"

Spatz flushed a crimson red that was noticed even in the relative gloom of the bridge when he realized the absurdity of his question. His fellow officers suppressed their grins at his discomfiture mainly because Captain Teebolt would surely and very sternly chastise them for making fun of a fellow officer. Stammering a bit, the crestfallen young officer replied rather quietly, "Yes Sir. It most definitely makes perfect sense that they would have radioed our position in long ago. I apologize for my rather stupid question."

"Mr. Spatz. An apology is not necessary because there is no such thing as a *stupid* question. It is quite within the realm of possibility that any of us older sea dogs could overlook even the most obvious, and then we would need you to ask your questions or make pertinent observations."

"Yes Sir, and thank you very much Sir."

"You're quite welcome. Now check with radar and sonar to make sure that there are no enemy submarines lurking about to inflict more damage to us while we dawdle making repairs."

With a quick salute and another thank you the young officer scampered back to the "eyes" and "ears" little rooms behind the bridge to make certain that *Gneisenau* and *Max Shultz* were the lone warships remaining on the vast empty ocean.

Scharnhorst

As the scheduled time for battle wound down to a few minutes, Chief Cook Manfried Strass came over the intercom loud and clear.

"Attila is safely housed in his battle station."

Kastanien stepped over to the intercom's mouthpiece and simply stated, "Thank you Chief Cook. Secure your galley immediately. Battle stations in five minutes."

Although they had heard it many times in the past but this time the galley had been forewarned by Attila's rocketing through the ship like a crazed ricocheting brown bullet. When the incredibly loud Klaxon horns permeated every cubic meter of the great battleship, every man in the entire crew was startled, skipping a heartbeat or two before plunging into their battle station preparations. Following the seven loud blasts of the horns, the equally loud voice of the first officer Herman Gott announced and repeated three times, "All hands, man your battle stations."

Manfried Strass had shut down all the cooking fires and secured the food that had been in preparation when he knew what was about to occur. Strass, along with three of the older galley crew, then hurried out of the galley dogging the hatches behind him. The battle station for the six galley crew medical members was either in the sick bay or if need be for more serious medical work, the galley's worktables.

To a man, the galley seamen said a silent prayer that they would have no business tonight. The remainder of the galley crew donned their uniforms and rapidly ascended the two decks to the main deck where they took up their positions as part of the gun crews. One by one in a matter of less than three minutes every battle station reported in, stating that they were manned and ready.

"Very well, Mr. Gott. Now Mr. Schmidt, what is our position relative to our friend?"

"We will be broadside of her in two minutes at a distance of three kilometers Captain. We are now less than four hundred meters behind her."

"Mr. Mueller, turn on all of our port searchlights and aim them at the target, most especially the rangefinders. These will effectively, but only temporarily, blind their watchers and give us a few precious moments of respite before, and if, they opt to open fire."

Within seconds five very powerful searchlights blazed into life traversing the three kilometers to the mystery ship. Her outline became very clear to the watchers on the bridge of the *Scharnhorst*. The four officers carefully studied the vessel for a full minute through their very powerful Zeiss Navy binoculars as the *Scharnhorst* came even with her. Seemingly always the first to break these protracted silences, second officer Karl Mueller quickly stated, "She appears to rather an ordinary merchant Captain. Maybe our fears were unfounded."

Before Kastanien could reply the intercom screamed into life, "Bridge, this is Heinz Alder in the crow's nest. I can see furious activity on the foredeck and right behind the bridge structures. They seem to be dismantling some crates. Now I can see the barrels of what appears to be a medium-sized, maybe six-inch deck-mounted guns in front and behind the bridge structures."

Kastanien reacted instantly.

"Open fire with the 5.9-inch guns immediately. Aim for the deck cargo just behind the bridge. Then concentrate on the foredeck cargo. These are the guns we anticipated. I want them knocked out immediately."

As Kastanien spoke the last words of his order, the *Scharnhorst's* three port-side 5.9-inch batteries opened fire as one.

Kastanien picked up the intercom to gun control and barked a quick order, "Mr. Rost, ten seconds from right now, I want you to light off your *fireworks* display."

"Yes Sir, Captain. Ten seconds from now it shall be."

Knowing that his rangefinder crew now had the distance calculated to within a meter or two, Kastanien took necessary measures to avoid any damage to his ship, if possible.

"Mr. Mueller, extinguish the searchlights and all running lights. I want this ship totally dark immediately."

All outside lighting, running lights and the brilliant searchlights went dark as the *Scharnhorst* vanished into the black of the North Atlantic on the cold April night. After the blinding light from the powerful searchlights, the night vision of the *Rawalpindi's* warriors was ruined for some time and even the rather bright moonlight was inadequate for them to see their nemesis. Then the eleven-inch guns from turret Bruno opened fire. The recent brilliance cast upon the rolling ocean and the *Rawalpindi* by the powerful searchlights paled in comparison to the pyrotechnic display that spewed forth from *Scharnhorst's* main armament. The fireworks gushed out of the three deadly eleven-inch guns as one gigantic, incredibly intense white cloud. The initial burst of magnesium was instantly followed by deep red blossoms of Erwin Rost's special fireworks mixture.

The visual effect was so mesmerizing that none of the spectators seemed to even hear the thunderous assault on their eardrums. Although almost everyone knew what was going to happen, the incredible effect completely caught all the officers on the bridge as well as every crew member within visual range by surprise. No one would have ever guessed that the "fireworks" would be so powerful. Heads quickly turned to the captain with the unsaid question on all their lips, *"Did the guns blow up or was this the way it was supposed to look?"*

Even Kastanien was taken aback by the shocking display the gunnery officer had concocted and he reached for the intercom to gun control and inquired of gunnery officer, "Mr. Rost, are our guns still with us?"

Struggling to suppress his mirthful laughter, the gunnery officer quickly replied, "Absolutely, my Captain; there has been no damage whatsoever to my beautiful guns. I believe that all the evidence we will ever see of our little trick is some darkening of the brass tips and that will be cleaned off as soon as we have a little daylight with no unfriendly company to hinder our efforts."

"Thank you for your assurances and let me congratulate you for exceeding my fondest hopes."

Back on balance again, Kastanien snapped his binoculars to his now night-blind eyes and focused on the *Rawalpindi* to see what effects the 5.9-inchers had. He got his answer a brief second later as the *Rawalpindi* returned fire from her undamaged forward six-inch turret. Her gunnery was an accuracy match for *Scharnhorst* as the first salvo struck the now "disabled" eleven-inch turret. The eleven-inch gun turrets of *Scharnhorst* were made of incredibly thick and stalwart armor plate, so the puny six-inch shells did little more than scratch the paint and make small dents. Kastanien winced as the slight concussion from the shell strikes reverberated to the bridge. He quickly resumed scanning the horizon for the *Rawalpindi* to see what hits his shooting had scored and to what effect. He knew at this close range, even his opponents six-inch guns could do some serious damage if left in action. His eyes quickly found the forward fire where the enemy's gun had been. This battery was out of commission and no further threat to *Scharnhorst*. Quickly traversing the hull he was further pleased to see that the area around the aft turret was a confusion of small fires and scrambling sailors.

"No doubt they are moving the live ammunition out of harm's way until they get the fires out." thought Peter Kastanien.

Dropping his long range eyes to his chest on their simple leather neck strap, Kastanien barked out new orders. When he barked, the entire crew knew that he demanded immediate obedience and implementation.

"Cease fire with all guns immediately. Turn ninety degrees starboard. Maintain complete blackout throughout the ship. Fire two star shells at sea level to blind her remaining guns, if any."

The helmsman spun the wheel like a roulette croupier in Monte Carlo and the massive bulk of *Scharnhorst* heeled to the command like a well-trained race horse. Kastanien had quickly moved to the bridge wing to be able to see what was transpiring behind his apparently fleeing *Scharnhorst*. He watched intently to see where his star shells were going to explode. Once again the gunnery officer exceeded Kastanien's expectations as two star shells exploded into daylight brilliance ten meters above the sea's surface less than twenty meters from the ship. The enemy would most definitely be blinded, but they would surely have noted his turn and might start shelling him again with the hope of a lucky hit. Kastanien would have none of that. Wheeling his body around, Kastanien left the nose and cheek freezing cold of the exposed bridge wing and returned to the bridge proper, instantly barking an order that once again meant immediate execution.

"Port ninety degrees hard. Maintain full speed ahead."

These orders were instantly repeated and before the last repetition was finished, the massive 38,100 tons of the sleek battleship leaned into the sharp turn. Kastanien and the crew also leaned into the turn before

Kastanien went on, "Gentlemen did any of you get a good enough look at her to determine who she is?"

The executive officer Hans Schmidt spoke up immediately with conviction, "Captain, I am virtually certain that she is the refitted *Rawalpindi*. Although the British have removed the aft funnel and outfitted her with some teeth, her lines are still very distinctive. She was commissioned in 1925 and has a top speed of seventeen knots. Our intelligence tells us that they are refitting three more ships of her class similarly, but two of them are not ready for sea, and the third one called the *Rajputana*, is operating currently off the East coast of Africa. The *Rawalpindi* is equipped with (eight) six-inch guns and (two) three-incher's. Their main duty is to protect convoys from our U-boats and possibly do battle with our destroyers. Berlin mentioned these vessels in a communiqué a month back, but put little importance to their effectiveness against us."

"Thanks you Mr. Schmidt. At least now we know who we were up against."

Captain Kastanien fell silent for a few moments and no one spoke. All the officers knew that their brilliant captain was eschewing all this relatively new information, trying to make good sense out of all the anomalies that they had encountered these past few hours. Then abruptly Kastanien quickly strode back to the radar room and enquired, "Merlin, what is our position relative to the enemy ship?"

"Sir, she is about four kilometers off our port stern quarter and we are increasing our distance from her rapidly. She looks like about a kilometer and a half behind us now that we have straightened up and are running parallel to her. At our present speed and if she maintains hers, we will be increasing the range by a kilometer about every three minutes."

"Thank you Mr. Molter, I trust our officers will agree with you about our rate of progress."

Molter instantly realized by giving the captain tactical information, he had probably overstepped his bounds and immediately did a verbal back flip. He gulped out a stammering reply, "Sir, sir, please forgive me for my discourteous presumption. I meant no harm or offence. It's just that I get pretty excited when we are in a battle situation and I like to know what's going on and what the future of the battle is going to be like."

"My fine young Mr. Molter; in the future it would be best if you left the tactics and running of this great battleship to those of us who have had the benefit of many years of training and experience. None of us would presume to tell you how to run your mystical machine, but then again we all are very interested in and dependent on your ability to give us accurate information. We all, every last one of the nearly 1,700 men on this ship, has an important job to do and to do it well. Your job is to provide us with information so that we are able to make decisions that are to the safety and benefit of the *Scharnhorst*. You have done an admirable job at that and I know you will continue to do so."

"Thank you Sir, I will make sure that I never trespass on your authority and responsibility. Please accept my sincere apologies."

"Apology accepted. Now, we are running at high speed through this rather dark night with only the benefit of moonlight. Your responsibility right now is to keep a very, very sharp eye on that machine of yours and keep me up to date on any changes in what I am about to tell you. We will continue on this course at high speed until we are twenty kilometers ahead of our late friend. I want you to tell me when we at that position. Now, if you 'see' any vessel other than our latest shooting opponent, I am to be informed instantly, and I do mean instantly. You may shout at the bridge if necessary. Remember, no one can see us and at twenty-eight knots I surely do not want to run into any vessel, even a garbage scow. The lookouts have been given orders by First Officer Gott to double their watch, but the long distance eyes of our *Scharnhorst* are yours. None of us know if there might be a submarine recharging on the surface or another surface ship also running without lights. The submarine could be the enemy or one of ours. Submarines are by their very nature secretive and Grossadmiral Dönitz himself has cautioned me to be very careful not to run over any of his wolf pack members. And he was deadly serious."

Kastanien put his hand briefly on the radar operator's shoulder and then silently returned to the bridge. Marvin Molter silently breathed relief that he had not gotten a sterner discipline.

"Gentlemen, we are about two kilometers in front of our recent adversary and we will continue on at speed until we are twenty kilometers ahead of her at which time we will turn about and proceed back in the direction we have just come from. Are there any questions? If not, I suggest that you gentlemen take turns in going to the galley for a light bit of food to nourish your brains and body for the next hour or so. Secure from battle stations in ten minutes if nothing untoward happens. Mr. Mueller, please have Mr. Rost join me on the bridge as soon as he has his guns back in order. I want a damage report from Mr. Bock as soon as he can assess what that the *Rawalpindi's* shells did. I will not assume there were no casualties, so please report any to me."

There were no questions and the officers with a quick look and with a few simple nods split up and three officers disappeared into the black passageway leading to the galley after properly having themselves relieved in letter-perfect military fashion. They proceeded very carefully through the gloom until faint vestiges of light from below decks helped them navigate the stairways and passages a bit easier. All three of the officers passed by Attila's battle station and quietly uttered a greeting. Attila returned the greeting with a rather loud greeting of his own and the natural pent up tension of the officers visibly relaxed.

Erwin Rost, the genius of *Scharnhorst's* gunnery, appeared on the bridge less than two minutes after his summons, smartly saluted and enquired, "Captain, you wish to see me?"

"Yes, Mr. Rost. I most assuredly do. Do you know what damage those hits did to us? I have not gotten a report from damage control as yet."

"Captain, there is no damage to the operation of the gun turret. I believe that we will find a couple of dents and some minor scorching on the outer armor when we have light in the morning."

"Excellent, as was your gunnery tonight. Knocking out their pesky guns so quickly was pure artistry and allowed us to proceed as planned. I have no doubt that knowing they were hopelessly outgunned they were trying for our bridge with a lucky shot. Fortunately, their marksmanship was rather poor. Your 'fireworks' exceeded any of my expectations and should cause them to scratch their heads wondering what happened. Let us hope that they think we are seriously crippled and no longer a threat."

The two men had a quick chuckle and the Kastanien continued, "I also think that if there was ever a marksmanship contest for star shell guns, I would bet heavily on you. I imagine that those who were looking in the direction of the star shells when they exploded are still having trouble seeing very well. A job very well done Mr. Rost, thank you. Be standing by for some more action in an hour or so. Now, join the others in the galley for some food."

Gunnery officer Erwin Rost smartly saluted his captain, which was returned with equal perfection and then departed the bridge through the same black hole as had the three officers' minutes earlier.

Kastanien turned towards the radio room but stopped when he caught sight of the damage control officer materializing out of the gloomy passageway. He stopped and waited for the officer to come to him. The officer strode up to Kastanien and the two exchanged salutes.

"Damage Control Officer Horst Bock reporting Sir."

"What damage did we suffer during our engagement Mr. Bock?"

"There are no casualties Sir with the exception of one of my men who got banged into a bulkhead rather hard but he is now in sick bay and the doctor told me he is just bruised and a bit shaken. There is no damage to the proper operation of anything on the ship Sir. We have determined that the shells hit the forward eleven-inch turret close to the top and although they exploded on contact most of the blast vented itself upwards into the air. Although we will not be able to ascertain an accurate assessment until daylight, I assure you that the damage is nothing that we cannot repair as good as new in a very short time."

"Thank you Mr. Bock. If your educated assessment is correct and all goes as we expect, you should be able to effect repairs tomorrow morning, weather permitting. You will report to me as soon as you can establish visual confirmation. "

"Thank you Captain. If the Captain has no further need of me, I would like to go visit my man in sick bay."

Again the two men exchanged salutes as Kastanien granted Bock leave to go. Kastanien immediately headed for the radio room, opened the door and quickly entered, closing the door snuggly behind him.

"Mr. Weisboch, do you have the recent messages from our latest adversary and equally important, any responses from London?"

"Yes Sir. There are several outgoing but only two incoming. If the Captain would give me about ten minutes I will have finished translating them."

"Very well, Mr. Weisboch, bring them to me on the bridge the instant you have them translated."

"Yes Sir."

Kastanien then stepped across the darkened passageway and opened the door to the radar room. The light from the radar room was a dim eerie-green glow contrasting the brilliance of the radio room but he still pulled the door to. When the doors to these two very small rooms were closed, the places took on a definite claustrophobic feeling. When Kastanien had called for darkening the ship, every source of position-betraying light was blocked. Even the smallest chink could be seen at considerable distance, especially on such a clear night as this.

"Mr. Molter, what is our position now to the ship behind us?"

"Sir, we are now six kilometers ahead of her and opening the gap quite rapidly."

"Thank you; please inform me when we are twelve kilometers ahead of the *Rawalpindi*. And also very importantly, let me know immediately if you see any other vessels within the range of your 'eyes'. My best guess is that there will be another merchant of some sort about thirty to forty kilometers ahead of the *Rawalpindi.*"

"Yes Sir. I will inform you immediately."

Kastanien upon returning to the bridge spoke a simple order, "Mr. Schmidt, please accompany me onto the port bridge wing. Do put a heavier coat on as I believe it is a bit frosty out there."

Both men donned their very long and heavy greatcoats, wrapped pristine white embroidered scarves around their necks, slipped on heavy leather gloves and ventured out into the crackling-cold exaggerated by the twenty-eight knot wind generated by the ship's passage. The scarves had been made by the very talented wife of the second officer Karl Mueller. Each scarf had the name of *Scharnhorst* hand-sewn onto both ends along with each officer's name. Every officer on the *Scharnhorst* was dumbfounded into stammering little boys when the scarves were presented to them by Karla Mueller their last time in port. These scarves were one of, if not the top, possession of every officer and they took extraordinary care to wear them properly.

"Mr. Schmidt, join me in scouring the far horizon for any signs of the *Rawalpindi*. We need to see if she still has proper steerageway and the state of their firefighting."

For several long moments the two men braved the cold which was now beginning to creep inside their coats and then Kastanien spoke, "I do believe that she is still very seaworthy and that the fires will be out in a few moments. Do you concur?"

"Yes Captain. They are damaged very little except for their guns and the fires are quite under control."

"Very well, let us remove ourselves from this frightful cold and proceed with our plan."

Immediately when Kastanien stepped inside, the radar operator screamed, "Captain, Captain I have another vessel ahead of us on radar."

Kastanien almost ran to the radar room whose door was in the process of shutting and forestalling the closing, rapidly entered and closed the door. The night-time light popped back on when the circuit was reconnected at the shutting of the door. Almost all externally visible doors and hatches were equipped with a shutoff switch that broke the electrical circuit to the lighting system when they were opened. This system was rather elementary but eliminated any stray light escaping and being seen by the enemy and thus giving away positions at night.

"What do you have Merlin?"

Pointing to a barely perceptible specific bouncing bar, Merlin stated that this was a new contact and was approximately twenty-eight kilometers ahead and slightly on their port side. Kastanien leaned against the door jamb and entered his pensive mood for nearly two minutes all the while watching the squiggly green bars. Even to his untrained eye, he noticed a minor increase in the height that the bars were moving.

"Your opinion, Mr. Molter?"

"It is a trifle early to exactly determine the nature of this contact, but I can say for certain that she is not a submarine. The contact is too far away for a submarine contact to register, but not yet strong enough to distinguish between a merchant and a warship of size."

"Give me a report when you have a better idea of what she might be. And thank you for your diligence. I can see the little bouncing lines now that you have pointed them out and I thank you for educating me earlier as to their significance. What is our distance from the *Rawalpindi* now?"

"Ten kilometers Sir."

"Mr. Molter, in about ten minutes we will be reversing course and heading back towards the *Rawalpindi*. I wish to pass by her on our port side about eight kilometers distant. I am relying on you to guide us as close as you can to this new course. We will be running without lights as we pass. Our lookouts will be watching closely to help us in this matter. However, if the *Rawalpindi* chooses to go dark, we will be depending solely on you. Have you any trepidations regarding your new orders?"

"No Sir, I have the utmost confidence in my machine and I will keep us on your new course quite accurately."

"Excellent. Thank you and now keep a very keen watch on our new friend. I shall be back in a few minutes."

Kastanien returned to the bridge and ordered, "Do not stand down from battle stations yet, but have the men stand easy. Those who are outside in this chilly night are to be rotated inside every ten minutes to keep them warmer and sharper."

Kastanien then parked his lean and still rather athletic frame in his captain's chair and stared out the armored glass window at the night. He only had a brief moment before the radio operator Eric Weisboch approached him.

"Captain, here are all of the intercepts you wanted translated with about eighty percent accuracy. I have put them in the order they were received"

Kastanien nodded almost invisibly in the darkened bridge, accepted the several sheets of paper, thanked the sailor and rose. He proceeded to the radar room and quickly opened the door, entered and closed it.

"Keep watch Mr. Molter, I am only here so I can read the intercepts from the British. I still want to know when we are twelve kilometers ahead of *Rawalpindi*. Keep a sharp eye on the machine." Kastanien had barely read half of the messages when Molter piped up, "Captain, we are now twelve kilometers in front of *Rawalpindi* and my new contact is strengthening up to where I can tell with a high degree of certainty that she is another merchant class vessel."

"Thank you Mr. Molter, now we shall implement a new course heading back towards the *Rawalpindi*. Keep a very sharp eye. I want to know when we are five kilometers in front of *Rawalpindi.* "

"Yes Sir."

Captain Kastanien returned to the bridge immediately ordering the ship to reverse course heading back to the *Rawalpindi*. He informed all the men that they would be passing broadside to her eight kilometers off the *Scharnhorst's* port side. The orders resounded throughout the bridge and the *Scharnhorst* made a relatively gentle turn before straightening up on the new course. Kastanien noted a slight look of puzzlement on the first officer's face, which was very difficult to see with only the low intensity glow from the instruments illuminating his countenance.

"Don't be quite so concerned about plunging on at this speed in the dark. I have full confidence in Mr. Molter's ability to keep us out of harm's way with his eyes that can 'see' in the dark. We are twelve kilometers ahead of *Rawalpindi* and with our closure rate of thirty-eight knots, we will pass broadside of her in about twenty minutes. Have the lookouts relieved in fifteen minutes so that a fresh and unfrozen crew is topside when we are within sight of her. Have battle stations up to full alert in ten minutes. I am going to my cabin for a few minutes to digest the messages to and from the British Admiralty."

Kastanien was at his cabin's door in less than a minute. He entered into a totally ink-black space but with his unconscious training to find things in the dark that stemmed from working many hours in his home photographic darkroom, he confidently walked across to the porthole and closed the dark shutters. He then took a few steps to the desk— immediately finding his chair. He sat and reached for the light switch simultaneously. After the many long hours of working in the darkened ship, the light seemed very bright, causing him to blink a few times until his irises adjusted from their night vision mode to normal. Leaning back he silently read the papers through twice. And then he closed his eyes trying to read the mindset of the British as best he could. Three minutes later after extinguishing the desk lamp and giving his eyes a few moments to readjust to the gloom, he exited the cabin and returned to the bridge. He made a silent cursory tour of the bridge—checking the dimly-lit instruments. Satisfied, he proceeded to settle into his captain's chair. He mentally noted that all the officers had apparently rotated out for something to eat and were all at their proper stations and ready for his next orders.

Like a wraith floating unseen in the night, the radar operator was suddenly at Kastanien's side. He spoke softly in keeping with the tomblike tense atmosphere that was palpable throughout the almost ink-black bridge.

"Captain, Sir. We are now five kilometers ahead of *Rawalpindi* and by my best estimate, we should pass her by at a range of seven kilometers."

"Helmsman, turn starboard five degrees until we are eight kilometers from *Rawalpindi* broadside on and then straighten us up to pass on opposing parallel courses."

"Thank you Mr. Molter. You may return to your duties."

Kastanien had thought long and hard about his options when *Scharnhorst* came abreast of the *Rawalpindi* and followed each option through to possible outcomes. He had narrowed it down to two best case scenarios. Now he had only a few minutes to make his final decision on which course to take. Kastanien opted not to pose the options to his officers lest they might perceive it as a sign of indecision. This would be a very bad thing to infect the leadership of a captain commanding one of Germany's largest and finest warships. Kastanien reached for the intercom commanding gunnery officer Erwin Rost to the bridge immediately. Rost appeared within a minute from below decks where he was inspecting his men in the fire control room.

"Gunnery Officer Erwin Rost reporting as ordered Sir."

"Mr. Rost, in a very few minutes we will pass the *Rawalpindi* again, but this time our broadside exposure to her will be very brief as we are heading in the opposite direction at speed. We will also be at a longer range this time, notably eight kilometers. I want you to illuminate her with star shells shot normally above her. Ten seconds after the star shells brighten up the sky I need you to blind them with your star shells exploding in their faces just as before. As rapidly as you can calibrate your forward 5.9 inch gun and fire it and it only. Limit your shooting to no more than three volleys. Co-ordinate with our radar operator, Mr. Mueller, to approximate your range before she is lit up by the star shells. Your shooting will again be rather poor in their minds but needs to be accurate for our purposes. Target their guns again to hopefully render her completely toothless. We will know soon enough if she has repaired any of her guns but concentrate on the rear ones as I don't believe that we incapacitated them for very long and they still can give us trouble. Are my orders completely understood?"

"Yes Sir," replied the much respected gunnery officer.

Kastanien then inquired of his executive officer, "Mr. Schmidt, have the lookouts spotted any lights from *Rawalpindi*?"

"No Sir. She apparently has put any fires that lingered out and has darkened herself."

"Check with radar right now to verify her course, relative position to us and her speed."

Hans Schmidt hurried to the radar room and was back within one short minute.

"Target is maintaining her course and speed as before. Ten knots and course 020 degrees. Mr. Molter says we will be broadside in three minutes."

Kastanien returned his gaze to his gunnery officer.

"Very well then Mr. Rost. Prepare to execute upon my order. We are only going to fire when we are directly broadside so you will probably not get more than two volleys at her before we are past. I want *Rawalpindi* to think that our 5.9 inch guns have malfunctioned and can only fire a direct broadside from one turret. Remember, it would be better to miss altogether rather than cripple or even worse, sink her. Do you completely understand?"

Erwin Rost struggled to contain the huge smile that was invading his face before he could reply. Sensing Rost was caught in a battle between a proper straight-faced naval response and his obvious pleasure with his new duties, Kastanien also let loose a decent smile of his own. Rost then relaxed with a reasonable smile that easily read he was a happy officer. The smile only briefly flashed across his face before he regained his military composure. Kastanien and the officer exchanged salutes and Erwin Rost hurried to his battle station. Kastanien returned to staring into the night towards the port forward quarter and then he addressed the bridge in general, "Gentlemen, prepare for action."

The tension that was high in the bridge for the past hour became oppressively heavy as the time ticked away until the battle was to be joined. It mattered not to these experienced officers that the impending battle was overwhelmingly in their favor with the outcome never in doubt—regardless their tension mounted with each passing second.

"Fire illuminating star shells."

Even above the low rustling passage of the wind outside, the distinctive reports of the star shells being fired penetrated the silent and darkened bridge. After a few seconds Kastanien barked his next orders,

"Fire point-blank star shells and then open fire with the 5.9 inch gun immediately that you have a more exact range."

The orders were repeated instantly and within seconds they were being executed. The grim silent tension broken with the call to action, the bridge seemed to regain its reality on life. Every officer simultaneously snapped a large set of his own personal binoculars into his eye sockets and waited apprehensively for the star shells to illuminate the *Rawalpindi*. Barely had they gotten the binoculars in place before the night sky turned the sullen-black North Atlantic into an eerie blue-white undulating landscape. The harshness of the magnesium phosphorescing light instantly cloaked the *Rawalpindi* in a white shroud that left her nowhere to hide from *Scharnhorst's* lethal guns. Then the point-blank star shells exploded mere yards from the bridge observers and the deck guns of the *Rawalpindi*. Even at the range of eight kilometers, the flash caused the *Scharnhorst's* watchers to blink a time or two. Within seconds a different but familiar pounding reverberated throughout *Scharnhorst* as the forward 5.9 inch battery opened fire. *Scharnhorst* was now dead parallel to *Rawalpindi* and as the silent bridge watched, the uncanny accuracy of Erwin Rost finished off *Rawalpindi's* rear six-inch battery with his second volley

"Cease fire."

But Kastanien's order was two seconds late as another round of 5.9 inch shells blasted forth winging their way across the ocean. This time they struck the aft freeboard railings and blew some flimsy wooden crates blazing skyward leaving the upper stern section of the *Rawalpindi* a bit *rearranged* with a few small scattered fires burning.

The engagement had lasted a mere two minutes before the high star shells finished their languorous decent plummeting into the sea to be immediately extinguished. Every sailor and officer who had been watching the one-sided exchange on both the *Scharnhorst* and the *Rawalpindi* had lost what little night vision they had, so the scene was one of total blackness save for the small fires burning on the stern of *Rawalpindi.*

"Maintain course and speed. Maintain battle stations and darkened ship for the present."

The new and expected orders quickly came from Kastanien. Stepping back to the radar room Kastanien enquired of Molter, "Mr. Molter, I'm curious about something. While we were firing only a few star shells and three volleys of our 5.9 incher, could you 'see' them on your machine?"

"No, my Captain; the radar beam does not have sufficient time to travel to a high-speed shell and return with any accuracy. Also, the shells are really too small to register properly. Any 'blips' there might have been were no doubt lost in the vacuum between pulses."

"Pity, it would be nice to know that we could 'see' trajectories of our shells. However, that is a minor issue that we can easily handle."

Kastanien reflected for a brief moment and then issued his next order to the brilliant young radar operator, "Mr. Molter, we are now headed in the opposite direction from *Rawalpindi* at twenty-eight knots. She is traveling at ten. The gap between the two ships will increase rapidly with a departure rate of thirty-eight knots. I want you to inform me when the range has opened to eighteen kilometers. It should only take about thirty minutes."

"Yes Captain I will inform you immediately when we are eighteen kilometers from *Rawalpindi.*"

Kastanien opened the door; the light went out until the door was closed again. He stepped across the still darkened passageway and entered the radio room. Once more the light was out until he was inside with the door closed.

"Mr. Weisboch. Let me have any recent radio transmission to and from *Rawalpindi* that have been translated. Also, how many are still being translated?"

"Here are four deciphered transmissions from *Rawalpindi* and two replies from London. We are still working on the last two transmissions from the Admiralty in London. We should be done with them in less than five minutes Sir."

Kastanien leaned against the securely fastened door and after checking to make sure that the six messages were in the proper chronological order, he silently read them through. The messages were quite short, finishing with them in less than three minutes. More to himself than the radio operators, Kastanien looked vacantly at the myriad of dials and meters above the two young men's heads and quietly made a simple statement, "Well, well, the British seem to have come to the conclusion that we arranged for them to deduce. That is excellent so far."

Kastanien returned from his partial reverie and addressed the radio operators, "Thank you. Please bring the last two translations to me on the bridge the minute you have them."

Within a few seconds Kastanien was back in his captain's chair. The officers, whose night vision had by now almost returned to excellent, could distinguish him rather well considering that the only illumination came from the eerie yellowish-green of the essential instruments. Kastanien rested his left elbow on the arm of his comfortable chair and slowly stroked his rather handsome, immaculately trimmed goatee with his left hand. Kastanien's night vision had not yet returned so he stared intensely out into the utterly black ocean that raced by unseen. The officers knew that this was his most pensive and thoughtful trait. No one would dare crack this critical concentration except for dire emergencies.

They also knew that Kastanien would ponder for only a few brief moments before he returned from his thoughts and brought them abreast of his plans. Nor were they wrong for after less than three minutes, Kastanien dropped his left hand to the arm of the chair, straightened up and quickly rose. He walked deliberately over to the steering section and backed up against the forward shelf of the bridge. He chose this particular spot because he knew that the illumination from the compass was the strongest of the weak lights and his face could be seen by all.

"Gentlemen, without boring you with the more mundane details of the intercepts between the British Admiralty and the *Rawalpindi*, I shall summarize them for you. It would seem that the Admiralty wishes us to continue following and doing battle with or sinking the string of ships that we have intercepted so far. Our first opponent was merely an innocent merchant to whet our appetite. The *Rawalpindi* was a different matter altogether but really no match for our *Scharnhorst* and they knew it from the start."

At this point in his impromptu speech Kastanien paused and motioned the radio operator forward. Chief Radio Operator Eric Weisboch had mystically and silently appeared and was standing a few feet behind the officers for a few seconds with some papers in his hand which could only be the latest translations.

"What do you have for us Mr. Weisboch?"

"Captain, these are the translations from the last two intercepts."

"Thank You, Mr. Weisboch. We always appreciate your prompt and accurate work."

The radio operator saluted, expressed his thanks to his captain and vanished into the gloomy passageway as quickly as he had appeared. Kastanien held the papers up to the light from the compass and thoughtfully read through them before he uttered another word. Kastanien then let a sly conspiratorial smile transverse his face and the assembled officers immediately read this as good news and they smiled as well.

"These last two intercepts are most welcome news indeed. Our British cousins seem to have completely swallowed the bait. The report to London says that our main guns have blown up and are currently inoperable and that our 5.9 incher's seemed to be locked in place and cannot rotate from a direct broadside aiming position but still have elevation control. The *Rawalpindi's* captain put forth a rather colorful narrative on what we are doing now and the Admiralty seems to agree with him, albeit in a much more subdued and straightforward manner."

With this tongue-in-cheek pronouncement, Kastanien let out a mirthful chuckle and the officers joined in the celebration of their captain's rather clever subterfuge. Kastanien then went on, "We will now follow through with the original plan and drop back to twenty kilometers behind *Rawalpindi* and resume our shadowing for a bit longer."

"Begging the Captain's indulgence Sir, but might we hear the 'colorful narrative' part of the intercept from *Rawalpindi*?" Second officer Karl Mueller ventured forth.

With a hearty laugh Kastanien replied, "Yes, of course. First though we have a bit of ship's business to attend to. Stand down from battle stations and have Mr. Molter inform me when we are ten kilometers behind *Rawalpindi*. Have all compartments report their status and any problems. I also want to know the status of the man who suffered an injury during our initial encounter."

For a few moments the officers went about their duties and procured all the information that Kastanien had requested. The reports came in quickly and efficiently. There were no problems with any areas in the ship and the injured sailor had been released from sick bay with no lasting ill effects. When all this had been reported to Kastanien, he thankfully acknowledged the reporting officers and was about to commence telling the colorful "narrative" from *Rawalpindi's* captain when the radar operator announced over the bridge intercom that they were now ten kilometers behind *Rawalpindi*. Reaching for the intercom to the radar operator, Kastanien ordered that he be informed when they were eighteen kilometers behind *Rawalpindi*. Radar Operator Marvin Molter acknowledged the order and Kastanien went on, "Light up the ship so *Rawalpindi* can see that we are still in the neighborhood just in case their radar was knocked out."

In seconds the cold, dark and lonely North Atlantic suddenly had a brightly lit guest traversing her long smooth undulating swells.

"Now that our ship's business is shipshape giving us a few quiet moments, I will read you this interesting and rather amusing intercept. Do keep in mind that the author is captain of an enemy ship and his opinion is rather different and highly biased."

Having set the proper mood Kastanien began reading the most recent intercept to his audience, "*Rawalpindi* to Admiralty. The bloody Bosch bastard doubled back on us and with what had to be a shell guided by a fairy godmother knocked out our rear six-inch turret. But it seems that his big guns are not operable after the bloody great explosion earlier. If they were working the Hun could easily have finished us off like a crumpet at teatime. Additionally, his 5.9 inch guns seem to be locked up tighter than a tart's bloomers down in Soho. They can shoot but not traverse. Maybe our hit or two was lucky enough to clip his fangs where it hurts the most. Our radar has become a bit trifle touchy but the wee lad that operates it says it will be back running like a steeplechase stallion with a hot poker up his arse soon enough. Shall we turn on our lights so the wily fox doesn't lose us before dawn?"

Kastanien folded the intercept and stuffed it in his coat pocket as his officers had a good laugh. A few of the slang expressions baffled some of the officers but they were quickly explained which rekindled the laughter. Kastanien let the tension-relieving mood continue on for a few minutes until the levity of the situation had run its course.

"Well now that we've had a bit of entertainment, let us carry on with our duties."

With his pronouncement, the novelty of the moment was over. Kastanien strolled back to the radio room and enquired if there were any new intercepts. The radio operator replied negatively and with a mutual understanding that any new intercepts were to be translated and reported as quickly as possible. Kastanien then took the three short steps and entered the radar room. As soon as the order for the ship's lights to be turned on both the radio and radar rooms doors had been opened and dogged back to alleviate the stuffy, hot atmosphere that the equipment by its inherent nature generated.

"Mr. Molter, our distance from *Rawalpindi* if you please."

"Captain, we will be eighteen kilometers behind *Rawalpindi* in less than one minute."

"Thank you Merlin, I am returning to the bridge. You do not have to inform me when we reach the eighteen kilometer mark as previously ordered."

With that Kastanien disappeared and returned to his chair on the bridge.

"Mr. Schmidt, execute a slow reversal of course to port to bring us up behind *Rawalpindi* twenty kilometers distant from her. Slow to ten knots before the turn. I want us to be offset on her starboard beam by four kilometers. Co-ordinate this position with the radar operator. We will hold that position until further notice."

The orders were repeated rapidly to and from the responsible officers and crewmen. Almost immediately the ever present background humming from the great turbines dropped drastically and the *Scharnhorst* began a gentle turn to port. Kastanien continued to remain in his chair losing himself in thought for several minutes.

"Captain, we are in position twenty kilometers behind *Rawalpindi* and four kilometers off her starboard beam. We are holding position with her at ten knots," Executive Officer Schmidt broke through Kastanien's thoughts.

"Thank you Mr. Schmidt for the gentle treatment of our *wounded* battleship. I hope that the British made careful note of our rather lethargic maneuvers."

With his rejoinder, the officers again had a good chuckle at the captain's sardonic remark. Most of the officers on board *Scharnhorst* had served with other captains before being the lucky ones to sail on one of the Kriegsmarine's newest and most powerful ships. When they were relieved and went to the officer's mess hall, they would invariably talk about how different Peter Kastanien was when compared to their previous commanders. Kastanien always came out the superior man. The discussions never became heated but there were several diverse opinions as to which of his characteristics was the best.

Some said his sense of humor, others appreciated his straightforward style of command that came more like a request than a direct order; which everyone knew and acknowledged as a direct order to be followed out with dispatch and thoroughness. His battle strategies and tactics had all of them baffled because they could not anticipate his next unorthodox move. At first, some of the junior officers were silently aghast with the blatant contravention of what they had been taught at the Naval Academy, but as the *Scharnhorst* continued with its successes, they began to truly appreciate his interesting and brilliant strategies.

Kastanien reached for the intercom and spoke to the radio operator, "Mr. Weisboch, I anticipate *Rawalpindi* will transmit shortly. I need your ears on full alert. Their next message will determine our next move."

"Yes Captain. I will keep on full alert and bring you the decoded message as rapidly as I can."

"Thank you Mr. Weisboch."

Peter Kastanien then turned to the bridge officers and issued a new order that caught most of the officers by surprise.

"Mr. Mueller, signal U3200X to come alongside our starboard beam."

"Right away Sir."

Once more Kastanien used the ship's intercom and spoke to the galley. "Mr. Strass. Please let Attila out of his battle station and see to his appetite, which I'm sure is rather keen by now. When he has satisfied himself, bring him to me on the bridge."

"It will be my pleasure and honor Sir. We shall be there as soon as Attila has eaten and taken care of any other personal business."

Nearly fifteen minutes passed before the chief radio operator Eric Weisboch hurried up to Kastanien. Making a swift salute which was immediately returned, he handed a single slip of paper to Kastanien who told him to stand easy and wait. Eric Weisboch was much more mature than his mere twenty-one years and unlike many young seamen who would have been very nervous, he stood proud, straight and calm in the presence of the great captain. After only a short minute Kastanien, with a smirk on his lips, looked up at the radio man and asked him for a pad and pencil. Weisboch had already anticipated this request and immediately, with a touch of theatrical flourish, handed his captain the pad and pencil he had been holding behind his back. Kastanien began writing a message, verbalizing it at the same time.

"Will continue to shadow *Rawalpindi* until first light. We are affecting repairs to the guns and should be at least partially operational by dawn. Will advise condition of armament then."

Kastanien then handed the pad and pencil back to the radio operator and gave him an order to send this message to Kriegsmarine immediately to the attention of Grossadmiral Dönitz. Eric Weisboch instantly stood at attention, snapped a perfect salute and replied, "Yes Captain. Immediately."

"Oh, Mr. Weisboch, do not complicate the encoded message too much. I do wish the British to at least have a basic understanding of the message given that their cipher clerks have not had much success with cracking our Enigma code. If they are able to get the basic gist of the message, I expect the Admiralty to respond rather quickly. Keep your ears on high alert and continue to bring me any intercepts quickly. "

At that remark, the smiles returned on everyone who had heard. The smiles temporarily vanished as quickly as they had appeared when the starboard lookout broke in over his intercom.

"Captain, U3200X has surfaced on our starboard beam 300 meters away and is holding station with us."

First Officer Herman Gott acknowledged the lookouts message and looked to Kastanien. Kastanien alighted from his chair and strode towards the back of the bridge, issuing an order at the same time, "Mr. Schmidt, fetch the signalman. Both of you put on your cold weather long coats, hats and gloves, then join me on the starboard bridge wing. We are now about to execute our last maneuver in this *chase*."

Within three minutes the three men were once more braving the bitter cold on the starboard bridge wing. The temperature had dropped rather drastically over the past few hours and was barely above zero Fahrenheit. The wind had dropped to a rather gently breeze from the south which quieted the normally tumultuous North Atlantic at this time of year. The combination of a following breeze coupled with a leisurely ten knot cruising speed all but cancelled out a wind chill factor making the outside venture far more palatable.

"Signal U3200X to close up to one hundred meters. Instruct them not to use their lantern until they are on station."

The signal lantern clattered for a few seconds and then the men waited until the great gray shark was in position.

"Signal U3200X that we will execute Operation Butterfly ten minutes after she is in position. She is to follow *Rawalpindi* until first light and assess the gathering of ships that I expect will be waiting for us. After she has made her observations as best she will be able to, have her send the information to Kriegsmarine on the special channel which *Gneisenau* and we can also receive. Make sure that the name of *Rawalpindi* is mentioned twice in their communication and the second mention needs to be misspelled by omitting one letter only. Just to quell your inquisitive nature about the deliberate misspelling, let me explain. When I send messages that are shall we say untrue, the recipients, which in this case are those in our battle group and the powers that be at Kriegsmarine, the code for the untruth is the repetition of a ship's name with this particular misspelling of one of them. We have devised several other methods of saying one thing and imparting another through these 'mistakes' but that is a conversation for another time. We will not be responding to the message as our whereabouts shall be a mystery to all but those in the know."

After Kastanien finished dictating his message the shutters of the signal lamp continued to chatter away for several seconds before falling silent. The signalman and the executive officer silently looked at the captain for further orders.

Then Kastanien continued, "Personal to Captain Wittrock. Please be my guest and dispatch the *Rawalpindi* and any others that you can in the early light. After your little party is over please proceed to the rendezvous. I look forward to clasping your hand and hearing about your adventures of late. It has been too long a time since I had a good conversation with my old friend. Happy hunting."

The message was sent and the men waited for the acknowledging reply which came after a few moments pause while the U3200X absorbed the contents and formed a response.

"It will be my pleasure to take care of *Rawalpindi* and any other *guests* that may show up at the party. I am looking forward to our meeting in a few days. God speed, my old friend and happy hunting to you as well. Signing off. Captain Wittrock."

"Signal man Jorgen, acknowledge and sign off. Gentlemen, let us return to the warmer climate inside."

Very grateful for the brevity of the signaling, the three men returned to the not exactly cozy but much more comfortable environment of the bridge. Kastanien repositioned himself in his captain's chair and looked out the front window. Less than a minute later, Chief Cook Manfried Strass appeared at his left side with the ship's good luck charm.

"Captain, here is Attila. He ate very well, did his ablutions followed by a quick inspection of the galley making sure that our battle actions hadn't produced any new unwanted guests from the nether regions of the ship. He came up empty of rodents and returned to me where he spent a few moments grooming. And here he is."

As he spoke the chief cook gently placed the sleek feline onto his captain's lap. Attila looked up at his human friend with his almost fully dilated eyes blazing red as only Siamese cats eyes can. He then made two quick circles on Kastanien's lap before plunking down. Being quite content he began to purr loudly. Kastanien placed his left arm beside the cat's side and began to massage the cat's ears.

"Thank you Manfried for taking care of our Honorable Master-at-Arms. Please prepare some food for the crew as we will be out of any actions for some time. I know that some food, rest and relaxation will be very welcome by our seamen and officers alike."

"Yes, Captain. I will be prepared for dinner guests in about a half an hour."

"I am not terribly hungry so I will let you know when I'm ready for some nourishment a bit later. Now, off you go and prepare for a lot of late dinner guests throughout this night."

After a quick exchange of salutes, the chief cook vanished to be replaced immediately by the chief radio operator, Eric Weisboch.

"Captain, here are the latest intercepts from *Rawalpindi* and the Admiralty in London. I apologize for taking so long but the response from

London had some rather odd words in it so my second operator and I struggled for quite a while to make sure that we have the translation as correct as we could."

Taking the papers from the radio man, Kastanien looked enquiringly at the youth and asked, "Odd words indeed! Please remain here while I digest the messages and see what I can make of your 'odd' words. Stand easy."

The radio operator inwardly smiled and assumed the relaxed position. He waited while Kastanien slowly read the first transmission from *Rawalpindi,* silently nodding his head to acknowledge that it contained what he expected. Then he read the response from the Admiralty and a puzzled frown appeared on his face. He then reread the message from *Rawalpindi* and the Admiralties response. His silent demeanor was being watched by most of the bridge officers with anticipation, hopeful of more interesting tactics to come. They knew him well when he was pensive like this. He then read the third and final message that was only the confirmation from *Rawalpindi* stating that they would proceed as ordered.

"Mr. Weisboch. Please tell me completely honestly how accurate you believe this decoding to be. I want a completely honest answer, not what you think I want to hear. Understood?"

"Yes Captain. I completely understand the necessity for you to have this odd response as accurate as possible. I can say confidently that we feel that translation to be at least ninety percent accurate. But there are some words—that although we are pretty sure that we have translated them accurately, they do not make any sense to us. "

"Very well Mr. Weisboch. You may return to your duties. If you have any more thoughts about the missing ten percent mystery words, let me know immediately."

"Yes Captain and thank you Sir. We will continue to work on the strange words."

As soon as the radio operator had left the bridge, Kastanien resumed his watch forward. He was pleased to see the U3200X had moved into position directly ahead of *Scharnhorst* at a distance of about one-half kilometer. Turning to his Executive Officer Herman Gott he ordered that *Scharnhorst* maintain the separation between the two German ships for right now. Then he enquired of the entire bridge staff,

"Gentlemen, how many of you, and the crew that you know of, have ever spent any time in England?"

That comment raised more than a few eyebrows but no one spoke for what seemed a short eternity. Then, always one to jump into the fray first, Second Officer Karl Mueller spoke, "Captain Sir. There is no one on board that I know of that has ever been to England but I do know that First Officer Heinrich Lassen of the U3200X spent several years in London as a junior assistant to our attaché there before he returned home."

"Mr. Schmidt. Signal U3200X to come back close alongside our starboard beam immediately."

The order rang out through the bridge and down to the engine room via the intercom in a flash. When Kastanien used the word immediately, he meant before another breath was taken by anyone. The quick clanging on the deep part of the hull was heard faintly by the men on the bridge within three seconds of the command. When U3200X was within range of underwater signaling the chief engineer was never more than a second away from the large sledge hammer that was used to communicate with the submarine. The engineer was determined never to be of any source of displeasure to the captain.

Unbeknownst to the entire crew, chief engineer Johann Grabbel had received one of Kastanien's rare looks of displeasure shortly after *Scharnhorst* had left port on this voyage for a minor breach of cleanliness during one of Kastanien's regular inspection tours. There had been no verbal reprimand since it was in fact Attila who had discovered the offense. The chief engineer kept his engines so spotlessly clean that the comment about being able to eat off them had been heard and repeated many times. Grabbel had in fact been highly praised by not only Kastanien but Grossadmiral Dönitz during the first thorough inspection after *Scharnhorst's* first sea trials.

"Mr. Schmidt. Have the radio operator and the signalmen put on cold weather gear and join me on the starboard bridge wing as soon as possible. Tell the radio operator to bring the strange Admiralty response with him."

Kastanien once more donned his great coat, scarf and gloves and stepped outside, waiting for his crewmen. Even in the short time since his last sojourn into the frigid night the temperature had dropped another few degrees—noticeably stinging the small amount of exposed skin on his face. The two sailors appeared within a few seconds and saluted. Kastanien returned the salutes and began, "Mr. Oden. Signal U3200X to have First Officer Lassen join their group as the first message will be for him."

The shutters again clattered into life and the simple reply came immediately.

"Mr. Lassen is already here. Proceed."

Kastanien turned to his radio operator and asked him to have Oden signal the troublesome words. Weisboch handed a neatly printed sheet to Oden telling him to ask if anyone knew what the words meant. Oden studied the paper for a moment under a small patch of light that spilled out of the bottom of his signal lamp and then quickly transmitted the message. The U3200X did not respond for several minutes during which the bitter cold inexorably crept in, through and under their bulky clothing. With stoic patience the two junior sailors stood staring out at the silver black ocean illuminated by the pleasant moon that had risen earlier. In the moonlight they could make out the sinister gleaming smooth hull of Germany's newest U-boat. The aqua-dynamic rounded shape made no phosphorescing wake like her earlier cousins. The water just rolled up the hull and slid down the sleek sides unhindered by any ungainly protruding metal. This night the sea had a mystical look and feel to it. The moonlight, unhindered by any clouds, made the sea seem like an ocean of quicksilver that undulated like the fronds on a tropical palm tree. The cold, gentle ten-knot breeze coupled with the empty silence of the ageless ocean had been mesmerizing the human beings that had traversed her surface for countless centuries.

The two junior officers became quite certain that they were frozen solid under their clothing but young male pride would never allow them to show the slightest sign of weakness in front of their beloved captain. Kastanien felt the cold probably to a slightly higher degree than his two stalwart sailors did, but his was a different reason for not speaking or showing any outward signs of discomfort. Being the supreme leader on a warship did not allow him any of the human weaknesses that to a varying degree all of the rest of the crew were allowed to show. Kastanien looked over at the two youngsters and knew immediately their thoughts. He had been there many times before in his younger years at sea. Almost casually, without any inflection in his voice, Kastanien spoke in a rather ordinary conversational tone, "Well now Mr. Weisboch and Mr. Oden, does this night and the condition of the sea remind you of the forests near your homes in the dead of winter? It does me and it lets a few moments of nostalgic homesickness creep into my thoughts."

Kastanien knew that the youngsters would leap at the chance to have a simple conversation with the great captain and it would allow them to move a bit and temporarily forget the brutally numbing cold until the submarine replied.

"How about you Mr. Oden, where are you from?"

"Captain Sir. I am from Peenemunde. We have only a small forest but the North Atlantic tonight reminds me of many a night that I have stood on the breakwater almost hypnotized by this same moonlight gleaming and glistening off the sea. I used to think that it looked like the mercury in my chemistry professor's lab. But I never stood there when the temperature was this cold."

Kastanien laughed a little and quickly responded, "Gentlemen, it's quite alright to notice the cold but we must endure this minor discomfort, as all sailors must, when duty calls. Now, Mr. Weisboch, some of your thoughts."

"Captain Sir, I am from Berlin and I have never been to a real forest in wintertime. My parents would occasionally take me and my sister to the Black Forest, but only in the summer. The sea tonight has an allure to me that must be like the Mediterranean that seduced Ulysses and many of the other characters in Greek mythology. It is fascinating and beckons like a siren song to us mere mortals."

Kastanien was visibly impressed with the young sailors descriptions and was about to say so when the signal lamp from U3200X blinked into life. The signalman had never taken his eyes out of line with it. He immediately began translating while radio operator Weisboch wrote it down in his version of shorthand that he would properly type up exactly later at his station.

Message reads, said signalman Oden, "Braithwaite and Frederick are the two outstanding defensemen of the Manchester United soccer team and Rhodes is the star goaltender for the same team. They are considered heroes by most Englishmen and thought to be almost invincible. The two defensemen have also been known to execute brilliant tactics that the offense takes advantage of which results in Manchester United winning most games. The most notable victory came against Germany in the 1937 World Cup and the English victory was attributed to these three soccer stars. That made them legendary folk heroes to every Englishman so their names and deeds would be known to everyone in England and on the seas. Message ends."

"Mr. Oden, signal U3200X that message is understood and to please stand by for new orders. Gentlemen, let us step inside for a few brief moments while I digest this interesting news before replying. We might also thaw out a bit while there as well."

With grins on their peach-fuzz covered faces the two young sailors quickly held the door open for Kastanien before rapidly following him inside. The bridge was not exactly a cozy log cabin warmed by a blazing fire in the hearth but it hit the three men like a gust from a blast furnace in a Krupp's steel mill.

"Mr. Schmidt, please join me in my cabin immediately. Mr. Oden and Mr. Weisboch, please remain here until further notice," Kastanien ordered as he headed towards his cabin. Schmidt was right behind him and seconds later Schmidt closed the door. On the conference table was a naval map of the general area they were operating in right now. Kastanien had not removed his cold weather clothing; such was his concentration on this new development by the Admiralty. The map had tiny little ships in the positions that were known to Kastanien about an hour ago when he had assembled this comprehensive map.

The most outstanding model was that of *Scharnhorst*. It was a bigger and very detailed accurate model made of solid silver, a present from Grossadmiral Dönitz after their glorious South Atlantic foray. Kastanien repeated the translated message from the U3200X and gave Schmidt a moment to calculate what it meant. Opening a drawer on his desk Kastanien removed three more tiny models and placed them directly behind and to the left and right of *Scharnhorst*.

"Mr. Schmidt, I believe our English cousins have decided to box us in from the rear with two defensemen and a goalie just in case we do one of our disappearing tricks again rather than follow *Rawalpindi* into their trap. They are no doubt furious that we are never where they expect us so they are going to seal off every direction and use their superior numbers to get us. I have no doubt that they have two battle squadrons converging on what they think our position will be at first light. With the possibility of these three new squadrons we would have nowhere to go when the sun comes up. Would you concur?"

Executive Officer Hans Schmidt didn't utter a sound for several moments and Kastanien, ever patient when he asked his officers for their opinion, also remained soundless.

"Captain, where would the British get enough ships to mount such an encircling movement?"

"That Mr. Schmidt is an academic question. Remember that they do have a very large amount of battleships, battle cruisers, heavy cruisers, aircraft carriers and so on. They probably dispatched those weeks ago from patrols in the Mediterranean and off the South African coast. We must keep in mind that they absolutely must deal with *Gneisenau* and ourselves or continue to lose merchants at a pace faster than they, including Roosevelt's Lend-Lease ships, can replace them. So, it makes sense to me that they are committing a large percentage of their Navy for the express purpose of sinking or at least crippling us. If this is their plan, then our U-boats should have a fairly free hand in several critical areas. This would also cross their minds but they also know that even ten U-boats cannot do the damage to their shipping that we alone can do. Throw in *Gneisenau* and in their minds committing such forces makes sense if the outcome is what they envision.

"However, on the other hand, the British have had a few centuries more experience than ourselves and have been known sometimes to delve into rather unorthodox thinking. Be that the case, according to our sources and intelligence they are also burdened with cumbersome bureaucracies that dictate more set-piece maneuvers. Then again, we have that cagy Churchill who makes the tough decisions about the overall war strategy. He has always been known to have a cherished place in his heart for *his* precious Royal Navy. He, like me, admires the battle tactics of the famous Nelson and is likely in this dire situation for them to employ similar tactics. So, regardless of where the ships came from, I believe that they have them and are determined to surround us with vastly superior forces. I and a great many other brilliant naval tacticians have tried countless times to understand and predict what the British will do. I have on many occasions been frustrated by the innovative British moves. Any further comments?"

"No Sir. I concur that you have summarized the situation perfectly and they are throwing everything they have into the coming fracas in order to deal with us."

"Very well, let us return to the bridge and see if we can tweak the British Lion's nose one more time."

The two men exited the cabin arriving back on the bridge in half a minute. Kastanien laid his gloved hands on the back of his captain's chair for only a brief moment before he spoke, "Mr. Weisboch and Mr. Oden accompany me to the bridge wing again."

The three men once more stepped out into the crystalline night. The ever-present cold immediately began its insidious invasion into their puny armor made of wools and leathers.

"Mr. Oden, signal U3200X that we have a slight change of plans. Proceed with Operation Butterfly as previously planned but we are to rendezvous in three days for refueling at Grid AZ4 instead of our previous arrangement. Repeat this message as I need it fully understood and ask for a confirming reply."

The message was rapidly sent, then after a pause of twenty seconds the same message was repeated as ordered. It was fortunate for the U3200X that the message was sent a second time as the signalman on the U-boat had been ordered below to warm up and did not get the first few words of the first transmission. Captain Wittrock, like his old friend Kastanien, always looked out for the welfare of his men. Both men knew that without a happy crew that respected them, they would not have been so successful and a small thing like letting them take a respite from glacial cold and other avoidable discomforts went a long ways to maintain that respect. The U3200X replied quickly that the message was understood and they would see each other in three days. *Scharnhorst's* signalman quickly sent a confirming reply. He told the captain that his message was fully understood and they would rendezvous in three days.

"Thank you Mr. Oden. Now let us return inside out of this *brisk* night air and proceed with our revised plan."

The men were more than amicable to departing the cold which seemed even more intense than that of even a few minutes ago. The bridge wing was cleared in less than fifteen seconds. Once inside Kastanien ordered the chief radio operator to relay his change of plans to Kriegsmarine HQ and *Gneisenau* and bring to him their confirmation as soon as it was received. He also told the radio operator to make very sure that the message was properly encrypted so that even the best of the British cryptographers couldn't decipher it enough to make any sense.

The radio operator responded with a grin, flourished a smart salute before vanishing like a wraith into the relative darkness. Kastanien resumed his captain's chair after stroking the head of Attila who had been watching the goings on between naps on his cozy red blanket. The cat stood up and gave a quizzical look to Kastanien. Peter Kastanien let out a quick chuckle and acknowledged the cat's wish by picking him up and sitting back in his chair. Attila immediately did a quick tour of the lap before settling in for a seriously overdue lap-nap. Kastanien picked up the intercom to the radar room and enquired, "Mr. Molter, what is the position of U3200X?"

"Captain Sir, U3200X is directly ahead of us at a distance of four hundred meters. She is perfectly aligned with the *Rawalpindi* so that I cannot differentiate between the two. U3200X has been holding station there for the past two minutes."

"Very well, Mr. Molter. We are about to reduce speed and drop back some distance. It is imperative that we keep U3200X exactly in a line between us and the *Rawalpindi*. Please watch your little green bouncing bars and advise me if there is any deviation in the alignment. Before the U3200X moved into position how far were we from the *Rawalpindi?* "

"When I last had a good fix on *Rawalpindi* she was twenty kilometers ahead of us and had been maintaining the same course and speed for a long time."

"Well done Mr. Molter. I also want to know when we are ten kilometers behind U3200X. We will be reducing speed to four knots. It should take us slightly more than one hour to be in this position but I want you to let me know when we are in position for sure."

"Yes, Captain. I will keep you informed immediately if there is any deviation in the alignment and when we are ten kilometers behind U3200X."

Kastanien signed off the intercom with his normal courtesy. Clipping the intercom back in its cradle, he ordered, "Make our speed four knots and maintain heading. Darken ship."

The order reverberated throughout the bridge and within a short moment the pulsing of the 165,000 horsepower engines dropped to a whisper—noticeably slowing the huge battleship. Kastanien was grateful for the relative calm of the sea; for at this crawling speed his ship would have been a frightful rolling tub in a sea that had any gusto to it. Satisfied that the bridge officers could handle the boring chores for the next hour, he announced to them that he was retiring to his cabin. Before leaving his chair, he informed the radar operator where he would be when the requested position was obtained.

Alighting on the deck with Attila in the crook of his arm, Kastanien proceeded to his cabin and turned on the desk lamp. He let Attila land gracefully, as always, on the deck. Attila immediately bounded up on the desk obviously demanding some attention. Smiling, Peter again picked up the cat giving the sleek feline a good massage behind his ears and under his chin.

After a minute of this mandatory attention, Attila signaled that his demand had been met satisfactorily and leapt to the deck. Without a pause Attila loped over, ascending to the bunk where he nuzzled into the heavy wool blanket. He quickly proceeded to settle in for the remainder of the night. Kastanien finally removed his heavy clothing and after storing it properly went over to the conference table. He leaned over the large map of the current area with its little model of *Scharnhorst* by placing both his hands on the table. He contemplated for only a moment before he shifted all his support to his left hand and picked up one of the little models from a tray with his right hand. The particular one he picked up was the *Prince of Wales,* a front-line rather new, British battleship. Peter knew the all the important details of this grand ship as he did most all of the units in the Royal Navy.

The *Prince of Wales* had been launched only a few months short of 1940 and was one of the *King George V* class of battleships. The British had five ships in this class alone. More than all of the large capital ships of Germany combined if *Bismarck* and *Tirpitz* ever came out into the Atlantic. The *Prince of Wales* was 43,786 tons and sported (ten) fourteen-inch guns plus a secondary of (sixteen) 5.25 guns. Her top speed however was the normal for all British capitol warships—twenty-eight knots. Four, possibly very critical, knots slower than his beloved *Scharnhorst*. A slower but still a very serious adversary indeed Peter thought.

The models were all relatively-well detailed models that Willy in the carpenters shop had laboriously sculpted during his off-duty time. Willy was not to be outdone by the silver *Scharnhorst* that had been a present from Grossadmiral Dönitz. It was always the centerpiece of Kastanien's tiny fleet but Willy was rather handicapped by the absence of silver so he could not make a better model than Dönitz's without possibly raising some eyebrows. Undaunted by these restrictions Willy worked wonders with the brass, bronze and copper materials that he had at his disposal producing a matching semi-scale model of every British battleship as well as the smaller German fleet. The German models of *Bismarck, Tirpitz, Gneisenau, Admiral Graf Spee, Deutschland* and *Admiral Sheer* were works of art, painstakingly welded, ground and polished to a glistening golden shine.

The British model ships lacked the finesse and polish but were still quite laudable in their own right. All the ship models were proportionately sized to the *Scharnhorst* model ranging between three to five inches long standing about an inch high, including the superstructure. Each British ship had its name delicately painted on both sides with black ink in the Germanic style. The names on the German vessels were painted a shade of purple to match the color of the lettering on *Scharnhorst.*

Willy was not the world's best calligrapher so the task of painting the petite names went to the Second Officer Karl Mueller. The lettering was equally as fine as the ships themselves. When the first models were only a couple of weeks old they began to show signs of tarnish so the ever resourceful Willy retrieved them from Kastanien and polished them back to the original gleam. But this time he dipped them in shellac to ward off the corrosive effects of the salt air and human oils. This became the standard procedure for all models to follow. Willy held a secret dream that the great Grossadmiral Dönitz would someday come on board *Scharnhorst* and compliment him on his work. Little did Willy know that this secret dream would come to pass but in a way he would never have thought possible.

He knew absolutely in his heart-of-hearts that Peter Kastanien would give him all the credit for creating the miniature navies. Kastanien was not one to take praise for anything that he had not done himself. Many were the times that he gave more credit to his sailors than they warranted. This was another of the captain's traits that endeared him to the entire crew.

Kastanien looked at the glistening ship in his hand—his eyes taking on a faraway look for a few seconds. Then he deliberately placed the model on the nautical map and strode over to his desk. He opened the second drawer down and removed two more oak cradles that nested with each other. These cradles held all of the tiny ships in green felt cut outs to prevent scratching from the constant shifting of the ship. Each cutout was about half an inch deep and labeled on the bottom with the name of each ship. Like the tiny vessels the fine-grained oak gleamed from hours of loving sanding, staining and waxing.

Kastanien took the rather hefty cradles over to the conference table and deliberately and delicately removed each miniature warship and placed it on the border of the map. As he took each tiny ship from its nest, Peter Kastanien smiled the knowing grin of a contented husband. His mind quickly ran a cameo of the way his beloved wife Andrea picked up small objects. With longish fingernails, that were always filed and polished to perfection, she would use her thumb and forefinger like the beak of a bird. Laughing to himself he mimicked her pincher movement and continued to pluck the models free. When they were all out of their little homes, Peter walked over to the intercom and requested his executive offer to join him in his cabin forthwith.

Within a minute, Hans Schmidt gently knocked and entered the cabin. While Hans was on his way, Kastanien had turned the light out, maintaining the dark integrity of the ship. On such a clear night he was not taking any chances that a lookout on *Rawalpindi* perched high in the crow's nest might notice a light that was much further away than their radar operator determined that *Scharnhorst* was supposed to be. When the door was securely shut the lights came back on. Kastanien motioned Schmidt over to the conference table. Schmidt had never seen the entire collection of tiny ships. He audibly gasped at the quantity and beauty of them. Kastanien himself grinned and began the conversation, "Yes, Hans. This is the little collection of warships that Willy has lovingly made up for us to use for tactical planning. They're quite marvelous, are they not?" The question was rhetorical so Schmidt did not respond immediately as Kastanien went on, "what is the latest intelligence on the whereabouts of each of these British battleships, battle cruisers and aircraft carriers?"

Kastanien handed each of the models to Schmidt who delicately placed them on the map in where intelligence information said they were a few hours previously. More than half of the British twenty-two battleships were in waters or harbors unknown to Schmidt or the Kriegsmarine. Kriegsmarine diligently sent out any sighting or reports on every Royal Navy capitol ship within sixty minutes of its receipt. Dönitz was painfully aware of his opponent's vastly superior numbers and demanded that his few battleship captains, as well as the rest of Germany's small navy, be informed of the whereabouts of British serious capitol ships at all times and as expeditiously as possible. The ships that been reported within the past twenty four hours were placed on the map and if there was sufficient information the model was moved to where it would probably be at the present time. Within five minutes the map was weighted down with many miniature models. The side of the map held twelve British miniatures that were in parts unknown. Eight of them had been separated from the other four and deemed to be either in Scapa Flow for various reasons or patrolling the Indian Ocean. As efficient as the German Abwehr intelligence agency was, they had pitifully little to pass on to the

Kriegsmarine regarding the whereabouts of a large contingent of the Royal Navy.

The Kriegsmarine itself limited its theatre of operations to the North and South Atlantic oceans. It was simply too far from friendly ports to send their precious few large warships into other oceans. The logistics of resupplying the surface ships in the South Atlantic were daunting enough without going thousands of miles further out and back. At the present time the U-boat's were at their limit of operations going as far as the outer waters of the Caribbean. Consequently the German Navy only had reports and sightings in the Atlantic to go on.

"Hans, obviously the path ahead, if we followed the sacrificial goat *Rawalpindi*, would get us into an unequal duel with the Royal Navy. Now, if we interpret the last message from the Admiralty about the three *soccer* players coming into the game, then we must assume that these are ships or squadrons of unknown whereabouts, but doubtless to our south. They must be steaming north to prevent us from escaping their clutches again. I am guessing that they want to block our rear before tightening the noose—so to speak. Our previous *disappearing* acts must be driving Churchill and the Admiralty to drink. No, that's not exactly true. Churchill is already there."

The two men laughed heartily at this remark. It was well known by most every government in the world that Winston Spencer Churchill ran the British government and the war on at least a bottle of high class brandy every day.

"Pressing on, I can only assume that these missing vessels have been tucked in the Western Mediterranean where we also have poor intelligence from the rather lackadaisical Italians. We do know that several serious warships have also been steaming from the Caribbean. We have not received any messages noting the absence of the Royal Navy in the Caribbean, but those U-boat captains would simply just thank their lucky stars for an open season on shipping without any interference. Hah! Most of them including our dear friend Gordon Wittrock would attribute the easy pickings to their own cleverness. My, but they are an egotistical lot. But, one cannot blame them given those nasty cold, smelly steel coffins they scurry about in. Let us assume the worst possible scenario and place these three ghostly squadrons in the most likely places they would be to ensnare us. They of course have our position down to a kilometer and have tracked our path for several hours now. How many hours do we have before first light at this latitude and then at the latitude we would be at if we followed along this route like a tame puppy dog?"

Schmidt swiftly glanced at his pocket watch and took a moment to do some mental calculation before answering

"First light at this latitude would be in just under nine hours. If we were to steam at our present speed in this virtually due north heading first light would be fifteen minutes later."

Kastanien was always amazed at how his executive officer could keep track of such complex and constantly varying information—always ready at a moment's notice to dispense it with the accuracy of a slide rule genius. Although he did not have a warm friendly relationship with Hans Schmidt, he knew that this officer was one of the best that the German Navy had to offer; therefore he was delighted that Schmidt was part of the ships officer compliment. As well as being a mathematical intellect, his executive officer was a remarkable tactician that even had some inspired moves akin to his own.

"Hans, I have my own ideas and thoughts about where we and our British hunters are and where all the players will be in about nine hours' time. You have positioned Willy's little masterpieces where you think they are now. We will compare our thoughts. After we come to a reasonable conclusion or compromise, then you will reposition *Scharnhorst* where the British think we will be and where you think *they* will be at first light. I am withholding my thoughts because I do not want to jade your thinking by placing these beautiful miniscule warships where I think they will be."

"Yes Captain. I understand your thinking"
The executive officer decisively and very deliberately began picking up the little ships one by one so as to not scratch the gleaming finishes and began to place them on the map. He spent a short time to get all the models he thought the British would or could muster up on the map. Then he pondered a bit before sliding each one into the position he thought where they would be in nine hours. When he was finished he leaned back, looked over at Kastanien and with a quizzical look stated, "Captain, this is my best assumption as to their possible dispositions come the dawn."

Kastanien silently studied the map and the locations of the ships for nearly a minute before speaking. Schmidt knew that the lightning-quick brain of his captain probably went through as many possible moves as a chess master before he spoke.

"Very well Mr. Schmidt. Now, you have positioned everyone where you think they will be at first light which is nine hours from now according to your calculations. I want you to position *Scharnhorst* where we will be on our present course and speed."

Schmidt nodded an affirmative agreement. He again did some quick mental calculations. As soon as he had put the model in its projected position, Kastanien spoke, "Hans, before you continue, do you not find it a bit strange that this track and position still keeps us out of range from English aircraft? I want your opinion as to why the British would do something apparently either suicidal or just plain stupid."

"Captain, the British regularly do many complicated and unorthodox maneuvers but this one is really different. They must know that we would be suspicious since a simple course correction of five degrees to the east would easily bring them under their air cover umbrella. Then at first light they could easily launch a serious air attack against us. They must think that we are so slow-witted that we do not see this obvious error? To me, there are a few other possible answers. First they will have a powerful naval welcoming committee hoping to do us grievous harm. They do not have many submarines so it wouldn't be that. The only British subs that we have heard of in the past few days have been reported operating off the bulge of Africa and near Gibraltar. Our intelligence tells us that their main purpose is to sink our armed merchant raiders. And they haven't had much success with that enterprise.

So, it would surely be their surface fleet of which the *Ark Royal* aircraft carrier could be close enough to launch air strikes. She was last sighted three days ago by U-33 as part of the battle squadron guarding the Denmark Strait against a breakout by *Bismarck* and *Prince Eugen*. She would have had enough time to have sailed with or without the rest of the squadron to be close enough to launch an attack, albeit from a rather longish distance. But as desperate as the Royal Navy is to have at us, they would probably try anything that has even a ghost of a chance to sink or cripple us. The other possibility is that they have developed or modified existing fighter-bombers with extended range to get at us where they think we will be. My guess would be some *Handley Page Halifax* bombers. They could have added drop tanks and they definitely have enough bomb load carrying capacity to drop many, many bombs that could seriously hurt us. That is my appraisal of the situation we face. Have I answered your query sufficiently?"

"Yes, Hans you have. I do like your creative thought about the possibility, no rather the probability that they have extended their air cover umbrella out a couple of hundred more kilometers. However, to me the most obvious reasoning behind their thinking is that we could not resist such tempting, easy targets and blunder right into their naval trap. However, I talk too much right now. Please carry on."

"Sir, this is my estimate of their strength and possible positions. It is where I would want to be when smoke becomes visible on the horizon just before dawn. There are many, many more combinations that could be considered—however I have always found that my first instincts are much more accurate than when I start to second guess myself."

"Hans, you and I think very much alike and my first guess would be the same as yours. There are simply too many variable to pursue this any further. Let us proceed to really stump the British by simply not being where they will *know* for sure that we be."

Both men lightly laughed with each other since they both knew what had to be done again as it had been done a couple of times before. Kastanien reached over the map deftly returning the *Scharnhorst* and the possible Royal Navy ships to the positions at the present time.

"Hans, we are here right now. If your guess and mine are correct and I think we are relatively accurate in anticipating their moves and motives, then our best course is this."

With the last statement, Kastanien reached out and turning the *Scharnhorst* in an easterly direction he slowly moved it towards the Bay of Biscay. Then he changed course and continued to slowly move the model ship in a direction just a bit west of due south. When he reached the vicinity of the Azores he stopped and lifted his hand from the map. Glancing over at his executive officer, he raised his left bushy eyebrow and waited for a reply. Hans Schmidt obliged immediately with a grin and spoke, "Excellent maneuver Captain. The British will greet the dawn and each other without our illustrious presence to give them something to do with their guns."

"Yes Hans, they should even find time to have tea and crumpets while they try and figure out where and how we vanished without a trace. Now, if we turn east very soon, hold that course and steam at twenty-four knots, where will we be at first light?"

The executive officer reached over and taking the beautiful shining *Scharnhorst* he unerringly placed it a few inches directly east of the previous placement.

"Now Hans, if we turn to a course directly for the Azores from the position you have just marked, and we take into consideration some more variables about the disposition and courses of our rivals, what are the chances that we will be steaming into them and have to do battle with what no doubt will be a squadron made up of at least one battleship with cruiser and destroyer escorts?"

"Captain, I believe that the chances are very slim of running into the Royal Navy but all of our conjecturing is just that—conjecturing. They could be doing a great variety of things with their large Navy and we don't have the intelligence reports to even make a decent educated guess. My only suggestions are to keep a constant watch on the radar screen and at first light reduce our speed so that we will not be making much smoke. The Royal Navy on the other hand will be steaming all out to intercept us where they feel assured that we will be. They will be making much more smoke than we would be and that would enable us to see them and take evasive action before they know we're in the neighborhood."

"An excellent analysis and some very good suggestions. That is exactly how we will proceed."

No sooner had Kastanien uttered his last syllable when the intercom announced that they were ten kilometers behind the U3200X. Kastanien immediately straightened up to his full six-foot height and began walking towards the door. Pausing for a moment he did a quick reflection and turned back to the table.

"Hans, return to the bridge and prepare to make our not so famous course reversal when I finish up here in a couple of minutes. It has been proven that my friend Attila thinks that the beautiful model ships are cat toys created for his amusement when I am not present. I need to store them back in their cozy little berths because they will surely be, shall we say, *rearranged*, around the room when I return."

The executive officer responded and saluted in perfect naval fashion before departing the momentarily darkened cabin. Kastanien walked over to the bunk where Attila was now fully awake, very casually lounging on his side with all legs outstretched. As Kastanien got near he heard the familiar rumble of the cat's purr motor and smiled. He reached down and picked the cat up, nuzzling his nose and chin behind the felines ears. Attila loved this gesture and after receiving this gesture of love and affection, he reciprocated by rubbing his head up and down Peter's jaw line. This mutual show of affection lasted but a brief minute or two before Peter let the lithe creature plop back down on the bunk. He then strode back to his desk and took out a pair of cotton gloves. He slid his rather handsome slim fingers into them. The lightweight thin cotton gloves were normally used to handle film negatives but in this case they were specifically designated to handle the models. He again reached into the drawer and brought out a roughly eight inch square piece of lamb's wool. With gloves on and a lamb's wool cloth he walked the few paces to the conference table. One by one he picked up the models, polished each one spotlessly and then carefully replaced them in their little felt-lined cutout berths.

Although Willy had reassured him that the models would not be adversely affected by the sweat and oils of human touch, Kastanien insisted in making absolutely sure that this prized collection would always remain in mint condition. He, like Willy, secretly hoped that the great Grossadmiral Dönitz would one day grace him and the *Scharnhorst* with a visit and then Kastanien planned to show off the complete collection of models that his old friend the carpenter had fashioned for his use. Finishing this pleasant task in only a few minutes Peter Kastanien donned his immaculate jacket and cap. He took a few steps over to the mirror and studied his appearance minutely. He found a couple of offending pieces of lint on his lapel but they were gone in a flash. Satisfied with his splendid appearance that he knew meant a lot to the officers and crew, he exited the cabin arriving on the bridge in a brief moment.

"Mr. Gott. How far behind U3200X are we now?"

"Just a bit more than twenty kilometers Sir."

Kastanien acknowledged his first officer before retreating back to the radar room.

"Merlin, are we still in perfect alignment with *Rawalpindi* and U3200X?"

"Yes Captain. We are and have been since reducing speed and dropping back."

"Thank you Merlin. We are now a slight bit more than twenty kilometers or fourteen English miles behind *Rawalpindi*. In your opinion and expert knowledge of the mysteries of radar would the British radar that is surely on board *Rawalpindi* be able to 'see' us if we were not in alignment with U3200X?"

By now Marvin Mueller was almost getting used to the captain asking him questions and opinions that could result in grievous trouble if he erred in his judgment. But he was not that used to them and he felt his heart race a bit before he answered, "Captain Sir. If the British radar is as good as ours they should be able to see us rather easily up to about thirty kilometers and we should become invisible at any range beyond forty kilometers. If their radar is better than ours which I sincerely doubt; then I would say fifty kilometers to make us totally invisible. A lot depends on the height of the radar mechanism above the sea and higher it is helps see over the curvature of the earth. I hope the Captain doesn't think poorly of me for talking so much but you have been very kind to me in the past when I have overstepped my bounds."

"No, Merlin you do not talk too much. It is far better to be somewhat loquacious than to miss a salient fact or two. I rather enjoy you espousing your knowledge and insights about radar to me. I am in need of more, much more, information about this new device, so do not fear my wrath if you ramble on a bit too much. If my duties require a brief answer, you will know immediately. Thank you 'Merlin'. Oh, any one thing more. You have been on duty far too long and are no doubt suffering from fatigue and lack of rest. I and all the crew sincerely appreciate your dedication to duty, but there is a limit. We will need you at your very best come first light. You are hereby ordered to have your relief take over your duties in one hour."

Placing a fatherly hand on the youth's shoulder he continued, "I myself will be getting some rest in an hour or so, because it is of the utmost importance that all of us are at the top of our form come first light which is a little more than eight hours from now."

Removing his hand Peter Kastanien left the tiny enclosure and returned to the bridge. Entrenching himself in the comfortable captain's chair he remained silent for the better part of three minutes. All the while the bridge officers kept glancing at him awaiting orders. The executive officer had briefed them on the upcoming maneuver consequently they were a trifle apprehensive. Finally Kastanien stood erect, strode over to the ship's wheel, casually resting his right hand on the casing.

Then he spoke, "Gentlemen, slow us down to two knots. We will wallow a bit with barely enough steerageway but the sea has been mercifully calm this night so we should not pitch around like a piece of flotsam."

The order and following remark broke the tension and when the order rang out the mood of the bridge was noticeable brighter; despite the blacked-out gloom that had prevailed for quite some time. Very soon the massive ship began to roll, pitch and sway much like a drunken sailor as she almost lost headway in the relative calm of the North Atlantic. Again an order was given to reverse all engines and bring the ship to a complete stop.

"Is the wind still quartering into us from the port side Mr. Mueller."

"Yes Captain, at ten kilometers per hour."

"Very well; full ahead port engine, full reverse starboard engine, maintain central engine at stop, maximum right rudder. Straighten up when we are turned exactly 180 from our present course. Make the turn as tight as you can. We do not want the British radar to detect this turn, which they might, if we stray very far from a straight line between the *Rawalpindi*, the U3200X and ourselves. After the turn is complete, speed up to twenty-eight knots."

Kastanien's orders this time were very sharp and clear. The orders again rang out though the bridge and were almost instantly telegraphed to the engine room. Some of the previous tension returned as the newer officers wondered what the monstrous ship would do in a maneuver like this. The massive 38,100 tons of *Scharnhorst* shuddered like a giant sea lion as the two outboard screws fought against each other while the central screw remained idle. Behind the stern the sea frothed like a giant ice cream float as the now virtual dead weight of the ship began to turn sharply to starboard, aided a bit by the rather mild wind. Once more the genius of Dönitz showed as the giant rudders that he had installed made the ship turn in little more than triple its own length. As soon as the ship had steadied up on her new course the twelve giant boilers delivered a goodly portion of their 165,000 horsepower to the three shafts and the *Scharnhorst* was back plying the high seas at speed. The graceful giant leviathan steadied up on her new course quickly accelerating to twenty-eight knots.

"Mr. Schmidt, hold this course and speed for forty minutes and then turn to put us on course for the island of Flores in the Azores group. Maintain our current speed of twenty-eight knots now and for the first hour during the run to the Azores. After one hour on our southwesterly course, reduce speed to eighteen knots to conserve some fuel. Please have the course plot and estimated arrival time ready for me thirty minutes before first light. After you make the turn and have steamed twenty kilometers you may light up the ship. This plodding along in the darkness has been debilitating to everyone, including myself. Then I want you to properly rotate the officers and crew through four hours each of rest and needed sleep. I need the ship's crew to be rested and ready for whatever we might encounter at dawn. Make sure that the replacement radar and sonar operators are especially alert for any signs of the Royal Navy.

"I am now retiring for a few hours but notify me immediately if any vessels are sighted by our radar. Maintain a lookout at all times, but rotate the position every thirty minutes. With the temperature what it is and possibly colder, those youngsters will be turned into icicles if they stay out in this cold more than thirty minutes. Mr. Schmidt, you have the ship. I shall see all of you in a few hours."

With the ship in good hands and all seemingly going well, Kastanien turned smartly on his heels and disappeared into the gloom. Unerringly he grasped the handle on the radio room door and entered. Eric Weisboch was looking directly at him when the light came back on as the door clicked shut. Kastanien smiled at the young sailor and made a simple but important statement.

"Mr. Weisboch, I am retiring to my cabin for hopefully a decent nap. You will be relieved shortly by my orders to the executive officer. I expect you or your replacement to alert me immediately if there is any more radio traffic between London and the *Rawalpindi*. Do not hesitate to call me. No matter how innocuous the message may seem, regardless of who sent it, I want to know immediately. Always remember that the English have ruled the high seas for centuries and they didn't accomplish this or maintain their singular lofty domination by being careless or simple-minded. You will not be disturbing my sleep but briefly, as I have taught myself over the years to awaken instantly, and am able to resume sleeping almost as rapidly. Please relay these orders to your relief, strongly stressing to him that it is vital to our ship that any enemy radio traffic is to be communicated to me as rapidly as it can be translated. Are you quite clear on this point?"

"Yes Captain. You will be informed immediately upon our translation of any radio traffic. Sir, may I be so bold as to wish you pleasant dreams? "

Kastanien's demeanor changed from the rather stern and militaristic captain of a major capitol ship to that of a warm and understanding father figure as his face and posture softened noticeably. Unconsciously he placed his right hand on the radio operator's shoulder in his typical friendly and understanding way that all of the junior sailors gossiped and bragged about. After a reflective silent pause he softly spoke to Eric Weisboch like a gentle uncle, "Thank you Eric for your very kind and thoughtful words. I had dreaded the thought of trying to get some sleep knowing full well that it would come quite hard grinding the myriad of possibilities that can confront us over the next few hours and days. That is the nature of war. But now, thanks to you I will let my mind relax somewhat and concentrate on thinking about my family back home in Cologne. This fox and hounds game we play with the British Royal Navy does occupy most of my thinking. I shall now dream of my lovely wife Andrea, my children and maybe a tiny bit about Attila's mate, Sasha. I'll also think of their offspring cavorting about, raising general mischief in the house and hope that all of them can play in the garden and woods—if spring is at hand. Well, enough of my maudlin, but pleasant thoughts. I shall be off and again I thank you for your kindness."

Kastanien then left suddenly because he knew that for the youth to see the tear that was forming in his eye would not be good for the discipline of the ship. By the time he had closed his cabin door behind him the tear had streaked down his cheek with another that was definitely going to follow shortly thereafter. He paused and wiped the droplet off his chin before it dripped onto his coat and fondly looked across the room at the curled up feline snuggled deeply into the blanket. Attila returned his gaze before resuming his nap, knowing that his bed companion would join him soon. As Peter Kastanien partially undressed his thoughts returned to Cologne and his comfortable, cozy little house nestled at the end of a quiet residential street. He was enjoying his pleasant thoughts and kept expanding on them lest his fearsome responsibilities for the ship and crew returned to rob him of this moment of pleasure.

The radio operator, like his compatriot radar operator across the passageway, knew positively that there was no better captain in the entire world. He wished that he had a nickname like Merlin so his heart would be gladdened if the captain were ever to use it. Maybe he could come up with one and let the ships grapevine do the rest.

Executive Officer Hans Schmidt kept to the schedule left to him by Kastanien and made the turn to the Azores without incident. After steaming towards the new destination for a trifle more than an hour, he lit up the ship and began the rotation of the officers as ordered. He had requested that the galley prepare some light fare for the officers and sailors rotating off duty. He had specifically ordered some hot broth for the semi-frozen lookouts as they came in from the cold making it an order that they partake of it as soon as they could navigate their way to the mess hall. None would admit that they felt the cold all the way to their bones but not a one of them passed up the warming soup which had the desired effect. They all knew that the officers were looking out for them, as always. They had not spotted anything but the liquid reflections of the moon which was what they all knew the captain wanted. It was dreadfully boring duty maintaining this vigil which became a test of their mettle on which they all prided themselves. Even the highly efficient radiant heaters in the semi-exposed tiny enclosures could not stave off the tentacles of the penetrating cold amplified by the wind that the recent rapid passage of the ship created. When the normal night lighting had come back on, the atmosphere in the ship noticeably improved making moving about significantly simpler.

In his cabin, Peter Kastanien had laid down with a contented look on his face and pulled the comforting wool blanket up to his chin. He closed his eyes immediately hoping that sleep would not be long in coming. Attila pretended to be nonplussed about the disturbance that his human caused, but he knew that it was an opportunity to get even more comfortable. The cold permeated through the ships steel walls and even the rather decent insulation was not up to the job of preventing the now bitter cold from penetrating most parts of the ship that were close to the outer sides. To Attila the cold was something not to be tolerated if there was an alternative. So he wormed his way under the blanket and shimmied down to the crook in Peter's knees. After performing the typical double circle, he heavily flopped against the back of Kastanien's knees and went to sleep. Peter's heart warmed with the cat's presence. Now he was able to relax somewhat and drift off to sleep thinking of his family and that of Attila's. The large cat's natural body heat warmed much more than his knees, it seemed to travel to every limb and most of all, it warmed his heart and soul.

Before he achieved the much needed sleep his mind transported him to Cologne and his beloved Andrea. He pictured himself at the last home visit coming through the front door unannounced and managing to sneak up on her as she was doing typical female industrious puttering in her kitchen. He could see the slight flush on her cheeks from the nearby kitchen fireplace along with speckled splotches of white flour. What a magnificent woman she was. Stealthily approaching, he caught her completely unawares with a bear hug from behind and a tender kiss on the nape of her neck. Naturally she uttered a screech and pirouetted around. Her surprise instantly turned to joy. She came rather close to crushing the breath out of him with her reciprocating hug. Smothering his entire face and lips with apple flavored kisses—her rapture seemed to know no bounds or limits.

To complete his homecoming, Attila's mate, Sasha leaped from her close-by perch on the wooden icebox and landed like a ten pound bowling ball on his right shoulder with her purr motor running at full throttle. The cat was obviously as happy as her mistress to have the human male back at home, but then she spotted her true love bounding up the basement stairs to join in the reunion. With effortless grace, Sasha dropped to the floor.

Peter had let the guardian of his small garden estate run loose outside to check and make sure that all was in proper order before he came inside. Attila took pride in keeping his property under a close governorship as Peter did with their ship, the splendid *Scharnhorst*. Attila and Sasha circled and sniffed each other for minute making sure that all was well with each other. When they were satisfied that each other was in fine health and none the worse for wear over the past few months of separation, they bounded off into the large living room and began cavorting with each other in their whimsical game of chase, pounce, bowl over and then they would rather realistically sink their four fangs into the other's neck in a playful death grip. Peter and Andrea were so wrapped up with each other that for once they did not even notice this enjoyable display which had constantly amused them so often in times gone by.

When the lengthy embrace ended and they stood silently drinking in the essence and presence of each other, Kastanien strolled over to the stove. He was about to lift the lid on a rather large iron pot when without warning, Andrea whacked the back of his hand with a sturdy wooden spoon she had just picked up admonishing him to keep out of *her* kitchen business. At this thought Peter laughed out loud; remembering how territorial she was when it came to her culinary artistry. Instantly he returned to his daydreaming and thought about the apple sauce that would have been simmering in the forbidden pot. Looking around, he took in all the glass jars filled with last summer's bounty, which had been lovingly preserved for enjoyment throughout the long winter. There were dozens of glass jars properly sealed and filled with red and gold apple slices, green and purple plums, half sections of pears and that very special sauerkraut. He could almost taste her prize- winning sauerkraut and closed his eyes to savor its true delight. He pictured the earthen floor cellar, its wooden shelves that he had built many years past burgeoning with a dozen or more varieties of root vegetables that would keep for months in the cool darkness.

As good as the bill of fare was aboard *Scharnhorst*, it paled in comparison to Andrea's magical touch with food—whether it was simple country fare or a gourmet's feast. He had been to many of the finest restaurants in Berlin and always came away with a greater appreciation of the skills that his bride of twenty years possessed. He chose to bypass thoughts about the typical rough spots in their marriage and concentrate on the myriad of happy times. He spent a moment or two reflecting how it seemed that there were too many times that he had been at sea, meetings in Berlin, teaching the new generation at the Naval Academy in Wilhelmshaven etc., when he would much rather, and should have, been at home to celebrate another anniversary with his delightful wife. He had to have a little chuckle at that thought.

Delightful was probably the wrong choice of a descriptive word for her. He smiled to himself at the many mercurial moods of this industrious, energetic woman that he had married on that cool sunshiny day two decades ago on the eleventh of November. He knew that she could be disappointed with his assignments and maybe take her wrath out on Dönitz himself—in person, if Dönitz was foolish enough to cross her path at the wrong time. Again he smiled, this time a much broader grin, as he remembered the two formal occasions on which the two had met. She had reigned in her volatile temper knowing it could injure her husband's career if she became too vociferous about the excessive demands she felt that the Kriegsmarine put on her Peter.

Instead she displayed a very believable façade of a contented, yet intelligent, and politically astute typical wife of a high-ranking officer in the new German military. He knew beyond any shadow of doubt that she would be very disappointed if they were together for the rather special twentieth anniversary that would roll around in a few months. Hopefully she would understand that they were now at war and his duty was a very important one for all of Germany. But his much annoying anniversary absences of years past were a different story altogether. When Peter had returned on those occasions she had shelved her anger. She understood the reason, or simply put the tempest aside for a more appropriate time when she would hit him harder with a verbal blast than that of a shell from *Scharnhorst's* main guns.

His mind wandered aimlessly for a bit and then wondered when the last snow of the year would come and then melt heralding out the gray and cold winter in his home at the edge of Cologne. He thought about how clean and fresh the first snow was as it drifted lazily out of the dull, somnolent sky. The last snow was almost always large moist gentle flakes that settled and drooped themselves on the budding branches of Andrea's prized rose bushes. The snowflakes brought a new sort of life to the thorny stems that had turned rather ugly since they had shed their leaves. He pictured the barren garden as winter eased its icy grip. All the bushes would be covered like the ghostly sheets that one puts over furniture, in a house or cottage that has been shuttered up for a season or a lifetime. *"A time to rejuvenate and rest."* His mind skipped over the brown ugliness that the city streets turned the pristine snow into and traveled to the woods directly adjacent to the back fence line of his property. The back of the yard was delineated by a neat and orderly line of fruit trees that provided his home with the delightful preserves that his family enjoyed all through the long winter months and into the spring. He thought that winter in Germany as a whole was generally dreary and overcast, but this atmosphere suited the woods perfectly.

He loved the woods in the fall with their blaze of variegated colors when the more oblique angle of the sun's rays cast long starkly-contrasting shadows. He vividly remembered the sharp crackle and crunch of the crisp dark-brown oak leaves as his feet trod over them. In the depths of winter a covering of white fluffy snow covered the fallen leaves and perched an inch or so deep on every branch. Sunshine seemed to be an unwelcome intruder on this muted and mystical monochromatic scene. Kastanien truly loved the solitude that the silence of the hibernating woods created around him as he wandered hither and yon with his camera and tripod attempting to capture the slumbering rapture of nature at rest. With his artistic eye for beauty and composition, combined with his mastery of photographic manipulations in his superbly equipped home darkroom, Peter Kastanien succeeded in his artistic quest by creating images of classical elegance.

The melancholic daydreaming was soon replaced by a deep sleep accompanied with fantasy dreams of the woods at home. Attila knew that his friend had fallen asleep and being a lifetime accomplished grand master of sleep himself, he knew that this was not the time to get restless, so he relaxed even more and the two friends slumbered on in dreamland.

U3200X

"Captain, *Scharnhorst* is directly behind us in a straight line with the *Rawalpindi* and holding station," The barely restrained excited voice of radar operator Erich "Marvel" Marsten came over the intercom to the U-boat's command center.

"Very well, thank you Mr. Marsten. Mr. Lassen, proceed with Operation Butterfly immediately. I will take command of the boat from the sail and we will co-ordinate our efforts from there. Make haste as Kastanien will lose no time before he begins to slow and we must replace him as the enemy battleship without the English being any the wiser."

The solidly built first officer of Germany's newest and most advanced U-boat responded with a short staccato blast in his distinctive, deep, foghorn voice, "Yes Sir, Operation Butterfly, immediately."

First Officer Heinrich Lassen slid down the ladder from the conning tower in the blink of an eye into the command center and within two minutes accompanied by four burly sailors he emerged from a small scuttle on the rear deck of the U-boat a few feet aft of the sail. Lassen signaled up to the sail with one burst from a deep-ruby-colored flashlight that they were ready. A double pulse from the flashlight's twin immediately blinked back signifying that that all was in order and to raise the "butterfly". The four powerful men were already at their assigned stations when the foghorn that passed for a human voice blasted out to get on with it and be quick about it as well.

The U-boat had been ready for this maneuver for more than an hour—running with only the night-vision retaining ruby lighting to move about inside the submarine. When the men came on deck the moonlight was actually brighter so they were able to perform their orders with ease. They had performed this operation many times as a drill and in much more adverse conditions. The commanders of *Scharnhorst* and U3200X knew that they would rarely have ideal conditions for this operation so they had drilled the men until they could do it in a medium sea and on a moonless night. The slow rolling sea with the moon illuminating the scene akin to a pale blue searchlight in the night sky made their labors progress rapidly and took less than ten minutes for the "butterfly" to be raised. Lassen had been watching and timing the men all the while and when the men stood at ease beside the metal structure that had arisen from the deck like a skinny wall of a skeleton building, his craggy face split into an enormous grin and his foghorn blared out again after the silence of the past few minutes.

"Wonderful, wonderful we have done it in record time. You have beaten your past record by nearly a full minute. This time was only eight minutes and twelve seconds. Wonderful, wonderful."

Lassen then faced forward and flashed the blood-red lantern three times up at the sail and was instantly rewarded by a like signal of three flashes signifying that the procedure was over and they could return inside the ship. The bitter cold that the sailors worked under was sloughed off with the unexpected praise from the first officer. Most of the time he was a rather somber individual seemingly without compassion for anyone aboard, so the praise meant an awful lot to the submariners.

The high command of the U-boat arm of the German Navy knew that the men who volunteered for underwater warfare had to be of an especially cooperative temperament because of the close proximity that they lived and worked in with their fellow sailors. They had questioned placing the rather sullen Lassen as second-in-command of the newest and technically superior undersea boat but his character flaw was overruled by Dönitz himself because of his previous service in the last conflict. Back in early 1917 when Lassen was only a boy of eighteen he had displayed an uncanny knowledge of U-boat warfare and could tell you within a few kilometers where the boat was without the benefit of position information from the command center. The high ranking naval officers in Berlin were about to dismiss these stellar traits as rather unnecessary and relegate the experienced submariner to duty on a surface ship when Dönitz overruled them in a rare breach of protocol for him.

After a last look at his handiwork, first officer Lassen disappeared down the hatch after his men. Submarines are notorious for being cool and dank but the temperature inside seemed almost tropical after several minutes in the biting cold on deck. Lassen once more broke character by casually ordering the men to warm up with some coffee and tarts in the mess.

Standing with only a sharp-eyed young lookout for company on the enclosed front of the sail, Captain Wittrock stoically, while braving the icy fangs of the ten knot breeze, looked back at the butterfly and grinned briefly. He reached down, undoing his coat and brought out his powerful binoculars. He had rather they be slightly warmed by his body heat than to put frigid rubber eyepieces on his now seemingly numb face. With the powerful glasses in place he scanned the rear horizon hoping he might get a glimpse of *Scharnhorst* reflecting in the moonlight. The gently rolling sea refused to give up any of her secrets this night. Even his imagination could not conjure up even a slightly darker shadow against the ink-black of the barely perceptible horizon.

"Good hunting and a safe exit my friend. I will once more make the British slightly crazy with your *impossible* escape," Wittrock spoke softly out loud to himself.

The lookout glanced briefly over at his captain and without uttering a sound returned to scanning the sea for any unwanted company. Boring as this duty was, it was what the submarine needed right now and for the many hours until dawn. Then maybe they would go on a hunt to liven up the drudgery of plodding along after a ship he wasn't sure that they were even going to shoot at let alone possibly sink.

Ducking down behind the cowling of the sail, Wittrock called down to the command center. The slight respite from the cold wind was welcomed, "How far behind us is *Scharnhorst* now?"

The answer came back in a flash from Lassen, "Sir, *Scharnhorst* is now about thirty-five kilometers behind us. She has just now turned southwesterly."

"Very well Mr. Lassen. Are we still maintaining station with *Rawalpindi*?"

"Yes Sir."

"Very well, please relieve me on the sail and send up a replacement for Johann. We are both a trifle cool up here and some hot coffee would do both of us some good."

Wittrock replaced the intercom; put his binoculars back inside his coat and waited for the replacements. Lassen with a new lookout appeared in a few minutes after donning their arctic gear to fend off the cold that would quickly sap the energy of even the hardiest of men. All seamen knew that the relative inactivity of the watch would emphasize the cold, but the submariners knew it more than most. They spent the vast majority of their time inside the relative warmth of the U-boat and extended stays outside were rare. Their mission was to not be seen and to strike unexpectedly from beneath the waves. U3200X, unlike her sister U-boats, did not have a visible deck gun, relying almost entirely upon torpedoes to claim any merchants or warships that were unlucky enough to have wandered into her periscope's watchful eye.

With a major improvement in battery power and oxygen reserves, this newest stealthy warship could remain submerged more than double the time of her predecessors. Like virtually all submarines, she only surfaced at night to recharge her batteries, so fresh air mixed with sunshine was a luxury rarely enjoyed by most of the sailors. When it became a dire necessity to recharge batteries during daylight hours, the U3200X like all of her smaller sister submarines would barely let the tip of the boat's sail poke through the surface and run the diesel engines on fresh air through a schnorkel system.

Every submariner hated this system as the air intake on the snorkel was barely above the waves so as to reduce the possibility of detection. Regularly but with an unpredictable irregularity the schnorkel would be washed over by an errant wave. When this happened an automatic flap shut the opening to the outside air but the diesel engine continued to inhale the air necessary for combustion. The result was an instantaneous decrease in air pressure that played havoc with everyone's ears. It was not unusual for several submariners to have bleeding ears and severely injured eardrums throughout this seemingly endless torturous ordeal that went on for hours upon endless hours. Wittrock had made it a point to avoid this nasty maneuver if at all possible. His men knew this and respected him highly for his concern over their well-being.

This night's fresh air was a bit too brisk to enjoy for long before it became an endurance test of one's mettle. Wittrock along with the semi-frozen lookout quickly descended into the blessed warmth of the ship's interior. The cowling around the sail kept the cold draft that cascaded down the hatch from above from being too much of a nuisance. The standard procedure on the boat was to always keep the hatch to the inside open when surfaced. This would allow the boat's topside crew to clamber inside a few, but very critical, seconds quicker if a surprise happened upon them. Quickly assuring himself that the boat was in good hands with the officer and the very all-important lookout, Wittrock strode into the tiny room that served multiple purposes but mainly as a place to relax and get a warming cup of coffee.

Although many of the officers and men would have preferred tea, it was considered rather poor form politically and socially to imbibe in an "English" beverage. Wittrock preferred the American coffee so the rest of the crew did without tea and because they were proud and loyal to a man, there was no grousing about the absence of their beloved tea. The coffee was plentiful thanks to a captured merchant that had been carrying half of her cargo load in wonderful Columbian coffee. The U3200X had stuffed her store rooms and every available nook and cranny with the wondrous delightful, quite rare, treats from the merchant that had originated in Caracas, Venezuela before turning her over to a prize crew that would sail her back to occupied France. The wily Captain Wittrock used this plentiful supply of a much sought-after prize to haggle with Kastanien for some of the special culinary treats that the heroic battleship was blessed with. His bargaining was more of a light-hearted game without the normal efforts of both parties to best the other. Wittrock never harbored any intention of besting one of his best friends at this ancient game of bartering.

After only a short twenty minutes to warm up and with two cups of the regenerating caffeine coursing through his bloodstream, Wittrock returned to the command center, silently looking over the sonar operator's shoulder. Satisfied with what he didn't see, he turned the boat over to the second officer, with a command that the men in the sail were to be rotated every thirty minutes. He also ordered that other crew members to rotate in four hour shifts to get some desperately needed sleep. Lastly, he spoke through the intercom telling Lassen to awaken him thirty minutes before first light. He added that Lassen was to have the boat at action stations and ready with all torpedoes loaded. Lastly, but critically important the boat was to be prepared for a crash dive if the Royal Navy showed up—as he was guessing they probably would.

Rawalpindi

While Kennedy slept, his crew worked tirelessly to repair the almost-serious damage inflicted by the *Scharnhorst*. The most forward six-inch gun turret was hopelessly smashed beyond any chance of repair short of the shipyard. The second forward turret had escaped crippling damage and was now relatively functional. Two of the guns in the rearmost aft turret were out of commission leaving the *Rawalpindi* with (four) six inch and the (two) three inch guns. With less than one hour to go before first light, the damage control party informed First Officer James Cook of the battle readiness of the armed merchant. Cook immediately went to Captain Kennedy's cabin and gently knocked on the door. Before the echoes of his rapping had faded, the door burst open and an obviously refreshed Kennedy inquired about the status of his ship. No matter how Cook tried to garner just one simple token of his appreciation from Kennedy, the old man never gave any one more than a curt "Thank You."

As Cook began his short litany, Kennedy closed the door and rapidly began striding to the bridge. By the time the two reached the bridge Kennedy knew that his ship was going to be hard pressed to inflict any serious damage on the German with only half his guns operational and relatively small caliber ones to boot. When he arrived at the bridge he perfunctorily thanked Cook and then grilled the other officers about the status of the German. He listened patiently while his second officer related that there had been no change whatsoever with the German. He was still back there keeping the same station with them as when Kennedy had retired.

"Well then." Kennedy began, "in about an hour or so, I am looking forward to seeing our Royal Navy pound the living stuffing's out of our German friend. Maybe, just maybe, we'll get our licks in as well. After all, it was us that lured him into the lion's den. Mr. Cook, what about the weather now and for the next few hours?"

"Captain, the skies are still clear with a very moderate sea. The forecast for at least the next eight hours is for the same. Temperature outside has begun to rise during the past few hours and is now just above the freezing mark. If the temperature rises much more we could expect some fog to form."

"Thank You Mr. Cook. Now, have the lookouts spotted any signs of lights back there from our nemesis?"

"No, Sir. The lookouts have not seen any sign of lights or even glimpsed the ship."

"Damnation, that wily bastard must be working by moonlight and has all his lamps inside repairing the damage we caused. Well, no matter, pretty soon our boys will be done with him for good."

Kennedy slowly strolled over to his captain's chair, heaved his bulk into it and leaned back—a pensive look on his face, *"This whole kit and caboodle stinks. I hope to the Almighty that those prissy armchair pettifoggers at the Admiralty have got this right. I surely don't want to take on that Bosch bastard by myself with only a few puny popguns left."* Kennedy thought rather angrily to himself.

His mind traveled back a couple of weeks when he had been informed of this mission. He noted then that they had used the word *mission* instead of convoy. Giving the Admiralty their just due, he had to admit that they had not understated the extreme danger that this type of mission entailed. So far things were going rather as planned, except for the unpredictable German. What the German had been doing made no conventional sense. The plan, as was explained to Kennedy, was to lure the *Scharnhorst* and/or *Gneisenau* into a pitched battle with the Royal Navy and sink the bloody bastards. Kennedy chuckled to himself as he remembered the unbridled vehemence that the First Sea Lord had imparted to that overly misused word, "bastards". The plan was to string out, in a straight line, seven merchant ships right at the extreme edge of the aerial reconnaissance of the *Condors*. The timing had to be such that the ships would come into range near the end of the day as the lumbering German giant birds were making their last arcs before heading home.

Kennedy was impressed that the Admiralty at least got that part right because the *Condor* had showed up right when and where it was supposed to. They had also told him that the big bomber would probably not bomb them as this particular enemy had proven that they would much prefer to hang onto their bombs to attack warships, oil tankers or stragglers on their way home. So far so good! The sinking of the *Gay Lily*, which was the last ship in the chorus line, was not unexpected as the plan was to keep the German doggedly chasing after one ship at a time until the fateful rendezvous at dawn. Being an old-line warrior, Captain Kennedy listened patiently and quietly as the High Command outlined their plan to dispense with *Scharnhorst* and *Gneisenau*. He quietly nodded when it became painfully apparent that this was most probably a suicide mission for him and the other "sacrificial goats."

Although the thought of deliberately sending these overmatched and mostly unarmed merchants into such grave danger was, at first glance, appalling. He and the other captains had taken very careful mental note of the staggering figures. The tally sheet was the same one that Dowding had used a few days before to show how many merchants this double menace had sunk, except now it had even larger figures. The seven captains, all long-time veterans, quietly came to the same inevitable conclusion that they truly must give this highly-dangerous scheme a chance. All of them chatted with the congenial hierarchy of the Navy before leaving the meeting with high hopes for success. It was simply too obvious that the *Ugly Sisters* absolutely had to be dispatched and damnable soon. At the rate the *Sisters* were sinking ships, it was almost inevitable that their own turn to face those deadly guns would come up sooner or later as the Battle of the Atlantic went on.

Kennedy fervently hoped that the German would stick to his normal modus operandi and rescue any survivors. On this point he had his doubts as the battleship did not seem to have paused after the sinking the *Gay Lily*. Then the plan seemed to go askew as the vastly superior battleship played cat and mouse with him. Why did the bastard simply not charge in and sink him? He could easily have stood off and pounded him to the bottom with his superior guns and range. But then maybe that tremendous explosion had really crippled his guns badly? Kennedy suspected that his enemy's rather odd behavior before and after the critical blast had something to do with his firepower. There was no doubt in Kennedy's mind that something rather wicked had happened to the enemy's guns; which was a fateful stroke of good luck for him along with the rest of the virtually helpless little lambs.

The normal blast from large caliber guns makes a big enough fireball with its attendant black smoke as it is, but that one was an unusually tremendous coruscation of blinding white, yellow and red flames. So, Kennedy again came to the inescapable conclusion that the battleship was temporarily almost toothless. He also knew that typical German efficiency would have the damage repaired by dawn when he would come after him or even before when his guns were again operational. There had been several hours until first light so the enemy would have ample time to effect repairs. He hoped that the damage was such that the German had little, or at least reduced, firepower, when the Royal Navy showed up. Kennedy wanted the high seas rid of this fearsome monster along with her sister so he could go back on the offensive against the slimy, slinking, sneaky submarine menace.

Bored with the inaction before the anticipated battle, Kennedy jerked himself from his reverie and his chair. Silently he slowly paced the deck, checking the clock every two minutes, seemingly to will it to go faster and get on with the show. None of the officers dared speak when he was like this other than to issue normal operational commands. The clock seemed to have a bad case of arthritis to Kennedy, but nevertheless inexorably moved forward. It was at thirty minutes to first light that the omnipresent quiet of the bridge was shattered by the loud and excited stammering voice of radar/radio operator Ian Kerrwin resounding through the scratchy, tinny intercom, "Captain, the German has vanished from my screen."
Instantly Captain Edwin Coverley Kennedy sprang to the intercom, "I'll be right there Kerrwin, hold fast."

In a short sprint worthy of an Olympic athlete Kennedy was in the radar/radio room.

"What the world are you saying man? How in great blazing Hades could he have just vanished?"

Kerrwin who was obviously overwrought made a valiant effort to answer the captain without showing he was scared out of his mind. Kerrwin replied just a bit calmer than his intercom announcement, but fear still lay couched in his words, "Captain Sir. He was there less than two minutes ago before he just rather quickly faded away. Sir, I checked my machine twice to make sure it was working properly before I called you. I have no explanation for his disappearance. It's like the sea just devoured him."

"And there had been no change whatsoever for the past few hours?"

"No Sir. He never once strayed more than a cables length—as best I can tell."

Kennedy was stunned into a lengthy silence. Before he could speak again the young lad sitting in front of him began to blubber, "I'm so dreadfully sorry Sir. I just don't understand. Please forgive me."

Kennedy, who was normally untouched by frail human emotions such as this boy's obvious despair, placed both his hands on the slumping shoulders of his radar operator and squeezed them a bit.

"Now, now laddy it's not your fault. You've done an excellent job all the time we've been at sea and you've always been spot-on with your deductions. Now, tell me how long did it take for the German to vanish."

With the calming touch and voice of Kennedy, Kerrwin ceased shaking, blew his nose rather loudly and in a sincere and much calmer voice replied, "Captain, the signal had remained very constant throughout the night and then in a matter of less than three minutes it was completely gone and I have not been able to raise even the slightest flicker of anything since. It has me totally befuddled."

"You're positive nothing is wrong with your machine?"

"Sir, there is always a slight possibility of a malfunction but I can say for certain that my machine is functioning perfectly."

Kennedy lifted his hands from the youngster's shoulders. Slowly, very slowly he returned to the bridge and clutched the handrail on the bridge. His grip tightened fiercely until his knuckles turned white. The officers stood silently and waited for the thunderstorm that they knew from past experience was shortly forthcoming. Much to their relief Captain Kennedy disappointed them when he began speaking in a low, very uncharacteristic voice that had a definite twinge of defeat in it, "Gentlemen, the German has simply vanished from our radar screen. Young Kerrwin assures me that his machine is functioning perfectly and has no explanation for this *disappearing* act. We were told that this has occurred a couple of times before, but then it was considered to be either a malfunction or the weather. I believe what Kerrwin says—but it makes no sense whatsoever. I pray that when we can see well enough in less than half an hour that the clever bastard following us is still there. He simply must be. If not then the *Gay Lily* will have been sunk for naught."

Shaking off the defeat and despair, Kennedy continued but now with his normal loud and strong commanding voice, "Have the lookouts doubled and make bloody sure that they are our best eyes up there. We are not going to change speed or course. Our boys will be here soon enough. Carry on."

Gneisenau

Although he was quite apprehensive about the perilous situation he was in, Captain Teebolt showed no outer signs of his fear. With barely enough speed to maintain steerageway he knew he was no better than a deer frozen-in-the-headlamps for any prowling enemy submarine. The minutes ticked by with agonizing slowness. He steeled himself to refrain from calling his damage control officer any more often than every twenty minutes. He did not want to undermine the morale of these men who risked grave danger repairing an underwater breech, which was difficult and dangerous in the best of conditions. He only gave away his inner tension by frequenting the radar/sonar room every five to ten minutes. After each trip back to the little room he would return to the bridge a bit more relaxed but that was very short-lived. He had done everything he could to throw the enemy off his scent. Within an hour after he issued the orders to secure the merchants, he was alone on the high seas dawdling along towards the rendezvous with *Scharnhorst*, with only the destroyer *Max Schultz* to keep him company.

The *Max Schultz* was a relatively new ship being commissioned in 1937 and although not very big, she was nimble and fast. With her high speed of thirty-six knots, (five) five-inch gun, (two) 1.5-inch, (six) .79 inch guns, eight 21 inch torpedo tubes and four depth charge racks, Teebolt felt that she could adequately protect him against any enemy submarines that chanced upon them in their current perilously vulnerable state. The tiny guard-dog ship was not much company since neither dared to use their radios for fear of tipping the enemy to their position. Even excessive use of signal lamps was chancy since they could be spotted many kilometers away. Especially if the enemy happened to be dead-on to the shuttered directional powerful lamps.

He had earlier given orders to the captain of the destroyer *Karl Galster* accompanying the captured merchants to send a message to Kriegsmarine when he had steamed at least eighty kilometers away from *Gneisenau* and pretend to be the *Gneisenau*. He knew the British would have by then have known that their precious convoy was either totally sunk or captured. With *Gneisenau* headed for the Azores and the captured convoy steaming for occupied France, Teebolt felt relatively secure that the Royal Navy would not trip to his real position and surprise him. Finally after the endless eternity of two hours the deep-brassy voice of damage control officer Frederick Mansel broke the brittle silence that had descended for the duration of repairs on the bridge.

"Captain, I am coming to the bridge to apprise you of our progress."

Less than two minutes later a quite large human apparition appeared on the bridge. Still almost dripping wet, covered with dirt, grease, grime and a myriad of other soiling marks that had turned his clothing into virtual rags, Damage Control Officer Mansel approached Teebolt, stopped and saluted.

"Damage Control Officer Mansel to report Sir."

"Very well, Mr. Mansel, you may report. First, give me the casualty and injured status."

"Very good Sir, there are no casualties, but we do have some injuries. Only two are considered serious but not incapacitating. One seaman has multiple fractures of his left arm and the other a broken leg. The medical officer has looked at them both and has assured me that they will both be right as rain in four to six weeks. Many of us have minor burns, scratches, cuts and various other inconsequential injuries that are being treated as I speak. The breach to the sea has been completely sealed and we are now fully seaworthy. The armor belt and hull where the torpedo exploded has some rather ugly spurs sticking out of our side. We cannot repair the outer hull without being in a proper dry dock. However, the only detrimental effect that these blast spurs will have on us is to reduce our top speed by about one knot, possibly as much as two. Damaged compartments have been pumped dry and the damage to electrical circuits is almost completely repaired. It will take maybe three more hours to rewire the communications as they were the most heavily damaged. It's still a bit of a mess down there but we will have it cleaned up and shipshape shortly. We can now increase our speed without any problems. I believe that is all. Do you have any further questions Sir, before I return to my men?"

"Excellent work Mr. Mansel. Truly excellent work and completed in an amazingly short span of time. Please pass along my sincere and heartfelt thanks to your crew for a damnable difficult and dangerous job well done now that everything is under control. My sincere congratulations. Now, take yourself to the infirmary and get some of those ugly cuts and scrapes tended to before you inherit some nasty germs or infections."

"Yes Sir. It will be my greatest pleasure to pass on your compliments to my men. Thank you very much Sir. Is there anything else the Captain wishes me to do?"

"You might consider consigning your current wardrobe to the bottom of the ocean as it makes you look like a down-on-his-luck sixteenth century pirate."

With this witty comment the built-up tension on the bridge collapsed into raucous laughter that completely evaporated the gloomy miasma that always prevailed over damage control reports. Damage Control Officer Mansel immediately blushed so strongly that it actually could be seen through the oil and grime that checkered most of his face and throat. He felt a twinge of embarrassment about the captain's left-handed compliment and now dropped his head which now gave him a very good view of the tattered remains of his uniform. Then he got the humor of the moment and began a thundering good old-fashioned laugh at himself. When the light-hearted moment passed, Mansel straightened up, saluted Teebolt and finished, "Very well, Sir. It will be done as quickly as possible."

Teebolt returned his salute and Mansel returned below decks to finish up and clean up. Seconds later Teebolt returned to his primary duty of guiding the mammoth battleship.

"Helm, maintain course for the southern coast of Flores in the Azores. Ring up turns for twenty-eight knots. I want to feel how our patched up 'wound' reacts to speed. Signal *Max Schultz* to maintain station with us a kilometer off our starboard."

The orders were cheerfully repeated with gusto throughout the bridge. Every officer was visibly relieved and breathed much easier now that their potentially disastrous predicament was now behind them. Everyone sported a self-satisfying smile as the powerful engines quickly brought the

38,100 tons of warship up to speed. Within a few short moments *Gneisenau* was once more slicing through the black ocean with ease. Frederick Mansel had just returned to the damaged section when he felt and heard the powerful engines increase their tempo. He quickly, but with obvious sincerity, relayed the captain's praises before he inquired of his senior damage repair specialist the state of the welded patch.

Even though this competent seaman reported that the patch was solid and secure, Mansel held the normal reservations of command. He ordered his men out of the immediate area of the patch. Several of them stared intently at the repaired wound for several minutes from the relative safety of catwalks above the area. When ten minutes had passed without any signs of weakness or water seepage, Mansel released the men from their relatively safe perches and told them to finish the minor repairs. He then proceeded to the infirmary where the doctor spent half an hour cleaning and bandaging some dozen or so of his minor and half-serious cuts and abrasions.

On the bridge, Teebolt and all the officers maintained a heightened sense of alertness hoping that they would neither hear, nor feel any effects from the repaired section of the hull. The ship attained twenty-eight knots and maintained it for nearly an hour without incident other than an ugly sounding meshing of the sea as it was churned into froth by the jagged obtrusions marring the sleek hull. Fortunately this unwelcome noise was audible only if one was outside near the damage. Feeling comfortable with the condition of his beloved ship, Teebolt ordered the ship to stand down from alert status and proceed to the Azores at twenty knots. He ran a bit slower than his normal cruise speed of twenty-four knots for two important reasons. His main concern was not to arrive at the rendezvous too soon resulting in having to cruise aimlessly around waiting for *Scharnhorst*.

Although the Azores were the protectorate colony of neutral Portugal, the German intelligence agency had informed the High Command that the British retained several paid informers throughout the islands to keep track of passing vessels. His second reason was to conserve fuel for both himself and the destroyer who had a much more limited fuel supply and subsequently shorter range.

With his ship secure and steaming safely through the night on relatively calm seas, the adrenalin high of the past few hours slowly ebbed away. The stress was inexorably replaced with a slight weariness. Teebolt realized that he had some log work to do and needed some rest. He ordered his officers to rotate some rest cycles for themselves and the crew, but to be at battle stations thirty minutes before first light. Then without further ado, he simply retired to his cabin and proceeded to update his log entries before slumping onto his bunk. Within minutes he was virtually dead to the world.

The U3200X

At exactly 0700 local time, Captain Wittrock ordered the "butterfly" be taken down and stowed away. First Officer Lassen scrambled up through the sail followed by his crew. The well-trained "butterfly" crew made short work of folding up the metal latticework that had simulated a radar signature of a much larger vessel, namely the *Scharnhorst*, for the past many hours throughout the night. Within the short span of less than seven minutes, the cleverly constructed ten meters wide by fifteen meters high grid of black steel mesh had been folded into a compact package that fit comfortably into the streamlined housing aft of the sail. The housing resembled an upside down double-ended canoe about twelve meters long, five meters wide and protruded up from the deck barely more than a meter. Had the U3200X not been so streamlined itself, a cursory glance by most people would never have noticed this small streamlined hump on its back as the sharp-eyed crewman from the *Gay Lily* had. Everything about the U3200X had been designed with minimum resistance to its passage through the ocean depths.

There was no visible deck gun, handrails or wooden flutes on the deck. The sail was elliptical in design, somewhat similar to a teardrop when viewed from above. From the side the sail was a normal boxlike protuberance whose front tapered slightly rearward as it rose about three meters above the deck. Rather than a sharp knife-like prow, the front of the U3200X resembled the back-end of a big black Cuban cigar. Extensive testing had proven that this design slid through the water with far less resistance than the traditional keen edge.

When Admiral Karl Dönitz had brought his plans and beautiful model to the shipyard at Kiel, the builders were stunned and amazed at the radical design with the attendant specifications that the top man in the Kriegsmarine had conceived. They had insisted on two months to go over his plans and come up with their own ideas of how to achieve what they at first thought impossible. Dönitz gave them one month—without any hope of an extension. With this seemingly unattainable deadline, the doubters were too busy meeting the deadline to bother with devising arguments as to why it could not be done. With only two days to spare they had summoned Dönitz to go over their slight revisions and plans for improvements as well as construction schedules. When Dönitz saw the revised version of the unattractive blunt bow that was his brainchild, he was taken a bit aback. Sensing his discomfiture with the design, they took him to the test tank in a large research shed and demonstrated all the various bow designs they had previously tested and showed him the impressive results with this new design.

Satisfied that this rather plain design was definitely the best way to proceed, Dönitz then questioned the finishing designer how he came up with such an innovative idea. The designer was a middle-aged, rather small character, with thinning hair and thick glasses mounted in the typical scientist's skeletal wire-frames. He was about to postulate mathematical theorems, occult physics and a few other obscure scientific facts that were meant to impress this imposing and important Naval officer, but after a brief eye encounter he thought better of his little prank. Instead, he simply told the truth. The truth was that he had also studied the design of aircraft and noted that the noses of multiple engined planes all had this basic shape. He realized that their design was for strength rather than streamlining so why not try it out underwater? He and his very skeptical colleagues were amazed at the results. With this admission, the slim scientist bowed his head and waited for a reprimand of sorts. Instead, Dönitz laughed lightly and reassured him that many great advances in science came from unexpected sources. Buoyed by his success with the great Admiral, the quiet little scientist went on to develop the entire outside shape of Germany's newest submarine which greatly exceeded all of Dönitz's expectations for speed.

"Captain Sir. The butterfly is stored and secured. We are no longer a *battleship* on anyone's radar," First Officer Lassen almost laughingly reported to Captain Wittrock when he entered the control room of the submarine.

"So, Mr. Lassen. Once again the mighty *Scharnhorst* has mystically vanished in a figurative puff of smoke. What must our British colleagues be thinking now? I'd love to hear them explain this *disappearance* to London when the sun comes up shortly and they confirm their radar operator's conclusion. Well, enough of that for now. Dive the boat to twenty-five meters, steer fifteen degrees to port and increase speed to eighteen knots. It is now 0710. First light in twenty minutes. At 0740 reduce speed to ten knots and bring the boat up to periscope depth. Have all torpedo tubes ready to fire on short notice. That is all for now."

With these orders delivered, Wittrock took a quick trip to the galley and grabbed a stout chunk of pickled pork from a platter the cook had just laid out. With his other hand, he picked up two thick slices of nourishing black bread and deposited his meal on a plate that the cook had instantly produced for him. The cook handed his captain a large mug of spicy cider. Wittrock quickly took a seat in the smallish room that served as a mess hall. Although it was small, at least there was room to sit and eat, read or indulge in idle gossip that had not existed in earlier model submarines. Gordon Wittrock wolfed down the impromptu meal, washing most large bites of bread down with the delightful cider.

The cider was a specialty of his friend Peter Kastanien's next door neighbor. Kastanien's neighbor was a slim, almost willowy lady a few years younger than Kastanien's wife. Kristine Sheerdan was almost as good a cook as her neighbor friend Andrea. Her one advantage over her friendly rival was her age-old recipe for a special spicy cider that no one could duplicate; although many had tried. She shared the recipe with no one, but generously distributed many, many five-liter jars to her neighbors. Peter and Andrea Kastanien were always excessively grateful every fall when she made the magnificently tasty cider. Peter Kastanien inevitably sweet talked her out of enough of the delightful drink to supply his friend Wittrock.

Gordon Wittrock would almost salivate uncontrollably with his first taste of the cider each fall, and because of his obvious delight, Peter, with Kristine's help, made sure that he had enough to last him through an entire patrol at sea, and maybe another. While Kristine was making her cider,

Andrea Kastanien harvested cabbages and preserved enough sauerkraut to sustain not only her family but to supply Kristine's family with enough of this traditional staple to last an entire year. Kristine's husband, Robert, cherished the sauerkraut with the same relish that Wittrock relished his wife's cider. Kristine's husband Robert was an electronics engineer at a nearby laboratory, so when Peter Kastanien was home on shore leave, Robert related the latest developments in electronic sensing equipment that weren't absolutely top-secret. Peter reciprocated with how things electronically were holding up and to what degree they fulfilled their original purpose. Most importantly, Peter told Robert what the Navy felt they absolutely must have to stay one or two steps ahead in the enemy-detection game. Such was the way critical knowledge was exchanged and science marched forward.

"Periscope depth Captain."

"Very good, thank you Mr. Lassen, up periscope."

With a snake-like hiss of hydraulics, the polished, gleaming, silver-like periscope post bolted upwards and protruded its non-reflective dark-gray head a meter above the waves. Within a second of the headset coming to rest in the operational position, Wittrock, with his cap reversed, wriggled his eyes into the rubber eyepieces and began a rapid 360 degree scan of the surface for any ships that might be critically near. Although he had just moments before checked with his sonar operator, he always needed visual verification to assure himself that he did not have unwanted company close by on any quarter. Sonar had reported that only the *Rawalpindi* showed on his screen at a range of twenty kilometers and aft of their starboard quarter. Satisfied that there were no troublemakers within a few short kilometers, Wittrock then began a very slow and deliberate scan of the far horizon. It was still far too dark on the surface to discern any telltale smudges of smoke except for the slight lightening of the cloud-free eastern horizon. Captain Wittrock was not expecting the British to come at 'his' *Scharnhorst* from the eastern quadrant as against the brightening sky the British would be blatantly silhouetted, allowing *Scharnhorst* to have more than enough time to get their range and pump a few salvos at them before the British even glimpsed their nemesis. Even the Royal Navy would avoid this very bad situation with its attendant, highly probable, catastrophic results.

Wittrock had also popped up his periscope to the west of *Rawalpindi* to similarly avoid being silhouetted by his night-long companion.

However, Wittrock silently, slowly and deliberately continued to transverse the horizon which now continued to brighten rather rapidly. After he made three complete circumnavigations which consumed eight minutes he stopped, retraced a few degrees, paused, then moved the periscope forward through a few degrees and stopped again. With his eyes still imbedded into the periscopes rubber eyepieces, Wittrock barked an order.

"Mr. Lassen, we have additional company at fifteen kilometers. Bearing?"

"Bearing 285 true. Eighty degrees off our port bow."

Wittrock smiled and thought to himself, *"That's where you were supposed to come from my friend and right on time."*

Wittrock, now even slower, continued traversing the Atlantic's surface, knowing that this new vessel was surely a warship and it would not be alone. The sun had now risen like a huge bronze searchlight illuminating all points of the compass where no one could hide as opposed to the predawn gloom of minutes past. Within a few degrees he spotted four more smudges in a loose line slightly to the north of his first sighting but not close enough for their outlines to show above the waves. That would no doubt change soon enough. Wittrock expected more company to arrive soon enough. He had no desire to be caught in the middle of a virtual armada of bewildered, confused and very angry commanders of the Royal Navy.

"Down 'scope. Dive the boat. Depth one hundred meters, steer course 180. Speed twenty knots."

Lassen responded immediately. Within the span of less than two minutes the periscope and its effervescent foamy trail had vanished from sight leaving the ocean's surface uninhabited to further confound the Royal Navy. Wittrock descended from the periscope room to his command center and proceeded to sit on a convenient stool next to his sonar operator.

"Anything new Mr. Marsten?"

"No Sir. I just have the *Rawalpindi* as we have had for the duration of the night."

"Well then. We have reversed course as you no doubt have noted and increased speed. Does either of these changes affect your ability to 'see' any newcomers to our neighborhood?"

Wittrock noted immediately that his junior officer seemed to hesitate before answering.

"Come now Mr. "Marvel" Marsten, out with the truth. I'm not the fire-breathing ogre some make me out to be."

Visibly relieved by the captain's use of the nickname, the sonar operator slightly stammering told his captain.

"Well Captain Sir; we are listening to noises that are generated by other vessels. At speeds up to fifteen knots underwater, I have no problems whatsoever detecting any vessel within a radius of a little more than ten kilometers. As we speed up the passage through the water creates a disturbance that reduces my machine's ability to hear quite so far. At twenty knots my effective range to detect other ships is reduced to about six or seven kilometers. When we are traveling at top speed underwater which I understand is nearly thirty knots, my effective range is barely a myopic two kilometers."

"Well stated 'Marvel'. Thank you. We will be slowing down shortly to twelve knots, say about thirty minutes from now. Keep your 'ears' wide open and on high alert. I sincerely expect much more company in the next hour or so. When you get even a slight hum or blip on your machine, please inform me at once."

"Yes Sir. At once, Sir. And thank you Sir for you kind words."

"You're welcome. An awful lot depends on that machine with your interpretations. I know positively that you will never miss even the slightest murmur that signals us of visitors on the surface. Carry on."

With that expressed, Wittrock strolled over to the plot table and stared for a few moments at a map showing the greater area around his position. Setting his calipers by the scale on the side of the map, Wittrock walked the pointers in several directions from his position, mentally cataloging with his extraordinary mathematical memory, several distances, and then silently calculating times to several possible destinations. After several minutes, Wittrock seemed satisfied with himself and then replaced the calipers in a side pocket. Leaning casually on a bulkhead, Wittrock pondered for an additional few moments before snapping back into action.

"Reduce speed to twelve knots. Bring us up to periscope depth."

The U3200X slowed rather gently and silently. The designers had done an exemplary job of streamlining such that any reduction in speed was minimally hampered by the resistance of the sea. This streamlining worked very advantageously when she sped up. The very slight drag by the ocean allowed this rather large submarine to rapidly accelerate out of harm's way when under a depth charge attack. As yet the U3200X had not been under any assault of any sort by any enemy. Nobody on board, especially Captain Wittrock, was anxious to *test* this theory any time soon. With this being only her second patrol, her explicit orders were to take all orders from *Scharnhorst's* captain. It seemed rather remote that she would come under a direct attack.   Although the restriction placed upon him regarding independent action against enemy shipping rankled a bit, Wittrock understood the strategy behind the thinking of those above him, most notably Grossadmiral Dönitz.

Again the gleaming periscope hissed up and once more Wittrock did his rather amusing quick-step dance revolving the periscope through a cursory, yet important complete circle of the surface for any new occupants. This time was a bit different now that all points of the compass were brilliantly lit by the early spring sun, coolly shining down from a cloudless sky. Although Wittrock had made note of a few new but still far away blemishes on the crystalline skyline, he maintained his ingrained habit of a quick look first for any serious nearby threat. His first look complete, Wittrock rotated the periscope back to the general position where he had spotted the telltale smoke. Within the span of a few heartbeats he had locked onto a new threat. And threat he knew it was, simply because the smoke was trailing off too quickly to be anything but warships plying the ocean at high speed.

"Mr. Lassen, we have more *guests* approximately thirty kilometers away. Bearing?"

"Bearing 165 true; fifteen degrees off our port side."

Wittrock made a grunt of approval and then continued his deliberate and seemingly tedious search for any more neighboring vessels. After two complete revolutions, Wittrock was satisfied that he had pinpointed the directions that trouble was coming from.

"Down 'scope. Dive the boat. Depth one hundred meters. Rig for silent running. Steer course 010. Speed twenty knots."

Satisfied that his orders were well under way, Wittrock once again dropped down to the control center and took the few steps over to the sonar console.

"Mr. Marsten. What have you now on your scope?"

"Captain Sir. I have just now picked up some new vessels off our port quarter. Please give me just a few seconds and I will pinpoint them more accurately."

Wittrock waited patiently and true to his estimate, Erich Marsten placed the new arrivals precisely where he himself had placed them only a moment earlier.

"Well done Mr. Marsten. Now what has become of the *Rawalpindi* and our other recent northern arrivals?"

"The *Rawalpindi* is still proceeding on the same course and speed as over the past night. Our quick dash to the south took the northerners out of my range a few moments ago but I should hear them relatively soon with our new heading and speed."

"Very well, inform me when they do reappear and of course any other new or changing developments."

"Pardon my impertinence Captain, Sir, but do you expect more warships to show up in addition to the enemy group already on the scene?"

Wittrock stared the young electronic whiz-kid straight in the eye, whose anxiety was written all over the smooth complexion of his youth. Before the sonar operator could understand the captain's gaze, Wittrock's face cracked into a knowing smile and he replied in a conspiratorially whisper close to the boy's ear.

"Marvel. I wouldn't be the least bit surprised to see the entire Royal Navy show up for a chance at *Scharnhorst* and *Gneisenau*. Lord Churchill himself would of course be leading this charge of the Heavy Brigade with cane, cigar and his ever present brandy close by."

Marsten was at first enthralled by the captains familiarity but suddenly realized that the captain may have been making fun of him and he blushed as crimson as a setting sun. Wittrock then stood behind his sonar man, clapped both hands on the boy's slim shoulders and started a monologue. He finished with a deadly serious tone.

"The first part of that could very well be true, but we should not fear or hope that the bombastic and vociferous Grand Master of the English language would show up for a sea battle, considering the way things are in England now. However, being the old sea dog he is, believe me when I say he will be back in London giving the Lords and Admirals Holy Hell to get *Scharnhorst* and *Gneisenau* at damn near any cost. Now let me return to my duties. I want you to inform me when the nearest vessels are ten kilometers from us."

"Yes Sir Captain. I estimate we should be in that position in about twenty minutes."

"Thank you Mr. Marsten."

Wittrock slowly strolled back to the control room and stood by the relatively large square plot table just off the center of the control room. The periscope trunk occupied the dead centre of the room so the port side of the plot table was so close to the lateral bulkhead that only one man could pass through at a time and then only if he wasn't sporting a rotund middle.

Submariners, as a breed, were seldom on the chunky side, but occasionally a few were a bit oversized in the middle. Wittrock stood for a few moments lost in concentration with his hands clasped behind his back. After a few quiet moments, his hands flowed from behind his back to the slightly nearer side of the table, where he began to move the small black and red simple lead symbols of ships. The black symbols represented the enemy and the red ones his countries warships. There was a single yellow lead symbol that was his boat. This one he moved first to a position east of their present position and then moved the black ones to different places. The red ones he moved completely off the chart as he knew that *Scharnhorst* and *Gneisenau*, the only two friendly ships anywhere close, were anything but close by now. Wittrock studied these new placements for a brief moment, then moved the yellow U3200X a small distance and with the calipers that he had casually picked up with his left hand, earlier preset to a specific distance. He danced them forward three quick twists with his fingers and parked the U3200X where the last point of the calipers landed. Before he started moving the enemies black pieces to the positions he felt they would occupy when he reached his new position, Wittrock pranced the calipers from his projected new position to St. Nazaire on the coast of France and the Azores, pausing slightly to calculate his sailing times to both.

Setting the calipers back in their little nest on the side of the plot table, Wittrock drew his pallid but beefy left hand over his bushy goatee a few times while he cogitated over several different strategies. When he was satisfied that he had come up with the best plan to continue to baffle the British and still accomplish his main mission to sink ships, he drew himself up to his full height of a few inches over six feet tall and reached for the ship's intercom.

"Attention all hands. This is your Captain speaking. Here is our battle plan for the next few hours. We will be heading north underwater at moderate speed abandoning our close observance of the British. They will no doubt by now scouring their intellectual powers to figure out what happened to their intended victim, the *Scharnhorst*. Well, we will not be in the neighborhood to allow them to connect the dots and deduct that it was our boat that befuddled their radar. When we have steamed for three hours, we will turn back. Then when our sonar makes contact with some of them we will then execute an aggressive attack. Exactly what that will be is up to the Royal Navy. Unfortunately, the Royal Navy does not always follow our plan of battle so we shall see what we shall see in a few hours. That is all for now."

During the captain's speech, the entire boat's company had remained motionless and silent, but when it was over, all eighty-seven seamen let loose with such a rousing cheer that any competent enemy sonar operator within ten kilometers surely would have heard. The crew of the U3200X, like virtually every sailor that volunteered for this most hazardous sea duty, abhorred most everything that did not have to do with what they cherished most—the adrenalin-fueled thrill of battle at sea. They were relieved that the boring job of imitating the *Scharnhorst* for endless hour after hour was over and soon they would get into a real battle.

Wittrock clipped the intercom back in its cradle then splayed his hands on the plot table, leaned into the map and let a mischievous smirking smile dance across his mouth while his eyes sparkled with the anticipation of real action against real enemies.

"Helm, steer course 015. Depth fifty meters. Speed fifteen knots."

Then Wittrock, just like his two dearest friends, Kastanien and Teebolt would do, ordered the crew to rotate through some rest cycles and be prepared for action in a few hours. He motioned his First Officer Heinrich Lassen over to his side and calmly handed over control of the boat before excusing himself. Within five minutes, Gordon Wittrock was in his tiny cabin asleep on his utilitarian bunk fully dressed with the exception of his boots and cap. Those he had neatly set down by the foot of the bunk available to don within seconds. He had curled up on his side with a cozy warm but rather plain woolen blanket covering him up to his neck. Crewmembers passing by could not but help hear his stentorian snoring and smiled to themselves that the captain was content with the state of affairs for the present.

With little to do for quite some time, the crew amused themselves by imagining how many ships of the Royal Navy would fall prey to their torpedoes. Within an hour, they had sunk nearly twice the amount of battleships that the British possessed before they started on the lesser ships. The banter was all light-hearted until one painfully young, fuzzy-faced torpedo man informed his fellows that what they had debated would take nearly three times the amount of torpedoes that they even had to accomplish. This reality was rewarded with a unanimous blast of catcalls. The young man, stunned with the response dropped his head and looked like he was about to cry. Since joining the U3200X, he had tried so hard to fit in with the older men, not one of whom was over twenty-eight years old. This desultory blow to his fragile ego was almost more than he could withstand. Then, all the previously jeering men began to laugh raucously at themselves and one of the older hands, still laughing, grabbed the lad in a friendly bear hug. This had the immediate effect of letting the forlorn youngster know that they had finally accepted him. His ear splitting grin, so obviously reflecting the pride his heart and soul now felt, infected the men closest to him resulting in a crush of good-hearted back-slapping, all the while accompanied with high spirited laughing

Battleship King George V
0815 Hours

First light had come and gone. *King George V* slowly sidled up close enough to *Rawalpindi* to commence signal lamp communications. Battle group "C" formerly stationed just West of Ireland on *Bismarck* watch was led by the battleship *King George V.* The group consisted of the two heavy cruisers *Berwick* and *Cornwall* along with five destroyers. Battle group "C" would have given the Royal Navy overwhelming firepower superiority over *Scharnhorst* but mysteriously there was no sign of the *Scharnhorst. King George V* opened the interchange of signals with one simple, curt scathing question.

"Where in God's name is that bloody Bosch bastard?"

Rawalpindi's Kennedy knowing he needed to be the one to answer paused before replying. He had no explanation for the inexplicable disappearance of his nightlong shadow, but true to his irascible temperament, he responded in a like fashion, not allowing the plainly implied accusation to get the best of him.

"Where indeed? The bloody son-of-a-bitch was stuck to my stern all through the night until less than an hour ago when he just simply disappeared. Much as I would like to have sunk him, unfortunately I didn't."

Frustrated by the terse reply, Captain John Parks, commanding the battle group from his flagship *King George V* ordered the *Rawalpindi* to increase revolutions to her fastest speed immediately. At the same time, he ordered his great bulking 42,200 ton, almost-new battleship, to pull alongside the *Rawalpindi* to within hailing distance and to maintain station until further orders. *Rawalpindi* complied and within a few minutes, her twin screws were propelling her along at quite a respectable seventeen knots. *King George V* smartly pulled up parallel to within a hundred yards, adjusting her speed to keep the close rendezvous with *Rawalpindi* at a consistent distance. The two heavy cruisers and five destroyers had been ordered to provide a cordon around the two vessels while the two captains tried to figure out the bizarre situation and come up with a plan of action. With the seas still relatively quiet, the close proximity of the two ships made for rather easy and very loud conversation.

Recriminations flew back and forth with increasing intensity until after a particularly nasty reference to the Royal Navy's current heritage by Kennedy. The comment was so virulent that the battleship's Captain Park was taken aback by its intensity. Quickly composing himself back to the demeanor of a senior naval officer, *King George V's* fifty-four year old Captain John Parks decided that the time for useless verbal recriminations was long past. The interchanges had possibly served some obscure purpose, although he could not fathom what at this juncture. In a conciliatory gesture, Parks ended the tirades.

"Captain Kennedy, let it rest. Now, since the clever German has managed somehow to vanish into thin air or by some stroke of luck on our part, scuppered himself, he must know where you are. I believe that we could carry on our conversation much less stressful over the radio. Do you agree?"

"Thank you Captain Parks. Please accept my sincere apologies for my unwarranted outbursts. How in blazes that damn giant floating tub of Kraut iron simply vanished unraveled my proper senses. Unfortunately, you bore the brunt of my aggravations. Once again, my apologies for my abominable outburst. However, I disagree that breaking radio silence is prudent at this time. I do agree that the devious German probably knows where we are but he might not know that you are keeping me company. I have no desire to give that slimy sod any help whatsoever."

"An excellent point about the radio silence. Agreed Captain Kennedy. Do you have any suggestions as to our course of action from this point onwards?"

"Well, thank you for asking the humble opinion of a half-arsed warrior. As for myself, now that I am a bit busted up with only a few of my pop-guns operational, I plan to make best speed to England, effect repairs then come back out to deal with those slimy, sneaky submarines that have given us so much anguish. All I can suggest is that you and yours somehow find the blighter and do him in."

Before Parks could answer, the bridge wing intercom screamed to life.

"Radar room here Captain. I am picking up several blips on my radar headed our way. They are definitely aircraft and most probably the Luftwaffe since we are still far beyond any possible fighter or bomber coverage from home."

Several centuries of British Naval training immediately took over. Parks verbally sprang into action.

"Sound battle stations for aerial assault. Flank speed. Signal all ships to make smoke and hide in it when possible. Independent evasive actions if attacked. Destroyer *Grafton* to guard *Rawalpindi*. Do not break radio silence until the aircraft are definitely identified either friend or foe."

Similar to pealing a banana, all the warships steaming along in the orderly cordon slewed away from the center ship, *King George V*. The immediate air above the sea was soon polluted with dense, rather nasty black smoke, rapidly covering an area of several acres. The almost total lack of any wind assured the smoke would hover motionless, gathering itself denser and denser until it created a huge island in the middle of the ocean, which was over two miles wide at this location.

King George V immediately frothed the sea with her four screws driven by eight boilers generating 125,000 horsepower quite smartly pulled away from *Rawalpindi* who was heading directly for the incoming aircraft. No less than eight lookouts had rapidly assembled on the bridge wings and were intently staring at the black specks in the early morning sky that grew slowly at first, and then rapidly increased in size. The first to grab the intercom was a slight lad of only nineteen from the Faeroe Islands with incredibly keen eyesight.

"Seaman Ian McGinnis here. Aircraft are most definitely German *Condors*. I make out two formations of four planes each about 10,000 feet, fifteen miles out and closing fast."

Captain Parks now went from frustration and disappointment regarding the missing German battleship to apprehension. He thought to himself how the cleverly laid trap set for the *Scharnhorst* and *Gneisenau* had been deftly reversed—putting *them* in serious straits. Not one to dwell on the change of fortunes and to wallow in self-incrimination, Parks, the epitome of Royal Navy discipline, barked out fresh orders, "Break radio silence. Make to Admiralty. *Scharnhorst* has again vanished without a trace. We will be under heavy attack from two flights of *Condors* shortly. We are taking evasive measures under cover of smoke. *Rawalpindi,* with destroyer *Grafton* escorting will maintain original course at best speed of seventeen knots for home. Give our position and when they reply come to me immediately with the response."

Battle group "M" that had shown up earlier on the sonar of U3200X was still over the southwestern horizon when the shattering black-edged news of the failed and now reversed trap reached across the ethers almost physically assaulting the listeners in the radio room of the flagship *Duke of York.* Battle group "M" was one of the Admiralty's "backstop" groups that had steamed from their station east of the Lesser Antilles a few days earlier to guard the western rear quadrant of the vast ocean if the *Scharnhorst* tried to slip out of harm's way by reversing away from the battle groups "B" and "C" descending on the "bait ship" *Rawalpindi's* position. Battle Group "M" was a bit slower than the other battle groups due to the simple fact that one of the two battleships, notably the fifteen year old, 38,030 ton *Rodney,* could only muster twenty-three knots. Accompanying this majestic old girl, who still had notable firepower with her potent nine sixteen-inch guns, several smaller caliber guns and torpedo launchers, was the much newer *Duke of York.*

The *Duke of York* belonged to the *King George V* class of battleships, all of which were launched either in the previous year or earlier in this one. By launching four very serious new battleships in the short span of only two years, the British were showing the world and especially Nazi Germany that they were dedicated to maintaining their absolute sovereignty on the world's oceans. The other two *King George V* class battleships were currently plying the far western reaches of the Pacific. *Anson* and *Howe* had been sent specifically on this most distant patrol to be a constant reminder to the Japanese, whom and what they would be dealing with, if they overstepped their bounds into any of the Britain's many varied Far Eastern colonies. Shanghai, Burma, Australia, New Zealand and many others were important links in the chain of British controlled territories that completed the British Empire's circumnavigation of the globe.

The Royal Navy was the most important symbol of the global power wielded by the small North Sea Island. The sun never set on the British Empire or the Royal Navy whose prodigious presence seemed to be cruising about on every patch of ocean in the world.

Captain Parks had stepped out to the bridge wing to see for himself the grave peril that was rapidly approaching. Within a moment of his arrival on the bridge wing, the air began resonating with a faint but growing thrumming from the eight four-engined bombers. Each of the feared *Condors* was powered by four nine-cylinder BMW-Bramo 1,200 hp radial engines and carried a bomb load of slightly more than two tons. As Parks watched, the right hand group of four turned to the south and reformed into a straight line fore and aft. Parks knew from the many reports that were relayed to him by all Royal Navy commanders that this was the favorite attacking mode of the giant birds. Parks, along with every captain in the Atlantic, as well as the Home Fleet, had been made privy to the overall strategy that the Admiralty had given to Operation Twin Sisters, a code name that was rather uninspired and completely obvious to any dullard.

The operation's objective was simply to send as many ships as necessary to assure that *Scharnhorst* and *Gneisenau* were cornered, overcome by a vastly superior, bludgeoning force of arms and summarily sunk. As Captain Parks maintained his vigil on the other four *Condors,* they too gently slid into their classic fore to aft formation and took a bead on his precious battleship. In the split seconds before Parks again took firm command, his thoughts centered on the *Condors* that had turned away from him but had assumed their attack formation.

"Their actions mean one of two things. Either they are coming around behind me for a one-two punch or they have spotted additional prey beyond my horizon."

The loudspeaker, connected directly to the bridge areas from the radio room, crackled to life rather loudly a mere second before he was about to snatch the mike from its cradle to issue his new orders. A welcome squawky and tinny voice erupted from the grey megaphone-styled speakers mounted under the overhang a few feet over his head.

"King George, this is Captain Jarvis on *Rodney. Duke of York* and I must be just over the horizon from your group since we have just verified two flights of German large bombers. Not much doubt that they are the perennial, persistent, pesky *Condors* that we noticed on radar a short time ago. One flight of four is headed my way with the other probably zeroing in on you and yours. We have gone to action stations, making as much smoke as possible and turning west. We will shortly turn back to the east ducking into our own smoke, hoping that the smoke will botch the Bosch

bastard's aim a bit—giving us a bit more fighting chance to do them in with our anti-aircraft guns. We are planning to throw up so much flak that they might just have to drop their landing gear and drive over it. Well, quite enough of my warped humor for now. Keep in touch old chum and let us know how you fare with your bunch."

Parks picked up the microphone, a quick humorous memory flashing through his razor sharp mind before activated the intercom to issue new orders.

"Good old Jarvis, a realist with optimistic humor. God love him and bless the Royal Naval College for turning a bit of a blind eye to his youthful antics. Well, at least they graduated him but giving him the old Rodney *was a bit of a slap on the wrist."*

Parks smashed down on the connect button to the radio room and barked sharply, "Signal all ships on the radio we are turning starboard immediately to course 270 at twenty-eight knots, Execute smoke pattern for five knot wind from due east. We will hold course for three minutes then come about by turning sharply starboard to course 090 to hide in the smoke as best we can. Maintain sighting distance from each other, which should be at least half a mile but no further than one mile. When the *Condors* make their final run, throw everything you've got at them. That is all."

The superbly trained officers of the Royal Navy had been practicing several smoke maneuvers ever since it became all too obvious a couple of decades ago that aircraft would be a seriously deadly foe in any coming war at sea. Although every warship from every maritime nation bristled like a porcupine with anti-aircraft guns, the relatively high speed of airplanes and their natural ability to change altitudes rapidly made them extremely difficult targets to deliver a killing burst to. Only when aircraft were zeroing in for a torpedo launch at close range did the warships have a decent chance for a kill.

Battle groups "C" and "M" began executing identical smoke maneuvers at virtually the same time. The flight of *Condors* arrowing in on Battle Group "M" looked on in partial amazement as the two battleships and their escorts launched into their intricate choreographed ballet. The nine ships of battle group "M" consisted of the two battleships, *Rodney, Duke of York*, two *Leander* class light cruiser veterans of the failed *Graf Spee* campaign, *Ajax* and *Achilles,* along with five very nimble destroyers. As the pilots of the *Condors* watched, the sprightly destroyers wove in and out of the much slower battleships belching out much more smoke than the pilots thought such small ships could produce. The surface wind was a mere two knots allowing the black, brown, gray and white smoke to lay rather calmly on the surface increasing its coverage as every minute passed. The original edges of the smoke slowly, much too slowly, were dissipating for the *Condor's* needs. The two battleships were now heading in opposite directions plunging desperately to reach the temporary sanctuary of the thickening smoke.

The flight commander of this flight section ordered two of his planes to split off and attack the *Rodney* with the classic stern-to-bow attack. He and his partner would take on the *Duke of York*. Because of the camouflage that the smoke temporality created, the pilots were strictly ordered not to guess where their intended targets might be if they indeed did reach the smoke cover. The orders were to either circle around for a clearer target or take out one of the cruisers.

Both *Rodney* and *Duke of York* scurried into the smoke screen just in the nick of time to thwart the Germans bombsights. The two attacking pairs flew over the roiling smoke eight thousand feet below them and sought out the cruisers. *Ajax* was missing somewhere in the rapidly expanding smoke that now covered the better part of several square miles of ocean, but *Achilles* had wandered too far from the smoke to cover herself before the *Condors* could press home a serious attack without the blinding hindrance of the smoke.

The captain of the *Condor* flight was a true warrior at heart that had not so mildly voiced his displeasure at being relegated to the bomber squadrons of the Luftwaffe. He knew he was in much superior physical condition for his thirty-three years than most of the eager, barely twenty year old young men that who were flying glamorous fighters in real aerial battles at 350 plus miles an hour. He had always romanticized the Gladiators from olden Roman days, so to him the dogfights between the ME109's and the *Spitfires* over England were just a modern day version of man against man in the Roman Coliseum. However, the Luftwaffe High Command would not grant his wish to be a fighter pilot solely because of his advanced age, so here he was about to make his first attack on an enemy ship, which to him should be pretty straightforward. He was determined to sink a warship or maybe two and then, with this to his credit, present his case again to the Luftwaffe High Command. The new commander, Adolph Galland, would surely understand his hopes and thoughts.

Spotting the lonely *Achilles* off by herself, the *Condors* quickly realigned themselves convoy attack-style less than a kilometer apart, lined up directly on *Achilles'* stern and pressed home their attack. The lead plane went into a shallow dive slightly increasing airspeed but mainly to throw off the anti-aircraft barrage he had been trained to expect. The black splotches of the *Achilles* air-defense guns began to pepper the sky above, below, and to the right and left of him long before he thought they could reach out to clutch at his precious airplane. As he dove, the black exploding popcorn seemed to close in a bit closer allowing him to hear some of the exploding shrapnel shells over the screaming drone of his four engines.

Undaunted by the close proximity of the deadly flak, the thirty-three year old native of Dresden single-mindedly pressed on seemingly impervious to the thick barrage outside, then handed control of the bomber to the bombardier for the final run. The bomb bay doors snapped open and seconds later two 500 pound armor-piercing ship-destroyer bombs tumbled from the *Condor's* belly. Gravity and a streamlined design quickly took flight command of the accelerating bombs arrowing toward the *Achilles*.

Achilles captain screamed an order for hard to port when his keen eyesight spotted the bomb bay doors opening on the lead aircraft. Knowing he had but far less than a minute until the bombs finished their travels, he hoped that it was enough to dodge out of the way and duck into the smoke screen that was now so tantalizingly close. The dodge worked and the two bombs vanished into the North Atlantic with just a negligible splash about fifty yards off the starboard beam of *Achilles*. Knowing the second *Condor* had adjusted his final run to his new prey's new position the *Achilles* rapidly turned to starboard and once more, the bombs missed by about the same not-very-comfortable margin, but a miss still counted as a miss. The third *Condor* anticipated the turn to port as the *Achilles* was just entering the thin edges of the smoke cover. What he didn't expect was a lucky shot from one of the anti-aircraft guns that flew into his now open bomb bay and detonated when it hit one of his eight 500 pound bombs still racked neatly in the bomb bay, exploding it in a titanic blast. Not one of the five crewmembers in the *Condor* ever knew what had instantaneously snuffed out their young lives.

The fourth *Condor's* pilot wrenched the rather unwieldy 24,000 kilogram craft into a hard port turn and pushed the yoke as far forward as he dared. These quick actions probably saved the *Condor's* life as the massive fireball that seconds ago were his wing mates, engulfed the morning sky with flaming petrol, screaming metal chunks and concussive forces strong enough to tear the wings off his sturdy aircraft if he had flown through it. The *Condor* did not escape totally unscathed. Several shards of metal peppered the fuselages rear section and a few small rents hindered the elevators and rudder operations slightly. Well within half a minute the steady hands of the seasoned pilot eased the bomber back to level flight, assessed the "feel" of the giant bird, then after receiving the minor damage reports from the three gunners, turned his attention back to his task. The barrage of anti-aircraft from the fleeing *Achilles* quickly resumed after reacquiring the general range of the last *Condor.* With his heart grieving for his vanquished comrades, the youthful pilot steeled himself to make sure the offending warship paid a high price.

Determined to make his bomb load count, the emotionally-driven pilot shoved the yoke forward, immediately changing the normally languid bomber into a gigantic four-engined *Junkers* JU87 *Stuka* dive-bomber. The *Condor* with all four engines pushed to their limit and beyond, rapidly exceeded her nominal maximum speed of 360 km/h. The air rocketed over the wings and slightly damaged rear control surfaces at over 440 km/h creating a shrieking sound that threatened to rip the plane apart. The *Stukas* dove nearly perpendicular in their terrifying bomb runs, but the *Condor's* pilot knowing his airship would never withstand that kind of stress, held his dive to a much milder, but still very dangerous forty degrees.

Downward the bomber screamed, jinking slightly side to side to throw off the now panicked anti-aircraft gunners, whose gun sights rapidly filled with the black death-dealing missile plummeting directly at them. The pilot pulled back slightly on the yoke when the altimeter read a mere twelve hundred feet. He had ordered the bomb bay doors opened right after he began his revenge-driven dive—their turbulence adding another high-pitched howling to the banshee-like cacophony of the excessive speed. The *Condor* filled the *Achilles'* entire gun sights making it nigh unto impossible to miss, however the gunners were so unnerved by the piercing, screaming wail that penetrated their hefty ear protectors, they couldn't maintain enough composure to keep their guns steady enough to accomplish more than near misses.

The *Condor* finally, after what seemed an eternity to both the *Achilles* and *Condor's* crew, pulled up level five hundred feet above the disinterested slate-gray Atlantic a couple of hundred meters behind an *Achilles* that was corkscrewing violently in a forlorn attempt to dodge the inevitable. Seconds later four 500 pound bombs were loosed like a hunting pack of falcons. The *Condor* leapt higher after shedding a ton of dead weight, arrowed up to port and with the throttles still wide open began to climb erratically enough to avoid the fusillade of inconsistent flak that had never abated. The low altitude of the released ton of projectiles of destruction did not allow them to spread over a large area, but the close proximity to *Achilles* virtually assured they would score hits. The bomb release mechanism was cleverly designed to release their captives nearly two seconds apart to insure close hits but still cover an area that the target would theoretically occupy.

The two front-running bombs ploughed harmlessly into the fathomless Atlantic just shy of the *Achilles* bow. The last two smashed into the forecastle, detonating with devastating effects. The first bomb to hit penetrated the thin armor plate fifteen feet aft of the bow, exploded, blowing a gaping hole in the port side of the bow. The second bomb hit twenty-five feet further back, again punching through the thin decking before detonating. The blast ignited the hundreds of gallons of highly flammable paint along with the sundried supplies in the stores lockers. Billowing dense black smoke immediately spewed out of the deck entry point, creating an unwanted smoke screen that all but blinded the bridge, hiding the intense fire raging inside. Alarms blared throughout the ship instantly. Very well-trained damage control teams immediately sprang into a coordinated chaotic scramble to stem the unseen fire before it raged out of control.

The *Achilles* was holed just above the Plimsol line so there was no imminent danger of massive flooding. Watertight hatches had all been dogged shut beforehand as standard procedure when the ship was at action stations, so the fire could not spread until in its fury it breached the watertight integrity between the bulkheads. The fire control team was determined not to let this happen. Three-inch fire hoses snaked across the deck like giant spaghetti strands as the fire fighters burdened with heavy, clumsy protective gear edged towards the noxious smoke-plume that was now gushing vertically through the five foot wide jagged hole pushed skyward by the intense heat of the chemical fire. With three men holding each of the powerful hoses, the teams moved around the deck obstacles and approached the black inferno from the sides where the visibility was best.

The hoses bucked like monstrous caged snakes as they were played out to the leading fire fighters. Every man aboard the *Achilles* knew the fearsome killing power of an unfettered high-pressure fire hose. A loose hose could scythe down men like a field of wheat more than likely killing them instantly with their brutal impact or by slamming them into hard steel. Many lives had been lost even before the hose depressurized automatically when the safety grip mechanisms were not firmly held by brave but frail human hands.

Relatively safe for at least the next few moments hidden by the smoke screens, *Achilles* slowed to a crawl inside its protective cocoon allowing the fire fighters to get their seawater and chemical hoses into the gaping hole to begin extinguishing the blaze. Although everything possible was being done to alleviate the visibility and control the fire, the hazards were still dangerously daunting in the extreme.

The *Condor* regained a reasonable bombing altitude of four thousand feet and searched for Royal Navy ships that were in the clear to drop their remaining four bombs on. None were clearly visible as the Royal Navy continued to make as much smoke as possible and hide themselves in it. The smoke screens also worked against the British insomuch as they could not see the prowling *Condors*, consequently their many, many anti-aircraft guns were silent.

The three remaining *Condors* still had half of their bombs with no visible targets and their time over the enemy was becoming rather limited before they would be forced to head for their home base in France with enough fuel to make it. After some inter-plane radio chatter and planning, the *Condors* opted to head east for a few minutes until they were out of the British radar range. They hoped that the Royal Navy would break out from its cover and they could press home a final attack.

The *Achilles* fire fighters, once they could direct the high pressure hoses on the base of the inferno, had the paint locker fire out within ten minutes. Then repair crews began welding a temporary water tight patch on the inside of the breach in the hull, just forward of the still hot and smoldering scene of the recent blaze. Only twenty minutes passed from the initial bomb hit until word was passed to the other warships that *Achilles* had her fires out and was relatively seaworthy.

Inter-ship radio traffic confirmed that the *Condors* had left the scene heading east. Subsequent to verification that the danger from the skies was now gone, the Royal Navy desisted making smoke and steamed out of their own fog bank into the clear morning on a north-west heading towards the other battle group. They were more than anxious to assess the damage done by that batch of *Condors,* which had also departed to the east after partially ravaging *King George V* whose radio had apparently been knocked out.

Before battle group "C" steamed over the horizon into visual range of battle group "M", the all too familiar black smoke trailing into the clear morning air could easily be seen by the naked eye. As the distance between the groups rapidly shrank, the radio traffic between the group commanders blazed back and forth. The second flight of *Condors* had apparently been repulsed by intense anti-aircraft fire that had done some damage to two of the big birds. They were last seen by many eyes and ears retiring to the east. All four had concentrated their attack on the *King George V* inflicting dangerously serious damage, enough such that the viability of her ability to stay afloat was still in question.

Listing nearly ten degrees to port and burning furiously, the proud battleship still maintained a decent speed of fifteen knots. The two heavy cruisers formed a protective shield on her flanks. Both slowed to match her forward progress. The five destroyers scampered around the three capitol ships like sheepdogs from the Scottish highlands—ever on the alert for the unseen undersea enemy. Fifteen long agonizing minutes passed with the *King George V* still valiantly struggling to stay alive. Suddenly, finally, hope soared as the signal lantern on the bridge wing of the *King George V* clattered into life aiming at the heavy cruiser *Berwick* keeping station less than a third of a mile off her port beam.

"Am holed badly port side. Bomb penetrated decking and blew crew quarters into a bloody shambles. Thank God no crew killed in there. Bomb left a nasty hole a few feet underwater. Flooding is under control and we are affecting repairs, which damn it all to Hell will probably take several hours. Bomb hit forward has twisted gun turret "A" rendering it unusable. Stern bomb hit was the least troublesome but made one damnable nasty bonfire that is almost out. We have suffered eighteen dead and forty-two wounded, only five serious enough to require services of a London surgeon. No officers are amongst the dead or injured. We can handle our wounded as sickbay is simply doing a smashing good job. When we get close enough for signals only, I will relinquish command of this battle group to Captain Dunn on *Duke of York* and with a watchdog or two for company, I shall trundle my merry way home for repairs, fresh crumpets and tea. Captain Parks out."

Captain Soames on the bridge of the *Berwick* read the message and along with his entire bridge officers sighed relief at the much hoped for news that the *King George V* was going to make it. The eighteen dead, although sobering, was nowhere near the much higher figure everyone dreaded considering the conflagration and a serious list. With a crew compliment of 1,422, the casualties were grudgingly acceptable. The officers, to a man, realized that the last light-hearted comment about home was that they were going to make the best of a rather bad situation. Quite rudely, the intercom speaker squawked to life with a desperate urgency.

"Captain, radar room reports aircraft approaching from the east at low altitude closing fast. Will report as soon as we can fix distance, altitude and speed more accurately."

"Bloody Hell, the damnable Germans doubled back on us. They will no doubt target *King George V* to finish her off, but the Germans are not necessarily predictable all the time so maintain battle stations for another aerial assault and prepare for emergency turns."

Soames wrenched the radio intercom from its little nest and literally yelled loud enough for the radio operator to hear him without the amplification, "Radio all ships of the imminent danger from returning *Condors.* I recommend all ships to form up tight line abreast to give them a single target thus also giving us concentrated firepower. Radar and lookouts, how far away are *Rodney* and *Duke of York*?"

The First Officer replied immediately, "*Rodney* and *Duke of York* are still about fifteen miles off."

"Very well, signal *King George V* and put her captain on line for me."

The signal lamp chattered to life sending the short request. "Parks here. What do you want Soames?"

"With all due respect Sir, do you intend to remain as battle group commander given your condition and *Duke of York* is too far away to signal transfer of command?"

"Excellent point Captain Soames. I have ordered my engines to best speed so as not to be a hindrance and increase our flexibility, however, I am still badly crippled and as such will no doubt be their prime target. Steering has not been affected so we can turn with the best of them. We cannot jeopardize the situation in case I am finished off. As of right now, I am transferring group command to you Sir. As my last command order I concur with your tactic of line abreast, let it be so. Good luck to us all and do your damnedest. Parks out."

Captain Reginald Soames took only a single breath before ordering a transmission to all ships. Mere seconds passed before the radioman said he was ready to transmit. Soames had patiently worked his way up the chain of command in the Royal Navy for many years so when he suddenly became a battle group commander the mantle of this awesome responsibility rested comfortably on his broad shoulders. A tiny detail, which did not go unnoticed by any bridge officer, was that Soames now stood a shade taller and straighter. When Soames issued his first command order to his ships, it came so smooth and natural that no one even cocked an eyebrow with his assured delivery.

"Signal *Cornwall* to form line abreast on *King George V's* port side immediately, we will cover the starboard side. Separation four hundred yards. Keep station with *King George V.* Her Captain Parks will make his best speed, which will be a mite slower than optimum but it should not make a great deal of difference. All destroyers fall back behind us and open up with all you've got as soon as the bloody bastards are in range. Soames out."

The *Condors* came on relentlessly but now there were only five. Two of their group had suffered flak hits that made further attacks difficult at best and far too dangerous to do anything but head for France immediately. Ever the optimists the two returning, wounded *Condors* held onto their remaining bombs just in case a stray target presented itself. If not, when they were near the coast of France, the Atlantic would be the recipient of the bombs and their final resting place. One of the two *Condors* was running on only three engines. The other had rather a large number of holes in its port wing. A couple of the holes had penetrated a fuel bladder, allowing a substantial amount of precious fuel to scatter to the winds. Fuel sorely needed for the long trip home.

With one engine out on one, the other plane critically low on fuel, the two *Condors* eased back to 335 km/h, which was considered their best fuel economy speed and headed for home.

As the *Condors* flew towards the ships that had just about finished moving into their defensive positions, they spread out into a revised attack mode. As the British had predicted, it became obvious soon enough that their goal was to finish off the battleship that was still listing a few degrees, but at least her fires were now out. Three *Condors* again lined up nose-to-tail while the other two with six bombs each fanned out wide. This maneuver was to avoid the withering anti-aircraft fusillade that began spewing forth from the destroyers—their angry black talons greedily grasping at them. The three central *Condors* immediately nosed forward and began jinking erratically to throw off the English gunner's aim, while doggedly persisting in their purposeful pursuit of the ailing battleship. Very soon the combined anti-aircraft batteries, 40mm pom-poms and even the four and six inch guns on the three capitol ships added to the destroyers barrage making the sky a very dangerous place to be.

The *Condor* pilots blanched at the amount of fire they were taking, but refused to break off before losing their remaining bombs. Knowing their comrades were about to attack on the beams of the outer heavy cruisers, they flew into the maelstrom with teeth clenched behind tense, pursed lips. The lead *Condor* took the first deadly hit as a flak shell exploded a mere two feet from the bombardiers nacelle, smashing the Plexiglas into deadly shards to accompany the metal fragments killing him instantly. Feeling the hit bounce his ship rather roughly, the pilot looked down through the access hatch and saw what had happened. He immediately took control back from the now-dead bombardier and with only a few seconds left to the drop point, he nosed over a bit more and released all four remaining 500 pounders at the slewing battleship.

Three of the four were near misses but the fourth bomb narrowly missed the smokestack and made kindling wood of two lifeboats before penetrating into the tender spot abaft of the bridge superstructure—exploding with devastating results. The concussive force that reached the bridge either killed or knocked out the entire compliment of officers present. The main brunt of the explosion obliterated the radio centre, plot room, radar control room, officer's quarters, sickbay, mess hall and galleys. Fortunately, the ensuing fire was relatively minor, being as there was no quantity of flammable materials to feed it. The ship was blind, leaderless and with no one to regain command of the steering immediately, she naturally began curving rapidly to port into her list. The sudden change in course saved her. The remaining *Condors* had committed their bombs, which dropped harmlessly into the starboard sea.

The concussive blast had shaken up the gun crews for a brief moment or two before they resumed their attack on the now rapidly vanishing *Condors,* which flew straight over the bow climbing swiftly out of reach.

Momentarily forgotten, the two flanking *Condors* were upon the *Berwick* and *Cornwall* before the defensive guns had spun around to meet the newest threat. Both sides opened up at the same time. From 4,000 feet the two *Condors* unleashed four 500 pound armor-piercing bombs at each of the cruisers. With their bombs away, the *Condors* clawed for altitude all the while executing wiggling, rolling evasive tactics.

All the bombs from the one *Condor* missed the *Berwick* but the *Cornwall* was not so lucky. One bomb penetrated the rather thin deck armor exploding in the engine room, detonating when it struck one of the eight Admiralty 3-drum boilers dead on. In the confined space, the brutal concussive force killed twelve men outright, seriously wounding six more. Only nine dazed, temporarily disoriented men remained to cope with the ensuing fire. Their lone battle with the blaze lasted only two minutes until the superb firefighting crew poured into the smoke and fire-filled cavern. The stricken boiler had erupted from its moorings, slamming into the neighboring boiler, knocking it enough to render it useless. The wrenched boilers bent the shafts that they powered enough to put them out of action.

Mere minutes passed in the engine room before the fire was extinguished. Powerful ventilators cleared the smoke rapidly allowing visibility of more than a few feet. The damage was almost total. Just as the *Condor* that had scored the hit on *Cornwall* thought they had reached a safe distance, a last ditch effort by an optimistic gunner at near maximum range aboard the *King George V,* scored a fatal hit to the bombers wing root. The stricken *Condor's* starboard wing simply fell off in a fiery blaze spinning all the way down to the remorseless sea. The remainder of the *Condor* flipped and pin wheeled itself into the sea, sinking within a minute, without giving any of the crew a chance to parachute or struggle out of their harnesses to reach the surface.

The *King George V* was mortally wounded, but the fates had smiled upon her this morning by sparing the magazines from exploding—although it was a near thing. Only the courageous Herculean efforts by dozens of determined seamen stemmed the fires that raged near the hatches leading into the magazines. This effort was just in time as a not-much higher temperature and the shells and powder bags would begin cooking off. Knowing the ship's turn into the list was the last thing the bridge would consider, a plucky, fast-thinking Canadian-born lieutenant directing the aft guns raced forward to appraise the situation. Within seconds, he determined that the bridge had been wiped out but was grateful that he did not have to contend with a fire. William Hay plunged into the shattered bridge, snatched the dangling intercom that was bouncing errantly on the deck, calling steering amidships to straighten them out—immediately. Through the star-crazed windshields, he realized the imminent danger the turn was creating to both his ship and the *Berwick*, now perilously close on the port side. The *Berwick* began to turn when she realized the possible impending collision would certainly occur if she did not maneuver out of harm's way and damnable fast.

What seemed a very sluggish starboard turn to those who could witness it, was in fact a desperate measure by the chief engineer who pushed the two port screws past their maximum, while simultaneously reversing the starboard pair. The ponderous 42,200 ton battleship shuddering under the strain of reversed power actually regained her proper course quite rapidly, avoiding a rather nasty collision. At the closest point, the two ships had come within forty feet of each other, close enough to hear the shouts and bedlam from each other rather clearly.

The flanking *Condors* had missed with fifteen of their total compliment of sixteen bombs blessedly leaving the *Berwick* unscathed. Launching their bombs at the beams of the two cruisers from four thousand feet was a mistake that wouldn't be made again. The target area was much narrower but longer, even though moving perpendicular to the falling bombs. Two of the 500 pound bombs straddled the aft deck of the *Berwick*, which was as close as any got. The rest simply fell behind the cruiser and vanished with tiny splashes. Relieved of their offensive destruction, the remaining *Condors* turned lazily eastward and headed for France with saddened hearts at the loss of their friends.

Badly mauled, communications reduced to signal lamps only, but still afloat, the *King George V* was soon encased by the floating walls of steel of her flock—the two cruisers and five destroyers in a classic defensive position. The escorts had signaled that they were returning to their original course that would join them up with *Rodney* and *Duke of York* within the hour. When they were within signal range, command of the battle group would be transferred to *Duke of York* if the Admiralty concurred. Communications with London had been sporadic during the attack by the *Condors*—everyone's time being desperately occupied staving off the big black birds. After being assured by the lookouts and radar that the *Condors* were a nasty thing of the recent past, Captain Soames sat glumly in his captain's chair aboard the *Berwick* solemnly, slowly dictating the grim news of his battle group's casualties and the grievous damage sustained by *King George V*. The bridge was as quiet as a tomb with no one even breathing hard, fearful of shattering the brittle atmosphere of dismay. Captain Soames ended the rather bleak message stating that he would make another report shortly regarding the state of affairs with Battle Group "M" when they met up in twenty minutes or thereabouts, and received firsthand information from the silenced battleship. The junior radio operator, once dismissed, hurried to the radio room to send the dour message, silently hoping that the Admiralty wouldn't keelhaul this messenger if ever they met up with each other.

The battered, bruised, fire-blackened battleship made a slow starboard turn to a heading slightly east of due north as the two battle groups were now close enough to merge. *Duke of York* easily slid alongside *King George V's* port quarter inspecting the damage.

The Admiralty Building
One hour before first light on Rawalpindi

Nearly three weeks after the audacious plan to corner and dispose of the *Scharnhorst* and/or *Gneisenau* had been formulated, the architects of the highly dangerous plan were once more assembling in the old conference room. Dawn had come to London over an hour ago with a soft cool light streaming through the old windows. High wispy, cirrus clouds had slightly dampened the normally stark early spring sunlight. A light fog had settled in the garden below masking most of the denuded shorter bushes and trees. With no wind, the traffic noises all but non-existent, the atmosphere should have been one of peaceful tranquility. However, that was not to be the mood in the conference room this morning.

First Lord of the Admiralty Ian McLeod stood motionless with his hands clasped lightly behind his back, staring into the nothingness of the garden below. No one had the slightest inclination to disturb his solemn reverie. They rather all simply took on an air of disinterested indifference. First Sea Lord Robert Stark tried his best to desist from fidgeting, but it was a losing battle to which he succumbed after ten minutes of excruciating nervous restraint.

"Where the blazes is Dowding? It was his bloody plan so he should at least be courteous enough to show up on time."

The pent-up emotions of the past few weeks waiting for this morning were so high that his simple question and statement came out more like a squawk from a rooster. The deathly silence snapped like a brittle twig.

McLeod slowly wheeled about-face, straightened his jacket, and then very softly replied.

"Oh, do be quiet Robert. Maybe the Air Marshal had some last minute desperate emergency to attend to that would affect this morning, or maybe he simply had to make a trip to the loo."

The quietly delivered levity broke the crackling atmosphere as the cabinet minister hoped it would. The impeccably proper manners of the assembled high command, all in the blink of an eye, roared with laughter at the thought of the dapper Air Marshal reduced to such a simple human function. The laughter continued for a short while with no one wanting to break off and return to the soul-sucking silence of the previous few minutes. The large door to the conference room opened. The ever stone-faced Air Marshal strode in with his head held high. The laughter stopped as if it had been smitten by an axe. Dowding glanced around at each man and chose not to enquire into the nature of the joviality.

"Gentlemen, I apologize for being a trifle late. I personally do not think that there is ever a good reason for tardiness. All I have ever heard are rather lame excuses. However, be that as it may, my reason is a rather valid one if you will."

Sensing the import of the moment, the ever-sensitive politician Ian McLeod plunged into the minute gap left when Dowding took a breath, "Gentlemen, before the Air Marshal tells us his reason, which I know damn well will be more than enough justification for our forgiveness, let us make ourselves comfortable. It will still be nigh onto an hour before dawn appears on the *Rawalpindi* and the action begins. Please seat yourselves while I step outside and tell the steward to bring us morning refreshments."

The minister snappily strode down the length of the room and exited. Everyone quickly chose the chair they had occupied at the previous meeting, seated themselves and turned their heads towards Dowding. Their anxiety was palpable. Curiosity is no stranger to high-ranking military officials; consequently, they were almost physically itching to know what could be of such importance to delay a man, who was considered by his peers, to have never been late for any meeting in his entire life.

Dowding passively gazed at the portrait of Nelson with an air of studied insouciance. Ever the first to plunge into any situation without correct political respect or forethought, the First Sea Lord Robert Stark loudly demanded, "Dowding, for God's sake tell us what's happening! The next hour or so will be hellish enough waiting without *something* to bash about."

Dowding impassively, slowly looked at Stark.

"My dear First Sea Lord, what I have to tell you, all of you, is of utmost importance. However, I do require the presence of the Minister before I begin. Furthermore, some light refreshments should make the news more palatable."

Before Stark could unleash a trademark tirade, the main door opened and two stewards followed by the impassive First Lord of the Admiralty silently entered. With a practiced flair, the stewards eased two rather large silver platters onto the sideboards and began distributing their goods. The goods were classic English breakfast fare. Admiralty design bone china cups of ubiquitous Earl Gray black tea, no doubt from the famous purveyor Twining & Co. was served accompanied with silver containers of sugar and milk, piping hot crumpets, toast, Wilkin's & Sons orange marmalade, lemon curd and jams. The last two silver platters placed on the grand old table were heaped with a cornucopia of delightful Walker's shortbreads.

Total silence reigned until the stewards left, gently closing the heavy door. No one paid the slightest attention to Stark who was beside himself, preparing to launch his invective before he had an apoplectic fit. Sensing that he just might be ridiculed or dressed down, he quickly regained some semblance of composure and quietly prepared his own tea and crumpet. When each man had settled back in his own chair, munching a crumpet and sipping tea, Dowding stood, wiped the fleck of raspberry jam from the corner of his mouth and began, "Gentlemen, as I was walking out the front door of my offices, my aide rushed up, damn near breathless, and handed me a decoded dispatch. Knowing I had a minute or so to read it before trundling over here, I did so. The news was, shall we say, grimly interesting. Hold your tongue Stark; I'm getting to it in a moment. As I was saying, the news was interesting and I trust you will agree with me, most distressing. Early this morning one of our *Sunderland* flying boats nipped through a hole in the rather dense fog that has plagued us for the past several days. The *Sunderland* was on *Bismarck* watch over Norway. Gentlemen, the *Bismarck* is gone.

"As of right now, we do not know when she sailed or where. I took a moment of *our* time to dispatch every available reconnaissance aircraft that was available to conduct a thorough search of the North and Norwegian seas. Fortunately, the air between the Faeroes and Iceland has been unusually clear for over a week allowing our air patrols to assure me that she has not slipped out into the Atlantic via this route recently. The bad news is our patrols out of Iceland have been grounded due to very nasty weather in the Denmark Strait. Assuming the very worst, she has now escaped into the North Atlantic and will commence raiding our merchant convoys shortly. If we're rather lucky, she has not been gone too long, allowing us to locate her before she is out of sight of our air patrols. To conclude my dispiriting news, we have every reason to believe she is escorted by the heavy cruiser *Prinz Eugen* and possibly the "pocket" battleship *Deutschland*. If true, this would be a small but quite serious battle group to deal with. I have instructed my staff to dash over here immediately if there is any more news regarding this issue."

To say the audience was stunned would have been classic British understatement in the extreme. Catatonic paralysis would have been a closer description to the frozen posture of the assembled top brass. After a graveyard silence for but a brief moment, all heads swiveled towards Stark, knowing full well he would burst forth first. Nor were they completely disappointed. This time however, even the perennial, vociferous First Sea Lord was so shaken, he started his diatribe barely above a whisper, but loud enough for everyone to hear clearly in the mausoleum quiet room, "God, help us. In our plan to rid the seas of the two smaller battleships, we've left the gate open and the real monster is loose, probably with a gargoyle or two along."

No one had anything to say—the tremendous shocking news had temporarily paralyzed them. One does not get to be the First Sea Lord through timidity or lack of objectivity. So, shaking off the news as simply fact, daunting as it was, Robert Stark took the lead to address the situation as succinctly as he could. The stunned cabinet minister along with the equally numbed others watched and listened as the First Sea Lord resumed, this time with a stronger timbre to a slightly faltering voice. It was appallingly apparent that this paragon of the Royal Navy was fighting an internal battle akin to physical torture.

"Esteemed colleagues, let me summarize the situation as it stands right now. For the sake of whipping up a decent plan of action, we must look at the worst-case scenario. Naturally that would be that *Bismarck*, along with her nasty escorts, has made it into the North Atlantic undetected and is no doubt steaming into our convoy routes. Our previous plan to rid the Atlantic of at least one of the *Ugly Sisters* is but an hour hence. It is my intention to let the converging battle groups deal with the battleship that has been shadowing *Rawalpindi* all night here within the hour. Here are the current positions of the groups. Battle group 'A' will still be nearly one hundred sea miles from *Rawalpindi* at first light, however our carrier *Ark Royal* will by now have launched a couple of dozen aircraft equipped with torpedoes and should show up on the scene approximately in the correct time frame. *Hood, Repulse* and the destroyers will plow onward into the area where our wily enemy should be.

"In addition, the *Ark Royal* has launched eight reconnaissance planes to look for the other battleship, which very well could be steaming to meet up with our intended target. We must remember that all of the intelligence so far on these two pesky predators is that they are the *Ugly Sisters* and as such are rarely separated. It is the Royal Navy's fervent hope that we can get both of them this morning. If we are fortunate enough to spot the other sister, Battle group 'A' will split off from its intended course and go after her at best possible speed. Battle Group 'B' is still a ways off but in a right ducky position to change course and go after *Bismarck*. We could also redirect Battle Group 'H' which has been coming on strong from just east of Newfoundland.

"But I get ahead of myself. This group is part of the backstop to head off the battleship if she disengages us and then skedaddles to the west. Battle Group "C" is now just over the northern horizon from *Rawalpindi*, ideally situated to pounce on the German at first light in less than an hour out there. Battle Group 'M' is also coming up on the *Rawalpindi's* position from the south-west. The only discouraging news about our encircling trap is that *Prince of Wales* has had some mechanical trouble. She is consequently hove to near the Azores effecting repairs. The remainder of her group 'G', minus three watchdog destroyers, is closing the backdoor to *Rawalpindi's* south. That, gentlemen is the status of the Royal Navy as of a few minutes ago. The German will not slither though this trap. We will be done with him and then possibly take on the *Bismarck*. Now, I surrender the floor for questions or comments."

"Thank you for an excellent update on the situation and especially for bringing us back to the business at hand. I fear that the bulk of us, including myself were rendered speechless with the *Bismarck* news, subsequently losing sight of what we know for sure is about to happen with our sacrificial goat, the *Rawalpindi*; who I might remind everyone is still afloat," The First Lord of the Admiralty stated without much enthusiasm.

Always the one to loosen up these staid somber meetings with a touch of levity, Rear Admiral Max Horton interjected a light comment that smashed the tension that was crackling throughout the room.

"My dear Minister, you most assuredly did appraise our silence quite correctly. I was definitely in a stunned stupor with the *Bismarck* news. However, it simply goes beyond human comprehension that you yourself could ever be rendered speechless."

When the laughter subsided, a slightly crimson-faced First Lord of the Admiralty parried the harmless trust with a rejoinder of his own.

"My dear Admiral Horton, you are most assuredly correct regarding my legendary oratory talent. I stand corrected. I am never at a loss for words. I rarely miss even the slightest notch in conversations to expound my fathomless knowledge. Alternatively, as you military types might rephrase it to say; boring drivel, fit only for early morning University classes where nodding off is the preferred option."

The harmless barbs expended, the pastries reduced to crumbs, Stark rapped the table with his knuckles bringing everyone back to the grim realities.

"Air Marshal Dowding, you've not uttered a chicken's chirp all morning since your bombshell. What have you got say? We wholeheartedly endorsed this plan and shortly will see its virtually inevitable conclusion. I need your thoughts regarding the big fish, *Bismarck*."

Slowly getting to his feet, Hugh Dowding strolled over to the large map. He picked up the slightly curved pointer and grasped it tightly with both hands, one at each end. After clearing his throat rather noisily, he solemnly began, "Gentlemen, for the past few hours I have eschewed the *Rawalpindi's* status. The plan we developed was a sound one. Lure the predator with the prospect of easy prey into an area of our choosing and then bludgeon him with massively superior firepower. But, and this is a very big but, he's not quite played by the rules we laid out for him. Inconsiderate bastard!"

At that uncharacteristic remark, the small crowd of wise military leaders could not suppress a slight chuckle. Attempting to retain the atmosphere of high hopes, the consummate politician chimed in with his own slightly cryptic remark, "Well now, I shall agree with our sage Air Marshal in that this particular German does not seem to follow anyone's guidelines—even Hitler's. Nevertheless, I might also throw in the antique adage that all military leaders have spouted for several centuries now. The rules and plans of warfare become null and void once the battle is joined."

After a brief round of slightly louder laughter the Air Marshal continued, "Well taken First Lord. Nevertheless, I need to point out to you that the old military adage we have worked with for untold centuries did not have your polite politician's turn of a phase."

Again, there was a ripple of laughter that Air Marshal Hugh Dowding stilled instantly with a quick about face—slapping the pointer rather loudly on the large map of the North Atlantic.

"Gentlemen, in a short while we will know for certain if the German has played into our hands. If he has, then we can all wait here for the results of the battle to come in. However, I would like to take some of your valuable time to consider what the options available to us are should we not be able to rid ourselves of at least this one big nightmare to our shipping. What if the battle turns poorly for us and the German escapes? Then there are two options. One is that he is badly damaged and must return to France for repairs and the other, Heaven forbid, he escapes unscathed. Now, let us hear from the fidgety First Sea Lord what his proposals would be given the last two outcomes."

First Sea Lord Robert Stark had been squirming in his seat as if he had a mound of angry ants in his pants. With the desperately overdue call to speak, the First Sea Lord bounced out of his seat and almost ran to the map, snatching up the pointer with a potent grip. Now on station, he visibly relaxed after taking a slow deep breath. Then astoundingly, he opened his remarks in a barely audible voice.

"Esteemed colleagues, if, and I may say it is a very highly improbable if, we do not carry the day, then none of the options ventured by the venerable Air Marshal are palatable. I have every confidence that the Royal Navy will prevail and we will have one less king-sized monster to keep us awake at nights. Nonetheless, I have been asked to venture forth my opinions on a reversal of fortunes. If the German is wounded requiring he return to France, then we will have temporarily removed him from the scene. When he is affecting repairs in Brest, we can let the Air Marshal send over some of his vaunted bombers with ship-killers and then we will be rid of him. If we fail to injure him, then ……."

Stark froze in med sentence staring at the entrance door that had very silently opened. The movement had been so discreet that none of the other high-ranking officers had noticed. They implicitly knew that the sanctity of this room had never, nor would ever be broken without at least a warning knock. Now all heads turned to the open door, which now framed the unmistakable figure of none other than Winston Churchill himself. No one spoke. The seasoned politician smiled at the effect he had on these men, and then strolled into the room trailing a slight cloud of blue cigar smoke. Churchill calmly seated himself at the end of the table, motioning for Stark to continue.

"Prime Minister, you grace us with your presence with fortuitous timing. Soon we shall receive reports from our ships of the demise of *Scharnhorst*."

"Robert, I had been listening for a brief moment before joining my most senior officers. I did hear that there seems to be some possible doubt about the outcome of the forthcoming battle. Moreover, my arrival here is not fortuitous at all. I deliberately rose early to be with you men for a fine celebration that will conclude your ingenious plan for the destruction of an enemy battleship. Please continue with your opinion, let not my presence concern you in the least."

His brief speech finished, the Prime Minister settled back in a chair, puffed his cigar back into life and waited. Although Robert Stark had the reputation of always being the one in charge, the formidable presence of his predecessor, now with the heavy robes of Prime Minister on his shoulders, visibly upset the First Sea Lord, and left him mute for a mite too long. Then shaking off the temporary paralysis, Stark picked up where he had left off.

"As I was about to say when the Prime Minister suddenly appeared— if the German escapes unscathed to continue his predatory ways then we shall simply, doggedly pursue him until we can be done with him once and for all. After that is accomplished, we shall then hunt down and destroy the other *Sister*. That gentlemen, is really all I have to say, as I'm sure several of you will be relieved to know. As the hour of battle nears, I shall quietly await the first reports."

No one seemed the least bit inclined to either comment or add to Stark's succinct summary. Then the ingrained political necessity to spout off about damn near anything seized the First Lord of the Admiralty, Ian McLean, who slowly stood, then walked over to the large map. Picking up the pointer, but letting it rest at his side, he began rather solemnly.

"Thank you First Sea Lord for a neat and concise opinion. I also want to express my pleasure at having the Prime Minister take time from his demanding schedule to be with us at what I am positive will be a joyous occasion when the German is dispensed with. However, until we hear reports from the North Atlantic, I would like to add my non-professional's opinion regarding the worst-case scenario as stated by the First Sea Lord. If *Scharnhorst*, by some bloody miracle, slips from our net, she has but a very few options as to where to head as she is attempting to evade our Navy. Now, would someone please come up here and show us the most likely options the German has to slip out of the net."

Oddly enough, the ebullient First Sea Lord, who normally would have leaped at this invitation, remained quiescent but alert in his chair. Field Marshal Montgomery took up the challenge. As he passed the military man, McLeod ceremoniously handed the pointer to the top officer in the British Army. The rather diminutive Montgomery was noticeably bow-legged which affected his walking style. Unlike his peers in high military office, whose posture was unwavering ramrod straight and true, Montgomery rather lopped forward swaying equally side to side like a coordinated drunkard. No one ever dared comment about his rather unorthodox mode of locomotion knowing full well his tinder-dry explosive temper. Ignoring the pointer, Montgomery pointed rather loosely to the area of the impending sea battle at the same time launching into his trademark friendly lecturing style.

"Right! Now laddies, as we know this frustratingly clever German must constantly be on his guard because he should have suspected we will probably be just over his horizon or damnable close by. I have firsthand experience with this new breed of German officers, namely General Erwin Rommel.

"This relatively new Nazi General showed up a couple of months ago and took over the Africa Korp. We had put the Axis armies on the run and were confident that we could rid North Africa of them rather quickly. Then suddenly, Rommel goes on the offensive and it is now we who are on the defensive. This German sea captain operates in much the same manner as Rommel, much to my dismay and the detriment of our Expeditionary Force in North Africa. My troops have even given Rommel the sobriquet of Desert Fox. It seems to me that we are now dealing a very similar mindset with this—shall we call him the 'Sea Fox.'"

Churchill leaned forward in his chair, unmistakably ready to interject his read on the subject. Montgomery, ever alert to his Supreme

Commander's mannerisms, bowed slightly thus relinquishing the floor, and seated himself. Churchill stood, paused a moment, then began.

"My dear 'Monty', I am suitably impressed with your use of the rather obscure word for the simple nickname Desert Fox. I shall add my approval of your character read on the German captain, whose name if I recall correctly is Peter Kastanien. From all that I have read about this adversary and studying this unfolding drama, I must whole-heartedly agree that we are indeed dealing with a clever individual who blatantly refuses to play by our rules. I most fervently desire that the battle trap will proceed as we have planned, however, I for one wish to hear your solution if, Heaven forbid, this 'Sea Fox' slips away from our hounds. Please continue."

The Prime Minister reseated himself, a pleased look on his face.

"Right! Assuming Kastanien breaks free from the pack, he has really only one option—that is to head for Brest in France with its attendant air cover. Hugh, can you send a few *Sunderland's* with bloody big bombs in his path to polish him off?"

"If *Scharnhorst* escapes our clutches and heads eastward, I will send three squadrons of *Sunderlands*, currently based at Plymouth. They will carry our newest ship-buster bombs weighing in at 700 pounds each. Even one decent hit from these gargantuan shells will either sink him or at least cripple him sufficiently enough that he is forced to slow down, allowing your boys to catch him before he can scurry back into his foxhole."

"Very good, thank you Air Marshal. I hope it doesn't come to that but at least we have a contingency plan of action. Now, although it is highly unlikely that he could slip through in some other direction, what can be done about it? First Sea Lord Stark, please elucidate your plan of action if the German heads where he shouldn't—according to our plan of battle."

Stark, who had been quite calm until now burst out of his seat ablaze with defiance.

"Field Marshal Montgomery, do you really think that he could possibly escape? My God, man, we have bloody near all of our Atlantic fleet converging on him. That is one huge amount of ships coming at him from every angle. I will concede that this so-called Sea Fox is more clever than your average Hun, but the simple fact of the matter is that we simply have him surrounded with so much devastating firepower that he will be forced to deal with us very shortly."

Sensing an impending clash of personalities, Churchill sprang to his feet, commandeering the discussion.

"Enough of this puerile bickering. Please let us be objective about this most serious matter, which must be resolved in the most unlikely event our German nemesis escapes to wreak further havoc. Stark, I believe that you were speaking. Please continue."

Before Churchill could take his seat, there came a rather urgent knocking on the door. Being the closest man standing to the door, Prime Minister Churchill rose and walked quickly the few paces, almost wrenched the door off its hinges; such was his anxiety to receive news about the battle being waged in the North Atlantic. The Staff Sergeant holding the sealed envelope instantly recognized the most recognizable face in all of England, second only to the Kings. Snapping a perfect salute, he handed the envelope to the current warlord of Great Britain. Churchill accepted the envelope, and then stared at the man's nametag for a moment.

"Thank you Staff Sergeant Ames. Do I have to sign your tally sheet for this?"

"Beg your pardon Sir, but I really didn't think it necessary being as you are the top man."

"In that regard you are dead wrong Ames. Never break from standard operating procedures unless absolutely necessary. Good Lord Man, if you were to start skipping with me, you might rapidly progress to skipping a chimneysweep. These types of procedures have been serving us exceptionally well for a very long time. Do not alter them in the slightest. I shall end this lecture by telling you a very short story.

"A few weeks ago, when I was conferring with King George, a messenger arrived with an important document for him. That messenger was correctly polite to the King but he too felt that asking the King himself to bother with such a *meaningless* trivial procedure would embarrass the King as well as himself. How wrong he was. The lecture he got from the King, who as we all know is generally rather mild-mannered, made even myself blanch at its ferocity. Naturally, the Staff Sergeant shrank a few inches regardless of his valiant attempt to stand as rigidly straight as he could. The essential message that the King delivered is the same as I am going to tell you now. Let us suppose a lucky bomb blast kills the recipient, without a record of the delivery there would be much time and energy spent rechecking and reconstructing whatever the message contained to a new owner. I hope you understand that time and energy are two commodities of many of which are in very short supply these days. Now, be on your way and thank you again."

"Yes Sir, Prime Minister. I shan't ever forget. Thank you very much Sir."

Churchill smiled a knowing smile to himself, after the Staff Sergeant flew away down the staircase, turned back to the room quickly reacquiring his famous English bulldog face. Gently closing the door, he slit the wax sealed envelope open with his index finger and removed the single folded sheet. Very slowly, he ambled to the head of the table rapidly reading the type-filled page. First Lord of the Admiralty Ian McLeod moved aside knowing this was a momentous piece of history that the master historian would most definitely read himself. Churchill remained silent for what seemed an eternity. He took several deep breaths, three major puffs of his barely operational cigar before he straightened up from a slightly hunched stance.

"Gentlemen, before I read this combined signal from our battle groups, I must implore you to restrain yourselves from any outbursts until I have finished every last word. If I told you the news was bad—that would be a drastic understatement for which we British are famous. Although it is not what I would call cataclysmic, it definitely fits into the category of a major catastrophe."

Churchill paused speaking and again puffed serious life back into the half-cigar that remained. The muted daylight streaming through the windows penetrated through the smoke exuding a dazzling display of multicolored shafts of light, radiating it seemed from Churchill himself. After a long moment or two, a visibly deflated Prime Minister raised up the sheet of paper like it was a viper, straightened his glasses and began, "It begins with the normal salutations to us and then immediately dives into the situation."

Churchill stopped—letting the offensive paper slip down onto the great table. After a few breaths, with a very tired, slightly trembling voice he announced in a volume so low that some of the men furthest away never heard.

"Ian, would you please read aloud the contents of this missive. To do so again would be much, very much too distressing, even for me."

"Most certainly Winston. Seat yourself while the rest of us find out the nature of this grim news."

First Lord of the Admiralty Ian McLeod rose, delicately recovered the offending paper, raised it to reading height and began. He got about as far as the Prime Minister had before slouching back into his chair—catatonic with obvious dismay. The silence was so thick; one could almost hear the minute dust particles crashing thunderously onto the great conference table. Finally, the military dispelled the crushing silence in the human form of a stern-faced Robert Stark, First Sea Lord of the British Navy. Stark grasped the odious paper from the trembling hand of Ian McLeod and without even a downward glance at the body of the offending missive, gave voice to the words that had paralyzed the politicians.

Stark had not risen to the pinnacle of the British Navy by being a political toady or wimp. He had served on many ships, with distinction on all of them. He knew war at sea firsthand. He also knew that reversals of fortunes were to be dealt with decisively. However, even this paragon of fortitude blanched halfway through the longish message. Stark stopped speaking, sat down rather heavily, bowed his head resting it in his hand. His eyes were covered so no one could see the unashamed tears that began to streak down his face. The man, whom many thought had battleship-gray blood, cried from his heart for a long moment. Shaking off the black blanket of defeat that had all but encompassed him for a short span of time, Stark resumed the narration. The rest of the men had sat stoically through the three aborted readings without uttering a word; such was their shock.

Stark finished the message with a stronger timbre to his voice that belied his inner turmoil. He knew that it would now be up to him, probably alone, to make the necessary decisions that could alter Britain's position of world power if he were wrong. Stark knew in the deepest recess of his soul that he would rise to the challenge—since there was no other acceptable option. He looked over to the portrait of Nelson and took heart. He might not be on the high seas crushing the French, but like Nelson, he believed that when in command, command. Stark intended to do just that, command. He would get rid the German surface ships, clearing the sea-lanes for the beleaguered convoys.

Scharnhorst

Scharnhorst was majestically steaming southward several hundred kilometers from where the Royal Navy had converged to deliver their deathblows to her. Dawn had finally, fitfully, scrabbled itself to a puny semblance of life despite a heavy sea-fog which prudence demanded even the gigantic battleship to slow. The ship was lit up resembling an Oktoberfest celebration. Dawn was more imagined than real. The plethora of lookouts could barely see the foredeck from their perches, such was the thickness of the fog that enshrouded the *Scharnhorst* in an ethereal swirling cocoon. *Scharnhorst* crept forward at eight knots—enough to maintain decent steerageway but slow enough to prevent serious damage in the unlikely event of a collision.

Captain Kastanien had stood motionless, leaning on the bridge shelf without speaking for the past forty-five minutes staring at the dark gray shroud. No sea captain can rest easy when blinded by fog. Kastanien was no exception. His unseen inner agitation chewed away at his innards like a feasting leopard. Suddenly the tension that gripped all the bridge was snapped when Attila gracefully sailed up to his red blanket. The ship's hero/mascot parked his hind haunches dead center on his special blanket, before proceeding to meticulously wash his face.

"Well now, my fine feline friend, it seems like you've had a fine breakfast courtesy no doubt of our Chief Cook Manfried. Judging by your ever-fit form with its magnificent, lustrous coat, I would be not be the least bit surprised that cook fed you better than the captain and officers."

Attila paused cleaning for a brief moment and looked Kastanien directly in the eyes. As only a cat can do, Attila silently conveyed confirmation of his friend's observation. Several close-by officers who had witnessed the exchange silently smiled to each other. They knew who really ran things throughout the ship. Peter Kastanien began stroking his friend rather delicately—so as not to disturb the mandatory cleanup. After a brief moment or two, Attila finished his grooming and then turned to face directly out the bridge glass at the gray miasma. Hind legs slightly askance to steady against the slight roll of *his* ship in the rolling sea, Attila looked identical to the statues prolific in King Tut's tomb. Kastanien, feeling comforted by the cat's presence mounted his captain's chair and once more silence reigned in the command center of the gargantuan battleship. Long moments passed with a deliberate unhurried snail's pace for nearly half an hour without any brightening of the gloom.

Unexpectedly, with an inborn grace, Attila stood bolt upright at full attention. Kastanien who had been daydreaming of home caught the sudden movement with his peripheral vision. Attila's ears were on full alert as was his body language. Attila was staring with his machine-gun eyes slightly to the port side of the great battleship. Split seconds later, Kastanien bolted from his chair sharply issuing an order,

"Full Stop! Tell radar/sonar to be on top alert."

In one seamless motion, he snatched a microphone and yelled into the outside address system.

"Lookouts, especially those of you stationed on the prow, keep a very sharp eye on our port side. There may be something out there."

Instantly, the officers and crew were at full alert—filled with an unknown apprehension. The echoes of the exterior speakers hadn't quite faded when a forward lookout excitedly reported to the bridge.

"Captain, I can hear some unusual wave noises in front of the ship. I cannot determine yet what is causing them, but it must be some large floating object disturbing the sea. Wait, I can see it now. It is just slightly off our port bow about 200 meters in front of us. It appears to be ----, yes, it definitely is the bow section of a ship sticking almost straight up and bouncing around. We might just miss striking it unless it swings our way."

Kastanien reacted with lightning speed, "Full reverse. Sound collision alarm."

In the blink of an eye, the first officer smashed his palm into the big red button of the collision alarm. Instantly the most feared noise on any ship blared into life. There is no more terrifying sound to a sailor than the collision alarm. Whether it is a torpedo, rocks or another ship, sailors universally fear collision. Nothing good can ever come from a collision.

The *Scharnhorst* had already, fortunately, slowed to a mere four knots when the three massive propellers reversed themselves. They gripped the sea with a savage fury, which sent a shudder throughout the entire ship. The proximity to the offending flotsam was too close for the powerful blades to have enough effect to avoid a collision. However, the monstrous battleship was almost stopped when the port side of her bow struck a glancing blow on the prow of the large steel mass floating haphazardly in the middle of the heretofore empty ocean. The collision was mild enough that no one was knocked off his balance even in the slightest. Only a moment passed before the triple screws were taking a very serious bite out of the sea. *Scharnhorst* slowly reversed herself away from what could have been a serious situation. Thirty seconds later, Kastanien knowing his ship had avoided disaster, issued new orders. This time they lacked the strident urgency of his earlier ones.

"One third reverse. Cancel collision alarm. Damage control parties, assess any damage."

Forgotten for the few tension-filled moments now past, Kastanien, along with most of the officers, looked over to the red blanket perch of their savior. Attila had curled up, appearing to be going to sleep. Kastanien walked over to his friend, laying his left hand gently on the cat's shoulders, then spoke quietly, "Attila, we thank you for your warning. You have once again kept us from serious danger. Now, rest up a bit as you digest your breakfast."

Turning to the grinning officers, a likewise grin splitting his face, Kastanien spoke, "Gentlemen, once more we need to pay homage to our smallest crewmember. If not for him, we could easily have suffered some very serious damage banging into the nasty remains of a ship. Let us salute him."

The officers, to a man, snapped off their very best salute, holding it for double the normal time. Just then, the intercom crackled to life.

"Captain, Damage Control Officer Bock reporting. We have suffered no discernible damage. We have checked our watertight integrity and found no breach. There might be some scratches on the hull paint, which we will determine when light permits, however I think that will be the extent of it."

"Thank You Mr. Bock. Have your men say a prayer of thanks to Attila. It was he who gave us the first warning."

The *Scharnhorst* had backed sufficiently away from the offensive floating danger that it was now invisible in the persistent fog. Kastanien issued new orders.

"Dead slow ahead, steer three points to starboard until we can see what we hit."

Scharnhorst slightly shuddered again as the engines reversed themselves into forward motion. Ever so slowly, the upended rusting-prow of a merchant ship materialized from the fog as *Scharnhorst* came abreast of it two hundred meters off her port quarter.

"An old freighter, no doubt but the rest of her lies on the bottom. The bow must have parted company with the main body, allowing the trapped air to keep the prow afloat. Put a few 5.9 inch shells through her letting the air out so she can take her proper place on the bottom. This kind of left-over battle garbage needs not to be left for some other vessel to plow into with results that are more serious. As our English compatriots would say, 'it simply wouldn't be cricket to leave such a nasty hazard out here.'."

With her amidships batteries at full depression, four 5.9 inch shells flew across the short distance. All four high-explosive shells unerringly smashed into the aging iron with dramatic results. The highly-compressed trapped air exploded from the rusted steel with a shrill whistle. Within seconds, the remains of a once-proud merchant ship slid beneath the gentle swells—never again to be a hazard to navigation. Every officer on the bridge and all those in positions to see watched solemnly the final death throes of the ship. Although not quite maudlin, all men of the sea feel sad to see one of their kindred vanish beneath the impersonal surface of the ocean.

The tenacious fog had begun to thin a trifle, so Kastanien ordered a speed of twelve knots to make up for the time they had lost crawling through the ever-dangerous fog. Tension was still heightened on the bridge, knowing that they couldn't possibly have the misfortune to endure a repeat incident, but human nature as it is, harbors nasty thoughts for a time following narrow escapes with disaster. Every few seconds every man on the bridge glanced over at the slumbering cat for any signs of danger. To a man, they all knew it was the cat's incredible hearing that had altered the ship, but also to a man, they partially believed the cat was the small furry embodiment of some mythological deity from antiquity.

Attila, probably aware of the awe in which he was held, simply chose to ignore the unspoken adulation, continuing with the very serious business of sleeping off his excellent breakfast.

Three hours slowly passed before the stubborn fog began to thin much more. As the fog lost its grip on the ocean's surface, the potent rays of a more southerly sun rapidly burned gaping holes that soon joined up to quickly letting a spectacularly azure blue sky provide the *Scharnhorst* with a beautiful serene day. Kastanien rapidly ordered the ship back to a cruising speed of twenty-four knots.

Then he announced, "Gentlemen, I shall retire to my cabin to log this morning's incident. I shall also attempt to take a few moments rest. Although it's needless to say, please inform me if there are any significant occurrences. Attila seems to be enjoying the warm sunshine so I shall leave him to guide you through until I return."

Kastanien quickly exited the bridge, stopping only for a brief word with his radar operator. Soon he was in his cabin. Settling into his chair, he pulled open the right hand middle drawer of his desk, retrieving the two logbooks. With a steady hand he recorded the slight scrape with the dead ship and the obligatory other, rather mundane ships operations throughout the night and morning. Satisfied with what he had written, he closed the ship's main logbook and opened the second one. This logbook belonged to Attila—however the cat was simply terrible about keeping his own adventures recorded, so his friend the captain assumed the secretarial duties of this important crewmember. He wrote in the first person as usual—emphasizing the importance of the early warning given to avoid a nasty collision.

When he was done, he requested the executive officer to join him. Han Schmidt entered the cabin shortly after being summonsed. Kastanien let his executive officer read Attila's log, then the two men signed their names verifying the accuracy of their beloved crewmate's daily activities. That done, the executive officer departed back to the bridge leaving Peter Kastanien to his much-needed rest.

The Admiralty

When Stark finished reading, silence reigned supreme for a brief moment before the indomitable Winston Churchill stood, his expression commanding everyone's immediate attention.

"Well, Gentlemen, let us not cry over the spilt milk any longer. That ingenious German quite skillfully turned the tables on us, leaving us bereft of several important warships. I believe Admiral Stark needs some time alone with his capable staff to formulate a new plan that will let his hounds run this wily Sea Fox down—ridding us of him once and for all. I suggest we adjourn until after lunch. We MUST do something while we still have a very serious presence in that spot of ocean. Return to your offices for a couple of hours, then let us meet back here at one and start over. I also suggest you come up with an answer to a question that really bothers me. How did we have the bugger damn near in our sights and then he mysteriously disappears? Ideas, Gentlemen, we need ideas. Think creatively. We must solve this mystery or suffer more frustration and loss of desperately needed ships. Thirty thousand plus tons of steel simply cannot vanish without a trace. Good day for now."

Winston's "suggestions" were always a politely-put command to be obeyed without question. With only courteous nods, the top military men that commanded the British fighting forces silently filed out of the gloom-shrouded room heading for their offices, which were all quite nearby. A blustery wind lashing large raindrops almost horizontal greeted them on the street. Hunkered down against the nasty weather the men hurried from the minimal protection of the portico into the waiting staff cars that swiftly whisked them away. Only Stark was spared the typical inclement weather that was April in London. His office was located downstairs in the august building where the worlds' most respected Navy had been directed from for nearly a century and a half.

Ensconced in the office that had served countless icons of the Royal Navy, First Sea Lord Robert Stark stalked around the perimeters of this rather spacious room like a caged leopard. Like the rest of the venerable Admiralty building, the décor was definitely from the last century with the exception of the myriad of stunning oil paintings. The paintings had been commissioned for decades to a premier naval art firm located in Portsmouth. The consistency was almost uncanny considering the nearly four dozen pieces of art covered a time span of over one hundred and fifty years. The centerpiece of this awesome collection was naturally Nelson's flagship *Victory* at Trafalgar. The most recent, only three weeks old, was the *Prince of Wales*, sparkling as a precious jewel bathed in the warmth of a spectacular sunset. With his hands clasped behind his back for nearly thirty minutes, the First Sea Lord spoke softly to the paintings as he eschewed the recent unpleasant events.

Stark was not a man who dwelled on things gone by which were irreversible, but there was still nagging questions rattling around in his brain, desperately groping for answers as to why their plan had gone so awry. His thoughts always ran to solutions.

"The loss of so much naval power is bad enough, but not critical since much of it is merely a setback before our ships are repaired and once again guarding the oceans at near full strength. Worse than the losses will be the disparaging effect on moral, which is in a desperately dire need of a boost. The military arms of England will of course know damn near immediately, then inevitably the entire population of Great Britain and the rest of the world. Of this there is no doubt whatsoever. It will be the headliner on tonight's broadcast from Berlin by that bombastic buffoon Lord Haw-Haw. He will no doubt extol the battle savvy of the German Navy and denigrate the obvious ineptness of the grandiose Royal Navy. Be that as it may, we will endure this firestorm of propaganda until we have a magnificent victory of our own. Of THAT, I am sure. It now occurs to me how the Germans knew our exact strategy. It was foolish not to institute radio silence much earlier. We, no I, should have deduced that those clever bastards could easily triangulate our positions given that Scharnhorst *and*

Gneisenau *were quite far apart and could easily have done so .However,* Scharnhorst's *last radio transmission was nearly nine hours prior and* Gneisenau *over twelve. One must presume the German High Command assumed, rightly so, that we would doggedly pursue our strategy. The only conclusion I can come up with for Winston is that* Scharnhorst *was just plain lucky in choosing her exit direction after they gave up the stern chase of* Rawalpindi.

"*Next questions. Why did they not sink her at night? Moreover, why give up the chase when* Rawalpindi *was such an easy victim? The bloody Luftwaffe damn sure knew where we were.*

Enough of this self-flagellating abuse! It serves no useful purpose. Now we must utilize whatever knowledge we have and use it to thin the numbers of the German Navy. Could the Germans have developed some sort of radar-jamming device that fooled our lads into thinking that the Scharnhorst *was behind them, when in fact she may have departed much sooner? Now that makes a bit more sense.* Scharnhorst *was no doubt warned by Berlin of the air attack and was ordered to steam out of harm's way. That being the case, we must redouble our intelligence gathering to discover the radar-fooling system they may have cooked up. If they have that confusing capacity coupled with their accursed heretofore-unbreakable Enigma code system, we shall continue to be seriously handicapped in our efforts to maintain dominance of the North Atlantic. Now then, what is to be done to salvage this bad state of affairs?*"

Stark stopped pacing, discontinued his one-sided silent conversation, paused for a brief moment, then purposefully strode over to his imposing desk and seated himself solidly. He lifted the phone and barked into it, "Get me the communications officer, IMMEDIATELY!"

Less than seven seconds later, the slightly terrified officer in charge of naval communications was on the line.

"Send this communiqué immediately, if not sooner. TO: Ark Royal. FROM: First Sea Lord. Launch all aircraft to conduct search pattern for *Scharnhorst* and/or *Gneisenau*. Concentrate your search to the south and east of your current position. Break radio silence if necessary. I'm quite certain that the Germans already know where you are and even if they don't, it doesn't matter since I'm positive they will not come calling today. Nonetheless, keep a sharp lookout for them AND maintain high alert for roving U-boats. Stark out."

Stark replaced the phone none too gently, then immediately snatched it up again. This time the recipient of his lash was the naval intelligence office located only three doors down the hall from his office.

"Bring me the latest information on the disposition of *Bismarck, Tirpitz, Deutschland, Graf Spee, Scheer, Prinz Eugen, Hipper* and *Blücher.* Bloody Hell, I might as well have the information on all their light cruisers as well. I also need all information regarding any sinking's by U-boats, surface raiders and any reported sightings within the past twelve hours. That is all. Make it fast."

Knowing the irascible, explosive temperament of their leader, the naval intelligence office was always ready at the drop of a hat with the most up-to-date intelligence regarding enemy vessels. Consequently, within two minutes, a messenger knocked firmly on the stout oak door. As per many previous orders, the messenger did not wait for a reply; he simply entered, walked seven paces to Admiral Stark's desk and deposited the single sheet of close-typed information on the spotless desk. Stark merely nodded, waved the messenger away and savagely snatched the sheet up. He read it but once. A slight look of dread flitted across his face for a moment before he stood and resumed pacing around the room.

This time he more resembled a stampeding rhinoceros, such was his churning turbulence. The news was not good to say the least. In less than two hours, he would have to drop this bomb on his colleagues, including the Prime Minister. That he most assuredly dreaded. He fervently hoped that he could keep a tight rein on his emotions and temper. Without warning, the words, oft repeated, of his wife sprang into his mind.

"Darling, when you have the most serious business to discuss, please do yourself a huge favor. Put some sustenance in your stomach. Don't eat so much to make you drowsy, just enough to keep your brain in top running condition."

Stark outwardly and inwardly had to smile at this errant thought. Since he really had done all he could for now, he might as well make a trip down into the basement cafeteria to fortify himself with some hopefully still-fresh crumpets and some of the excellent tea that they still had. As he progressed down the stairs, his mind, for once, was clear of the dreadful situation out in the Atlantic. His mind was transmitting delightful taste messages throughout his entire being. Crumpets, dripping with melting butter, and smothered with his favorite Seville orange marmalade simply overrode any thoughts of the sea war. He was blessed with nearly half an hour of this bliss before the reality of life outside the cozy cafeteria intruded, sending him back to his office.

Admiralty Conference Room
One O'clock.

Stark strode into the somnolent room with an air of confidence that he most assuredly did not feel. His effected optimism was wasted as the room was still bereft of any live human presence. Stark thought it rather odd no one had yet shown up at the appointed time but rather than fret about it, he simply took a chair and waited. He had barely time for a mental review of his forthcoming solution before the door burst open letting the missing members pour in—most dripping water courtesy of the continuing downpour outside. The two ever-present stewards scuttled in behind the military High Command, relieving them of their outer raincoats before they drenched the stalwart chairs and conference table. A third steward magically appeared mopping up the blizzard of puddles before they had a chance to do any serious damage to the ancient oak flooring.

Less than a minute had passed before the stewards exited; satisfied that the brusque mannerisms of England's High Command had not caused any serious damage to their cherished conference room. The door closed with nearly an inaudible snick. Stark seized the moment to maintain control, as he knew this gathering could easily turn into a gentleman's donnybrook. He would not be disappointed.

"I do hope that you fine fellows enjoyed your respite with a bite of lunch. Pity you couldn't get back here in time. You should be mighty grateful that Winston is delayed for some obtuse reason; otherwise, he would probably flay the skin off your backsides for tardiness. You know how he is."

None of the slightly chagrined men were of a humor to tolerate Starks' miserable sarcasm, mainly because to a man they also had railed at unpunctual subordinates on many an occasion. Sensing a bout of verbal bashing about to break out, the First Lord of the Admiralty, Ian McLeod slapped his hand noisily on the table, instantly stifling any further conversation.

"Enough bickering, remember who the bloody enemy really is. If we descend into childish, antagonistic prattle, we will only increase our chances of losing this war. Now, Stark, for your enlightenment, we were all there assembling in the entryway off the side portico with time to spare when a minor army of fuddle-brained dissidents stormed us as we exited our autos. I suppose it was some sort of grog-rationing protest. The Bobbies on guard literally slammed us into the corner in case any of them had a weapon. It took a bit of time to rid the premises of them before they would let us go. Oddly enough, none of us became indignant with the rather rough handling to which we were subjected. The point being is that we all respected the quick, decisive actions taken by London's finest. Gentlemen, we're all on the same team. Now, let us get down to solving our dreadful dilemma. Admiral Stark, please be so kind as to begin. The rest of you keep your flapping gums together until asked to render your opinions, and more importantly, your solutions."

"Thank you Minister. I apologize for my ill-conceived sarcastic remarks. It's a rather bad habit of mine to spout off without thinking first. Again, my apologies. Now, let us get to the real business of salvaging this rotten state of affairs. We need to be getting on with gaining the upper hand over the Germans. The *disappearing* battleship still has me stumped; however, please allow me to summarize what we know for sure to this point. One, *Scharnhorst* was last physically seen by real human eyes from the *Rawalpindi* early last night when she made a rather feeble attack on *Rawalpindi* heading south at speed from a distance of about two miles. She fired a few 5.9-inch shells at us without any serious damage, except for more damage to *Rawalpindi's* guns—which made her virtually toothless. Even though the *Rawalpindi* was mostly blinded by star shells, the eyes on the bridge shaded from the illumination by binoculars actually did see *Scharnhorst* quite distinctly. *Scharnhorst* continued to run south until she was about five to seven miles behind *Rawalpindi* when she lit up her night running lights. Up to that point, she had made the run with no lights whatsoever. She continued south for a few more miles and then slowed and made a very, very wide turnabout, dropping in behind *Rawalpindi* at a range of fifteen or sixteen miles. Right at the maximum range for our lookouts to barely able to discern her. She held station for about thirty minutes before shutting down all her lights.

"Rather odd behavior I thought. However, her 'signature' as those radar types like to call the bouncing blips, remained constant throughout the night until just before first light when radar said she just slowly faded away. I have had detailed information about this 'fading' forwarded to me and it is mysterious to say the least. *Scharnhorst's* signature did not change course, did not speed up or drop back. She simply faded off the screen as though she had gone down. Don't we wish that were the case? What I have concluded is that more than ten hours elapsed before our fleet could physically see her and that we only had radar to tell us *Scharnhorst* was there shadowing *Rawalpindi*. In that critical ten hours, somehow the *Scharnhorst* slipped away leaving an electronic signature on the radar.

The Fairey Swordfish torpedo bombers from our carrier *Ark Royal* that were sent out just prior to first light to attack *Scharnhorst* were instructed to simply range as far as their fuel would permit to search for her after she had vanished. They completely covered an area much further than *Scharnhorst* could possibly have steamed in the time she dropped from our radar sight. However, if she headed away, most probably to the east with air protection from France, when she doused her lights last night she could now be bloody near anywhere within a three hundred and fifty mile radius given she was traveling at twenty-five knots or thereabouts. My conclusion is that the Germans have concocted a method of tricking our radar system. I, for one, do not think she scuttled herself which is the only other plausible option."

Stark paused for a brief sip of water from his truly exquisite goblet. The stewards had thoughtfully provided every member of this select group with matching goblets with three full pitchers of water to slake their thirsts during the preordained strain on their vocal workings. Stark then held the goblet at half an arm's length admiring it, "I don't believe I am familiar with this replacement crystal. When did this arrive?"

The question had barely been asked when the door literally flew open to admit Winston Churchill with Ian McLeod in tow.

"The crystal glassware you are quaffing your thirst with arrived just yesterday forenoon. It comes courtesy of the Nazeing Glass Works. They have only been in business here in London since 1928 but their heritage stretches back to 1610 in Vauxhall. The company has delivered simply outstanding design and quality for this past decade to those who can afford it. Buckingham Palace, Windsor Castle, Balmoral Castle, 10 Downing Street et al. They have all received complete sets of their wares over the past few weeks. In exchange for the coveted Royal recognition, the company has agreed, temporarily, to suspend manufacture of such superfluous luxury items. They will turn their manufacturing resources, which includes many considerable talents, into manufacturing delicate instrumentation for our military. We promised them full Royal support, as well as political, when the war is won, allowing them to return to their centuries old love of beautiful leaded-glass crystal ware. Now, Gentlemen please continue with this odious business."

Before Stark could continue, Air Marshal Dowding raised his hand akin to a schoolchild asking to be excused for a quick trip to the loo. Stark, who was just a trifle unsure of how to proceed from where he left off, grinned slyly and with a rather exaggerated flourish, waved a hand for the air marshal to pick up the conversation. Dowding stood, paused only for five or six heartbeats before quietly beginning, "Thank you Robert. Before I expound my theories about the mysterious *vanishing* battleship, let me recap what has transpired to this point so that the Prime Minister and First Lord of the Admiralty are brought up to date. If that's all right with you Admiral?"

"Go ahead Dowding. You no doubt have gone through the same frustrating exercise about this as I have. I'm quite sure you'll get it spot on."

For the next few minutes, the Air Marshal eloquently reiterated essentially all that the first sea lord had stated. When the summation was complete, Hugh Dowding himself took a long drink from his goblet. No one broke the brief silence, not even Winston or the routinely bumptious Ian McLeod.

"Now then." The air marshal resumed, "Given that *Scharnhorst* didn't sink herself willingly, nor donned a cloak of invisibility, I have one other possible theory to explain this disappearance. My question is mainly directed to Admiral Stark—but please let all of you bring forth your opinions. Let us assume that a U-boat stationed itself forward of

Scharnhorst in a direct line with *Rawalpindi* and then drew closer so that her signature on *Rawalpindi's* radar overlapped. My limited knowledge of radar tells me that radar could not separate the two as long as they were in perfect alignment. When this mysterious U-boat drew close enough to *Rawalpindi* her radar signature would override that of *Scharnhorst*. Then *Scharnhorst* could slowly drop back until she was out of radar range before scooting off wherever she damn well pleased. Your comments please gentlemen."

The concept was so intriguing to these very sharp-minded men that a heavy silence reigned supreme for a protracted time. Then, as if on cue, First Sea Lord Robert Stark stood, glanced thoughtfully at Hugh Dowding and began, "Hugh, your concept of the Germans method of deception is very, very interesting. I shall not discount it as impossible but I must point out the limitations of our radar system.

"The Royal Navy has done exhaustive testing with the newest radars we have and found that even a surfaced submarine at any distance, including being close enough to kick a football into, did not register on the radar at all. The whiz kids in their dark caves that conjure up these new gadgets tell me that the frontal surface area of the submarine is of insufficient area to register. They did say that if the submarine was perpendicular to our ship and close enough, we *might* just be able to see her. Ever optimistic and fawning to please, they assured me that in the future they will be able to pick up even just a periscope at a mile distant.

However, they would not commit to a time frame. Nevertheless, that is not our concern today. I also brought up the idea of the Germans being able to implant somehow, if that is the correct word, a false reading on our radar so we *thought* that *Scharnhorst* was behind *Rawalpindi* all through the night. They of course, would not give me a straight yes or no answer. The best I could squeeze out of them was; *'We suppose that is possible, in our world most everything is— in theory. However, we cannot imagine how.'*

"At this stage I am at a loss to come up with a definite conclusion."

As Stark lamely finished Churchill stood, removed the omnipresent cigar from the corner of his mouth and then with a determined manner strode to the map-stand still present in the far corner. He flipped the security covering over the back to reveal a section of the eastern Atlantic from Gibraltar all the way to the Arctic Circle. Clutching the slightly curved pointer with both hands he began what the assemblage feared was going to be a severe tongue lashing. They were only partially correct considering they had to read between the lines for his hidden threats.

"Gentlemen, we most definitely have a sticky conundrum with this clever Hun. Speaking for myself, I do not have the faintest glimmer of an idea how they simply disappeared like a fogbank when the sun came up. However, I fervently hope that this tactical problem will be resolved soon. Knowing you gentlemen as I do, I am quite confident you will have already assigned some very brainy types to solve it. Nonetheless, even if we cannot be confident in nighttime tracking, we must employ a maximum effort to stop these bloated commerce raiders quickly. As you are all well aware, the tonnage sunk by their two *light* battleships alone has already partially crippled some of our important industries.

The populace has managed to cultivate every possible square inch of arable land for food production. Vegetables will keep them alive but we are in dire need of meat from the commonwealth countries and the United States. Their U-boat wolf packs in conjunction with the *Ugly Sisters* are sinking or commandeering over twenty percent of our convoy vessels. This has got to stop or we will be in very serious straits all too soon."

Before Churchill could go on a frantic knocking threatened to unhinge the stout oak door. Stark bellowed out, "Stop that infernal pounding and open the door."

Immediately, the door was jerked open and a freckle-faced lad no more than sixteen years old breathlessly plunged into the stony-faced group of senior officers.

"Begging your pardon Prime Minister, this just came in and I was dispatched to deliver it to you post haste."

Churchill motioned the frightened youth forward to where he stood. When the boy handed him the wax-sealed envelope, Churchill put his free hand on the youngsters shoulder and thanked him. The messenger cracked a smile that spoke volumes for the respect the common folks had for the lonely leader of the endangered British Empire. Then remembering his place, the youth politely asked the Prime Minister to sign for the envelope before being excused. He then left, not in quite such an agitated state. Churchill split the red wax seal, unfolded the single sheet and quietly read the newest bad news. His shoulders sagged a trifle as he silently read on. After only half a minute Churchill neatly folded the note and thrust it into his jacket pocket.

"Gentlemen, I'm afraid our troublesome situation just deteriorated. *Bismarck* has sailed. We are not exactly sure when, but our intelligence agents on the ground in Norway finally got through to us a few minutes ago. Because of the damnable efficiency of the Gestapo, the SS, and all their other vile watchers, our spies took nearly three days to forward their information to a safe haven for transmission.

"Essentially, *Bismarck* accompanied by the heavy cruiser *Prinz Eugen* sailed approximately three days ago. At normal cruising speed she could have easily covered the distance from Trondheim to the Denmark Strait and now be on the verge of being loose in the North Atlantic. If, God forbid, that monster joins up with *Scharnhorst* and *Gneisenau* it will be a battle of the Titans when our lads tangle with them. Gentlemen, it appears you have your work cut out for you. There is one other piece of quite interesting, possibly disturbing news, which our brave lads sent along with another rather mysterious tidbit. It seems that the Luftwaffe's pompous peacock Air Marshal Hermann Göring was sacked about two or three months ago by a very agitated Hitler. His replacement is none other than General Adolph Galland.

"Another scrap of strange information stems from an overheard short conversation at a local pub in Trondheim. The second officer from *Bismarck* was deep in conversation with a junior officer—not much of what was overheard. However, the second officer made a very intriguing remark loud enough to be heard clearly and accurately. This is the quote. *'Ours is the greatest battleship ever built. I only wish we were blessed with Attila. He alone has made* Scharnhorst *a legend in the Kriegsmarine. How fortunate captain Kastanien is to have him for divine guidance.'*

"Who is Attila? Probably he is one of those flaky mystics that abound around Hitler. It is astounding to me that Hitler can trust so much of his fate to the occult and other fanciful ethereal folderol. Well, let us not delve into that mystery right now. It will no doubt clarify itself in the near future. Now, Hugh, please give us your honest opinion of how this change in the upper hierarchy of the Luftwaffe will affect us."

Churchill returned to his seat, stuffed the temporarily abandoned cigar defiantly back in place, and then waited as the air marshal gathered his thoughts. Air Marshal Dowding stood, shrugged his immaculate uniform a trifle so it hung perfectly before beginning.

"Gentlemen, all I will say at this time regarding *Bismarck* is that the Royal Air Force will assist in every possible way to rid this additional very serious threat to our shipping. As soon as we are finished here, I will dispatch a few, no several, fast *Spitfires* searching to their limits just in the slight off chance *Bismarck* did not sail three days ago bound for the Denmark Strait and the North Atlantic.

"Now, to answer your question Prime Minister regarding the removal of Reichsmarschall Herman Göring and the effect Galland will have as his replacement. My opinion is mainly guesswork, but it is a quite good educated guess given the facts that we have accumulated regarding Galland. The new Air Marshal, former General Adolph Galland, is a superb aviator and leader. What might cause any disfavor with Hitler is the well-known fact that he is most definitely not a polished politician. Therefore, bumptious posturing, fancy uniforms, and fawning political prattle are totally off his agenda. As best as we can tell, all that matters to Adolph Galland is simply getting the job done with the correct results.

"Oh, he does some nominal party politicking that is required, but absolutely nothing more than the barest minimum. The men of the Luftwaffe idolize him and the General Staff has ignored him to this point, virtually shunning him as diplomatically best they could. You see, Galland does not come from the privileged aristocratic class like most all of their High Command. I suspect there will be some significant attitude changes towards him amongst those preening Prussian Generals surrounding Hitler—now that Galland is part of their sanctified inner circle. I do not for one minute think that they will sabotage him since they have, or I should say had, even much less regard for the now departed Göring. We have heard rather slim rumors regarding a few highly secure meetings between Dönitz and Galland, but could not substantiate what were regarded as little better than whispered rumours. Now, this news lends serious credence to those rumours.

"The two of them are the purest sort of warrior. By that, I mean they avoid politics, more so than they would the Bubonic Plaque. We must assume that given the like mindsets of these two formidable military men, they will no doubt co-ordinate their forces to much more devastating effect than Herr Göring ever would have. In his own mind, Göring thought that he had the whole bloody world by the tail and could do no wrong. Well, that is before he met up with Englishmen in *Spitfires* and *Hurricanes,* not to mention a flush-faced fuming Adolph. If Dönitz and Galland co-coordinate their considerable weapons of war, we could be in for a nasty spot of bother. It is now crystal-clear that since Galland apparently took over complete command less than three months ago, the marked increase in sinking's which continue to rise sharply each week, can be attributed to this cooperation. Gentlemen, especially you Admiral Stark, we must come up with a better plan to rid the ocean of that wily Sea Fox in *Scharnhorst,* his equally clever, audacious partner *Gneisenau,* and now the monster out of our nightmares—*Bismarck.* I am very sure that the dramatic rise in sinking's has been brought about by Galland's strategy. His redeployment of the *Condors* to south-western France had made them virtually untouchable by our bombers and it is definitely too far for any fighter to have a chance.

"Göring had previously based the *Condors* just north of Paris and at Brest. Apparently, Göring wanted some of them close to him for ego-stroking, selfish reasons. However, since the *Condors* were used almost exclusively for sea reconnaissance, it makes far greater strategic sense to station most, if not all of them closer to their nefarious work as well as being much distanced from British bombers. Moving the squadrons to three separate airfields to the south and slightly north of St. Nazaire allowed the previously Paris-based *Condors* to be over the critical Atlantic approaches four hours sooner than before. By simple mathematics, each *Condor* could now patrol an additional eight hours. Multiply eight additional hours each, by the fifty or sixty *Condors* that they currently have and one can easily see why their effectiveness has skyrocketed. They are damnable good bombers who prey mainly on our merchants who have little or no defensive firepower.

"Geographically, the move now puts their airbases and planes virtually out of range from any air attack by our Royal Air Force. The few sorties we sent to St. Nazaire, even at night, accomplished virtually nothing regarding destruction of their airfields or aircraft. Our cost was horrific. As I have already mentioned; the distance was too far and too dangerous to allow our precious few *Spitfires* and *Hurricanes* to provide fighter cover. The Luftwaffe with its new improved night fighter version of their tough old *Messerschmitt* Bf 110 easily chewed our *Wellington* bombers to shreds.

*   *   *   *   *

When first flown in May of 1936, the Bf 110 was classified as a heavy fighter that could double as a high-speed bomber. The Battle of Britain quickly changed the roll of the original version dual-purpose fighter-bomber when the much faster, more maneuverable Spitfires *and* Hurricanes *literally used them for target practice. Losses were unacceptable, topping fifty percent and even higher on some missions. The* Bf 110's *found their niche as night fighters and medium bombers. Now powered by much better twin Daimler-Benz DB 601B inverted V-12 engines that generated 1,455 hp each, the* Bf 110 *had a top speed of 348 mph; a hundred miles per hour advantage over the lumbering* Wellingtons *which immediately became painfully easy prey. The Luftwaffe quickly had the night fighters outfitted with upward firing cannon. This improvement in armament allowed a* 110 *to swing up under a* Wellington, *the best possible firing position for them, and blast away with high explosive and incendiary munitions at the soft underbelly and wing fuel tanks.*

*   *   *   *   *

"When the *Wellingtons* were raiding Brest, losses averaged less than fifteen percent; however, the longer trek over Frogland to St. Nazaire, losses ballooned to over forty percent. Britain could not tolerate these losses so the program was dropped until a better plan was developed for hurting the Luftwaffe's deadly FW 200 birds where it would really sting without our suffering such heavy, unacceptable losses."

"Well Gentlemen, let me again summarize our situation," Churchill stated as he strode purposefully to the head of the table.

"We have a lot of our eggs in one big empty basket out there, namely four major battle groups steaming around hunting for two deadly enemies that have vanished. Two of the groups came under very serious aerial attack and we suffered dearly. Just moments ago, we learned that a third, even more potent enemy, to wit *Bismarck,* is possibly now loose in the North Atlantic. Her mission will be the same as *The Ugly Sisters,* aided and abetted by those accursed U-boats. I know you know all this, but I repeat it nonetheless—mainly for emphasis. They mean to sink as many merchants as they can, denying our populace of food and the military the necessary materiel to continue our fight. Those ships are very deadly and have been extraordinarily blessed with an overabundance of good luck so far. I will task our spies to discover what electronic wizardry bamboozled the radar on *Rawalpindi.* Their second new mission will be to discover the identity of 'Attila' and what mysterious, mystical sway he or whatever has over the Kriegsmarine.

"Yes gentlemen, the Royal Navy and our beloved Island face rather a grim, nay, grave state of affairs that we are charged with reversing. Can we do it? There is no doubt in my mind. We must not succumb to the malevolent black scourge that has enveloped most of Europe. Once more, I task you with this critical duty. Sink the Germans and do it quickly, very quickly. Please inform me immediately, and I mean immediately, any time of day or night, of new developments however seemingly insignificant. The temporary defeat of the Luftwaffe last summer will be for naught if we are deprived of the fuel and munitions to stave them off again very soon this year.

"Oh yes, they will come back, and I fear with a battle-hardened resolve thirsty for revenge. Unfortunately, for us, it appears that they will have improved leadership. Hitler's secret agenda is to neutralize our threat, so he can turn east and plunge his considerable forces into a titanic battle for Russia. Yes, gentlemen, that has always been his true objective. France was a practice round that expunged the Germans humiliation of the Versailles Treaty—formulated by those addle-brained Froggies. We are next on the list. He simply must neutralize any danger in the west before he can unleash his Blitzkrieg on Stalin. The non-aggression pact that gave Stalin half of Poland was a short-term placating, exchange for Hitler's freedom to ravage in the west.

"Men, I thank you for your patience listening to an unnecessary, impromptu, rather bombastic speech—far better aimed at those pretentious laggards in the House of Parliament. You know your duties. Please carry them to a victorious conclusion. Moreover, do it expeditiously as supplies run dangerously low—everywhere."

Churchill smartly wheeled and headed out the door bound for 10 Downing Street. Silence reigned for a long, long minute before Stark plunged into his plan with a zealous fervor that had formed during the prime minister's speech. He stood, aiming unerringly, with a new spring in his step, for the map while expounding his overall strategy.

"Well now, gentlemen, I presume our first priority has now switched to *Bismarck*. We do have two submarines patrolling the exit from Denmark Strait. The bad news is that the ice pack has been shrinking daily out from Greenland. The exit passage is considerably wider than just a few weeks ago. I hope that our lads can spot them and give us a decent idea where they are. So far, there have been no sign of them. I am turning Battle group "A" around immediately and tasking battle group "H" to co-ordinate with them, which will flank *Bismarck* and *Prinz Eugen* from the south-east and west. When *Ark Royal* gets closer in a day or so, they will launch their *Fairey Swordfish* planes, weather permitting, to scour the ocean for those other two large, nasty *bastards*. Sorry for the offensive language, the desperate urge to clean up our ocean momentarily got the better of me. Well, maybe I shan't apologize for using that much overused word since it seems that our esteemed Winston uses truly derogatory terms for our Frog allies. Some allies they were—collapsing slightly faster than the Germans could drive their tanks."

At that welcome bit of levity, the men responded with a rousing cheer and much-needed laughter. All of them felt the same way, but rarely voiced their opinion of the worthless French military. When the gaiety had almost subsided, Stark continued.

"The wounded groups "B" and "C" will dispatch the crippled ships back home with the remainder continuing the search for *Scharnhorst* and *Gneisenau*. As Winston so succinctly stated, they did not vanish nor sink. They are not phantoms that can dematerialize. They are simply and positively out there somewhere. Even the vast expanse of the North Atlantic cannot hide them forever. We are also overdue for a bit of luck ourselves, but I will base our search patterns on rather basic common sense. As much as I would embrace Lady Luck right now, we cannot base our strategy on the mercurial moods of chance. If we eliminate the obvious directions the *Sisters* would not steam, then we can concentrate our forces in a much smaller, yet still expansive sections of the Atlantic. Now, that should be quite enough for the moment. I will keep all of you, especially Winston, apprised of any developments as soon as there are any. Please meet me back here after dinner this evening at eight o'clock when I will outline my plan to run these cagey Huns to ground."

Scharnhorst
Same Day, late Afternoon

As the weak, yellow-orange sun sedately exited the sky on the smooth and calm sea, Attila slowly awoke. His sapphire-blue eyes blinked open and then his head, moving as smoothly as if it were mounted on ball bearings, began a slow, penetrating circuit of the captain's cabin. Satisfied that all was as it should be, he yawned mightily for several seconds before silently slamming his jaws shut. Rising slowly to all fours, he stretched his front paws forward an almost impossible length, and then forced his front torso downwards into a deep shoulder bend. He then straightened up and one at a time extended his back legs out to their maximum to shake any lethargy out of them. With his ritualistic calisthenics finished he assumed the classic statue pose, known worldwide amongst cat lovers. All cats do this regal position with cultured grace—however Attila managed to exude a majestic, imperialistic aura to his perfect posture. After a moment or two, the sleek feline decided that his human companion needed to be awakened—mainly to take care of his needs. His needs were very simple but incredibly important. It was time to eat. Then inspect *his* ship to make sure there had been no new developments of late.

Attila marched purposefully from the foot of the bunk until his head was but a few millimeters from Kastanien's stern but relaxed face. Then he began to wash the captain's chin stubble with his sandpaper-like pink tongue. Kastanien had felt the cat awaken but he pretended to be asleep so that his mostly silent friend would perform his daily ritual. The rasping noise of the tongue along with the predictable minor irritation caused

Kastanien to blink his eyes wide open immediately. Kastanien grinned, and then clutched the powerful predator to his arm. Attila desisted his licking, settled in to the crook of his friends arm and commenced to purr contentedly. The two companions passed several moments peacefully before Kastanien gently moved his furry friend while whispering in his ear, "Time to arise my friend. Let us prepare to go about our respective business for the evening. I am sure you need to visit the galley before inspecting *our* great ship."

Kastanien smartly wheeled from the bunk and took the few steps to his desk. Picking up the intercom to the bridge he quickly received the current conditions of the ship, the sea, their position along with a plethora of other sundried information. He informed the bridge staff that he would be amongst them within the next half hour. His second call was to the galley.

"Mr. Strass, our Honorable Master-at-Arms will with you shortly. Of course, you know he expects dinner for a king, which I am sure you will gladly provide. Several of the officers and I will descend upon you in about an hour or so. I will give you ample notification of our arrival. What may I tell them will be your bill of fare for this evening?"

Kastanien listened, commenting and slightly modifying the main course of the day before hanging up the handset. He then crossed to the cabin door with Attila close behind. As soon as he opened the door, the cat vanished after turning his head and giving out with a muffling noise that was his way of thanking Peter for letting him loose to indulge in dinner with his ardent admirer, Manfried Strass. The admiration was quite mutual but for vastly different reasons. Manfried had never forgotten how Attila had intervened in the pantry when he plucked the vicious rat a fraction of a second before a mid-air collision with Manfried's face. Manfried could replay the incident in his mind like a motion picture, and did so most every time he chanced to gaze back at himself in a mirror, grateful to have been spared what would have been nasty scarring at best. Attila on the other hand admired the rotund cook for the phenomenal bill-of-fare that he always received. Even when fresh meat supplies ran low on the ship, there were always prime dishes for Attila.

Kastanien, relatively confident that all was well with the *Scharnhorst*, undressed, took a short but thorough shower, shaved then generally brought himself back to being the immaculately-groomed captain that the idolizing crew expected him to be. Feeling totally refreshed, Kastanien donned a completely fresh uniform, checked it for perfection, and then proceeded to the bridge. When he arrived a moment later, he silently admired the last vestiges of the setting sun on the horizon. Feeling quite content with the state of his watery world, Kastanien inquired once again of the bridge officers the general and specific details regarding the status of the noble battleship. Satisfied with the ordinary, non-threatening reports, Captain Kastanien then sincerely asked his officers about their status. After sharing a quip or two with each officer, Kastanien was about to end the conversations when Executive Officer Hans Schmidt interjected, "Captain, we have intercepted several radio transmissions from the British which I feel are of no immediate concern of ours. However, I feel that you should read up on the havoc that we left behind last night."

"Thank you Mr. Schmidt, I shall do so shortly. Right now I want you to relieve the bridge officers for the evening watch."

Schmidt went about executing the watch change for the next few minutes while Kastanien took the few steps back to the radio room.

"Mr. Weisboch, please bring all the latest radio intercepts that are translated to me on the bridge as soon as you can. Also, please make certain they are assembled in chronological order."

Kastanien almost absently replied to the radio operator's affirmative response before returning to the bridge. He was about to seat himself in his command chair but made a quick turn and headed for the starboard bridge-wing door. When he opened the door, he took the few short paces to the railing where he lightly grasped the gray steel and gazed at the ocean which was painted with a tinge of warm orange coloring from the almost vanished sun. The temperature outside had risen dramatically in the past twenty plus hours that they had been steaming south. Although it was barely above fifty degrees, it felt almost tropical compared to the below freezing weather they had left 500 or so kilometers behind. Even the eastern sky had taken on the aura of the Caribbean with its azure blue clarity. Pleased that he had chosen to give the crew a change of climate, even if it proved to be of short duration, Kastanien re-entered the bridge and settled comfortably in his chair. The radio operator, who was patiently waiting, handed over the sheaf of radio intercepts.

Kastanien casually gripped the considerable wad of messages, did a quick but penetrating scan of the bridge before he settled comfortably back in the chair. Then with concentrated Teutonic thoroughness, he began reading. The large amount of messages took more than a few minutes for the first read-through. When he finished the last paper, he paused, deep in thought before beginning reading the messages through again. This time the reading went quicker as he could skip some messages that were somewhat redundant or made irrelevant by later dispatches. Captain Kastanien, still gripping the intercepts that were now cradled in his lap, pondered over their content for many minutes, before rising and heading once more for the radio room.

"Mr. Weisboch, I can find no mention of any submarine or torpedo attack in these messages. Do you have any other intercepts that are either undecipherable or otherwise?"

"No Captain. You have all of the messages that have been transmitted from the Royal Navy to London, as well as all London's replies and orders. We have been able to decode every message with a very high degree of accuracy. There is nothing else Sir."

"Very well Mr. Weisboch. I will be on the bridge most of the night after dinner. Please bring all decoded messages to me immediately. If any message comes through in the near future that you deem urgent, please bring it to me here or in the officer's mess."

Kastanien then strode across the darkening passageway into the radar room. As usual, the rooms lighting was so dimly lit it reminded him of a cave with only candlelight to penetrate the gloom. Early on into their first sortie, "Merlin" Molter had explained to the captain that the almost total absence of ambient light made his job much easier in that he could perceive and interpret the subtle variances of the radar reflections. After Kastanien's eyes had adjusted to the rather eerie pulsing-green light, he spotted Attila. The comfort-seeking feline was contentedly curled up in "Merlin's" lap obviously digesting his recent dinner.

"Well 'Merlin', it appears that you have truly made a good friend. I trust that he assists you well."

Marvin Molter had not heard the captain silently enter his domain, so he jumped a little hearing the familiar voice. Attila with his incredibly acute hearing knew it was his friend but remained motionless.

Knowing nothing was amiss, he merely cracked one eye a trifle before resuming his early evening nap.

"Good evening Captain. I am so very proud to have earned Attila's friendship. Thank you for allowing him to visit me occasionally. Yes, actually he is of some help.

"Sometimes he will stand, just staring at my screen for lengthy moments. If there is even the slightest change, he lets out a low murmur that alerts me. There have been no ships in sight on our radar for over twenty hours but when our scout seaplane left and returned in the early morning, Attila was here and became fascinated with the action on the screen. That is when he signified the changes with the rumbling noise from deep in his chest."

"Interesting. I had half wondered where he had spent the morning, but now I know he was in good hands. You have told me what I came by for already, so I bid you a good night. I know you are scheduled for relief in a few minutes. Get a good night's rest so as to be on your very highest alert tomorrow afternoon when we rendezvous with *Gneisenau*."

"Yes Sir Captain. I promise I will be on my utmost top alert when I return to my duties tomorrow."

Peter Kastanien snapped off a return salute and returned to the bridge. He inquired if the officers scheduled for dinner had left for the officer's mess. He was told that the bridge had changed officers only a few moments earlier and that all the slated officers had departed for dinner. Satisfied that everything was under control, calm and orderly, Kastanien himself left, heading for the culinary treat promised by his excellent chief cook.

After a very satisfying dinner of succulent roast pork, delightful ship-made tangy sausages, scalloped potatoes and perfectly cooked cabbage, Kastanien returned to the bridge. He immediately exited onto the starboard bridge wing. Once more Kastanien spent several minutes outside on the starboard bridge wing savoring the pleasant change in climate. He cherished the crystalline clarity of the heavens—much bejeweled with millions of sparkling diamonds. He especially enjoyed the fresh new aroma of the sea. Kastanien had always felt that the grim, dark sea that was the North Atlantic had a dank, slightly sinister scent to it, except possibly in high summer. Peter Kastanien barely held onto the railing—more out of habit than necessity. He was relaxed in the solitude of the empty ocean. The familiar whispering hiss of the ocean passing along the *Scharnhorst's* flanks, the revitalizing sea breeze, and the powerful, confident background hum of the mammoth engines, were like a friendly siren's song to Peter Kastanien.

At peace with himself, he calmly let his mind ramble—unfocused on past and possible future events. Peter Kastanien had learned long ago that many brilliant, inspirational ideas came to him when he did not force issues. The solitude at night was one of his favorite times to indulge in what some might consider daydreaming, although none dared voice this opinion to anyone. As *Scharnhorst* knifed southwards through the mild sea, Kastanien's mind stumbled once more onto a recurrent theme.

"What will be history's judgment of Scharnhorst *and me? Will it be complimentary or contemptuous? I alone am responsible for the honor, reputation and conduct of* Scharnhorst*, my crew, and most of all myself. I must be forever on guard to hold to the highest standards of conduct."*

Finally, feeling that his spirit and soul were quite refreshed, he re-entered the realm of command. Strolling about the large bridge area, Kastanien passed a few friendly words with each of the evening watch officers before seating himself in his chair. He had only been seated for a few moments when an ethereal movement caught the corner of his eye. Noiseless as a ghost, Attila had floated up to his reserved seat to assist during the night watch.

"Ah, Attila, my good friend. Thank you for joining me. Your new friend 'Merlin' must have been relieved and perhaps you're not quite so chummy with his replacement or maybe I could hope that you really missed me."

Attila rotated his head, staring his penetrating stare at a grinning Kastanien who began to chuckle quietly. Both knew what really went on unspoken between these two close friends.

"Thank you for your loyalty my friend. Shall we settle ourselves in for what I hope will be a rather long, tedious and boring night?"

Attila replied with a combination of a chest-rumbling mixed with a barely audible meow, which Kastanien knew was his way of agreeing affirmatively. The dim spectral-silhouette of the cat assumed the statue pose, his piercing eyes aimed over the bow. As on the many quiet nights, he was the self-appointed, very special watch-cat on duty. Both captain and cat stared silently into the night for a long time. Then Attila began to groom himself, a seemingly never-ending chore that all cats indulge in. Kastanien absently noted the methodical, yet seemingly haphazard way his companion worked varying areas of his thick glossy coat. After some work on his shoulders, Attila began to wash languorously behind his right ear. This telltale sign brought Kastanien's mind out of the doldrums. He didn't move, but his eyes focused intently on Attila. Attila was probably aware of the increased scrutiny by his friend, but never hesitated in his ablutions.

After a few moments watching Attila massage and clean behind both ears, Kastanien calmly announced to the bridge in general.

"Gentlemen, our infallible weather-cat has forewarned us of some inclement weather ahead. Judging by the low intensity of his washing, I would venture to say that we are heading into nothing more than a heavy rain, which should not stir up the ocean too much. However, please prepare for heavy weather should I have misread Attila's actions."

The Admiralty
Early Morning

"Stark, you cannot be serious. Are you trying to lighten up the atmosphere in here with some ludicrous bloody fairy tale? Maybe I should have rephrased my last question to go like this. First Sea Lord, have you gone *stark* raving mad? Your intelligence people must have had far too much to drink or something else entirely," The First Lord of the Admiralty loudly announced.

The First Lord of the Admiralty seated himself amid the light laughter of the High Command, mostly over the deliberately intended pun. Stark was not smiling or laughing. He was still standing bolt upright exactly where he had the made the astounding announcement a few moments earlier that set off Ian McLeod on his short but derisive tirade. Stark had prefaced his statement with several sober assurances that the intelligence was accurate and had been triple-checked since it was literally absurd.

Stark had found out the identity of Attila. When he was informed that *Scharnhorst* was being divinely guided by a mere housecat, he continued to dig and verify the sources before he would make this ridiculous sounding pronouncement. Stark had made absolutely certain that there had been no confusion or embellishment by anyone in the intelligence chain from the source to himself. None would dare invoke the legendary wrath of the first sea lord.

After intense questioning, cajoling with a touch of badgering thrown in, the First Sea Lord Robert Stark was as convinced as he could be that the intelligence was accurate. Robert Stark did not achieve his lofty position in the Royal Navy by having less than bulletproof skin, so without so much as a blink he picked up the conversation where he had been so rudely interrupted by Ian McLeod's sarcastic remarks.

"Gentlemen, and I still include you in that class Minister, please allow me to fill you in on a few more details of this not-so-ordinary *cat*. From very, very reliable intelligence sources right in Kastanien's home town of Cologne we have garnered a rather comprehensive picture of this extraordinary feline."

The first sea lord spent only a few moments describing the home life of Captain Kastanien and his family's love of cats. Thanking the attentive silent crowd for their tolerance, he ended the subject, and then seated himself comfortably.

Air Marshal Dowding was the first to speak.

"Thank you for enlightening us Robert. I myself have a deep love of cats and from what the First Sea Lord just told us, I could well understand why this clever captain takes his favorite cat to sea with him. In addition, we must remember that it was not so long ago that every ship that plied the oceans, including our own Royal Navy, had a ship's cat. When steel replaced wood for ships, the ship's cat inexplicitly slowly faded into history. Cats were considered a necessity back in the days of wooden sailing vessels—mainly for rodent control. I can personally attest to the fact that there is no better method of ridding, or at least keeping these nasty varmints under control. Now, I wonder how my cat would get along in a bomber for a few hours a day?"

The High Command of the British military had a good-hearted laugh at Dowding's ending remark.

Politician to the core, Ian McLeod stood. With a mirthful smile on his face, he made a short conciliatory speech.

"Please accept my apologies First Sea Lord. I made those unfortunate remarks before proper consideration. I too have a love of cats. At last count there were at least a couple of dozen of them on the grounds of my estate in addition to the four housecats. I most heartily agree that without them, the grey plaque would overrun me. Now, I have an honest question to put to the First Sea Lord. I know, I know, when a politician uses the word 'honest' everyone goes into a defensive mode. Nevertheless, this is most truly sincere.

"First Sea Lord, please educate us lowly landlubbers about rodents on our warships. Has steel eliminated the need for the services of our feline friends?"

It was almost more than these normally stolid men could contain. However, to a man they restrained outright laughter at the bizarre direction the conversation had taken. This light conversational moment had most definitely helped to relieve the taunt atmosphere.

"Actually the rodents adapted quite well to the transition from wood to steel. Unfortunately, the Royal Navy never saw fit to keep rodent records so, without detailed historical facts to back me up I can only venture a guess. Fellow officers, I do not think the problem ever went away on board ships. For well over several centuries the Royal Navy has kept very detailed medical records on all injuries that occurred during a deployment cruise. Anticipating a question such as yours I had one of my aides do a little investigating regarding rat bites.

"Without boring you with the static details, I can tell you without hesitation that the incidence of rat bites has remained a very consistent constant for the past 300 or more years. No, the steel ships of today did not have any noticeable, reducing effect regarding rat populations. Maybe our clever German Captain Kastanien has taken a step back in time to keep his vermin under control. Moreover, maybe it's an idea that we should look into seriously. A ship's cat is not such a loony idea after all. However, I cannot brook the thought of a cat determining a warship's destiny. Must be the influence of that maniac Heinrich Himmler, who we all know puts an inordinate amount of faith and trust in arcane, occult claptrap."

"That's enough of this ridiculous prattle. Let us get on with the real matter at hand," Field Marshal Montgomery blasted out from his seat stilling any further comments about Attila.

Ian McLeod stood, retaking control of the meeting.

"Gentlemen, gentlemen enough of this. We know that Attila is merely a cat. Let us not waste any more time on pursuing this subject. We must come up with new strategies to deal with the serious matter of the German surface fleet, which has been rapidly delivering us more bad news heaped upon more bad news. First Sea Lord, please be so kind as to share your new plan of actions with us."

"Very well Minister, my apologies for getting rather carried away on that tangent. My last word on the subject is that I found it quite intriguing. Now, on to my new strategy. As I informed you earlier, I have dispatched battle groups 'A', and 'H', to seek out, contain and hopefully dispatch with *Bismarck* and her escort. Battle group 'G', headed by *Prince of Wales* is currently steaming north-west to pass on the eastern side of the Azores. Her group, in addition to her (ten) fourteen-inch guns is comprised of the battleship *Nelson* with (nine) sixteen-inch guns, the heavy cruiser, *Cumberland* and eight destroyers.

"*Nelson* is twenty-five years old with a top speed of only twenty-three knots, which unfortunately hinders a quicker response. Should they happen upon *Scharnhorst,* there is more than adequate firepower to deal with this damnable German. When the group is close enough to assure that any gaps where the *Sisters* could escape through are properly plugged, I shall send *Prince of Wales* along with three destroyers equipped with torpedo launchers to close in on *Bismarck.* The slower ships, *Nelson* and *Cumberland* can slog around hoping to get a shot or two at our sly opponent. That is at least a day or two in the future, but by then we should most definitely have more information to go on. That, Gentlemen, is our basic plan of action. Do any of you have comments or questions?"

Silence reigned supreme for what seemed a protracted eternity. Finally, Field Marshal Montgomery shattered the crystalline silence.

"First Sea Lord, I assume that you either have or intend to right smartly inform Winston these details of your plan?"

"Field Marshal Montgomery has asked the obvious. By now, Winston will have received by urgent carrier the details of this forthcoming operation. If the Prime Minister has anything to say, I daresay that we will know rather shortly."

As if on cue for a stage play, the door once again burst open—the plump figure of Winston Churchill appearing. No one even twitched an eyelash—all were anxious with apprehension for the words that would be forthcoming. The door quietly closed with only the slight metallic click of the latch.

"My fellow warriors; I have perused the First Sea Lord's strategy most carefully. Being the Prime Minister as well as a former First Sea Lord, the politician in me screams to modify your plan so that I might be able to garner some of the accolades when it succeeds. However, the safety of England and our Empire is far, far more important than any aggrandizement that my modest ego needs. Robert, your plan is sound. Please expedite it immediately without further ado. Now, you may all breathe easier since you have my blessings.

"In deference to our fellow countrymen up North in Scotland, here is a fine bottle of single malt Scotch from one of their vaunted distilleries. Take a drink now to calm your nerves while we wait out the news from the Atlantic."

The stunned men stared at the bottle, breathed long sighs of relief but held their tongues. Winston evaporated from the scene like a ghost, his leaving marked only by the light click of the door latch. Air Marshal Dowding was the first to emerge from the stupor that gripped all of them.

"Well done Robert. I for one am going to have a tiny nip of Winston's gift before getting back to my own turf. Shall I pour a tot for any of you fine gents?"

Attila

Shortly after midnight, Kastanien relieved himself from duty on the bridge—retiring to his cabin to do the necessary paperwork and catch a few hours needed sleep. When Kastanien opened and closed his cabin door, Attila's incredible hearing picked up the unique snicker of that particular lock. Attila knew his friend would be gone from the bridge for a while at least, probably several hours. Since he himself had not had a decent nap for some time, he decided that some activities, ending in a prolonged catnap, were overdue. The eighteen pounds of fur and fluid sinew bounded to the deck with only a minor humph from his lungs compressing. Executive officer Schmidt noted the ghostly exit with a knowing grin.

Attila jogged through the darkened bridge to the radar room where "Merlin" Molter was on duty. The youngster, as usual, was intensely concentrating on his machinery, so it came as a startling jolt when the hefty cat mystically landed in his lap. Recovering quickly, "Merlin" reciprocated the cat's loving attentions by giving him a light hug, then scratching under his chin and behind the ears. Attila was in cat-heaven with this boy's knowing caresses. The two brought exquisite pleasure to each other for nearly ten minutes. Then, remembering the overdue catnap, Attila vanished into the gloom as suddenly as he had appeared. On the short distance to Kastanien's cabin, Attila thought that a midnight snack was in order. Now he raced down the stairs and passageways to the galley. Bounding into the brightly-lit room, he searched for his good friend. Spotting Manfried Strass, the chief cook, he bolted over to the table where some delicacies were being made ready for late-watch diners. The cook had caught the brownish blur from the corner of his eye. He was ready when Attila silently sailed up onto his worktable—as he knew from many previous visits that is what his beloved friend would do.

Instantly trapping the cat in a miniature bear-hug, the two friends lovingly greeted each other. Manfried gently set the cat down, and then staring intently into the sparkling sapphire eyes he asked the obvious, "Would you like a bite to eat so to sustain you through the night?"

Attila responded by nuzzling the cook's scratchy day-old beard while engaging his loud purring engine. Manfried backed away laughing so hard his rotund belly rocked mirthfully. Stepping back to a side table, Manfried chopped some choice chunks of beef into cat-sized bites. Glancing back at the cat whose neck was outstretched watching the procedure with anxious anticipation, Manfried inwardly glowed. His heart swelled with an inner warmth that he had only felt many years ago when he fell in love with his long-departed wife.

Manfried had steeled himself against any emotions that day over ten years ago when the love-of-his-life was abruptly taken from him by a drunken lout on a motorcycle. Manfried became a changed man with this new love in his heretofore rather lonely existence. Attila had returned humanity to his friend freely without any need for recompense. Manfried did not fully appreciate this aspect of their relationship on any conscious level, but he would never forget how he had been saved from a frightful scarring by this magnificent feline.

Captain Kastanien and virtually the entire crew of the *Scharnhorst* gave Attila the credit for the wonderful change that had come over their chief cook. Consequently, Attila ate far better than any of the crew. On many an occasion Attila's meal was even better than Kastanien's himself. Fearing reprisals regarding the special treatment accorded to Attila, Manfried surreptitiously made every effort to conceal the cat's bowl from prying eyes. It was one of the most poorly-kept secrets aboard the *Scharnhorst*. The only two crewmembers who still thought it was a closely guarded secret were Manfried and Attila, who naturally could have cared less.

Although he had been a good Navy cook when *Scharnhorst* first set sail, Manfried's culinary skills dramatically improved after the rat incident. The entire crew immediately noticed and appreciated it when they savored the much-improved meals. Manfried was soon overwhelmed by a torrent of compliments. With his newfound humanity, this flood of praise made him one of the happiest sailors in the entire German Kriegsmarine. His ebullient, bonhomie became infectious, spreading universally throughout *Scharnhorst*—dispelling most all of the typical military griping about their bill-of-fare.

Satisfied that the midnight snack was perfect, Manfried turned, presenting the gleaming special bowl of cat delicacies to his friend. Attila flashed a glance at Manfried, and then settled in to devour the chopped-beef treat. Manfried simply leaned back on the prep table watching the cat enjoy his simple creation. Every time, and there were many, too many times to recount, that this midnight ritual took place, Chief Cook Manfried Strass could feel an inner joy coursing throughout his entire being while he took time from his duties to quietly observe his beloved friend.

When the bowl was licked clean, Attila methodically began to wash his face. Manfried always marveled at how the cat invariably kept every square millimeter of his small personage immaculately clean. After a few moments, Attila shook his head vigorously; signaling that he was done. Manfried took the single step back to the table and again embraced his friend, softly whispering into his ear.

Attila responded by again purring contentedly. After a few minutes, Attila decided that it was time to go. Manfried, recognizing the body signals, released his light grip. Attila turned his head, affixed Manfried with an appreciative look, then launched himself off the table—vanishing like a phantom into the darkened labyrinth that twisted and turned throughout the heart of the enormous battleship. Manfried reflected on his great fortune for a moment, and then returned to his temporarily abandoned task—still feeling a warm fulfilled contentment inside.

Attila was in no big hurry as he trotted through the darkened ship, bouncing up stairways, strolling down passageways until he arrived at the captain's cabin. Pushing his head though the leather flap of his private entranceway, which was unlocked, he glanced around before committing fully to come into *their* cabin. Kastanien was softly snoring on their bunk, a small circle of light emanating from the desk lamp, dispelling the total darkness. Attila knew that all was well with his world so he silently entered the cabin, proceeding to his nighttime sleeping spot on the bunk. Kastanien paused for a brief moment in his snoring as he sensed the presence of his friend settling down at the foot of the bunk.

The two companions quickly dozed off for a few hours rest, lulled to dreamland by the gentle whispering motions of the prodigious battleship, as it slid effortlessly through the ocean. The perpetual background thrumming of the colossal engines permeated their beings with a calming reassurance.

Tomorrow, they would rendezvous with friends near the Azores, probably in a rainstorm of sorts.

Nelson

The destroyer escorts of Battle Group "G" chafed at the slow, plodding speed of twenty-three knots. The hundreds of sailors in this potent battle group were spoiling for a crack at Germany's best warships, knowing that they would surely prevail. Waiting to join battle with *Scharnhorst* and *Gneisenau* taxed the patience of these stalwart sailors heavily.

Twenty-three knots was the top speed of the older battleship *Nelson*. Any murmured grumblings were instantly stifled if an impatient officer voiced such a thought by a gentle reminder from the captain that he should consider her armament.

*   *   *   *   *

Nelson sported (nine) sixteen-inch guns, oddly arranged in three triple turrets, all forward of the superstructure. Supplementing this ferocious firepower were a (dozen) six-inch, (six) 4.75 inch guns along with (two) twenty-four inch torpedo launchers. Her internal belt armor of twelve to fourteen inches was amongst the best in the Royal Navy. Even the deck armor was unusually thick, varying between seven inches over the magazines to nearly four inches over the machinery. This plodding leviathan could dish out ruinous devastation to an enemy all the while shrugging off sustained brutal punishment, which would rapidly reduce lesser vessels to nothing more than useless smoking, sinking scrap iron.

*   *   *   *   *

Captain David Parker perched in his captain's chair on the bridge of *Nelson*, contentedly puffing on his favorite Meerschaum pipe. Parker had served the Royal Navy for nearly forty years, beginning his officer's career as a junior officer aboard the then newest armoured cruiser in the Royal Navy—HMS *Cornwallis*. Parker idly gazed at the endless parade of waves that passed beneath this Goliath of a warship. It was a very pleasant afternoon on a quiet ocean. David Parker's mind was at ease for the near future. He knew that soon enough this period of calm would end—no doubt in a Herculean clash of guns. Parker had total confidence in his outstanding crew. Every seaman was extraordinarily proud to serve on *Nelson*—the namesake of England's greatest fighting Admiral.

The warmth from the afternoon sun penetrated the bridge with a soothing calmness. Captain Parker reminisced of his early days aboard *Cornwallis*. The fifty-eight year old captain recalled how he had thought the *Cornwallis* was the grandest warship that had ever sailed. He thought that she would never be surpassed in size, armament, speed or grace. "*My, how things have changed.*" The *Cornwallis* displaced 10,000 tons—quite large for her day. However, this was slightly less than one-third of his *Nelson* which displaced nearly 34,000 tons. *Cornwallis's* (four) twelve-inch guns, although bigger than *Scharnhorst's* eleven-inchers were puny compared to *Nelson's* (nine) sixteen-inch monsters—the biggest-bore guns now arming several Royal Navy battleships.

Back then, the incredible speed of nineteen knots for *Cornwallis* made her one of the fastest battleships on any ocean. A snail's pace when one considered that *Hood* could race along at thirty-two knots and *Hood* weighted in at whopping 41,250 tons, more than quadruple the old *Cornwallis*. He wished that *Nelson* could do better than twenty-three, because he knew how frustrating it must be for the others in his battle group to hold back their superior speed. However, he thought, should we be fortunate enough to tackle the Germans, our firepower will surely redeem us.

Parker was about to let his colorful career continue forward when the silence of the bridge was shattered by a sharp announcement from his second officer.

"*Prince of Wales* is signaling Sir."

"Very good Mr. Kent. Please bring me the signal."

Several tense minutes dragged by before the signal from the beautiful new battleship was delivered to him.

Captain Parker read the note calmly. The signal was not good news. *Prince of Wales* had developed some troublesome problem with one or more of her four shafts. Captain Reginald Sullivan, commanding *Prince of Wales,* stated that he had to partially shut down his ship until the damage could be known for certain. The signal also stated that much of the repair time would have to be done with his ship at a standstill and in calmer waters since he would have to inspect the problem underwater. He requested Parker to reply with a solution as to the best way to deal with this untimely delay. Parker had already reached the chart table in the rear of the bridge. He quickly issued a command.

"Signal *Prince of Wales* to stand by for a few moments."
Parker snatched up the calipers from their side tray, then leaned over the map showing their position in the Atlantic. With deft movements, he adjusted the calipers then twirled them on the map. After double-checking his calculation, he moved outside to the signal station on the bridge wing.

"Send this to *Prince of Wales*. Calculate that you are only six hours steaming at eighteen knots to the most southeastern island in the Azores, called Santa Maria. I am familiar with these waters. They are quite deep with no outcroppings to disrupt your barnacle families. This island would shelter you from the weather, which according to my meteorologists has a reasonable chance to turn a trifle nasty in the next twelve hours. I would also suggest we send two destroyers to accompany you as watchdogs. These are Portuguese islands and as such, we have good reason to suspect German intelligence reporting stations on the islands. Additionally there has never been any reported U-boat activity within a hundred miles or so. Respond with your decision."

Captain Sullivan, along with an audience consisting of three officers, performed the same calculations on their identical map. Sullivan stood straight pausing for a long moment.

"That old seadog knows his stuff. Knowing that eighteen knots would be our most efficient speed comes only from many years' experience. We will take his learned advice."

Sullivan, like his counterpart, quickly went to the bridge wing signaler.

"Signal *Nelson* with this. Thank you for your suggestion. We will proceed to Santa Maria at eighteen knots with destroyers *Kashmir* and *Jervis* as babysitters. Once repairs are made, we will proceed northeast exiting into the Atlantic through the wide channel separating the islands of Terceira and Sao Miguel. Hopefully we will rejoin you in a couple of days. Suggest you continue at best speed on original course east of Azores. In addition, I am officially transferring overall command of this battle group to you. Please concur."

Parker read the signal as fast as the signalman did. Captain Parker knew all the jobs on board his vessel, most of them better than his officers and crew. This had earned him the sincere respect of the crew, which in turn gave him peace of mind, knowing that his ship was in competent hands—always. He chuckled a bit at the "babysitters" word before responding with a short reply.

"*Nelson* acknowledges your plan as sound. Your transfer of the flag is noted and logged. Thank you. If we chance upon those Bosch blighters, we will give them your regards in the cleverly disguised form of some Royal Mail sixteen-inch shells. God speed and good luck. David Parker, Captain of *Nelson*."

Captain Sullivan quickly read the signal. A distinctively satisfied grin grew rapidly. Receiving carte-blanche approval from Parker was tantamount to a blessing from King George, or maybe even God himself. Although they had been rather close acquaintances for nearly twenty years, Sullivan wouldn't exactly call Captain Parker a close friend. He felt that Parker was just a bit too much Royal Navy for his liking, especially when the two met off-duty.

The transfer of command completed and a plan of action verified, Captain Sullivan issued orders to his staff.

"Make turns for eighteen knots, port thirty degrees, and come to heading 280 degrees. Chief Engineer, please advise me regularly if eighteen knots is the best speed considering our condition."

The orders were repeated quickly through the chain of operations on the bridge. *Prince of Wales* heeled slightly before straightening up on her new course. Her speed dropped off to eighteen knots within a quarter mile after assuming the new course. The bridge intercom squawked noisily.

"Chief Engineer here Sir. Eighteen knots seems about right. Any faster and we could worsen the damage. If I feel any need to reduce speed further, I will consult you first. Engineering over and out."

Captain Sullivan then went out to the starboard bridge signal station.

"Signal *Kashmir*. Position yourself a mile ahead of me. Run a zigzag pattern with your superior speed, listening for U-boats. At our reduced speed we make a very tempting a target for them. *Jervis* will be guarding our flanks."

After receiving confirmation of his orders from *Kashmir*, Sullivan then briskly walked through the bridge to the port bridge signal station with the signalman in tow.

"Signal *Jervis*. Repeat the orders given to *Kashmir* then add; position yourself a mile abreast my port side for fifteen minutes. Then drop back and come up on my starboard side for fifteen minutes. Repeat these maneuvers every fifteen minutes until further notice. If you pick up U-boat sounds, immediately signal *Kashmir* and myself. Then attack with everything you've got. *Prince of Wales* over and out."

Within minutes, the two "babysitters" were positioned and the tiny flotilla slowly steamed towards the Azores with a setting sun obscured by a dense, deep purple line of low clouds. With his years of experience, Captain Sullivan knew almost certainly that they might be in for a spot of rainy weather, maybe even a light storm. However, his on-board meteorologist refused to verify his experienced insight. The weatherman, with all of his sophisticated equipment, stated categorically that there would be no rain, let alone a storm. All he would concede was that it would be somewhat cloudy.

Since arguing with this rather pompous twit, as Sullivan had pegged him, was futile, Sullivan continued to hope for rain. In addition, being wrong might just imbue a dose of humility on this particularly pretentious prig. A storm at night, while lying in the lee of Santa Maria, would make him invisible enough to avoid detection, except perhaps for an unlucky fluke of chance. The two destroyers would be further insurance against unwelcome guests that might just drop by. He would have them scurry back and forth in a classic racetrack pattern, a mile or so off his beam. With any kind of luck, he would be able to resume his quest for *Scharnhorst* about dawn.

Without any substance or for any particular reason, Captain Reginald Sullivan was apprehensive about tomorrow. The necessary repairs and the inherent danger of stopping for many hours were not necessarily the reasons for his uneasiness. Nonetheless, he could not shake the anxiety that persisted just below the surface of his conscious mind and in his gut, which experience had taught him to trust implicitly.

Scharnhorst

Kastanien awoke but did not rise. His subconscious had registered subtle changes. Listening he heard the light splattering of rain washing over *Scharnhorst*. The sea had also risen a bit, slightly increasing the roll of the battleship. Kastanien propped himself up on an elbow checking on Attila before rising fully. The cat lay curled up exactly where he had settled a few hours previously. Kastanien smiling thought to himself, *"Old friend, you knew for sure that this weather was in our path so you just carried on totally unperturbed. I sometimes envy your confident style more than I should."*

Just then, Attila raised his head, glancing back first at Peter, then swiveled his head around covering the entire cabin. Satisfied, the cat stretched all his legs thoroughly before standing erect. The compact eighteen pound feline went through his ritual for waking by shivering, yawning and lightly shaking his coat into place.

Kastanien rose, donned his boots and jacket. He strode over to the cabin lights, turned them on and then inspected himself in the full-length mirror. After brushing his slightly ruffled hair into place, he donned his cap and did a final check of his appearance. After a few minor adjustments, Kastanien was satisfied that he exuded the confident demeanor of a battleship captain.

Exiting the cabin, Kastanien slowly strode to the radar room. The door stood open with only a dim green glow of light emanating from the radar screen to dispel the gloom of the darkened hallway. Kastanien had not been heard approaching, which was his intention. He was pleased to note that his radar genius Marvin Molter was not staffing the post. A blond-haired youngster, who looked even younger than his tender age of nineteen, studiously switched between checking the screen and reading a technical manual on the inner workings of radar. Peter Kastanien knew this boy's name, as he did know virtually all of his crewmembers names. A rather prodigious feat of memory, considering there were nearly 1,700 seamen aboard *Scharnhorst*.

"Good Morning Mr. Munster. How do you read this rain on your machine?"

The radar operator literally jumped several inches out of his chair when he instantly recognized his captain's distinctive voice. No matter that the captain had surprised him on many a previous occasions, he still felt an adrenalin jolt from the suddenness of his captain's appearance. Quickly recovering from his momentary fright, the second radar operator rapidly stood bolt erect, smartly saluting Kastanien. Kastanien returned the salute with a polished smartness that only came with thousands of repetitions. Peter Kastanien then quizzically looked at the boy awaiting an answer.

"Yes Sir, Captain Sir. I have been watching this storm forming for about two hours now. It seems to be strengthening forward of our position. I expect we shall have a drenching rain, at the very least, in about two hours. The wind will probably kick up the sea considerably as well."

Before Kastanien could reply, Attila sailed up onto the small table in front of the radar screen. Both men remained motionless watching the cat perform his endless check of this area. Satisfied, Attila then cast one of his trademarked questioning looks towards the junior man. Kastanien helped the lad interpret the look.

"He wants you to seat yourself Mr. Munster. You are about to become *privileged* by having Attila reside in your lap."

Looking anxious at this wonderful turn of events, the blond youngster reseated himself. He had barely settled in the cushioned dull-green chair before the hefty cat gracefully stepped down, settling himself in a position to observe everything in the room. He seemed especially interested in the radar screen, probably because it was jumping much more than normal. With Attila in place, Kastanien made a slight noise, which drew the attention of his radar operator. Looking up into his captain's penetrating eyes, Irvin Munster awaited the captain's remarks. With a twinkle in his eyes and a slight touch of humor in his voice, Kastanien responded to the weather forecast.

"Very good Mr. Munster. That is exactly the weather that your newfound friend predicted late yesterday when we took up this new heading. It comforts me to know that my human crewmembers seem to be equally astute, at least in this department. However, the night is still young. Let us see how your dual predictions play out before dawn. Please inform me at once if there are any new developments of significance with this weather front. I shall be on the bridge for the next hour or so."

"Yes Captain. I will let you know immediately if the storm disturbance changes much."

The radar operator snapped off a perfect salute, which was returned with an equally perfect one, and then Kastanien vanished into the darkened hallway. Attila naturally made note of Kastanien's departure before retuning his undivided attention to the fascinating wiggling-green screen. The young radar operator, after remaining motionless for a minute or so, tentatively began gently stroking the cat. After only a few feather-light strokes, Attila rotated his head around the tiny room, settling his stare square in the boy's eyes. Attila's sapphire-blue eyes penetrated the depths of Munster's light-cerulean eyes sending a silent, but demanding message. Unconsciously accustomed to the silent messages that cats deliver, the boy began stroking the ship's idol with conscious reassurance. Satisfied with his cursory, yet thorough, reconnaissance, Attila went back to studying the green squiggling bars, all the while purring contentedly with the lad's now acceptable stroking.

Kastanien silently arrived on the bridge. Before settling in his chair, he strolled rather nonchalantly over to the starboard side and studied the light slashing rain streaming back on the glass. Seemingly satisfied, he proceeded to the port side, studying the rain that was only barely perceptible in the dim light emanating from the instruments, "Turn on the two forward searchlights if you please Mr. Mueller and point them both perpendicular to our beams."

The black smothering grip of the night was shattered by the intense light from the two powerful arc-lamp searchlights. However, all that Kastanien and the bridge officers could see were millions of scintillating diamond-bright streaks filling the black void. The rain had intensified enough that it created an almost impenetrable shield of aerial water surrounding the battleship. Kastanien studied the direction and wind deviation of the rain for nearly three minutes.

"That's enough for me Mr. Mueller. Please shut the searchlights off for now. I am leaving the bridge for the radar room and then to my cabin. Please awaken me an hour before our rendezvous."

Kastanien once more silently startled Irvin Munster, but this time the young seaman was partially prepared when he spotted Attila rotating his ears towards the hallway. Although he couldn't hear Kastanien's silent approach, he knew that the cat's vastly superior hearing detected someone approaching.

"Well Mr. Munster, what is the latest on our storm?"

"Captain Sir. As best I can tell, the rain should be a bit heavier now, however, we will drive into the heart of the storm in about an hour at our current speed."

Kastanien pondered this information for a moment before responding.

"Can you tell me the heading, speed of the storm and its probable intensity?"

Realizing the importance of his answer the young radar operator paused for a moment before deciding that his opinion was of some serious consideration. Before he could answer, the astute Kastanien eased the obvious tension gripping the boy.

"Come now, Irvin, I value your opinion, but you must always keep in mind that I, and I alone make the final decisions. There is no disgrace in making a bad guess when you only have very limited instruments to work with. Before you give me your best estimates, I suggest that you grasp Attila lightly by the shoulders with your thumbs resting at the back of his ears, close your eyes and feel his energy pulse into you. Your compatriot radar operator 'Merlin' is also one of Attila's favorites, and he cherishes any special knowledge that Attila imparts to him this way. Before you answer let me remind you as I have 'Merlin', I must always have your best opinion, right or wrong. Do not answer with what you *think* I want to hear. What I want to hear is the best evaluation you have concluded. Contrived answers to please '*The Captain*' will not be tolerated."

Irvin Munster with his eyes still closed felt his anxiety dissolve with the gentle but explicit words from his esteemed hero. Kastanien firmly grasped the boy's shoulder and squeezed firmly. Suddenly there seemed to be a minor jolt of electricity infusing his fingertips that rested on Attila's shoulders. Opening his eyes, Irvin Munster felt as well as saw the intense look aimed directly at him by the ship's incredible cat.

"Captain Sir. I felt Attila's energy infuse itself into my being. The energy message confirmed that my first estimation was correct. We will be in for some rather heavy weather in an hour or so. The storm is coming in from the east, with its center just now passing over the southern islands of the Azores. I estimate its speed over the ocean at about fifteen knots. We are just a few kilometers inside the western edge of it. If the storm's track and speed remains constant, we would collide with the heart of it in about four hours. My instruments are not sophisticated enough to determine the intensity of the wind but as a guess I would say they could be as high as forty kilometers per hour."

"Very well Mr. Munster. Thank you for your prediction. I do realize that, like all weather predictors, you can only estimate any weather pattern. I have no training in meteorology, but my many years of cruising around this unpredictable ocean have almost given me a sixth sense about impending storms. Moreover, that sense tells me that you are quite correct. However, we shall not be keeping our present heading much longer, as we have a rendezvous shortly with some friends. So, let our storm carry on its merry way. The rains along with considerably darkened skies suit my purpose quite well. Well, that is enough for now. Keep a close watch on the storm and if there is any significant change inform me at once. I shall be in my cabin until an hour before first light."

Attila watched Kastanien disappear into the passageway for a brief moment until he heard the distinctive click of their cabin door. Satisfied his friend was taking care of himself, Attila swiveled his head and attention back to the radar screen. Irvin Munster noticeably relaxed now that the captain was gone. His hands still resting on the cat's shoulders began a gentle massage. With his world humming along nicely, Attila began purring louder to show his appreciation.

Kastanien took only a few moments to log the weather conditions along with the predictions before removing his jacket. After his boots were off, he quickly slipped under the bunk's coverings. Within a few dozen heartbeats, he was snoring lightly. He had always thoroughly enjoyed the rhythmic tapping from this type of rain. The soothing patter on the porthole glass brought back wondrous memories of his honeymoon week with his bride Andrea.

*   *   *   *   *

Immediately after the traditional wedding feast, they had spirited themselves off for a week's honeymoon. Their destination was an old rustic cabin in the mountainous foothills, twenty-five kilometers south of Wiesbaden. The cabin was a surprise gift to them on their wedding day from Peter's favorite uncle, Artemus Jonas. Uncle Art had been very instrumental in generating Kastanien's passionate interest in photography.

The drive to the cabin had been uneventful, or more correctly stated, hardly noticed. The two lovebirds reveling in each other's company snuggled-up in the small Mercedes coupe. They had arrived two hours before dusk. The skies to west, partially obscured by some evergreen trees, were filled with dark, brooding clouds. The young lovers cared not what the clouds portended—they had very different plans for the interior of a wonderfully furnished, warm, cozy and romantic retreat.

While snuggled in each other's embrace, shortly after making long, fulfilling, sensuous love, a gentle, yet heavy rain began. The wooden shingles on the cabin proper deadened the sound of the rain, but the adjacent tin-roofed woodshed reverberated with the large raindrops sounding like a crew of very busy drummers. That wonderful memory of their first night twenty years ago had never faded from Peter Kastanien's memory. Their marriage, only two years after the Great War had ended, had been one of two souls destined for each other. This cherished time had sustained him through all the trials and tribulations of marriage and politics.

Whenever a similar rain came into his life away from home, Kastanien could close his eyes and relive every second of that magical night. Captain Peter Kastanien slept soundly, dreaming romantic thoughts of his beloved Andrea.

Prince of Wales

Night enveloped the battleship with a wet blanket. The sudden rain was torrential, accompanied by gusting thirty mile-an-hour winds. The heavy raindrops pelted the huge ship sounding like an endless barrage of machine-gun bullets. The seas inexorably began to rise to uncomfortable heights. Captain Sullivan anxiously paced the bridge. Calm and cool nearly all the time, he was clearly as nervous as a London alley cat. His bridge officers knew the fearsome responsibility that he carried with this command. None envied him the decisions that must surely be made soon. The weather only gave Sullivan a few choices, all of which were poor at best. No one spoke. All were waiting for a command. Only the pounding rain along with the cannon-shot smashing of the ever-growing waves on the bow invaded the tense atmosphere. Suddenly the intercom squawked to life, dispelling the tension almost immediately.

"Chief Engineer Thompson to Captain Sullivan. Sir, I respectfully request we reduce speed to twelve knots immediately. The heavy seas are playing bloody Hell with my cobbled-up temporary repairs."

Now that a decision could be made, Captain Sullivan made it in an instant.

"Request granted. Reduce speed to twelve knots. Mr. Thompson, we are still some distance from shelter off Sao Miguel Island, which will be our revised destination. The tiny island of Santa Maria, where we are still headed is too small to provide us adequate storm shelter. Sao Miguel on the other hand is a rather large, long island with a high mountain range, which should moderate the storm's intensity quite a ways out from the lee side. I implicitly trust your evaluation of the situation. However, the sooner we can get relief from this blow, the better your working conditions should be. The water is very deep there right off the shore. We will able to tuck in rather close to the landmass, giving your engineers the calmest possible situation. Moreover, I am sure you will agree that it would be best to finish our repairs before first light if possible. If you think a minor increase in speed would be in order, just do it, and then inform me of your actions. Captain out."

Sullivan replaced the intercom, strode over to the chart table, and then issued a new order. The order was short.

"Change course to the eastern tip of San Miguel Island. I'm sure all of you heard my thoughts and description of our new destination, so I won't bother repeating myself. I am leaving the bridge for the radar and radio rooms. I shan't be gone very long. Mr. King, the bridge is yours."

A few short seconds later Captain Sullivan entered the dim cave-like domain of his radar operator, a youngster not yet old enough to shave. The heavy footfalls of his captain had forewarned Alex Denham of the impending visit. Being rather quick-witted, Alex was prepared for the captain's regular visit. He and the captain both knew what would be asked. Both also knew the almost predictable answer. Sullivan opted to forego proper Royal Navy protocol.

"Well, Mr. Denham."

"Sir, the outlook is still the same. Heavy weather for the next several hours. I have not detected any significant change in the storm's pattern."

"Very well. Thank you. Carry on."

Sullivan exited the radar room, took a few strides, and then entered the adjacent radio room. The two rooms were identical in size, but the differences were quite significant. Whereas the radar rooms' impression was that of a dingy, subterranean medieval dungeon, the radio room was alive with light. The overhead lighting coupled with the seemingly hundreds of yellow, green, red and blue gauges and dials had turned the tiny enclosure into a miniature crystal palace. The plethora of electronic apparatus completely covered three walls and most of the tiny, heavily scarred oak desk, which abutted a monstrous machine, with a very large lime-green frequency band. One simply could not work in this environment with even the mildest touch of claustrophobia. There was barely enough room for one small chair, let alone a second. However, even in the cramped space, the radio operator was not alone.

Leaning over the shoulder of the radio operator, with his right hand supporting himself on the back of the chair was none other than Captain Sullivan's pompous meteorologist, William Clinton. Although the radio was crackling with bursts of static, the message was nonetheless clearly decipherable. The captain's presence had not been noted, so Sullivan left his presence unknown for a few moments while his radioman scribbled the incoming coded message on his work pad. The message didn't take but another few moments to be complete. Sullivan remained quiet for a few seconds before Clinton spoke up.

"Well John, what is that all about?"

Without turning about, radioman John McCambridge replied, a slight hesitance in his voice.

"William, you know perfectly well that I must take a few moments to decode this message and furthermore, until the captain reads it, it is nobody's bloody business other than his. If he decides to share the contents with the crew, that is his prerogative. Now, please leave me to do my job. This message is very important—as they all are."

Before the weatherman could put his other foot in his mouth making the situation much worse, Captain Sullivan gave a slight harrumph, and then spoke with a stern admonition.

"Mr. Clinton, Mr. McCambridge is absolutely correct. The message is for me and me alone. Furthermore, you should not even be here. It is not a Royal Navy regulation that an officer, however junior, cannot visit the radio room occasionally to maintain relationships with his fellow officers. However, it is at the captain's discretion to formulate individual ship policies. From now forward, you are forbidden to enter the radio and radar rooms without my express permission.

"Those two rooms are vital nerve centres of our battleship, and as such does not warrant unauthorized personnel eavesdropping, hoping to glean some nugget of classified information. No doubt if you had been able to cajole this fine young seaman out of the message's contents, you would have immediately posted the contents on the ship's grapevine. When stupid things like that happen, I am always the last to know, which make me look foolish, if not impotent. THAT, Mr. Clinton is wholly unacceptable to me. This warship, like all others, has a very efficient gossiping rumor mill, which is generally close to one hundred percent misguided. This gossiping is impossible to squelch and I do not intend to attempt dispensing with it. It serves the purpose of alleviating the crew's boredom when there is not much action. I am sure that even you can understand boredom. From now on, you might best spend your free time reading up on weather predicting rather than childish snooping. Your previous forecast, which you adamantly stood by, was pathetically erroneous. Thank our lucky stars that my simple experience of many years at sea was more in predicting with what we are slogging through right now. This storm, although a bit uncomfortable, is exactly what we needed to remain unseen whilst we seek some shelter for repairs. I sincerely hope that the rain continues through the night until we are being back to normal.

"If you still believe your prediction was correct, I suggest that you step outside and enjoy your pleasant evening. Good night Sir."

The verbal lashing had more effect on the junior officer than thirty lashes with a cat-o-nine tails. Lieutenant William Clinton, thoroughly admonished rather roughly by his captain, in those few moments of the brutal tongue-lashing had discovered some sense of humility. Snapping off a perfect salute, Clinton wheeled on a heel and vanished.

Sullivan squeezed in close to the table, noting that John McCambridge was furiously flipping pages of his codebook translating the transmission; pretending to be oblivious to the recent chastisement.

"Mr. McCambridge. I am quite pleased with your handling of our arrogant lieutenant. You stood your ground quite correctly. If Mr. Clinton even darkens your doorstep in the future, you will inform me immediately. Now, how much longer will it take you to produce a readable translation?"

"Thank you Sir. I shall do my best to inform you immediately of any other snoops that wander in here. The first part of the message from London is simply a weather warning. It states that our battle group will probably run into a light to medium rainstorm near the Azores."

Before McCambridge could go on, Captain Sullivan burst out into laughter.

"They don't say. Well, if we were not under strict radio silence we could give them a more accurate description of what we are gladly enduring. Now, what about the rest of the message?"

"Captain Sir, the rest is rather long. To transcribe it accurately will take me several minutes. From the beginning text, it seems to be a current update on the German warships and the Admiralties plans for our battle groups."

"Very well. I shall be in my cabin. Please bring me the transcript immediately when you are finished. Until then Mr. McCambridge."

"Good night Captain. I should not take more than fifteen to twenty minutes to complete the translation."

Sullivan made one last short appearance on the bridge. Satisfied that things were progressing properly, he left heading for his cabin. When he closed the door behind himself, he shook his head in frustration and thought to himself.

"Just because one graduates Cambridge with honors, it should not make one a pretentious snob. I sincerely hope that Lieutenant Clinton has learned the value of being a bit more self-effacing in his learned opinions."

Sullivan peered out the small porthole, checking the conditions outside. The ink-black night was broken only by slashing streaks of rain reflecting the lights on the bridge. Satisfied that the camouflaging storm was holding steady, Sullivan lay down on his bunk fully clothed except for his boots which he placed neatly near the foot of the bunk and his jacket which he hung carefully on a shaped wooden hanger. If trouble came a'calling, he would not waste precious time donning anything more than his boots and jacket.

Needing some desperately overdue sleep Sullivan closed his eyes, but he would not shut down his mind until he knew the contents of the latest Admiralty message. Still, he thought, closing his eyes was restful enough for now. Mother Nature had other ideas. Against his wishes, he was sound asleep when there came a knock on the door a few moments later. Blinking himself back to consciousness, Captain Sullivan was on his feet before the significance of the knock registered. By the time he opened the door, he was fully functional. The radioman handed him the message.

"Does the Captain wish me to stay for further instructions?"

"No, Mr. McCambridge. Return to your post. Thank you for this."

Closing the door rather loudly due to a sudden lurch of the ship, Sullivan returned to the bunk. Setting on the edge of the bunk, he read the message. He again silently chuckled at the weather forecast before delving into the current disposition of naval forces in the Eastern Atlantic. Slightly frustrated that he would be out of the hoped-for-action, he resigned himself to the fickle fates of life at sea. He carefully folded the message before stuffing it into his inside breast pocket. He lay down and resumed his nap, still fully dressed.

Scharnhorst

The few hours of pleasant dreaming were rudely interrupted by the tinny bark of the intercom.

"Captain, to the bridge."

Kastanien swung out of the bed, careful not to disturb Attila who was snoozing in his regular spot at the foot of the bed. In only a few seconds, he yanked on his boots, and then donned his jacket, fastening the sparkling brass buttons as he headed to the door. Less than two minutes after his dream was interrupted by the sharp words from the intercom, Kastanien was back on the bridge, once more in total command.

"Well, Mr. Mueller, what is going on that requires my presence?"

"Captain Sir. We are nearly at the point where we need to turn south. The island of Flores is thirty kilometers forward of our port quarter. We should rendezvous with our oiler and supply ship in a little more than an hour. Secondly, we have intercepted a message from the British Admiralty advising their convoy PG 26G to steer further west of the Portuguese coast. It seems that one or two of our surface raiders have been spotted plying the normal shipping lanes from Gibraltar to England. They further state that this convoy is escorted by only four destroyers and one light cruiser."

Kastanien thought pensively for a moment or two before replying.

"Very well, Mr. Mueller. We will make our turn as planned when we reach the proper position. Let us take advantage of this weather to refuel and take on fresh provisions as quickly as we can."

Kastanien then addressed all the officers present.

"The most recent radio intercept couldn't be better news. After we refuel and replenish our supplies, we shall head east to pass about fifty kilometers north of the island of Graciosa. Mr. Mueller, when I am finished, please plot our course after the refueling stop. Since we are not sure how far along the British convoy is I want to try to catch them somewhere near forty degrees latitude and fifteen degrees longitude. We will have to hurry a bit to accomplish this since we probably have three times the distance to cover than they do. However, if the British hold true to form, they will be using their older merchants which are notoriously slow. I imagine that their top speed is under ten knots.

After the rendezvous with our supply ship, we will steam at twenty-five knots, which should allow us to catch them in about thirty hours. Mr. Mueller, also please consult the charts to verify my estimates. The escort vessels should not be a problem if we dispense with them before they can launch their nasty little torpedoes. I don't imagine that the light cruiser will be very much to contend with since they are undoubtedly using their better ones against our U-boats further north."

There was nothing to see but the wavering light patterns of the heavy rain. Still, hundreds of random thoughts swirled inside his head. Kastanien closed his eyes. He pondered where the Royal Navy would be searching for him once they had discovered he had vanished from behind the *Rawalpindi*. He wondered if the Admiralty was losing an abnormal amount of hair figuring out his little ploy with U3200X. These thoughts put a brief but satisfied smile on his lips. His musing covered a diverse variety of subjects, most of which concerned the near future of the *Scharnhorst*. His family finally popped into his mind, creating a warm glow throughout his being. He was so very proud of his son and daughters, but his wife Andrea dominated his daydreaming. His mind was drifting over the memorial lovemaking sessions that improved with time when his reverie was broken by a command from his second officer.

"Execute thirty degree turn to port. Come to heading 225. Slow to twenty knots."

Kastanien flushed the pleasant thoughts from his brain.

"Mr. Mueller, how long before we rendezvous with the supply ship?"

"Captain Sir. We are less than an hour's steaming time from the rendezvous at our present speed."

"Very well Mr. Mueller. We should be right on time, if not a trifle early. I want to get this operation over while we still have cover of darkness and rain. We will not be able to launch our aircraft to scout for the enemy, but then neither can any enemy vessel so equipped. I am going to check the radar room, then to my cabin to do some paperwork. Inform me when the supply ship is in sight."

Sharp military salutes preceded the captain's departure. When Kastanien entered the dim radar room, he was pleased to see that it was "Merlin" operating the long-ranging eyes of *Scharnhorst*. His silent approach and laying his hand on the shoulder of his star radar man did not startle the lad, which he thought unusual. Then he noticed Attila curled in the boy's lap staring at him.

"Good morning 'Merlin'. I see that our friend whose hearing is far superior to us mere mortals forewarned you of my presence. I'm glad you are here on duty. The next few hours are quite dangerous for us as we must slow to a crawl during provisioning. Do you have anything on your radar?"

"Yes Captain. I have the island of Flores thirty kilometers off our port quarter. I can barely make it out because of the storm. That is all I have Sir."

"Thank you. Keep a sharp eye out. I expect we shall see a ship relatively soon and I fervently hope it is our supply ship. I shall be in my cabin. The instant you see anything new, report to me immediately."

At that, Kastanien vanished into the gloomy passageway.

Prince of Wales

Captain Sullivan slept fitfully for only three hours before the information contained in the last message could no longer go on without some serious thought. Although he would be idled for many, long, agonizing hours, he still had to mull over the seemingly endless scenarios that resembled a titanic chess game played without set rules in the vastness of the Atlantic. Rising from his bunk, Sullivan headed to the bridge. The scene outside was unchanged. Heavy rain continued to pelt the windows, preventing any visibility whatsoever past the guardrail that joined both bridge wings.

"Well, Mr. King, I see that the weather is holding up quite nicely for our purposes. What is our present position relative to our destination?"

First Officer Roland King, ever the proper Royal Navy officer, replied in an almost nonchalant manner.

"Captain Sir. As you can see, the weather has held steady for several hours now. I have just recently received an update from our radioman. We are close enough to the Island of Sao Miguel to pick up their strongest commercial radio station. They have stated that this rather heavy rain will continue for another eight to twelve hours. That forecast is nigh on to being exactly what the radar room has reported to me less than twenty minutes ago. Although the seas have not abated any since the storm began, they should be toning down rather soon. We are only thirty miles from the shelter of Sao Miguel. I should estimate that the seas will be much tamer in an hour or so when we come into the lee of their mountains. We are still steaming at twelve knots, which seems to be just about right according to Chief Engineer Thompson, whom I have spoken with every half hour."

"Very well. Thank you for such a complete report."

Captain Sullivan reflected for a moment. He moved to a position off to the port side of the bridge before continuing. What he had to say needed to be shared with all his officers.

"Gentlemen, let me bring you up to date on other matters regarding the Azores. First, they are not exactly friendly to us. We have had only unsubstantiated, rather sketchy, reports that the Portuguese government allows port facilities to German U-boats. With this in mind, it is to be assumed that if we are spotted by anyone on the island that it will be reported immediately to the German military. This would undoubtedly put us in great peril. Therefore, we will hope and pray that this fortuitous, camouflaging weather holds true until we have finished repairs. Now, I am going below to confer with Chief Engineer Thompson. Call me immediately if anything untoward happens. The bridge is yours Mr. King."

Captain Sullivan rarely had visited the nether regions of his great battleship after his first thorough inspection. That first inspection had been arduously long and agonizing to the junior officers that had accompanied him for nearly five hours. Captain Sullivan wanted, no… needed to know every nook and cranny of his massive battleship. *Prince of Wales* was 745 feet long with a beam of 103 feet—a lot of steel territory to inspect. And inspect every inch of it he did—meticulously. Sullivan was no novice to large warships; it was rather simple for him, thanks to his incredible memory, to assimilate every aspect with ease. Without hesitation, he took the most direct route down into the engineering power plants nestled within a cavernous space, deep in the bowels of his 43,786 ton warship.

Sullivan stopped on a catwalk directly above the rearward section of the boiler room. For a brief moment, he studied the men, all of whom were diligently laboring with the troublesome shaft. Not being a gifted engineer like his chief engineer, Sullivan could only assume by the orderly but frantic work that things were going as well as could be expected. Sensing his presence, the chief engineer looked up from his position near the troubled boiler and saluted with a very greasy black hand. Sullivan snapped off a return salute and headed down to the deck where the work was progressing.

"Mr. Thompson, what is the status of your repairs?"

"Captain Sir. We've done our damnable level best to reduce the time frame for full repairs. Once we can stop, hopefully in quieter waters, I will put some divers over the stern to assess if there is any unforeseen damage to any of the propellers. I should not think there would be any problem, but one never knows. Repairs to the propellers, braces, and seals outside the hull would be our only reason for a dead stop. Maybe we will get lucky—I pray so. The work here is coming along quite nicely. I am optimistic that we will not be stopped for as long as my original estimate. Stopping in mid-ocean during wartime scares the living daylights out of me—so I will affect proper repairs without wasting a single moment. When we are finished, our grand Lady will be right as rain. Speaking of which, is it still typical Scottish squall weather topside?"

With a bit of a chuckle, Captain Sullivan remembered his chief engineer's rather strong dislike of the entire Scottish population. Seems that his clan from Manchester had a nasty run-in with some Scottish rebels a few centuries back and they had not forgotten some supposed crime against them.

"Mr. Thompson, it's a bit more than a 'squall'. I would liken it to a small hurricane without the high winds. The wind is strong enough to make the sea restless enough, but in the lee of the mountains, it should be relatively calm. How many boilers do we need to shut down?"

"Only two Sir. The other six will be kept up in case we need them. Once repairs are made, we can be underway at nearly full power immediately. We're giving it our best and then some."

"I know you are Chief Engineer. I will let you know a few moments in advance of when we can stop engines. Now, carry on. We must be underway at first light or before the weather clears—if at all possible."

With that, Sullivan departed and the chief engineer sprang back into action. Sullivan had only just regained the bridge and resumed command when all noticed that the sea was suddenly becoming relatively calmer. Sullivan picked up the intercom to the radar room.

"Mr. Denham, how close in to the island are we?"

"Captain Sir. I estimate we are about ten miles off the shores of San Miguel Island."

"Thank you. Please let me know when we are three miles from the island."

Scharnhorst

Kastanien intensely disliked paperwork, especially the demand for every seemingly insignificant tiny detail. Some days it felt like that was all he did, and that the war was just one more way of generating mountains of paperwork. Kastanien would much have preferred to write the salient facts about each day in a simple logbook and let it go at that. However, his superiors at Kriegsmarine HQ had long ago dispatched explicit orders that this was the way it had to be. Shrugging off his displeasure, Kastanien plowed on.

Finally, he felt he had done more than enough to satisfy some goggle-eyed, mousy bureaucrat. Shoving the irksome paperwork into his desk drawer, Kastanien leaned back in his chair closing his eyes. The now-soothing ship's motion threatened to lull him off to dreamland, but Kastanien was too much of a dedicated warrior to allow himself any self-indulgence as a crucial time approached. His mind skipped forward to his plans for the next few days. Before he had much of a chance to formulate a decent plan of action, the intercom from the radar room in his cabin squawked to life.

"Captain. I have a slow moving ship twenty kilometers ahead of us. She is just two points off our port bow and heading towards us at about ten knots"

Before the echo of the message had died, Kastanien was out the cabin door headed to the bridge. Before speaking, he took in the officers that were manning his battleship. Satisfied with what he saw, Peter Kastanien issued an order to his executive officer.

"Mr. Schmidt, it appears our supply ship is twenty kilometers ahead of us and on course. We should meet up with her within half an hour. Make sure that the lookouts, all the officers and yourself verify her identity before we come alongside."

"Yes Captain. I have already alerted the lookouts to inform us the instant they know for sure who she is. We will not be surprised if she is not who we expect."

"Very well. Carry on."

Kastanien proceeded to perch in his chair and stare out into the blackness. The rain had moderated to where it was now only a misty drizzle. *Scharnhorst* was running with her normal nighttime lights, which were insufficient to penetrate more than a few hundred meters forward of her bow. Kastanien knew that the supply ship would be lit up with a virtual Christmas tree of lights. The theory of brightly lighting these supply ships, although odd to many seamen, seemed to work for their benefit. None had been attacked, let alone sunk, since the war began well over a year ago. The idea was to announce to the world's warships that this was a semi-neutral vessel simply going about its own business.

The minutes ticked by slowly for the bridge compliment. No one spoke. Only the water, now almost silently sliding along the steel sides, accompanied with the background soft grumble from the engines broke the deathly quiet. Eighteen minutes into the vigil the eagle eyes of Heinz Alder crackled through the intercom.

"Ship ahead, just a point off our port bow. Maybe eight kilometers away and heading steadily towards us."

Although all the high-powered binoculars on the bridge staff had been focused in the correct direction, none had yet seen even the faintest glimmer of lights. Ever impetuous, second officer Mueller turned to speak to Kastanien. Kastanien knew that the junior officer was about to question Alder's sighting. Before his officer could utter the first syllable, Kastanien sternly motioned him to silence. Mueller froze but complied, quickly returning his binoculars into the dark night out in front of *Scharnhorst*. He felt a little puzzled by the captain's silent rebuke but he chalked it up to captain's privilege.

Abruptly the misty rain stopped. The obscuring curtain of water parted comparable to that of an opera house. Hiding behind the curtain, albeit at a considerable distance, were the unmistakable swaying lights of a merchant ship, trundling over moonlit waves. Mueller now understood. Alder was above them and as well as the weather—which was why he spotted the ship sooner. The bridge officers, who for quite some time had borne a striking resemblance to department store mannequins, came back to life. In the sudden activity by his fellow officers Mueller took a few quick steps to where he stood not two feet from Kastanien. Kastanien glanced to his officer. Mueller quietly whispered, "Thank you Sir."

Kastanien simply nodded his head once. That was assurance enough for Mueller, who immediately started back to join his fellow officers. He got not one pace before Kastanien gripped his arm firmly. Mueller turned to question why he had be restrained. As soon as his eyes met Kastanien the knowing captain with a conspiratorial smirk nodded his head towards the bridge wing door pulling one of his favorite officers with him. When Kastanien opened the door to the port bridge wing, the wind noise snapped every other officer's head toward this disturbance. They had all forgotten the rain had stopped, which meant clearer visibility outside—let alone no nasty weather to deal with. After a quick conference as to who would be left inside the bridge to mind the store, the lucky ones scampered out the starboard door, happily taking up watching as the well-lit ship drew nearer.

The binoculars remained attached to every officer's eyes for a long time. Everyone was hoping to be first to identify the vessel. Kastanien stood casually gripping the railing with one hand. He knew by the arrangement of lights which vessel she was. However, he wished to see who had the best eyes amongst his officers and to trap anyone who made a guess, hoping only to curry favor with him. He had drilled it into everyone on board that guessing or assuming was fraught with disaster. Specifics were an absolute necessity to make intelligent decisions that could adversely affect every man on board with possible fatal results. He had also told them that if the worst came to the worst and the best that could be distilled from the available information was guessing, then the "guess" would be considered, but only if the pronouncement was strongly prefaced with the word "guess".

As these thoughts rattled around in his mind, Kastanien had to grin internally. Here he had almost bludgeoned the officers with his dictums, and then realized that all he could do with respect to the disposition of the Royal Navy was to "guess". *Funny how that worked.*

The minutes seemed to be endless—the ship barely closing the gap. Then, it just suddenly seemed closer. Now it was near enough to make out which ship she was, but still no one triumphantly chirped out her name. Kastanien became a trifle vexed with his officers who should easily have recognized the *Bremen Castle*. They had replenished stores from her before, so there was no excuse for this hesitancy. Finally, none other than second officer Mueller piped up loudly, "It's the *Bremen Castle*."

"Very good Mr. Mueller. Now we wait for her signal."

No sooner had Kastanien's words blew away with the wind, than the *Bremen Castle* made her recognition signal, which also included a secret coded phrase indicating that there was no trouble aboard, nor had she been commandeered by an enemy.

"The signal is correct Mr. Mueller. Have our signalman make the correct reply. Also, have our signalman tell the *Bremen Castle* to turn about so that we can run up parallel on her starboard side. Have her reduce speed to five knots. Maintain our present speed until I notify you of a change."

The signal lamp chattered away for a moment or two. After a very short pause, the *Bremen Castle* slowly turned to run in the same direction as *Scharnhorst*. In the lee of the island, the seas were quite moderate, which was a great blessing for the maneuver the two ships were about to engage in. Even though the *Scharnhorst* was now chasing *Bremen Castle*, the speed difference rapidly closed the gap. With everything under control, Kastanien ordered his officers back inside the bridge.

"Mr. Schmidt, have all qualified hands stand by on our port side to receive supplies and the oil hoses. Mr. Gott, reduce speed to ten knots and hold steady until our bow is opposite her stern. At that point, slow us down until we are running side by side at identical speed. Then bring us within thirty meters of each other. Mr. Schmidt when we have achieved these objectives please oversee the transferring's. I want this to go efficiently and quickly. This close to land at a crawling speed, attached to an unarmed ship full of volatile fuel is a precarious and perilous position. Let us not delay any longer than absolutely necessary. I will take command with the able assistance of Mr. Gott while you are seeing to topping up our fuel and taking on other supplies."

Scharnhorst slowly eased into perfect position abreast of the *Bremen Castle*. Kastanien was rightfully proud of his crew, especially the very talented first officer Hermann Gott. His ability to maneuver 38,100 tons of steel, even in this relatively calm sea, verged upon mystical.

Kastanien had witnessed Gott's first maneuvers of *Scharnhorst* out in the Baltic Sea during *Scharnhorst's* first sea trials. He politely inquired as to where his first officer learned to handle a ship so deftly. Gott beamed at the compliment from his legendary new captain. He replied that he simply felt that a great warship, like their *Scharnhorst*, likened unto a beautiful woman, who if you treated her gently with loving strokes, would implicitly obey your every command. Kastanien, with a knowing smile, had remembered that comment every time Gott was in charge of pinpoint accuracy in maneuvering his majestic *Scharnhorst*. Kastanien felt that his other officers were quite capable, but when his great Lady of Steel needed an artist's magical touch at the helm, no one could hold a candle to Gott's precision.

Scharnhorst dwarfed the supply ship. She was nearly twice as long as the *Bremen Castle* although *Scharnhorst's* beam was narrower by a few meters. With the two ships meandering along with equal speed and the gap consistent, Kastanien calmly ordered Gott to close the gulf to *Bremen Castle* down to twenty meters. *Scharnhorst* smoothly slid into her new position. Standard procedure for refueling at sea was to allow the supply ship to be in command of refueling and transferring of goods, but the warship was in command of maintaining position. This system had been adopted mainly because a supply ship handled like a pregnant sow, especially at crawling speeds, whereas warships, albeit much larger, were far more nimble. If the sea was troublesome, but not enough to forestall what needed to be done, the agility of a warship kept the two ships in proper proximity.

Only a few brief moments passed before bullhorns blared from both vessels and thin pilot lines streaked across the narrow gap. *Scharnhorst's* crew quickly secured the lines then began hauling in the attached heavier lines that would carry the cargo. The oil hose was first to be brought over and attached to the refueling connection. Within what seemed like only seconds of the "all is ready" bellowed order, the heavy-duty fuel pumps began pumping black lifeblood over to the steel leviathan. The oiling pumps transferring huge volumes of oil under pressure were so loud that the crewmembers monitoring them wore thick insulated ear protectors under their helmets. The cacophony of other shouted orders had cargo bales being swiftly shuttled from *Bremen Castle* to *Scharnhorst*. The huge rope containers swayed a bit wildly during their short voyage over the hissing sea below, but all made the journey without any serious mishap.

Scharnhorst's seamen were well trained in this maneuver. As soon as a heavily laden bale arrived, they rapidly disengaged the hoist mechanism, dropping the cargo carefully, but not too gently onto the deck. Within two minutes, a swarm of seamen emptied the rope bale and prepared for the next one to arrive. Calmly watching the beelike activity from the bridge wing was captain Kastanien. He firmly held Attila in his arms, as this was about the only time the illustrious cat was allowed to be on the outside of the warship at sea. Attila only partially enjoyed the fresh sea air. The gentle breeze caused by the ships momentum bothered his ears a trifle so he laid them back, not in anger, but for comfort. Sensing that his friend had had enough of a visit outside, Kastanien went back inside the bridge and deposited Attila on his red blanket. Attila looked up at his human friend and verified that he was pleased to be inside out of the wind. Kastanien smiled at the feline, and then strode over to his first officer.

"Well Mr. Gott, the sea has been kind to us today. The transfers go quite well. We should be fully topped up with most everything in record time today. Is there any message you wish to send across to our kindly friends?"

"No, Thank you Captain. I have sent everything I needed to over with the mail bag."

"Very well, carry on."

Always a bit nervous during refueling, Kastanien made a cursory visit to the radar room, more to have something to do than check up on his skillful operator.

"Well 'Merlin' do we have anything on your machine that shouldn't be there?"

"No Captain. My screen is clear except for the land mass and the *Bremen Castle*."

"Very well, carry on. Keep your vigilance high as I expect the *Gneisenau* to show up, hopefully quite soon."

"Yes Sir. I will be exceptionally vigilant. Would the Captain please tell me from what direction I should expect her?"

"An excellent question. She is supposed to approach from the southwest, but who knows what mischief Captain Teebolt had gotten into these past few days. He might come in from the northeast; however, he knows that from that direction we might assume he is the enemy. No, he most assuredly will show up from the southwest."

"Thank you Captain. I will pay special attention to both quadrants."

Reassured, Kastanien made his way back to the bridge wing where he could continue watching the furious but orderly transferring. The pounding of the oil pumps immediately assaulted his ears when he opened the door. He thought to himself that this endless brutal noise was almost as bad as the tremendous explosive blasts from his big guns. He was about to go back inside to fetch his ear protectors when the signal light from *Bremen Castle* sprang to life, aimed directly at him. The message was short but poignant. *Bremen Castle's* Captain was sending across a private message in the mailbag for him that required a reply during this rendezvous.

Kastanien did not query this message as it was a relatively routine procedure. Kastanien, becoming anxious and bored with the transferring, decided to retrieve the message himself. After perfunctorily handing off command to Gott, he quickly descended to the lower deck. Almost casually he strode towards the forward transfer lines. The view from eye level was drastically different that his previous birds-eye observation. His men were moving mountains of goods into open hatches. Quickly spotting second officer Karl Mueller, who he had put in charge of the forward loading, he rapidly moved to his side. Mueller was so engrossed performing his duty that he started when Kastanien tapped him on the shoulder. Wheeling instantly with his lips parted to shout—young Karl Mueller's whole being froze at the sight of his captain. Kastanien grinned at the boy's rictus.

"You were about to say, Mr. Mueller?"
Quickly regaining his composure and by necessity, his wits, Mueller blurted out, "Captain Sir. I'm sorry for jumping so. I'm afraid I've forgotten what I was about to say. You did give me a bit of a scare."

"Come now, Mr. Mueller, you can do better than that. Nevertheless, let us leave that behind us. I have an important message from the captain of *Bremen Castle* in the mailbag. Would you kindly fetch it for me?"

"At once Captain." Smartly saluting, Mueller sprinted off to a specific gray-green canvas bag that was snug up against one of the huge capstans. Quickly undoing the double watertight clasps, Mueller immediately found the bright yellow packet clearly marked for his captain. After properly resealing the precious mailbag, Mueller rushed the packet back to Kastanien who had casually been watching the many tons of stores vanish into the innards of his ship. Mueller stopped a meter from Kastanien and with a minor flourish, handed over the important message. The two saluted each other and then Kastanien returned to his chair on the bridge. When properly seated he broke the old-style wax seal and removed the two pages of news. Kastanien methodically read the two sheets twice before neatly folding them and then he slid them into his inside jacket pocket. He sat silent for many moments mulling over the news.

Due to the critical importance of radio silence, he was completely unaware of any meaningful events that had taken place in the Atlantic since his last communiqués a while back when they were playing games with the *Rawalpindi.* The only truly important item was about *Bismarck.* This was of such interest that it would definitely influence Kastanien's plans for the immediate future. Dönitz had sent *Bismarck* out under cover of heavy fog on an almost moonless night. That particular night was exceptionally black due to low snow-laden clouds which blanketed the entire North Sea area. This made aerial detection by the ever-present British spy planes impossible. *Bismarck* had been sent north to vanish into a fjord midway up the Norwegian coast. Dönitz planned to hoodwink the Royal Navy into thinking that the pride of the German Navy was about to go foraging into the North Atlantic. He had bolstered this charade with false radio messages that 'accidentally' were sent in a previous code that he knew the British had effectually cracked.

Supposedly, *Bismarck* accompanied by *Prince Eugen,* would enter the Atlantic by way of the Denmark Strait. Kastanien realized immediately that this ploy would divide the Royal Navy ships that were all concentrating on finding and destroying *Gneisenau* and himself. The Denmark Strait was a long ways from where they had been searching for himself and *Gneisenau.* The message had been relayed to *Bremen Castle* by an ingenious communications system devised by none other than his younger brother James.

James was nearly fifteen years younger than Peter, but had the gift of a brilliant, rather devious mind. A motorcycle accident as a teenager had left him with a bad leg negating his eligibility for active duty with any of the military services. Undeterred by his minor infirmary, James rose quickly within the cryptology department of the Abwehr. Although his famous elder brother had never used his influence to further James career, the stoical Admiral Dönitz, early on in the war, had dropped a casual "hint" to Admiral Canaris—head of the Abwehr. Dönitz knew how much the brothers meant to each other and if Kastanien felt that his brother was succeeding well, he would have one less distraction from the job at hand.

James's clever mind had devised this very innovative system to get ultra-top-secret messages to their warships, which were under strict orders for total radio silence, unless engaged with the enemy. The system was used very sparingly and only for information that must never be seen by the enemy. Like all military intelligence departments, the Abwehr was paranoid that sensitive material did not fall into the wrong hands where it could culminate in disastrous consequences.

Although no system is absolutely foolproof, this one had virtually zero chance of being intercepted. The last leg of the system was innocuously embedded in the daily news broadcast from Lisbon in clear Portuguese. Since the broadcast needed only to reach as far as the Azores, it was only of minimal strength. Naturally, the British could receive every broadcast emanating from Western Europe; however there were so many military coded ones to deal with, that they simply did not have the work force to pay any attention to a simple, short-range newscast from a neutral nation. The British guessed wrongly. Since the signal strength was so weak, no secret message could even reach the North Atlantic where the German Navy prowled.

Kastanien almost laughed aloud when he realized that his mind had flashed up the egotistical thought that Dönitz's ploy was almost ingenious enough to be equal with his own clever subterfuges. As Kastanien was calmly massaging the *Bismarck* information and the probable response of the Royal Navy, a messenger from Second Officer Mueller silently appeared before him. Kastanien looked the seaman square in the eyes.

"Good evening Seaman Hersing. What brings you up here?"

The junior seaman beamed at being recognized by the captain. This was his first time to speak personally to Kastanien. He had heard that Kastanien knew every man on board, which he thought nearly impossible—but that doubt had just evaporated into thin air.

"Captain Sir. Second Officer Mueller sent me. He has come across several cases of goods marked specifically for your personal attention and wishes to know where to put them."

"Well, that's interesting. I was not expecting anything special. Just tell Mr. Mueller to put them in the galley where I will inspect them later. Wait a moment Hersing, I would like to talk to you."

Hersing's heart skipped a beat or two. He turned about and stood in front of Kastanien rigidly at attention.

"Yes Captain." Were all the words his vocal cords could utter—and they were noticeably taut.

"Mr. Hersing, I'm not going to bite your head off. Please stand easy. That's much better. Now then, I would like to know how your father is these days. He and I spent a few congenial hours in an enjoyable Berlin beer-hall during the last conflict. We have kept in touch sporadically over the years but I have not heard from him in over two years. I would appreciate it very much if you would bring me up to date on him, your mother and siblings. I will call for you later when we are finished with this task. Now, you must go as Mr. Mueller will wonder what happened to you."

"Yes Captain. I will be ready when you summon me."

Hersing saluted and departed, overjoyed with the captain's attention. Kastanien, his anxiety returning, stepped outside to the bridge wing. The assault on his hearing was ignored as he descended to the main deck. With determined strides, Peter Kastanien made his way aft to the refueling stations. No one noticed him standing silently watching the precious lifeblood of *Scharnhorst* pulse though the huge pipes into her tanks. When her tanks were topped up to their capacity of over 6,000 tons of oil *Scharnhorst* would be able to cruise more than 13,000 kilometers at her optimum speed of nineteen knots. Executive Officer Schmidt finally noticed Kastanien and quickly strode over to him.

"Everything is in order Captain. The refueling is going well. Is there anything I can do for you Sir?"

"No Hans. I am just a trifle restless when we are so vulnerable. Please carry on."

Kastanien did not linger very long after Schmidt had taken his leave. Now that he had seen the crews laboring diligently he quickly decided that he could spare his nasal sense from the cloying, noxious smell of the fuel. While the slow passage of two ships carried the bulk of the fumes away, the sheer volume of the vapors, exiting the vents, and then swirling around the various turrets, was formidable. Kastanien rejoined Gott on the bridge and tried vainly to dispel his nervousness. Then he wondered where his friend Attila was hiding out from the invasive stink, let alone the noise and commotion of the very busy ship. On a hunch, he checked the radar room, into which the all-encompassing stench had also invaded. 'Merlin' told him that Attila had taken off much earlier for places unknown. Still a trifle fretful, Kastanien wandered down to the galley.

He was rewarded in his quest with the pleasant sight of the great ship's cat enjoying being hand-fed some tender morsels from his cherished friend. Head Cook Manfried Strass also seemed very pleased with this delightful pastime. Strass was enjoying the respite from food preparation. All of his cooking flames had been extinguished due to German Navy's strict orders that there be no open flames during refueling. Down here in the very bowels of the *Scharnhorst*, the fuel smell was, thankfully, considerably more tolerable. Kastanien breathed easier and walked over to the two companions.

"Well, Mr. Strass how is your friend?"

"Captain. Attila is in the equivalent of cat Heaven when he gets his special treat of liver."

Leaning over a little, Kastanien gently stroked Attila's luxurious coat which relaxed him for a few quiet moments. Then with a resigned sigh he straightened up.

"I must take my leave and return to the deck. Enjoy yourselves for now my friends. We shall soon be back to our normal work routine."

Reluctantly, Kastanien vanished into the night.

Prince of Wales

Captain Reginald Sullivan paced the bridge, fidgeting with his ear. His apprehension as to the sea's condition, when they were in position to effect repairs, gnawed at him like a hungry cancer. His brain continually worried a budding ulcer that of late had besieged his stomach. He never liked being reduced to a single option, but he could not conjure up any reasonable choice other than simply stopping for repairs. He had cajoled chief engineer Thompson to distraction in a doomed attempt to "invent" a more palatable alternative. However; one inescapable fact remained. Divers had to go over the side to repair the external damage to the shaft exit bearing. Thompson had used this waiting time juggling every aspect of the necessary repairs. Everything that could be done before the ship stopped had been finished for quite some time. The divers were ready at a minute's notice. All the equipment, necessary parts and sequence of actions were in place. Thompson's men had been drilled incessantly, until they could probably do their assigned tasks blindfolded. Time dragged on—tediously slow.

"Captain Sir. We are three miles offshore," the radar operator blared through the intercom.

"Mr. Denham. How deep is the sea a mile offshore?"

"Very deep Sir. The cliffs at this sector of the island drop off almost vertical. There are no beaches at the bottom of the cliffs. It is a sheer drop to several thousand feet only a few yards offshore."

"Thank you. Mr. Denham. Mr. King, bring us closer inshore until the sea has settled quite a bit more. Reduce speed to three knots. I would much rather take a trifle longer to reach shelter versus blundering into something nasty. With the offshore wind, we should not be in any danger of bumping into those cliffs while we bob around like an errant cork. We must give the engineers the best possible working conditions so that they can affect repairs quickly."

Slowly, ever so slowly, the 43,786 tons of steel edged closer to the invisible cliffs of Sao Miguel. The sea condition remained unchanged until the gargantuan battleship was only a few hundred yards shy of a mile offshore. Then, quite noticeably, the sea calmed to gentle swells.

"Mr. King. Take us in another quarter mile closer. Since we cannot anchor, I want the underwater repair crew to have time enough for repairs before we drift back out into a more restless sea."

First Officer Roland King waited only a few moments before ordering the helm to alter course. *Prince of Wales* slowly turned her stern out to sea with her bow to the land. When *Prince of Wales* had positioned herself, her length perpendicular to the now gentle rolling swells, he called for. *"Engines, all stop"*.

According to the plan devised by Captain Sullivan and himself, he ordered the tender and two lifeboats lowered. The plan was to have two lifeboats tie up to the bow and then hopefully keep *Prince of Wales* from drifting away from the island into rougher water. Even a gentle breeze caressing the monstrous bulk of the battleship would create a force that the two lifeboats could only hope to slow down a bit. The tender, using her more significantly powerful engine would act as a tugboat attached to the bow. Her duty was to keep *Prince of Wales* from slewing sideways to the waves. The consensus that the slight vertical motion created by the traversing waves, would be much more palatable to the dive crew than having the idled battleship roll side to side.

The well-instructed, disciplined crew members sprang into action with cheerful alacrity. The diving crew rapidly lowered their work barge and equipment over the stern. When the barge was secured in place, a profusion of equipment was lowered along with the prerequisite replacement parts. Immediately upon the equipment and parts being shoved into their proper places, the divers descended to the barge. Fortuitously, the rain had not slacked off. The minor inconvenience of a slick deck was grudgingly considered a blessing rather than a hindrance. The rain clouds, coupled with the cascading curtain of rainwater, would squelch the low level of the ship's lights—masking *Prince of Wales* to any observers more than half a mile distant. If it had been a clear night, the activity would have been visible for several miles. Quickly attaching themselves to the air hoses, the divers gave the sign that they were ready. Clutching the powerful underwater lanterns, acetylene torches, and the supremely important lifelines, they were slowly lowered into the ink-black water. With the plethora of tools festooning their bulky dive suits and the huge brass helmet with its reinforced glass ports, the divers looked like oversized medieval knights wielding short, strange-looking swords.

The barge crew very slowly inched out the strong lifeline cables of the two divers until they received the signal jerk to stop. Although the divers were not that far below the surface, the powerful torches were barely visible to the watchers on the barge. They were so close to the towering cliffs, that the returning wave action kept the relatively close-in waters cloudy with all forms of detritus. Visibility was no more than fifteen feet— if you were an optimist.

The divers laboriously paddled forward towards the outer starboard screw. Fortunately, there was virtually no current to make this tricky job even more dangerous. Also very fortunately, the water was relatively warm, which dramatically increased the divers endurance time and kept their minds off their body heat, allowing them to stay focused on the task ahead. After less than two minutes, the ghostly image of a massive propeller blade silently appeared from the green gloom. Then they saw the problem.

The huge propeller was wrapped with a heavy braided cable—the thickness of a man's thumb. The divers paddled to where the propeller was attached to the shaft. With one diver on each side they slowly moved forward, inspecting the cable that was wrapped around the shaft like a python squeezing the life out of its prey. When they reached the end of the external shaft where it exited the hull, they were relieved to find that the binding cable stopped a few inches from the crucial exit bearing. Since they could not converse with each other, they resorted to well-practiced hand signals augmented by printing notes on a slate. The apprentice diver wrote a quick question wondering why the cable had not dropped to the ocean floor.

The more experienced head diver wrote on his slate.

"Really doesn't matter much now does it? Good question though. I would like to know as well, since if whatever kept it afloat might still be with us. I prefer not to be unpleasantly surprised. Let's follow the cable inboard to see where it goes."

Using the cable for handholds the two divers maneuvered around the fourteen-and-a-half foot, three-bladed massive screw until they found a strand of the cable that headed straight out towards the inboard propeller shaft. Meticulously careful with their airlines, the underwater torches and all the sundried equipment dangling from every corner of their dive suits, the two divers moved hand over hand until the inboard propeller materialized out of the gloom. After a careful circumnavigation, they discovered the cable had wound around this shaft a few times before heading straight upwards. With practiced hand signals, they followed the cable upwards. After only a few yards, a ghostly greenish-white apparition materialized from the murk.

Closer inspection of the quite large, featureless object proved it was some kind of flotation device. The divers cautiously grasped the cables that crisscrossed the float and proceeded to survey its bulk. Reaching the far side, they found another cable that vanished into the deep. The lead diver, now satisfied that there was little danger, held onto a cable that was securely wrapped around the ugly float and tugged on the descending cable. The cable, although rather heavy, did not seem to be part of the mess that entangled his ship.

The two divers scribbled notes back and forth until they were unified on a plan of action. Quickly motioning the universal hand signal for all clear to proceed, the lead diver ignited his acetylene torch and began immediately to cut through the cable that dropped into the ocean depths while the second diver firmly gripped the section above where the cut was being made. The potent, knife-sharp flame boiled the water, sending volumes of hissing bubbles toward the surface. Once amputated, the cable dropped like an anvil into the abyss. There was only a minor backlash on the remaining cable as the strain from the hanging dead weight was liberated. After securely attaching a tough manila rope to the slime-covered float, the head diver quickly severed the cable holding the float to the propeller shaft. Loosed from its unnatural habitat beneath the surface, the ugly float popped upwards to the surface.

When the securing rope stopped after several seconds, the apprentice diver signaled to be brought up. Surfacing, he handed the rope to a brawny seaman, signaling him to hold tight. His faceplate was opened and the ghoulish countenance of Fred Thompson stared at him from less than two feet. Quickly, the diver blurted out what they had done and what the barge crew needed to do with the rope that was attached to the pestilent float on the other end. After the very brief summary of what they had done so far, he asked to be sealed up; which Thompson did with brisk efficiency.

Descending, he quickly rejoined his dive mate who had devised a course of action for tackling the vastly more complex mess that reminded him of the mythical Medusa's hairdo with its many dangerous writhing snakes.

The head diver, a cautious optimist, grabbed the cable strung between the two shafts. It was as tight as a violin string. Again, the divers conferred on their slates as to how to proceed. Severing the line with the torch would undoubtedly release far too much tension causing the cable to lash out viciously—with little doubt as to the dire consequences which could cripple or even end the life of a man. They concurred that the best plan of attack was to reverse the inboard shaft a turn or two and relieve the pent-up strain. The two divers quickly ascended to the barge, where they passed on their recommendations to the anxious chief engineer who had been chain-smoking ever since they descended. With something to do now, he flicked the half-finished cigarette overboard as he ascended the rope ladder to the deck.

Three minutes later, he was back on the barge. Knowing Fred Thompson's efficiency, the two divers had remained in the water, rather than going through the energy-draining procedure of clamoring onto the barge. With their faceplates open, they were informed that the inboard starboard shaft had been reversed three turns. The anxious look on the chief engineers face, made almost ghoulish by the harsh illumination, was all the instructions the divers needed. Thompson had signaled two seamen to latch the faceplates as he was relaying the information to the divers. Within a minute, the divers were once again bound for the fouled screws.

The scene they came upon between the shafts was better than they had hoped. The previously taunt cable now drooped slackly, waving gently with the slight swell of the ship. The divers quickly cut the slack cable and then backed away a few feet. The two ends of the severed cable end simply dropped. Supported by his teammate, the lead diver latched onto the recently severed cable and began loosening it from the inboard shaft. One loop after the other the cable was unwound. It had threaded itself to the shaft so neatly that it mimicked a well-organized windlass. After a few loops had been unwound, the cable, weighed down by the other end, sluggishly began to slip a bit. The lead diver immediately backpedaled away several yards pulling his companion with him.

Although they were now out of decent visual contact of the cable and shaft, the constant slight scratching noise of the slipping cable assured them that it was unwinding itself. The scratching suddenly turned into a screech as the physics of gravity vs. the co-efficient of friction swung dramatically against friction. Then through the murkiness, a Catharine Wheel of green luminance appeared. The divers knew this was created by the rapid acceleration of the short end of the cable, frothing the salt water into a reflector for their torches. The whole scene lasted less than a minute before the screeching stopped along with the eerie light.

The divers waited a full minute in the now dark, silent water before slowly moving forward with their torches held far forward of their bulk. They carefully checked for any possible trouble on or near the inboard shaft. Finding nothing but a gleaming shaft where the unraveling cable had polished all the ocean grime away, they then headed towards the snarled mess on the outboard shaft.

The outboard shaft and screw were both enmeshed with so much cable they resembled a big wicker basket. Slowly the divers began wrestling one loose end of the cable until it came up cinched by an overlapping strand. Careful not to let the torch chew into the bronze screw or shaft, they cut away the offending strand. Not much happened, but they could unravel a few more feet before the same problem presented itself. Working cautiously, the two divers managed to free some of the screw from the choking cable. With still more cable to be cut loose, the head diver signaled his companion to surface for a well-deserved break.

Surfacing, the two divers motioned for assistance to get on board the barge. Their faceplates were opened immediately when they were seated on a bench. The air pump stopped—making conversation much easier. Fred Thompson concurred with the head diver that they were about done-in and needed the second team to take over. The second team had already suited up and quite smartly they attached their umbilical cords. After a detailed briefing by the first pair, the second team vanished below into the quiescent ocean. After surveying the remaining tangled hodgepodge, the second team set to severing the tightly bound cable that strangled the driveshaft. Several lengths of cable were cut before the divers could unwind a few lengths without cutting further. Finally, the last of the cable gently eased its vise-like grip on the shaft, becoming loose enough for the divers to unclog the congested tangle.

With a few well-placed torch cuts, the cable lengths dropped from sight to join their brethren hundreds of fathoms below. As the last wrap unwound itself, an errant strand of wire sliced into one of the diver's suits slitting open a ten-inch gash. The water quickly began to fill the suit radically making the diver excessively negative buoyant. The barge crew immediately felt the additional strain on the lifeline and began to haul the diver back to the surface. The other diver, sensing more than seeing his companion in trouble, moved to assist. Before he reached him, the ailing diver was hauled up to safety.

The intact diver signaled to be surfaced as well and quite shortly the two men were grinning with the first team on the barge bench. Their euphoria was short-lived before Fred Thompson began grilling them about the status of the shafts and propellers. Thompson said little as the men described what they had done to remove the offending cable and float. When he asked about the status of the propeller blades, the four men remained mute. None of them had done a proper, thorough inspection either before or after the clean-up operation.

Thompson mulled over the facts for several moments as he paced the barge—smoking cigarettes, which he lit from the butt of each one when it was nearly finished. Ordering the divers and crewmembers to stand or sit easy until he returned, the chief engineer scrambled to the main deck, and then hurried below to his cherished engines. He personally engaged the Parsons single-reduction geared turbines one after the other, allowing the screws to turn ever so slowly. With his surgeon's skilled fingers he felt the huge shafts as they slowly revolved forward and then in reverse. Satisfied there were no real or imagined problems, he disengaged the shafts allowing them to stop rotating.

Barking orders to leave things as they are, Thompson returned to the barge and suited up for a personal inspection of his propulsion system. Thompson descended with only a powerful torch attached to his suit with a short lanyard. He was not an experienced underwater maintenance diver, however, he could hold his own when it was only a relatively simple swim-around, enjoying the sights.

Thompson found quite a few dings in the leading edge of the outboard screw most probably caused by the thrashing about of the cable. The inboard screw had only a few fresh scratches of no consequence; which was a great relief. Just to be on the prudent side of thoroughness, Thompson signaled for more line. When he had adjusted his suit to be as neutrally buoyant as possible, he swam across to the port propellers. Finding them in proper condition, he returned to the barge.

"Right, me laddies. We're back in business. Let's pack up this little lot and give the captain the good news."

The four divers who were still suited up with their faceplates open, along with the rest of the barge crew shouted a loud hooray three times and then with satisfied, grinning faces scurried about sending all the assorted gear back to the main deck. Less than ten minutes passed before all the equipment and men were back topside winching up the barge. When the barge was clear of the ocean, Thompson ordered the two lifeboats and tender to disengage and be stowed properly back in their divots. After double-checking to assure himself that all was returning to normal, Thompson reported to the captain.

"Captain Sir. Chief Engineer Thompson reporting on damage and repairs."

"Very well, Mr. Thompson. Please just give me the pertinent essentials for now. I wish to get underway with some sea room as soon as possible. We can go over your detailed report later."

"Yes Sir. As you know, we had a nasty bollixed proper mess of cables and net mesh wrapped tightly around both starboard shafts and screws. After my men cut all the hodgepodge mess loose, I went down and checked their work. They did an excellent job and best of all, there is no serious damage. I did find a few small nicks in one of the screws, but that will not create any problem other than possibly a miniscule flutter and vibration. We will need to repair those nicks when next we are in homeport. Until then, let us chase the Germans and give them bloody Hell."

"Excellent, excellent. A fine job Chief Engineer Thompson. Please give a 'well done' to your divers and crew from me. Especially for the short time they took to accomplish what might have been a rather longish challenge. Your idea of using the lifeboats and tender to stabilize us was brilliant. They kept your men from dealing with much nastier seas. Now, when can we get underway and are there any limitations to our speed?"

"Captain, I will return to the deck where I'm quite sure the boats are on board and properly stored along with all the equipment. The boilers are fully operational, needing only the word to engage the screws. I will give you the all-clear over the intercom, probably within five minutes. Captain, one more thing. Would you please start out at a modest speed while I keep a close eye on our propulsion system?"

"Very well, Mr. Thompson. I will await your consent to get underway and I will heed your advice on building up speed," Captain Sullivan replied with just a tinge of sarcasm.

Thompson scurried down to the deck. His second-in-command greeted him as he stepped off the ladder onto the main deck. The two men snapped off sloppy salutes then shook hands grinning like Cheshire cats.

"And now Second Engineer Marston, what is our status?" inquired Thompson.

"Boats all secured, barge and all equipment properly stored in their lockers and the men are in the mess having a hot toddy, courtesy of the captain who called me while you were on the way to the bridge. We are ready for sea, and hopefully finding those damn Huns who cannot continue to hide forever.

"Thank you Mr. Marston. That was right thoughtful of the captain— treating the men to a bit of warming libation. Guess that proves he's not the ferocious 'King and Country' ogre all the time. Now, while I give the captain permission to get underway, I want you to nip down to the mess and procure us some of the captain's largesse. Please make sure that we get a full measure."

With that last comment, Thompson slyly winked at his sometimes partner in nefariousness.

"Mr. King, be so kind as to get us underway. Slowly build up speed four knots at a time starting at ten knots every five minutes until we are cruising along at twenty-four knots. Set a course for the Iceland-Greenland gap. Maybe we can get in on the *Bismarck* action," Captain Sullivan ordered.

Knowing he was speaking for all the officers and probably most of the crew, the First Officer Roland King promptly piped up, "Captain Sir. Do you really think that we might get into some action with *Bismarck*?"

"Gentlemen, the Royal Navy has been chasing about pursing two smaller German battleships over most of the North Atlantic for some considerable time now. Our luck has been abysmal. We've not even gotten a glimpse of their smoke, not to mention the fact that our guns have been cold since we left England. I bloody well hope we can tangle with some

German capital ship. I don't even give a tinker's damn which one. I, Winston, and the entire Admiralty desperately need to rid the oceans of those ravenous predators before they sink so much shipping that we cannot continue to fight. Besides that, I want to fire our guns in anger for the first time."

The officers remained hushed by the raw vitriolic of Captain Sullivan's answer. It seemed to them that Captain Sullivan had a few more sides to his persona than any of them had even speculated on. Finally, after several longish seconds, First Officer Roland King shattered the ominous silence, "Thank you Captain. We feel precisely the same way."

Scharnhorst

"Mr. Gott, what is our status on refueling and taking on stores?" Kastanien asked immediately as he entered the bridge from the darkened passageway.

"Sir, we have all stores on board and our fuel tanks are topped up. Mr. Schmidt is down on the deck overseeing the disconnecting of the fuel lines. We should be ready to get underway within a very few minutes."

"Thank you Mr. Gott. When Mr. Schmidt gives us the all clear, carefully move us away from the *Bremen Castle*, set speed at twenty-four knots. Set us on a course north-east for ten kilometers and then head east for the area approximately one hundred kilometers due west of Portugal. Hopefully we can catch that convoy."

Just as the first officer was about to acknowledge the orders, the intercom squawked to life.

"Captain. Radar operator Molter here Sir. I am picking up another vessel west south-west of us on a course that would bring her up to us rather quickly. It has just barely registered on my screen but it seems to be moving faster than any normal merchant would. I will keep monitoring and relay any new information as I decipher it."

All the bridge officers' eyes scrutinized Kastanien silently, waiting for his orders. They had not long to wait.

"Mr. Schmidt. Turn us around and head for Mr. Molter's unknown ship on an intercepting course. Take us away from the shore so we will be positioned on her seaward side. It is almost certainly *Gneisenau* showing up for our prearranged rendezvous. However, we should be ready if perchance it is someone else—a bit less friendly. I want her up against the islands with no sea room to maneuver should she prove to be unfriendly. Go to battle stations in a few minutes. Send our best eyes up to their watch stations. When the men are at their posts and ready, darken ship completely. If our new colleague doesn't have radar to see us, then we shall have the marked advantage of surprise. Also signal *Bremen Castle* to maintain steaming on her current course at normal speed, but darken their ship totally and immediately. With the night now so clear, any light whatsoever could be seen from a very long ways off. We are simply going to vanish. Now I am going to the radar room to check our mystery guest's progress."

The leviathan, aptly named *Scharnhorst,* promptly executed a course change and then charged forward at twenty-four knots, which would close the gap in a relatively short period.

After the few hours of tedious tension, the call to action galvanized the battleships' crew into action. They all were looking forward to meeting the mystery ship after sighting nothing other than a dark foreboding shoreline. Most of the crew was hoping that they would see more action against the Royal Navy, especially if it proved to be one of the hounds from the pack sent out by the Admiralty. Their euphoria was so high that any thought of losing a slugfest with an English battleship never entered their thoughts.

"Mr. Molter, I can see that the blip on your screen seems quite strong. Please give me your updated opinion about our friend out there."

"Captain Sir. The vessel approaches at a speed over twenty knots. She has not changed course since she first appeared on my screen. She is now approximately twenty kilometers slightly forward of us on our starboard side maintaining the same course."

"Thank you "Merlin," I am returning to the bridge. Inform me immediately if she changes course or speed."

"Mr. Schmidt. We are closing rapidly on this 'mystery' vessel. If she is running with lights, we should see her within fifteen to twenty minutes. Are battle stations manned and ready?"

"Yes Captain. Just finished. I am darkening ship right now."

As soon as he finished speaking and getting a sharp nod from Kastanien, Schmidt used the ship's intercom ordering all lights visible from the outside extinguished. Within twenty seconds, *Scharnhorst* blinked from sight on the lightly rolling ocean. Only a dim, spectral glow from the critical bridge instruments remained—creating a Frankenstein effect on the officers' close by. For no reason whatsoever, the sudden eerie change, which was nothing new to these men, stilled every voice for several minutes. The tension became virtually audible as they waited impatiently—frozen in place for action or reunion. Suddenly with a shattering effect, the intercom snapped the hypnotic spell.

"Bridge, Radar man Molter here. Mystery ship is now fifteen kilometers ahead. No change in course or speed."

"Well now. Our friend either has no radar or is deliberately staying his course. At this range considering the clarity of the night, she must also be darkened or our sharp young eyes would have spotted them by now. That is what Captain Teebolt would do in this situation, regardless of whether we were friend or foe. Mr. Schmidt, please go to the radar room and tell Mr. Molter to inform us when she is eight kilometers away."

No words were spoken in the short span of time while Schmidt slipped into the darkness, returning in less than a minute. He silently stepped up to Kastanien and nodded. Kastanien returned the nod and then both men turned their eyes forward straining into the mysterious black night. Like a wraith, Attila silently appeared on his perch. His familiar statue silhouette gladdened the hearts of those who had witnessed the glass-smooth leap. Kastanien refrained from commanding his friend to hither to his battle station since he knew instinctively that there was little chance of danger forthcoming.

Abruptly, a piercingly bluish arrow of light erupted from the nothingness. It lasted only a few seconds before being extinguished. Any night vision the *Scharnhorst's* watchers had developed was now gone for many minutes.

"Return two flashes from our searchlight, each with duration of three seconds apart—immediately!" snapped Kastanien.

The forward searchlight, mounted on the foretop quickly sent two bursts of identical matching blazing brilliance light, once again piercing the blackness. They found their mark unerringly. In the short time they were lit, a smattering of reflections returned to *Scharnhorst*. Ten seconds after *Scharnhorst's* light ceased, one single burst from afar came back at them.

"Ahh, it is without any doubt, our companion *Gneisenau*, unless the Royal Navy has been eavesdropping on private conversations between Captain Teebolt and myself. Rest easy, but do not stand down from battle stations just yet. Let us continue to shorten the gap to truly verify her identity," Kastanien announced in a much less tense demeanor.

Only a few moments passed before the intercom blared to life.

"Radar room here. Vessel is now eight kilometers ahead, maintaining course with a speed of twenty knots."

At that instant, the night visitor illuminated his entire ship, which loomed rather large, even at this longish range. Kastanien ordered *Scharnhorst* to comply by turning on all her nighttime running lights. Suddenly the previous empty night sea had two large, sparkling travelers heading for a rendezvous with each other. Kastanien stepped back to the radar room himself.

"Merlin, how far is the ship from us now?"

"Six kilometers, Captain."

After perfunctorily thanking Molter, Kastanien strode back to the bridge immediately issuing orders.

"Mr. Mueller, have the signalman, along with yourself join me on the starboard bridge wing."

With a significant closure rate, the once distant ship had rapidly loomed larger when the three men reached the signal lamp on the bridge wing.

"Signalman, ask our friend out there what is the name of our honorary mascot."

Sporting a wide grin, the signalman clattered the shutters rapidly for no more than ten seconds. Within five seconds, the reply came back with the correct answer—Attila.

"Now, there is absolutely no doubt that she is *Gneisenau*. Signal *Gneisenau* we will reverse course and join her when she links up with *Bremen Castle*. Inform *Gneisenau* that *Bremen Castle* is steaming without lights several kilometers ahead of her. We will signal *Bremen Castle* to light up when we are in range of our signal lamp."

Now the signalman spent nearly two minutes transmitting Kastanien's orders. When the rattling clatter abruptly ceased, the three men waited for the reply. It didn't take very long before a short affirmative response flashed across the shortening void. Satisfied all was in order, Kastanien told the two men to maintain a watch for three minutes, just in case there were more messages forthcoming, then stepped back into the bridge, once more issuing orders as he strode towards his chair.

"Mr. Gott, reverse course and take us back towards *Bremen Castle*. Make the turn to port, slow and easy so as not to scatter all the provisions which Mr. Strass will still be in the midst of stowing away. Before you execute the turn, please inform *Gneisenau* of our action. I want to be three kilometers ahead of her and two kilometers to her seaward side. When we are there, hold that position with her.

"When we are in signaling range, signal *Bremen Castle* to light up. Neither *Gneisenau* nor we need to bump into her. Inform her that *Gneisenau* will be coming up between us shortly to refuel and take on provisions. Inquire of the officers if there are any messages that they wish to signal *Gneisenau*."

Kastanien had reached and settled into his chair when he finished with his orders. Now that the pervasive stink from the refueling was a dim memory, the night took on a much more pleasant atmosphere. When *Scharnhorst* began her leisurely turn, Attila's head swiveled at the same rate, never letting his gaze waiver from *his* sister ship. Soon the back wall of the bridge blocked *Gneisenau* from his view. Unperturbed with not much else to see or do, Attila began to wash his paws—no doubt to remove some miniscule remains of his recent late night snack. Not spending much time grooming, Attila leapt onto Kastanien's lap after Peter signaled him to come over. With a grace, exceptional even in the feline world, Attila handily soared the few feet from his perch to Kastanien's lap. He arrived more than landed, did a few mandatory circles, massaged Peter's stomach, and then curled into a ball gazing up at his friend. Kastanien silently returned the look and began softly stroking the luxurious fur as Attila tucked his snout into his tail.

Kastanien relaxed slightly in his chair, seemingly oblivious to everything around him. The truth be known, his thoughts were several thousand kilometers away. He continued to pet Attila, who never tired of his affection, while he allowed the war to recede in favor of Andrea, his children and all the other pleasant thoughts of his small estate back home. All of his officers gave their revered captain these precious few interludes a wide, silent berth. They all knew that Peter Kastanien needed some respite from the tension of war, and that when the time came, he would lead and command them better than any General or Admiral in modern times. Only the English Admiral Horatio Nelson from the previous century could lead outnumbered naval forces to resounding victories so adroitly, as *their* Captain Kastanien.

Abruptly the spell was broken as the lights from *Bremen Castle* blinked to life a couple of kilometers forward of their position off the port quarter. Kastanien leaned slightly forward, whispering into Attila's ever-alert ear. As Kastanien shifted to rise from the chair, Attila sailed effortlessly back to his perch. After settling instantly into his watch posture, Attila swiveled his head from side to side before settling with his gaze concentrated on *Bremen Castle*.

After Kastanien had collected Second Officer Mueller and his signalman, the three men once more returned to the port bridge wing.

"Signal *Bremen Castle* our intention to hold station with her until *Gneisenau* hooks up. She should be alongside within a few minutes."

After the staccato beat of the signal lamp desisted, the three men silently watched the lights from *Gneisenau* gradually swell in size. The sea remained relatively quiet, but now occasional feathery wisps of damp fog brushed their faces, growing minimally denser with every passing minute. Kastanien took careful note of the minor changes in the scend of the sea along with the growing fog. With a few decades of experience at sea, Kastanien could gauge what the future would bring with uncanny accuracy. The fog reached a thin density that was more a nuisance than a hindrance before remaining constant. Visibility was only slightly impaired. The lights from *Bremen Castle* and the looming *Gneisenau* took on ghostly halos, but were still brilliant enough to illuminate the scene with decent clarity.

"Mr. Mueller, I believe that we shall be in for a bit of weather come the dawn. Nothing ferocious, mind you, but a bit of a rough ride, hindered by medium to heavy fog."

Mueller nodded his agreement and the men continued their silent vigil. *Gneisenau's* giant bulk quite suddenly snuffed out all but the uppermost lights from *Bremen Castle* as she sidled up to the supply ship. *Scharnhorst's* watchers remained inactive while the umbilical cords supplying needed fuel were affixed on the far side from their view. After many minutes, the signal lamp from *Gneisenau* began flashing to *Scharnhorst*. Kastanien waited patiently until the signalman read him the contents of the message from Captain Teebolt. When he was finished reading, Kastanien addressed his signalman, "Signal *Gneisenau* that we are pulling alongside within hailing distance once Captain Teebolt informs us that he is secure to *Bremen Castle* with oiling and provisioning underway."

Kastanien waited until the message had been sent and acknowledged before turning to his second officer.

"Mr. Mueller, while we await Captain Teebolt's permission to close up, I have a question for you. It is part of your education regarding procedures, so do not struggle with your answer. I want only your truth. Here is the question. Why did I opt to move within hailing distance rather than simply flashing signals back and forth?"

Mueller, although he had had many such thorny questions put to him by Kastanien since joining *Scharnhorst's* compliment, he still felt uncomfortable with his answers. A couple of admonishments by Kastanien when he waffled had been enough to teach him that straightforward answers were always the best by far.

"Captain, honestly I do not have a solid answer but I do have a guess. My guess is that you would rather hear your friend's voice over that of impartial messages from the signalmen."

"Well now Mr. Mueller, that's quite perceptive of you and that really is my secondary reason. However, the main reason is a much more serious decision. You know that we are quite close to a foreign shore, which although they are marginally unfriendly to us, they harbor enemy agents. Moreover, unless they are totally asleep on the job, they will have discovered that there are two unknown quite large ships slowly steaming along their shoreline. If we keep them in the dark, so to speak, they will not know who we are.

"Also, keep in mind that we will be seaward of *Gneisenau*, so our signal lamp will be visible to any watcher on the shore. You will also note that our searchlights are all trained slightly over *Gneisenau*. From the shore, these powerful lances of light will nullify any night vision the watchers might have, thereby rendering accurate identification of us virtually impossible.

"If we were to use our signal lamp to transmit sensitive information, there is the possibility that the enemy could get their hands on it—much to our dismay. Therefore, Captain Teebolt and I will go over things by simple voice contact that cannot be heard from the shore."

"Thank you Captain. This is a lesson that I shall not forget."

"You're welcome Mr. Mueller. I have every confidence that you will someday captain your own ship and I know that you will do Germany's Navy proud."

Mueller was rendered speechless for several seconds with Kastanien's compliment.

"Thank you very much Captain. If I am fortunate enough to attain the rank of Captain, I shall always remember the valuable lessons you have taught me. I fervently hope that I shall be as great a Captain as you are, Sir."

"Mr. Mueller, one other thing to remember. Never try to think what I would do in any circumstance that you find yourself in—just use your own good judgment. Second-guessing what I would do will cause you to hesitate, and that is something that a good captain can never do. Now, let us concentrate on conversing with Captain Teebolt. Please hand me the megaphone."

While the two officers were talking, *Scharnhorst* had gracefully slid up to within fifty meters of *Gneisenau* and was now holding station with her. Kastanien aimed the powerful megaphone towards *Gneisenau's* bridge and began.

"Captain Kastanien hailing Captain Teebolt. Captain, are you able to converse for a few minutes?"

Immediately the response came.

"Captain Teebolt here. Yes, we are tethered to *Bremen Castle* and oil is flowing properly. Provisions are also being shuttled across. My Executive Officer Karl Ehrlich has everything under control for the moment. I am now free to talk to you, however, if something goes amiss, you will forgive me if I break off suddenly."

"Understood. Well now Kris, it appears that you have had a bit of trouble since last we were together. I have noted that your fine ship shows some battle damage. Have a bit of a tussle with the Royal Navy? Please bring me up to date on your recent activities."

Teebolt talked for nearly ten minutes relating his recent battle with the Royal Navy. When he was finished, he enquired of his friend Peter Kastanien as to any noteworthy adventures that *Scharnhorst* had lucked into recently. Kastanien replied relating the incident with *Rawalpindi* and the role U3200X played in 'vanishing' since last they saw each other. Teebolt guffawed at the clever deception, adding that he was a bit jealous of the maneuver. The two men continued to check with each other that the information gleaned from intercepted British transmissions had been deciphered similarly. There were a few minor discrepancies, which they quickly ironed out. Overall, the two captains had drawn similar conclusions.

"Kris, now that we are of one accord, here are my thoughts for our immediate future. I believe that the Royal Navy is expecting us to have headed back to the Caribbean area, so let us ply our trade where they do not expect us to pop up. I originally planned to head for the west coast of Iceland, but analyzing our facts with a goodly dose of guesswork thrown in—that destination might get us into a bad confrontation with a large number of Royal Navy ships. Instead, I suggest that we head eastward towards Portugal and hopefully pick up a Gibraltar-England convoy either inbound or outbound. I would prefer to decimate an outbound convoy laden with war materiel that could hinder Rommel's efforts in North Africa. However, reducing supplies headed for England would suffice."

"I totally concur that the Royal Navy thinks we have headed for the New World. Judging by the intercepts, they are now probably much more concerned about keeping tabs on *Bismarck*—since they can't ever seem to find us," Teebolt replied with much sarcasm in his last statement, "I wonder what our sly Grossadmiral Dönitz has in mind for *Bismarck*?"

"Kris, I appreciate your levity regarding the hide-and-seek game we have been playing with the Royal Navy, but let us not get too smug. They do have an enormous advantage over us with the sheer number of potent warships at their disposal. Unfortunately, most of their ships have also maintained radio silence for days, leaving us to ponder where they are. I do know that *Bismarck* has not headed out into the Atlantic, but the British think that she is headed for the Denmark Strait. Until the Royal Navy gets a whiff of us, I'm going to assume that the British have sent everything they have within reasonable range to keep *Bismarck* boxed in behind the Denmark Strait. If that is the case, then the sooner we can 'pop up' off the coast of Portugal, the fewer ships the Royal Navy can spare to concentrate on *Bismarck*. You well know that we have tweaked the mighty Royal Navy's nose, and they will come for us with the bit between their teeth.

"You still have a couple of hours to finish refueling so I shall bid you farewell and head for our new hunting grounds. I will cruise along at fifteen to twenty knots, depending on the density of this recently arrived fog, until you can catch up. That way we can cover more territory since you will be about sixty kilometers behind me when you are finished victualing. Being the optimist that I am, I am convinced that I shall engage a convoy soon enough. You can then make up the distance while I am cruising around in circles capturing or sinking a few merchants."

The two captains spent a few more minutes co-coordinating their courses along with several rendezvous points and when they were in accord, Kastanien concluded the conversations.

"It's been wonderful visiting you again Kris and I look forward to seeing you later today. If this fog does not lift soon, then you might just have to dawdle along at a slower speed. If that's the case, then we shall meet up the following day. In the meantime, do not dwell on unknown, unpleasant possibilities. Rather, let us enjoy the fruits of victory while they are still ours."

Kastanien handed the megaphone to Mueller and the two men once more took their stations in the bridge. Mueller went to his post while Kastanien issued orders.

"Mr. Schmidt, take us away from *Gneisenau* at twelve knots until we are fifteen kilometers ahead of her which should be adequate enough to tone down any nuisance waves we create that might hinder *Gneisenau* and *Bremen Castle*. Then ring up eighteen knots on a heading of eighty-five degrees. Darken ship immediately. With this growing fog, we should be able to slip away without the shore watchers deducing who we are or what we have been up to."

With these new orders, the bridge instantly was abuzz with activity. The officers moved with smooth alacrity honed by the countless drills that every sailor respected but detested nonetheless. *Scharnhorst* smoothly accelerated away from the two ships—quickly swallowed by the increasingly dense night fog.

Attila roused himself from his perch, checked out the busyness around the bridge, and then being assured that there was nothing to be overly concerned about, resumed his nap. Kastanien seated himself in his chair and once again evaluated all the fragments of information about the Royal Navy's disposition of their formidable forces. He mulled over the known and guesswork facts for many minutes before tiring of the futility of mind-reading the British. His mind drifted over the battle events that his friend Kris Teebolt had relayed to him, and realized that he was jealous of the real naval action between serious warships that had been missing from his life as of late. Once more, he realized that he was a warrior at heart, needing the dangerous exhilaration of deadly combat. How prophetic his thoughts would soon prove to be.

The Admiralty

The five haggard Senior Officers of England's military command silently sipped on their tea while munching on scrumptious tasting crumpets that oozed butter and orange marmalade. The past few weeks had visibly aged Robert Stark. His haggard face had sprouted several new lines giving credence to how fine he had been drawn. Stark finished his crumpet, wiped a speck of marmalade from the corner of his mouth, and then broke the silent gloom.

"Fellow Officers, while we await the Honorable Ian McLeod, let me----."

Stark stopped in mid-sentence when the massive door flew open, admitting a visibly agitated First Lord of the Admiralty who charged immediately into a loud diatribe, principally against the Gods of War.

"Damnation to the bloody Huns, Oden and any other of their godless Gods. Sorry to be rather testy this morning gentlemen and I do apologize for keeping you waiting. There was a critical communiqué that I absolutely needed translating before zipping over to show Winston. I say, those crumpets look positively magnificent. Since I cannot remember when last I ate, would someone be kind enough to procure me a few of them along with some tea to perk me up. Once again, my sincere apologies. I do seem to be wandering all over map here. Let me start from the beginning.

"On my way over here, a young chap rushed up to me and handed me a missive from Bletchley Park that had just shown up. He said that Head of

Signals regarded it to be of the utmost importance. Well, they understated the importance. Men, *Bismarck* has still not been spotted in or even near the Denmark Strait. The weather was exceptionally clear last evening and night, so *Ark Royal* launched every plane they had to search for her, but to no avail. With the ice pack shrinking from Greenland's shores, the navigable gap is wider, but still narrow enough that there is simply no way she could get through without our chaps spotting her.

"I immediately enquired if our patrols scouring the Shetlands-Iceland gap had had any better success. Now, please refrain from exploding when I tell you that they simply do not know. Right, they do not bloody well know. It seems that some addle-brained genius decided that it was unnecessary to adequately cover this entrance into the endless tracks of the North Atlantic. Robert, please tell me that it is not too late to rectify this foolhardy oversight."

"Minister, *Bismarck* has had more than adequate time to have slipped through this gap. Earlier, while we were waiting for you to arrive, my esteemed colleagues and I dissected every scrap of intelligence we have received for the past two or three weeks. There simply is no clue as to the whereabouts of *Bismarck* at this time. I fervently wish there was so we could plot a course of action. This interminable waiting is frustrating at best, and ulcer generating at worst. The only ray of hope, which we should fervently pray for, is that *Bismarck* and company have returned to port with mechanical problems."

"Stark, do you really think that she turned about?"

"No Minister, I don't think there's much chance of that happening. If you recall, we monitored her initial sea trials rather thoroughly, and she came through them with only a few superfluous problems. The Germans have built a damn fine, bloody big and supremely dangerous battleship which when, not if, she gets loose in our convoy lanes will be a formidable force to be reckoned with. However, I will not give up the hope that this is the case—however forlorn that hope might be."

"Come now Stark, you've always been the perennial optimist, albeit on the cautious side."

"My apologies Minister, gentlemen. I fear that lack of food, sleep and the comforting embrace of my wife have put a few nicks in my armor. Regardless of what does or does not transpire today, I shall rectify these deficiencies this evening."

In an attempt to lift their spirits with a touch of levity, Minister McLeod slyly inquired of Stark, "Robert, might I ask in which order you plan to resolve these critical shortcomings? Could it be that your last stated deficiency is the real source of your crankiness?"

The normally stoical, sage men-of-war immediately burst out into raucous laughter. Stark's face flushed crimson, but even he had to join in the doom-and-gloom shattering remark. Once the laughter moderated, Stark let fly with a piercing arrow of his own—a knowing smirk plastered on his partially faded red face.

"Well, at least I can still enjoy all the soft comforts of the female of the species."

Any vestige of humor left amongst the senior officers vanished. McLeod, with his political shrewdness interjected before the conversation turned sarcastic and nasty.

"Gentlemen, since I do not have immediate access to all of your intelligence reports, could I enquire if there has been any indication of where those two *Ugly Sisters* are of late?"

That sobering question quelled any further ribald comments and returned the men to the deadly serious reason for this almost daily meeting before sunrise. Stark, with whom the heaviest burden of responsibility lay, rose slowly from his chair, silently scanned each face, and then issued a curt statement.

"Gentlemen, the answer is a simple no."

McLeod, sensing that the fangs of despair had begun to chew through the tough hide of the first sea lord, again jumped in with a statement attempting to get the discussion back on track.

"Come now, Robert. Let us find a bright spot in this whole affair. Since we don't know where they are, could you please hazard a guess where they *might* be, so we can go hunting after them before they pounce on our convoys again?"

Stark, who had quietly sunk low in his chair leaned forward and then began pessimistically to appraise the overall situation.

"Minister, Gentlemen, for all we know right now, they could be headed for home, the Caribbean, the Indian Ocean, the South Atlantic or any other decent sized body of water on the entire earth. Sorry for that unnecessary snide comment however true it may be. Now, let us take into consideration that the *Sisters* have been at sea several weeks and unless they have managed somehow to meet up with a victualer recently, they would definitely be short of oil and provisions. This being the case, they should be homebound for Brest. *Gneisenau* suffered some damage from our boys yesterday, but at a big price. She simply blew our destroyers out of the water, sank a couple of merchants and commandeered several other vital ships. From the sketchy reports we have from the battle, it seems *Gneisenau* was torpedoed but with minimal non-threatening damage. Unfortunately, she seems to still be very seaworthy and dangerous.

"Let us park that thought for a moment while we pursue their other probable options. If they have sufficient fuel and supplies, my best guess would be the Caribbean. Kastanien's pattern so far in this war has been to alternate his hunting between cold and warm oceans. I would consider April in the North Atlantic to fall into the cold category; therefore the Caribbean seems his most likely destination. I should think that he knows about *Bismarck* and our concentration of ships going after her, so he is not very likely to steam into a serious firefight where the odds would be frightfully stacked against him. He might, since he is an adventurer that cherishes a good fight—but German Naval HQ most assuredly has ordered him to steer clear of the North Atlantic.

"The South Atlantic really does not have enough merchant traffic inbound to us for him squander time and fuel chasing after—therefore my first best 'guess' is home to Brest followed by the Caribbean."

All the senior officers sat quietly while Stark rambled on. Then suddenly Stark paused, closing his eyes for a brief moment as he stood. Then lifting his head high, he shook his entire body a bit much like a jungle lion—opened his eyes and studied the men around the table. On each man, his gaze lingered a bit before moving on to the next. Minister of Defense Ian McLeod was the last one to meet his piercing gaze. Then he began again. This time there was a firm steeliness to his words.

"Gentlemen, please accept my apologies for my wandering, maudlin thoughts. I think rather that I was thinking aloud. We are not here to mishmash past troubles or to shed tears over tactical blunders. Nay, ours is the task of formulating decisive actions that will wipe the Kriegsmarine's menace from the surface of the oceans. My first proposed action right now is to plug the gap between Iceland and the Shetlands. I hope that we are not too late, but if we are, our ships will be better positioned to hunt down *Bismarck*. I will appraise what larger ships we have available to patrol off the coast of France to catch the *Sisters* heading home. If the *Sisters* are headed for the Caribbean, then battle group "M" led by *Duke of*

York should be able to handle them. I shall inform you by messenger when I have put my thoughts into a workable plan. These are my proposals for the immediate future. Could I please have your input before I put these measures into action?"

The men remained silent for only a few seconds before McLeod spoke up, "Robert, as far as this old politician is concerned, your basic strategy seems quite sound to me. Then again, I am not a naval man, so I shall leave the decisions regarding disposition of the Royal Navy to you. Let us just get the damn Germans in our sights and be rid of them."

The discussion lasted only a brief ten minutes more since there were no serious objections to Stark's plan of action. Then with the briefest of courteous farewells the assemblage scurried off to their own offices all except Stark—who sat pensively for many minutes. Then he rose and exited the room, whispering a prayer to himself.

Prince of Wales

"Bridge, Chief Engineer Fred Thompson here. All shafts turning smoothly at ten knots. You may increase speed as planned. I shall keep a close watch for any anomalies, which if there are any, you will be informed of immediately.

"Mr. King. Acknowledge engineering that message understood and then commence building up speed."

The first officer responded immediately to the captain's order and then the bridge fell silent again as every ear tuned-in to the steady hum of the engines, which seemed to be even running smoother than before the snarl-up with the cable. *Prince of Wales* quickly cruised up to fourteen knots. After ten long, uneventful minutes, First Officer King ordered the next step up to eighteen knots. Again, the bridge officers listened with every portion of their being for any flutter, vibration or hiccup. There were none. Within thirty minutes, *Prince of Wales* was scything through the empty ocean at her maximum speed of twenty-eight knots. The propulsion system ran as smooth as a Swiss watch. Captain Sullivan remained impassive for thirty minutes after maximum speed was achieved. Then he gave a simple order. "Reduce speed to twenty-two knots to conserve fuel. We've a long ways to go to maybe get a shot or two at *Bismarck*. I do not want to lose any precious time going out of our way to refuel."

Prince of Wales settled into her optimum speed with relatively conservative fuel consumption on a course that would take them to the projected area of *Bismarck's* operations.

Scharnhorst

Soon after coming up to eighteen knots, *Scharnhorst* slid past the protection of Flores Island to be greeted by long swells two meters high. The distance between the swells was just the right spacing to make *Scharnhorst* roll considerably more than normal. Her reduced speed coupled with the swells being nearly parallel with her course made the roll even more pronounced. The fog still hung over the rolling sea like a thick, damp, gray blanket—akin to the fog shrouds that visit London on a much too regular schedule. Visibility was probably no more than three hundred meters, but no one could really tell since there was no reference point in the virtually total darkness. Kastanien excused himself from the bridge to get some sleep and catch up on paper work. As he passed the radar room, he popped his head in and told the secondary operator to keep a very keen watch on his screen since they were steaming along at eighteen knots at night in heavy fog—which made visually sighting anything in time to avoid a collision virtually impossible. The radar operator responded with a bit of humor, a good sign, thought Kastanien.

"Captain, no cat, not even Attila ever watched a mouse hole as intently as I have been watching my screen and will continue to do so. Instantly when the slightest blip occurs, I shall inform you at once."

"Mr. Munster, Attila might just take offense to that remark. As we all well know, catching mice and rats is rather a highly specialized trade, of which he is the undisputed master."

Before either of the two men could utter another word, Attila simply arrived out of the darkness, landing like a feather's touch on the radar console. Kastanien stepped into the tiny cubicle and closed the door, which turned the dim overhead light back on. Attila blinked three times to adjust his superior night vision to the sudden brightness. He then proceeded to put his nose within an inch of the flickering green light of the radar screen. After this minute inspection of the mysterious machine, Attila slowly looked around the room before settling a hypnotic gaze on the motionless radar operator. Munster stared back but could not break the piercing concentration of the felines dark orbs lined with blue. There was no tension apparent with any of the three—just silence.

Kastanien remained motionless as well, shifting only his eyes between the two. Finally, Munster reached out and began to stroke the revered cat. Attila responded by engaging his purring motor, which was inordinately loud in the small space. After a moment, Attila eased down into Munster's lap, rotated until he was staring square on to the radar screen. Munster wasn't sure what to do next, so he looked up at Kastanien for guidance.

"Mr. Munster, you've reacquainted yourself with our guiding force. I shall now retire to my cabin. Make sure that you come to a mutually respectful accord with Attila for your remarks before he leaves. I did appreciate your bit of levity. It confirms to me that we have a happy ship with excellent morale. One last thing before I depart. Would if agreeable with you for me to address you as 'Magic' when there are just the two of us?"

"Yes Sir, Captain. That would be a great honor for me. Attila and I will help each other watching the screen. When he leaves, I'm quite sure that I will have benefited from his expertise."

Kastanien chuckled a bit. Attila turned his head to Kastanien and the young radar operator was struck speechless. Content that his ship was in good hands for the rest of the night, Kastanien went to his cabin. After closing the door, turning on the lights, Peter Kastanien stood for a brief moment before opting to skip the paperwork and get some sleep. Dawn was still a few hours away when he would routinely command his ship at first light. Doffing only his boots and jacket, Kastanien eased under the blanket and quickly shut down his ever-active mind. He was asleep in minutes.

Gneisenau

Nearly three hours after *Scharnhorst* had been swallowed by the night, *Gneisenau* finished her refueling and slipped away from *Bremen Castle*. There had been a few problems in the refueling that had caused the rendezvous to take longer than normal, but in the end all was well. *Gneisenau,* now fully replenished, quickly slid away from *Bremen Castle* and Teebolt sped up his slightly damaged battleship to meet up with Kastanien. Like his friend, Peter Kastanien, Teebolt totally darkened his ship for two hours, which with the dense fog would guarantee that any shore watchers would have no idea what direction he took.

Teebolt wanted to use his best speed to meet up with *Scharnhorst* as soon as possible, but with negligible visibility, he prudently held *Gneisenau* to eighteen knots. He hoped that the fog would dissipate at dawn when he could speed up to twenty-eight knots. Although *Gneisenau* was capable of thirty-two knots, the engines simply drank too much fuel to use this marked advantage in non-crisis situations.

Bremen Castle turned southwest with all of her lights blazing. Kastanien had ordered her to decoy the direction taken by *Gneisenau* and *Scharnhorst*—one more tiny, little red herring to remain "lost" to the Royal Navy. As the very much depleted supply ship slowly trundled off into the fog, she finished tidying up her decks and re-trimming her remaining fuel and cargo—a much needed necessity after refueling and provisioning the two huge, ravenous warships. She left her lights blazing for two hours before reversing course, heading northeast to vacate the Azores vicinity by steaming through the gap between the islands of Flores and Faial. This course would keep her at least fifty miles from either island, making observation from any land-based spies impossible. With her holds now almost empty, she was not much use to any ship, so she was headed back to occupied France for fresh supplies.

The fog still hung heavy over the calm ocean. The wind had dropped to a gentle zephyr, which portended that the fog would persist long after sunrise. These weather conditions were ideal for the slow-moving supply ship, whose purpose was best served by plying the seas undetected. After making the course change, giving the island of Flores a wide berth, she reduced her lighting to minimal nighttime conditions to avoid collision with errant fishing vessels.

For the most part, the men of *Bremen Castle* were naval veterans of the First World War. They were a happy bunch since they knew that they were doing their part to avenge that hideously wrong Treaty of Versailles that had reduced the proud German nation to penury. Knowing that they were too old for combat duty at sea, very few of these men resented that reality of life. They were looking forward to a few pleasant days in their new home port of St. Nazaire. The increased German naval personnel presence in this cozy little port city had livened things up considerably. The pathetic attempts by the fumbling French Resistance to sabotage any of the new installations that serviced the Kriegsmarine surface fleet were summarily squelched before any real damage could be done.

The Frenchmen of St. Nazaire soon gave up their nefarious activities after dozens and dozens of their compatriots languished in very unpleasant jails. They constantly complained how bad the jail conditions were—quite conveniently forgetting that they had constructed these jails themselves, with deliberate consideration given to making inmates miserable.

The French women on the other hand, although they had no love of the occupying Germans, quickly adapted to their new circumstances. In typical female fashion, they actually likened to their new status and made the best of it. The Germans were lonely for female companionship and the French men were stubbornly sullen all of the time, making them poor companions for the lonely women. Consequently, the French women, the German seamen and shore personnel were having a grand old time, which made the Frenchmen all the more unsociable and morose. The Germans, along with their new French lovers could have cared less.

Scharnhorst
Latitude 39 degrees Longitude 26 degrees, 41 minutes.

Scharnhorst had steadily held course and speed for eleven hours with nothing to break the monotony of the fog—which had shrouded them in a grey cocoon all through the day. There was only an hour before sunset, which would only mean the dank weather would become even gloomier. Suddenly the partial stupor of the bridge officers was shattered by the excited voice of "Merlin" Mueller.

"Ship bearing twenty degrees off our starboard bow, heading north-northwest"

Kastanien, who had been listlessly ambling about the bridge, immediately shot to the radar room.

"Merlin, how far away is she and how fast is she going?"

"Captain, she is at the limit of our radar eyes—about forty kilometers. We will have to wait for several minutes until I can calculate the blips with reasonable accuracy to determine her speed. I wish I could be quicker but the machine has its limits."

"It's alright Mr. Molter, I can wait. I hope that it is a nice fat merchant ship filled with goods bound for England. I would like to commandeer her and send her home to France. That is after we have perused her cargo to ascertain whether there are any goods that are *vital* to us," the last said with a conspirator's smirk.

"It is unlikely to be a Royal Navy warship—for this is far from any of their normal patrol areas. However, excuse me, I ramble too much. We shall simply have to wait to ascertain her speed."

Ten minutes seemed an eternity as Kastanien silently, impatiently watched the bouncing green lines subtly change positions. Then "Merlin" Molter cracked the tense atmosphere like a thunderbolt.

"Captain Sir. She is traveling at high speed. I estimate that she is doing about twenty-plus knots. Much too fast for any merchant. Please excuse me Sir. I did not mean to be presumptuous."

"That's quite alright Mr. Molter. It shows that you have a thinking brain, and I do concur with your evaluation of her not being a simple merchant. Now, I must return to the bridge and do my job. Inform me immediately if our new ship contact changes course, speed or does anything different, and I mean anything."

The adoring youngster replied with a simple, "Yes Sir."

Kastanien quickly entered the radio room, startling Eric Weisboch.

"Mr. Weisboch. Radar has picked up a ship off our starboard quarter about forty kilometers away. Since this mystery ship is turning twenty-something knots it is definitely not a merchant vessel. Have you heard any new transmissions from either the ship or elsewhere that might give us a clue as to her identity?

"No Sir, the only radio traffic that I have picked up all has been commercial radio stations broadcasting from the Azores."

"Very well then. Please keep your ears turned up full. We need to determine who she is and rather soon."

"Yes Sir. I will put myself on extra alert and inform you immediately I hear anything."

Kastanien returned to the bridge briskly, walking to the center console. He turned his back to the forward window and addressed the officers as a whole.

"Gentlemen, we have a radar sighting about forty kilometers away from us on our starboard quarter. The ship is steaming at twenty knots or thereabouts, which negates any merchant vessel that I know of. In these waters, she could only be one of three things. She could be one of our heavy cruisers, a Royal Navy warship or possibly even a passenger liner. It seems that *Gneisenau* has been delayed for whatever reason. She should be approaching from our port quarter; however it might still be her coming up. In my opinion, the three options are almost equal in value. With the omnipresent fog still with us, night descending shortly, then coupled with radio silence, we are in a quandary as to what to make of it. Now, have I summed up the situation fully or do any of you have any further input? I am fully aware that it is I, and I alone, who makes the final decision regarding our immediate actions. Please speak up."

The entire bridge staff was silent for a few seconds before the oftentimes bumptious Second Officer Mueller ventured forth his opinion. This was not the first time that Kastanien had asked for alternative views. He felt that true leadership required all of his subordinates to have their say in most matters. In this, he was absolutely correct.

"Captain Sir. Not meaning to be impudent but there is one other slight possibility."

Kastanien spoke before Mueller could expound his opinion.

"Mr. Mueller, I would have hoped that by now that you would know me well enough to avoid apologizing before proffering your opinion. I want straight talk, not obsequiousness. Remember these few simple truths. We are at war. Our Navy is new but vastly outnumbered by our enemy, the Royal Navy, who has been damnable good for a very long time in controlling sea traffic on the world's oceans—most notably this one. Holding back any opinion on my bridge could prove fatal. I want the options, and I want them spoken clearly. Let me repeat. It is my duty, and mine alone to appraise each situation and act upon it.

"Someday, many of you will command your own ship. I sincerely hope that you will employ any lessons that you learn from me. Contrary to popular belief, I am not infallible. Mr. Mueller you probably did not deserve that mild chastisement as strongly as I put it, but this situation requires careful thought so that we can take the best action possible. Please do not take it as a rebuke."

The officers had stood stock still during Kastanien's speech and when he finished they all looked to Mueller. Mueller had taken the short speech to heart.

"Captain, is it a possibility the radar reflection, being as it is at the maximum distance we can detect, could be the U3200X running on the surface with her butterfly deployed?"

"Very good thinking Mr. Mueller. Yes, that is a possibility; however, it would be almost impossible for her to have covered the distance from when we last saw her, to be coming from the southeast. However, it could be one of her sister ships. The Kriegsmarine has two additional U-boats configured like our faithful friend the U3200X. I know that the U3201X had just successfully completed her sea trials when we set sail, so there is a reasonable chance that it could be her. The U3202X will not be ready for sea for at least a month or more. Now, if it is the U3201X what reason could she have to deploy the butterfly? Your opinions please, Gentlemen."

There was a brief silence while the men absorbed this question. Mueller, after hesitating long enough to give someone else the opportunity to speak, picked up the question.

"Captain, the only reason that I can come up with is that she is leading a British warship out where we might have a crack at her."

"A good thought Mr. Mueller; I'll keep that one in mind. Anyone else?"

The officers nervously shuffled a tiny bit to show their failure to come up with another alternative.

"Come now, gentlemen. Put your thinking caps on. Even far-fetched ideas could shed some light on this mystery ship."

No one spoke up so Kastanien resumed the conversation.

"Since we have no new ideas, let me summarize what we have at this point. There is an unknown ship heading approximately north-northwest that we are on a converging course with. She is traveling at a speed that eliminates her being a merchant marine vessel. That leaves us with four choices. They are. One, she is one of our warships, most probably a heavy cruiser, which will be no problem. Two, she is the U3201X and we are *seeing* her butterfly. If this is the case, then she is probably leading a hostile warship into the area that she thinks *Gneisenau* and ourselves will be patrolling. Three, she is a passenger liner in which case we avoid her enough so that she cannot identify us. Four, she is a Royal Navy warship and we are heading into a possible conflict.

"Since there is no indication as to which of these four choices she might be, I shall try to eliminate them one by one until we can ascertain what we will be meeting soon. It will be dark before we cross paths and coupled with this dense fog we cannot risk getting too close in case it is a serious British warship. Therefore, we will change course soon. If the ship is a passenger liner, it is very unlikely that she will change course. Those types prefer steaming in as straight a line as possible. The U3201X also will not alter course if she is leading an enemy warship. If she is one of our warships or the Royal Navy, assuming they are equipped with radar, they will in all probability make course corrections. We should be able, with reasonable certainty, to eliminate two possibilities within the next little while. "

Kastanien then picked up the intercom to the radar room.

"Mr. Molter is there anything new that you have deciphered about our new contact?"

The reply came immediately.

"No Sir Captain. The vessel is still maintaining her course and speed. She has drawn closer to us and is now only thirty-six kilometers away."

Kastanien thanked his brilliant radar operator and then resumed.

"Mr. Schmidt, alter course twenty degrees to port. Make the turn rather slow. Slow us down to twelve knots. I would like that vessel to mistake us for something other than what we are. Let us wait and see what our new companion does."

Scharnhorst leisurely turned to port, slowing during the turn. Kastanien strode back to the radar room where he quietly stood, watching the glowing green bars hop around haphazardly. Molter, who had felt the decrease in speed along with the course change, knew that his revered captain wanted to know immediately how the mysterious interloper would react to *Scharnhorst's* actions.

Prince of Wales

"Captain, the unknown ship has changed course and slowed," the strident voice of radar operator Alex Denham crashed through the speakers on the bridge.

Snatching up the intercom to the radar room Captain Sullivan replied in a normal voice, designed to reduce jumpy nerves.

"Mr. Denham, please inform me what direction she has taken."

"Captain Sir. She has turned to port and has slowed to twelve knots. I will inform you when she has straightened out and is on a constant course."

Sullivan acknowledged his radar operator and patiently waited for his radar man to give him the new course that the unseen ship settled upon. Three long minutes passed in funereal silence before the crackling of the intercom shattered the quiet.

"Captain Sir. She made a turn of twenty degrees to port, settling her heading at sixty-five degrees true. Her speed is still twelve knots."

Captain Sullivan thanked the operator, telling him to keep a sharp watch for any further changes and to inform him immediately if there were any. He then paced the bridge for a few moments, obviously turning the possibilities and probabilities over in his mind. At last, he addressed his officers, who had stoically awaited his decision.

"Gentlemen, I believe that our unknown vessel is one of the German's battleships; either the *Scharnhorst* or the *Gneisenau*. They simply just vanished into thin air a couple of days ago. They were presumed to be heading for the Caribbean, but that has never been confirmed. The other possibility is that she might just be one of ours. However, I am discounting that because all the Admiralty's transmissions have almost every available warship scouring the North Atlantic for that monster *Bismarck* or the *Ugly Sisters*. With this accursed fog and night about to descend, our best option is to shadow her until dawn—at which time I hope that the fog has lifted, and we can confirm my belief. If it truly is one of the *Ugly Sisters* then we shall have a go at her. We outgun them and our ship is slightly newer, which should also be to our advantage. We shall proceed to shadow her at a distance of ten miles through the night. If we are fortunate enough to have clear skies at dawn, we can bear our six forward fourteen-inch guns on her, while she can only reply with her aft turret of three eleven-incher's. Let us not be lulled in any semblance of smug superiority.

"Both of the *Sisters* have plenty of kills that attest to her damnable fine accuracy and her eleven-inch shells can wreck serious havoc—even to us. Now, Mr. King, plot a course and speed to shadow her at a constant distance of ten miles until further notice. Signal our escort destroyers to tighten up on our starboard quarter and to take their position at our direction. Unless the German radar is vastly superior to ours, the smaller destroyers will remain invisible on their radar, but only if we keep them in a direct line away from us and the other vessel. This is critical. If the ship turns out to be the enemy, I want the destroyers ready to surprise attack from her flanks. Now, if she makes any further course or speed changes, inform me at once. I am retiring to my cabin for some sleep. I desire to be at my best come the dawn. Rest as many of the officers and crew as possible for the hours until first light. We must all be tip top if we are to engage a formidable adversary."

Scharnhorst

"Captain, the ship has changed course. She appears to be on a course that would bring her up behind our starboard quarter at a distance of about sixteen kilometers."

"Very well, Mr. Molter. Keep tracking her, and if she deviates from her new course, inform me at once."

Kastanien mulled this new information for only a few heartbeats before addressing his officers, "Gentlemen, our friend has now eliminated two possibilities with her recent maneuver. We can now know almost certainly that she is a warship, either friend or foe. Her captain would have no choice but to assume the same of us. He will have one advantage, but that advantage is dangerous. If it is a Royal Navy heavy warship, her forward guns put us at a two to one disadvantage, especially if she is one of their battleships, which have decidedly larger caliber guns than ourselves.

"Her captain will surely just shadow us until first light. Let us wait thirty minutes or so to determine if shadowing is her intent for the duration of the night. If she does maintain a shadowing position, we will rest as many of the crew as possible so that they are in top form for a slugging match when and if she proves to be a Royal Navy battleship at dawn. That is all for now."

With his intentions made clear Kastanien wandered back to the radar room. He opened the door and entered. Attila, who had been wandering about doing his duties, bounced into the room and with an Olympic-class high jump, gracefully leaped onto the tiny worktable, purring rather loudly.

The sudden appearance of the most beloved crewmember slightly startled the two men. Before either man could utter a word Attila bumped his head into Molter's left hand—blatantly demanding to be stroked. Molter looked up at Kastanien as his free hand began to massage Attila's ears and neck. Kastanien smiled, nodded his head with permission and then asked, "Mr. Molter. Has there been any deviation in our companion's projected intentions?"

"No Sir Captain. She has just reached a position where she will be sixteen kilometers behind us off our starboard stern quarter."

"Can you see any other vessels near her?"

"No Sir Captain. My screen shows only the one vessel in every direction."

"Merlin, let me ask you a question. Is your machine capable of distinguishing between two ships that are in close proximity? I know that this sounds like I'm repeating the scenario with the U3200X that we employ, but to me there is a subtle difference. Please answer honestly."

Molter paused a moment before replying. With his previous experiences with the captain, his pause was not from nervousness; rather he was searching for the proper words.

"Captain that is a rather difficult question to answer because the answer is both yes and no. Please let me explain. My outgoing radar beams reflect off solid metal surfaces and return to me much like an echo. If there is a smaller ship directly between the larger reflecting ship and us I could maybe distinguish it as a separate entity only if it was separated by some distance. If the ship is smaller and on the far side of the main vessel and in a direct line, I would not be able to see it unless wave action raised it above the main target. Now, if the two ships were not in alignment with us, then they would both show up quite plainly. I'm sorry that I cannot give you a more definitive answer Sir."

"Merlin, no apology is necessary. You have confirmed my own suspicions about your magical machine. I can tell by your look that you are beset with curiosity as to the why of my question. This will be part of your ongoing education about warships. If our shadow were indeed a large Royal Navy ship, like a battleship or heavy cruiser, it would be very unlikely that she did not have some sort of smaller escorts in her company. That is just the protocol of the Royal Navy, since they have quite a large numbers of ocean-going destroyers to guard their capitol ships against our

U-boats and us. Please keep a very close watch for any sign of escort vessels.

"Yes Captain and thank you very much for educating me as to the enemy's order-of-battle. I shall remain especially vigilant for any change in the targets reflections, however minimal."

"Very well then. I shall stay with you for a few moments until we feel confident that we will be simply shadowed for the next few hours and maybe we can catch a glimpse of an escort or two. That is of course if it's quite alright with Attila."

Molter instantly grasped the sarcasm in his captain's voice and broke into lusty laughter. Kastanien temporarily maintained his composure but an instant later, he too began to laugh. Attila glanced up at Molter, swiveled his head to Kastanien—decided that humans did the most unusual things before returning to his enjoyable massage. With the only chair in the tiny cubicle, Molter offered his to the captain, who laid his hand on Molter's shoulder and told him to stay put.

The minutes slowly passed in silence, except for the background humming of the radar, and the deep rhythmic purring of the very contented Attila. The man and boy remained quiet, just enjoying the cat's peaceful tranquility. After twenty minutes, it was apparent that the mystery ship had settled into a quartering shadow position. There had been no telltale blips on the radar to indicate another ship's presence.

"Well now, 'Merlin', it appears our shadow is possibly alone and has opted to wait until dawn before making any move. I am bound for my cabin to catch up on some sleep. I need to be fresh and sharp for the morning. I want you to do the same. Please inform your replacement to keep an eagle eye on our shadow. If she should deviate whatsoever in speed or position, or an escort pokes her beak out, he is to awaken me immediately. I want you back at this post one hour before first light. Goodnight Mr. Molter."

With his ship in very competent hands and serenely sailing through the pitch-black night, Kastanien headed to his cabin. Attila opted to remain with 'Merlin' Molter. Once back in his cabin Kastanien informed the bridge of his whereabouts and then decided it had been much too long since his last shower. Quickly he undressed, and then ran the shower until it warmed up. The shower stall was rather tiny but adequate for his needs. Kastanien closed his eyes and turned his face into the stream of hot water. The soothing water slowly rinsed away the patina of mental fatigue that inexorably hung like a cloak on his shoulders. Reluctantly, after nearly five full minutes, Kastanien stepped from the now steaming cubicle. The room felt a bit chilly, so Peter Kastanien wasted no time drying himself and quickly putting fresh clothes on. He only left his jacket and boots off before slipping under the warming blankets. Relaxed now, he dozed off after his mind had churned through several details for only a few moments.

Prince of Wales

First Officer Roland King barked out orders. The first order was addressed to Second Officer Jerry Davis.

"Mr. Davis, make it your responsibility to co-ordinate signals and radar to maintain our destroyers in a direct line between the unknown vessel off our port bow and us. The captain wants the two destroyers on our starboard side and tucked up rather close. By close, I mean within 300 to 500 yards of us for the two of them. They MUST be kept in alignment else the enemy, which we must presume it is, will catch on that there are more than just us to contend with at first light. The captain did not mention it, but I have traced the history of the *Ugly Sisters* and I would not be the least bit surprised if the two of them are out there so tight together that we cannot determine if there is just one of them. They no doubt have spotted us quite a bit ago and would probably use the same tactic as we are employing.

"Much as I hate to admit it, it was these two lovely lassies who dreamt up the tactic in the first place shortly after radar came about. Moreover, they used it quite effectively on more than one occasion. So, strongly stress to the destroyers that it is of utmost importance to maintain their designated positions until further notice. Be sure to tell them why. The young jocks that drive those thin-skinned greyhounds are a rather unschooled bumptious lot—bless their little black hearts."

After the stern beginning of the orders, turned speech, the officers on deck relaxed—even lightly chuckling at the uncomplimentary jab regarding their fellow sailors. With the captain gone to his cabin, First Officer King quickly shuffled his officers, sending the bulk of them to get some well-deserved rest. The tension of lying to during the recent repairs still lingered in their subconscious. Although nothing untoward had transpired and the repairs were executed perfectly, the human psyche still requires sleep to recover and regenerate from highly stressful experiences.

Satisfied that all was in order, King stepped out onto the port bridge wing. The dampness of the fog hit him like a wet blanket, but the temperature was pleasingly mild. He strode over to the railing and stared into the Stygian night.

"Are you one of the Ugly Sisters? Which one? How good is your gunnery? Does it really matter?"

The silent questions rattled around Roland King's mind for several more minutes before the pervasive dampness of the fog became a bit chafing. With his unspoken questions unanswered, first officer King returned to the relative comfort of the bridge, which had settled in for a long, probably uneventful night.

The Admiralty

"What the Hell do you mean by telling me that we have not been able to locate *Bismarck* yet? I find it incredulous, nay, unbelievable that she could not have been spotted yet. If, as you say, the Denmark Strait is buttoned up tighter than a tart's behind and no sign of her in the open ocean, then where in the name of God could she be? You have dozens of ships out there and the planes from *Ark Royal* can cover a lot of territory in two days. We have two convoys headed our way smack dab in the projected path of that German monster, and even they have not seen hide nor hair of *Bismarck*."

The assembled High Command sat motionless—displaying not the slightest emotion for a full minute after First Lord of the Admiralty Ian McLeod had finished his vehement tirade and flopped down in his chair. As expected, the First Sea Lord Robert Stark shattered the brittle, silent tension.

"Come now Minister. That is one enormous patch of water out there to look for one or two little ships."

"Do NOT patronize me Robert. I am fully aware of the vast expanse of the North Atlantic. Furthermore, *Bismarck* and her escort, which she surely has, are not exactly *little* ships. She's a bloody gigantic beast that can and will surely cause us serious harm if we don't eliminate her. I understand from the weather bunch that there are no storms kicking up to camouflage her, so why can't we find that damnable German?"

Once more, a deathly silence settled over the men. No one had an answer and no one was about to incur any more wrath from McLeod by proffering up any excuse. All eyes stared silently at McLeod who had his head down cradled in his hands, much as if he was attempting to invoke God's help. Stark was about to make a feeble attempt to get the meeting back on track when the trademark scent of a special cigar permeated the room. All heads swiveled to the door. With one hand massaging his cigar, there standing silently in the doorway, was none other than Winston Churchill himself. Once noticed, the master politician launched into an impromptu speech.

"Gentlemen, I presume that you are eschewing the fact that our Royal Navy cannot find the *Bismarck*. I daresay that the Huns have outfoxed us—*again*. As the former First Sea Lord who ran the show back during the last fracas with the Germans, I vividly recall they did some rather unconventional stunts back then. Let us consider not where we expect them to be, rather delve into where they should not be. Keep in mind that we are in a new era of warfare where the old, predicable tactics no longer apply to the order of battle. Did not the Germans with their new Blitzkrieg land operations roll over Poland in a few weeks? Then during the winter's respite, the Belgians, French and ourselves should have taken careful notes regarding their new style and learned from it. However, we did not.

"Consequently, the German armored divisions did the same thing to Western Europe—begrudgingly I daresay even better. The French never thought it was possible to attack with heavy armoured strength through the Ardennes, where their vaunted Maginot line did not exist, consequently they were completely unprepared. The result being that the French army was defeated almost before they knew it and *we* got pushed into the Channel without having much of a go at them. The French army outnumbered the German army nearly three to one, but the German tactics negated that prodigious advantage on the first day of engagement. That gentlemen, was the classic example of the new warfare. Keeping those thoughts in mind, let us address our Royal Navy versus the German Navy. We outnumber their capitol ships over eight to one, plus, we have larger and more potent firepower. The *Ugly Sisters* are a classic case of popping up where they were not supposed to be.

"Now, shall we explore where the *Bismarck* should not be and do a little snooping there?"

At this precipitous moment, a strident knocking on the door stopped the Prime Minister before he could continue. Churchill, still standing just inside the portal of the closed door, opened it immediately. Standing there, quite out of breath was a staff sergeant. The staff sergeant snapped off a perfect salute and then handed Churchill a sealed packet. Churchill signed the receipt form and dismissed the courier.

Ever the consummate politician, Churchill seized the opportunity to dramatize the meeting by silently walking to the front of the table. No one uttered a sound. When he was standing just to the side of Ian McLeod, Churchill slit the packet open and read the contents. It was but a brief moment before he folded the single sheet of paper, looked firstly at First Sea Lord Stark, and then glanced around the room at the other men.

"Well now, this is a decent piece of good news. It seems that my interrupted speech has borne some credence. In short, gentlemen, *Bismarck* is quietly at anchor in Bergen. She apparently turned around for reasons known only to the Germans and returned to port. Much as I would like to tell you how to proceed from this point forward, I will keep in mind that I am no longer the First Sea Lord. However, as Prime Minister, I am permitted to task you men with the Government's overall grand strategy.

"Simply put, we must receive the essential materials to keep the Germans at bay, and even more importantly, we must feed our people. How you achieve these goals is your purveyance. My personal suggestions are to bottle up the Norwegian and North Seas, which should keep *Bismarck* out of the Atlantic, and set your sea hounds to dispense with the *Ugly Sisters*. Please inform me instantly, if not sooner, when, and definitely not if, either of these objectives is accomplished. Gentlemen, I bid you good day."

With his marching orders delivered, the portly Prime Minister deftly slipped away leaving his High Command looking rather stunned. All heads swiveled to Stark.

Scharnhorst
Two hours before first light

Kastanien arrived on the darkened bridge wraithlike out of the even darker passageway. He surveyed his officers, who were quietly going about the ship's business. Then, seeing all was in order, he strode up to his first officer quietly asking, "Mr. Gott. Since you left me undisturbed for the past few hours, I presume that there has been no change in the position of our shadow?"

"No Sir. Whoever she is has doggedly maintained her position off our starboard stern quarter. Radar has informed us every fifteen minutes for the past several hours that she is rock-steady back there."

Just then, Attila who had been dozing on his favorite red blanket, stood up, shook himself fully awake and then finishing his morning ritual, he executed a cavernous, drawn-out yawn. Now ready for the day, Attila affixed his gaze on Kastanien. Kastanien's peripheral vision immediately picked up the movement.

"Mr. Gott. Has Attila been here the whole night?"

"Yes Captain. He has been sleeping on his blanket the entire time with only one of his ears rotating occasionally. All of us felt very privileged to have him here keeping us company, and we know that he is always prepared to give us ample warning on any danger."

"Well then, I feel doubly assured that all is well—for now. However, logically and intuitively I know that this pleasant quiet is about to change. Please have all senior officers present on the bridge in one hour. We will begin operations then."

The next hour passed slowly for the officers who knew Kastanien's tactics well enough to be more than a bit apprehensive as to what he would demand of *Scharnhorst* and her crew at first light. With agonizing sluggishness, the clock ticked inexorably forward for sixty minutes. Kastanien stroked Attila, quietly whispering to him for some of the time. Few words were spoken—none were necessary. A few moments before the allotted hour was up, the entire bridge staff was present, awaiting orders. Right on cue, Kastanien began, "Gentlemen, I feel quite confident that our shadow is a wayward Royal Navy warship. Why she is in this sector of the ocean is her own business, which is about to become ours. Ready the *Arados*."

*　*　*　*　*

The Arado196 *was the mainstay of the Kriegsmarine seaplane fleet, designed specifically for shipboard use. As such, this aircraft was exceptionally sturdy to withstand the rigors of open sea use. The plane had a straight, broad wing with only a slight taper on the trailing edge. Powered by an air-cooled nine cylinder, 880-hp BMW radial engine, driving a three-bladed, variable pitch propeller, this seaplane was quite nimble and very maneuverable. With a limited range of about 800 kilometers and a top speed of 312 km/h, the* Arado *served the Kriegsmarine admirably well. The first versions featured a single center-mounted main float with two small stabilizing outriggers. In mid-1940, a modified version with two lower-drag floats increased its performance and allowed a torpedo to be fitted directly below the fuselage. The* Arado *series were not toothless leopards. The rear cockpit had two 7.9 mm machine guns— mainly used for defense. The impressive forward armament consisted of MG17 machine guns and two MGFF cannon. Overall, the* Arados' *could tackle most enemy planes which would be encountered over the open ocean with confidence—*Spitfires *and* Hurricanes *being the two notable exceptions. Used extensively from shore bases in the Baltic, Norway and the Mediterranean, the* Arado *had wreaked havoc on merchant shipping and enemy submarines caught unawares.*

*　*　*　*　*

"Battle stations in thirty minutes. Mr. Mueller, please take Attila to his battle station now. Mr. Gott, bring the *Arado* pilots to the bridge. I wish to brief them thoroughly on their missions. There will be no further orders for thirty minutes."

Mueller strode over to the red blanket and gently lifted the ship's cat from his restful nap. There was a slight protest and an accusing stare. Mueller, knowing the cat's temperament brought the cat close to Kastanien. Kastanien lovingly stroked his faithful companion and then whispered softly in his ear, "Sorry to disturb you old friend, but we are going to *battle stations* shortly. I want you out of harm's way in your magnificent castle."

Attila, upon hearing the dreaded words "battle stations", instantly snuggled down in Mueller's arms. He was definitely not opposed to being carried to his station during this frightfully noisy time.

Mueller returned in a short time, just as Kastanien started addressing the bridge along with the newly arrived two *Arado* pilots.

"Gentlemen, we could very well be in for a serious sea battle with the Royal Navy rather shortly. Therefore, we will first use our airborne eyes to see who has been shadowing us through the night. Pilots, make very sure that your planes are topped up with maximum fuel, as we may not be able to recover you in a timely manner. If that is the case, then you to head back for the Azores and meet up with the *Bremen Castle* for refueling. Mr. Schmidt will give you the course *Bremen Castle* would have taken and her approximate position. Once the first seaplane has been launched, fit the newer A-5 *Arado* with a torpedo on the catapult. If the other ship is a warship, which I feel almost certain she is, then we will be able to deliver a nasty surprise during the gunfight."

Kastanien then spent a few more moments going over every possible contingency that his eyes in the sky could possibly encounter, and the signal codes to be used—once the vessel was in sight. Radio transmission was to be avoided unless the stranger proved to be a Royal Navy capitol ship, then the quicker the information was relayed to *Scharnhorst*, the sooner the deadly armament of the superb battleship could engage.

Their orders crystal clear, the pilots saluted the captain and scurried off to their battle stations. The pilot of the first seaplane would of course be in the cockpit awaiting the signal to go. It only took the first pilot but a few moments to verify that he was fully fueled and had a full complement of munitions. With the aid of the second pilot, they verified that all the control surfaces were working correctly. After waving to each other with jaw-splitting grins, the two young pilots went to their respective battle stations. This would be their first time to engage in a real sea battle between capitol ships. Previously, all they had flown were scouting missions looking for convoys. Never tasting the nasty reality of war, the youngsters were still euphorically anticipating the glory of battle.

Time seemed to stand still for the first pilot. He looked lovingly at the tiny photo of his girlfriend sandwiched between two instruments—which made his heart soar. Then his eyes caught sight of the equally tiny photo of a very stern-looking Grossadmiral Dönitz, which Captain Kastanien had gently *suggested* he also keep in plain view. A wry smile accompanied his thoughts about how perceptive was his captain to assure that he kept his mind on his duty. Although it seemed at least two eternities, the signal to launch came less than ten minutes after he had strapped into his warplane. He ran the engine up to full throttle, and then gave the launcher the universal sign that he was ready. In his excitement he momentarily forgot to acknowledge the launcher's signal that he was about to be flung into the dim pre-dawn light. Snapping back to reality, he made the acknowledging sign and was instantly catapulted into the air. The *Arado* did not struggle to become stable; such was the beauty of her design. The pilot, Jorge Mogen could just make out the swells fifteen meters below, which was enough for him to fly the plane the way that Kastanien had ordered.

The plane had been launched to the port side of *Scharnhorst*, away from the prying radar eyes of the mystery vessel. He had been ordered to fly less than twenty meters over the slowly undulating swells and to take a circuitous route to the unknown ship. Kastanien wanted his reconnaissance plane to approach unnoticed by radar from the enemy's rear starboard quarter, which might just cause a momentary delay in the vessel's decision making. This wave hopping altitude kept the *Arado's* speed down to only 282 km/h. Nevertheless, since the unknown vessel was relatively close, even with the roundabout course he took, it was less than ten minutes before he began to see a vague shape materializing from the gloom. The fog was still quite thick, so the *Arado* had to close to less than two kilometers before the pilot could make a definite confirmation as to her identity.

The Royal Navy destroyers were not asleep, and they had heard the powerful BMW engine long before the *Arado* came into view. As soon as it did, their anti-aircraft guns opened up on the unsuspecting Jorge Mogen. Seeing the tracers speeding towards him, his youthful reflexes responded instantly to his training. He managed to make a rapid climbing turn to starboard and avoid all but one shell that punched a neat hole through his right aileron. The damage was slight and not the least bit dangerous since the control surfaces of the *Arado* were fabric covered. However, Jorge now had to contend with a slightly balky airplane. His dreams of glorious battle were quickly replaced by nervous fear. Recovering from his fright, he remembered that this was the one occasion when he needed to use the radio and right now. Five seconds later, the electrifying news was received that *Scharnhorst* was about to be pitted against one of the Royal Navies front line battleships, the *Prince of Wales*. Jorge also reported that he had also seen two destroyers tucked in close to the *Prince of Wales*. Within seconds, Kastanien again spoke the deadly word, "Fire."

Without being able to physically see their opponent the (three) eleven-inch guns of turret Caesar opened fire along with the (six) 5.9-inch starboard secondary guns. Turrets Anton and Bruno could not rotate far enough to shoot.

Prince of Wales

"Sir, German aircraft approaching from our starboard rear quarter. No doubt a German seaplane from our mystery ship," announced Second Officer Jerry Davis.

"And how exactly do you know it's a German plane since we can't even see it, Mr. Davis?" Captain Sullivan asked with a noticeable tinge of sarcasm.

"Begging the Captain's pardon, Sir. The engine sound has a very distinctive tone to it. I visited Germany before this fracas began and heard many of their engines first hand. This particular noise is made only by BMW radial engines—which are used exclusively on their seaplanes."

Deciding to let the slight impertinence pass, Captain Sullivan quickly exited the bridge and stared into the fog, hoping to get a glimpse of the airplane. Suddenly the mists were split asunder by a menacing black airplane whose snarling engine grew louder by the second. Warily Sullivan and several of the other bridge officers stared at the enemy wondering if the plane would send any bullets their way. The airplane quickly filled their fields of vision, but no tracer rounds heralded the arrival of nasty steel insects. Now confirmed the aircraft was the enemy, *Prince of Wales* anti-aircraft guns immediately opened fire but had little chance to sight in the plane before it executed a sharp right turn. The *Arado* climbed rapidly from a few feet above the sea into the cover of the still-thick fog. The turn allowed the captain and every observer to see the distinctive German Cross emblazoned on the fuselage along with the tail swastika. Almost before the first shells from *Scharnhorst* had time to reach the *Arado*, Captain Sullivan and all the other officers were back inside the bridge and orders flew.

"Open fire with all guns. The German is close enough that we might just get lucky shooting by radar. Radio the Admiralty immediately and tell them we are engaging *Scharnhorst* or *Gneisenau*—or possibly some other German ship big enough to have a seaplane on board. Give them our position and make sure to inform them that we are opening fire with all we've got."

Just as he finished issuing these few quick orders, the distinctive heavy whistle of large caliber shells passed over the bow of *Prince of Wales*. Three seconds after the German shells passed harmlessly overhead, the first salvo from A and B turrets of *Prince of Wales* erupted with fiery volcanic ferocity, sending (six) fourteen-inch missiles of devastatingly destructive potential towards the still invisible enemy. All six of the shells overshot *Scharnhorst* by a goodly margin. Unfortunately, the overshoots did not allow radar to dare venture a guess as to where they landed since the fall of shot was masked by the bulk of *Scharnhorst* and the fog.

In the short span of time between the deafening blasts from his own guns, Captain Sullivan continued to issue a seemingly endless series of commands. Centuries of Royal Naval traditions along with superb character infusions by equally prestigious English military schools were now in evidence. Captain Reginald Sullivan was the pinnacle of leadership under fire. His complete control over any outward sign of fear—knowing exactly what to do and when—infused confidence into every officer and seaman aboard the mighty *Prince of Wales*.

"Shorten shot and give radar a chance to plot our progress. Mr. King, is the engine room giving us all this grand lady can muster?"

"Yes Sir Captain. Engineer Thompson says that he—and I quote: *'My little darlings have pumped up their skirts pushing us past the stodgy Admiralty's maximum mark of twenty-eight knots all the way to twenty-nine. I've promised my darlings a proper pat on their arses when we are done with this bloody Hun—if they can just squeeze us out another half knot or more. I'll be sure to inform you when we get there Sir.'*"

Amidst the thunderous blasts from the guns, which had a fire rate of two rounds per minute, per gun, the descriptiveness of Fred Thompson created wide grins and a few chuckles amongst the bridge crew. Knowing many of his officers and most of the crew had never experienced a deadly sea battle, Sullivan, the ever-aware commander, opted to buoy up the men's spirits with a touch of his own levity.

"Well now, that's very patriotic of our Mr. Thompson. I think rather surely that his report to you Mr. King was a much watered-down version of what he tells his crew. That lad could do very well on the stage or perhaps Hollywood opposite—shall we say Joan Crawford. She would sure enough be his equal from what I have heard of her."

Now real laughter, tempered only with a tinge of trepidation, resounded throughout the bridge. Few had even heard that Captain Sullivan did have a sense of humour, let alone display it in the heat of battle.

"Gentlemen let us return to the business at hand. It has been accurately reported that *Scharnhorst* has a top speed of twenty-eight knots, which means she cannot outrun us thanks to Mr. Thompson. For simplicity's sake, we will call the enemy *Scharnhorst* until we can positively confirm who she really is. Keep up the maximum fire rate and close as best we can. Maybe the Gods of weather will do away with this troublesome fog and we can get a decent bearing on the German. Mr. Davis, please use your infinite knowledge of the Germans to track this particular Germans' maneuvers. I thoroughly expect that if it is indeed Captain Kastanien on the *Scharnhorst*, he will bear watching like a hawk. Remember that he and his partner in crime, Captain Teebolt of the *Gneisenau* simply vanished from our rather tight net quite recently. They do not run their ships according to any conventional logic—theirs or ours.

"My best guess is that he will make best speed for air cover from France. That is a goodly distance away and we will be with him all the way. We will maintain a chase just off his starboard rear quarter. This will give us the double advantage of our (six) fourteen-inch guns to his (three) eleven-inchers. However, lest we forget, experience has shown that both of these *Ugly Sisters* have proven deadly accurate with their shooting and those eleven-inch guns do pack a rather nasty wallop. In addition to their accuracy, which I believe is not one whit superior to our boys, they have a much faster fire rate. From the noise outside over the past few moments, it appears they are getting a salvo off every twenty seconds versus our thirty second reloads. Carry on."

The Admiralty
Same Time

Robert Stark's aide burst unbidden into the sanctuary of his superior. Stark, momentarily shocked at his aides presumptuous behavior, fixed a frosty glare at the aide, cocked his head and awaited an explanation for this apparent rude behavior. He had less than a second to wait.

"Sir, pardon my impertinence but I knew you would want to hear the news instantly. *Prince of Wales* is engaging a German capitol ship, presumed to be the *Scharnhorst*, north-east of the Azores."

"Bloody Hell, you say. That's the best news we've had for many a long day. Your unceremonious entry is forgiven and forgotten. Now out with the rest."

"Well Sir, thank you Sir. *Prince of Wales* had a spot of bother with her propulsion and had to lay up leeward of the Azores for several hours freeing up a cable mess from her propellers. Since she was under the strictest orders to maintain absolute radio silence, we didn't know ----"

Stark had held up his hand to silence his aide.

"Mr. Jeffries, please do not prattle on about what delayed them for now. Tell me only about the present battle conditions. Essentially all I need to know is what *Prince of Wales* sent us. Then I can make the necessary decisions. Carry on."

"Sorry Sir. I didn't mean to tell you your job. *Prince of Wales* reported that an *Arado* seaplane buzzed them for identification shortly after first light. She, *Prince of Wales,* had been shadowing an unknown vessel suspecting that it might have been a German heavy warship. All through the night and right up the present, the entire area was blanketed by heavy fog making visual identification impossible, except at very close range. When the *Arado* flew over them, barely above wave top height, there was no doubt that it had come from an enemy capitol ship. Captain Sullivan immediately opened fire with his forward two main turrets as well as his 5.25-incher's. The range was about ten miles. The German is returning fire, but only from his one main eleven-inch rear turret, along with his 5.9-incher's that can bear. Both ships are targeting by radar. Captain Sullivan is almost positive that his adversary is the *Scharnhorst*, whom he relates vanished recently. *Prince of Wales* is accompanied by two destroyers that were left behind for escort by the battle group when he lay to behind the Azores. They report that the German's shooting is still rather erratic, meaning too short, too long but improving. Nothing so far within a quarter mile. With the fog still so dense, Captain Sullivan cannot tell if he has scored any hits, but is doubtful. That is all Sir."

"Very well, signal *Prince of Wales* to press home the fight and then call up the other officers who have previously joined our discussions. I will not assume that the Prime Minister has been told, although he should have been—so I want you to dash over to 10 Downing Street. After you have messengered the others, then inform Winston. 'Tis a trifle early for him to be rattling around, even in his pajamas. Regardless, stress the urgency of seeing him to the guards. Do NOT take no for an answer. Now, be off with you and get my orders taken care of—immediately, if not sooner."

Kriegsmarine Headquarters, St. Nazaire
Same time

A strident knocking on the office door immediately brought Grossadmiral Dönitz thoughts out of a brief reverie about his family. Sensing the urgency of the knocking, he instantly commanded the knocker to enter. When his chief adjutant burst into the room, obviously very excited, Dönitz had donned his usual implacable face. Calmly, but firmly Dönitz asked what constituted this minor uproar.

"Grossadmiral Dönitz, Sir. We have just heard from *Scharnhorst*. She is exchanging fire with the British battleship *Prince of Wales*. There have been no hits from either side when the message came through. The message also related what they had been up to for the past few days. Then at the end, a coded message in English. Sir, here is the message. It would be best if you read it yourself."

A quizzical look replaced his normal stoic façade and then Dönitz tilted his head at his man and took the message. Before he read it, he motioned the adjutant to seat himself—obviously to await his orders. Dönitz silently read the entire first part of the message—noting that his adjutant had summarized it perfectly and then he read the last paragraph.

"Karl, meet my sister at the beer garden as fast as you can. They are having a grand party."

Dönitz replaced the puzzled look with an uncharacteristic smile and then motioned for the adjutant to come forward. When the adjutant was before him, standing ramrod straight, Dönitz spoke a few succinct words and orders.

"Mr. Hemmer, for your information, should it ever become necessary, I shall explain the last paragraph. Our decoders know that sometimes Captain Kastanien and even Captain Teebolt will send a message in our code, but worded in English for top-security reasons. This subterfuge was felt necessary by the three of us to doubly insure that the enemy would be confused by the language switch. We hope that they do not figure this out—even if they break our supposedly-unbreakable Enigma code. The message translates to mean that *Scharnhorst* knows that *Gneisenau* is relatively close and we are to signal them to make best speed to join *Scharnhorst* in the present battle. When our super battleships *Bismarck* and *Tirpitz* are let loose in the Atlantic, their captains will also use this double code.

"However, until then let us deal with the present situation. First, signal *Scharnhorst* this." *'Peter, I will be at the beer garden party as soon as my transport can get me there.'* Send this at the beginning of the message, also in English, and then end the transmission in German with: *'You are in command so do what you have always done best. All I ask is that you keep me informed at all times of the progress of the battle. All of Germany is cheering for you. Return to Breast when the action is over.'*

"Mr. Hemmer. Before you question me and embarrass yourself, let me explain. I have assumed that the British have been clever enough at least to decode the word Brest. Make doubly sure that the signaler misspells 'Breast' to include the 'a'. Kastanien knows that this is a deliberate error to mislead the British into positioning their other capitol ships in useless positions. Positions that will not be in Kastanien's path on his homeward journey. The British will probably muster up some of their *Lancaster* bombers in preparation to bomb *Scharnhorst* when she docks at Brest or on her way there.

"However, that is no longer her Atlantic port. The very large, complete dockyard and harbor are finished and ready for them at St. Nazaire. *Gneisenau* will also hear the message and understand that *Scharnhorst* could use his help as quickly as possible. Doubling our firepower with *Gneisenau's* guns, engaging the rather formidable *Prince of Wales* with her (ten) fourteen-inch guns should give our magnificent twin sisters the advantage. Because you are a vital part of my staff, I have let you in on these secrets. Keep this information entirely secret by telling absolutely no one, including that very lovely girlfriend of yours. The British spies have yet to discover that our newest facility is completely functional. We want to keep them in the dark about it as long as possible. Now, get the message sent immediately! Dismissed."

Scharnhorst
A few minutes later

The bridge intercom from the radio room screeched into life.

"Captain, message received from Kriegsmarine HQ. Shall I read it or bring it to you?"

"Neither, you must stay at your station and since it's rather noisy up here for verbal communication. I am sending Second Officer Mueller to retrieve it."

The blind battle had been continuing for nearly ten minutes without a direct hit from either warship. Some had come close enough to *Prince of Wales* to douse her stern decks with a few tons of seawater but no damage. One lesser caliber shell from *Prince of Wales* had clipped a forward handrail on *Scharnhorst* but not sufficient to detonate the warhead.

Within less than two minutes, Kastanien had read the message and sharply issued new orders, "Reverse port engine, maximum revolution, and maximum speed on starboard engine—hard to port. Steady up when we are running abreast of *Prince of Wales* in the opposite direction. Steady on speed twenty-eight knots when we straighten up. Set course to run parallel fifteen kilometers from *Prince of Wales* present course and maintain that distance if she should make turns; which is most likely. Inform Mr. Rost that I expect him to maintain maximum rate of fire from all guns that will bear even through the turn."

Without even a questioning glance, Kastanien's orders were executed instantly. Once more, the massive ship of solid Krupp steel shuddered slightly as she figuratively pirouetted on her large twin rudders.

In the fire control center, Erwin Rost smiled a cunning smile with a twinkle in his eyes when he received the orders. Disappointed that he had failed to inflict any damage on the bigger and heavier armed opponent to date, Rost took the challenge of aiming his guns though the wickedly rapid turn to heart. Without rancor, he silently said to himself. *"We'll show the English, the captain, and all our boys that we can dance to this tune, even without a decent bearing on the enemy."* Rost did not mistrust radar, quite the contrary; he embraced it as a wonderful new tool. However, his soul wanted to see his opponent in the iron-gray flesh rather than some wiggly green bars.

Scharnhorst was halfway through the sharp about-face when one of the massive fourteen-inch shells from *Prince of Wales* slammed into her side forty feet behind the bridge, exploding like a small meteor strike. Immediately flames broke out. *Scharnhorst's* damage control teams lunged into the inferno. Fortunately, the rent in her side was well above the waterline, and not excessively serious, thanks to the 350mm of armor plate. Had the builders not forged such high-grade armor, the damage could have been crippling, and would have created a completely different scene right out of Hades.

Men, burdened with heavy fire fighting gear to slow them down, nonetheless sprinted into the fray carrying very heavy water hoses. The power of these hoses was so potent that it took two burly men leaning into them to handle the pressure. Externally, the conflagration was quickly contained, and shortly thereafter the relatively light internal damage was under control and the fires extinguished. Standing by until the flames were out, the damage control repair crew immediately plunged in to repair the three foot by seven-foot jagged gash that the shell had made.

Prince of Wales

"This is the radar room. *Scharnhorst* is executing a tight turn to port. In addition, I believe that we have scored a hit. I will keep you informed as she continues her turn," the young squawky voice announced over the intercom to the bridge.

Captain Sullivan smiled at the news of a probable hit while the rest of the younger officers let out a resounding cheer. Then, after a few seconds, the raucousness suddenly quieted and all eyes turned to the captain. Sullivan pondered only a brief moment before speaking.

"Gentlemen, up to now we have assumed our enemy is either *Scharnhorst* or *Gneisenau*. However, I am definitely inclined to believe she is *Scharnhorst*, but until we have definite confirmation, that is how we will continue to refer to her. Even though Captain Teebolt does some interesting maneuvers, this tight turn, apparently to come at us head-on, smacks of Kastanien. Therefore, we will have to be very wary, because as we all know, he continually re-invents naval tactics and maneuvers. Or should I say that he is very 'creative' with naval tactics."

Captain Sullivan paused but a few seconds more before issuing new orders.

"Radar room, keep me informed immediately when he steadies up on a new course. I suspect that he will drive straight towards us so he can make use of his two forward turrets. That suits me just fine. He will duke it out with his six guns to our six. The advantage is ours if we hit him one for one, since we have fourteen-inch shells vs. his eleven-inchers."

Suddenly amid the thunderous din of the six monster guns, a very excited voice erupted from the radar intercom.

"Captain Sir. *Scharnhorst* has steadied up and is running a parallel course to ours and if she maintains that course, she will pass us broadside about ten miles to our port side."

Sullivan once again began thinking aloud.

"Nobody but Kastanien would do such a foolhardy maneuver. Taking on superior gunfire, literally broadside, at ten miles is tantamount to suicide, but that wily Sea Fox no doubt has a new trick up his sleeve."

"Guns, pound away at that devil before he does something untoward. While we have the chance, let us do him in. If I know him, he will not carry this course much longer. Prepare to adjust when he turns away, which is the only half-sensible thing to do. Then again, he might just try to cross our T, where he will have use of all nine of his guns to our six. But, none of this is Gospel gentlemen—for all we know he could just vanish like one of those damnable U-boats."

These sobering thoughts were enough to contain the captain's levity to a few chuckles. Again, the excited voice squalled out of the radar intercom.

"Captain, Sir. *Scharnhorst* is making a turn to port and heading straight at us. Distance is now eight miles."

Sullivan responded instantly, "The blighter has gone bonkers. At our combined closure rate, he will be on us in a few minutes. The fog works against both of us, but not for long. We should see him in less than five minutes. Hold course steady for now, but prepare to make a rapid turn."

Both ships had expended multitudinous shells but only the *Prince of Wales* had made one solitary hit. Then suddenly *Prince of Wales* shook slightly from a direct hit midway on the forecastle. The great battleship shuddered but her guns kept up their relentless fire. The eleven-inch shell penetrated the light armor easily before exploding which caused relatively minor damage and a small fire. Less than thirty seconds later, *Prince of Wales* took two more hits aft of the bridge causing more serious damage.

Alarms screamed throughout the ship. Damage control parties which had been standing by, immediately leaped into action. Once again, the squeaky voice from the radar room broke above the cacophony in the bridge, only this time there was a noticeable tinge of fear underlying the excited voice.

"Captain, Sir. *Scharnhorst* is now making a sharp turn to her starboard and heading away from us."

Scharnhorst

"Mr. Schmidt, starboard forty degrees and make it a very sharp turn to throw off the English guns. Mr. Gott, inform Mr. Rost of the turn and to put turret Caesar in action as soon as she will bear on the enemy and tell engineering to put up a dense smoke screen," Captain Kastanien calmly issued his new orders.

Scharnhorst again heeled into the turn smoothly and sharply almost like a racing sloop, albeit quite oversized. Within forty seconds turret Caesar began firing, adding three more shells every twenty seconds to the six missiles from Anton and Bruno already thundering towards the *Prince of Wales.* Caesar's gun crew was determined to score some hits after being idled. They were quickly rewarded with radar's confirmation that two of their shells had scored. Without missing a beat in the well-rehearsed firing sequence, a hearty cheer rang through the crew that could even be heard above the incredible clamor of the mechanisms that brought up the shells and the ramming home of the pistons.

"Captain, *Prince of Wales* is turning to follow us," the excited voice of "Merlin" Molter announced from the radar room.

"Mr. Mueller, have radar inform me immediately after *Prince of Wales* has steadied on her course."

Only a few brief moments later, the radar room announced that *Prince of Wales* had steadied on a course directly following *Scharnhorst*. After Kastanien determined the distance was about fifteen kilometers he issued new orders, "Helm, turn hard to starboard until we have made a complete circle, increase speed to thirty knots. I want to come out of the smoke screen, hopefully without the nuisance of the fog to hinder our shooting. We will then head at 225 degrees to meet up with *Gneisenau,* who by now will have been apprised of the situation and be on her way to help us deal with *Prince of Wales.*"

Gneisenau

Captain Teebolt read the message from Kriegsmarine twice before issuing a statement to his bridge staff and giving orders.

"Gentlemen, our sister ship *Scharnhorst* has run into the *Prince of Wales* and is dueling it out with her. *Prince of Wales*, as most of you should know, is one of the newest battleships in the British navy, therefore making her a seriously formidable opponent. She has (ten) fourteen-inch guns plus assorted smaller firepower and doubtless, the latest radar the English have. We are 'requested' by Grossadmiral Dönitz to join the 'party' that is going on. Captain Kastanien should have a fair idea of where we are and will no doubt be steaming in our direction so we can add our firepower pounding away at *Prince of Wales*.

"Helm, take a bearing on *Scharnhorst's* radio transmissions and head for her at maximum speed, and then some if we can squeeze more out of the engines. Our friend Peter no doubt has his hands full—especially being outgunned by a sizable margin. I intend to bracket the British and split some of their firepower away from *Scharnhorst*. If we are lucky, the British, being pre-occupied, will not notice us on their radar—probably a pipe dream of mine since they won't make the same oversight they did when we surprised them in the South Atlantic picking on our little sister— *Admiral Graf Spee*."

Gneisenau had been steaming along at a reasonable twenty knots in the general direction of the battle so only a minor course correction was necessary. The warship shuddered a bit as the full power of the twelve boilers transferred 165,000 shp to the three shafts. After only a few short moments, the 38,100 tons of gray steel was racing through the Atlantic a trifle under thirty-two knots. Teebolt resisted the temptation to radio that he was coming to his friend's aid. After determining the exact direction where the battle was raging, Teebolt mulled over his options. He knew that if Kastanien headed his way, then the closure rate of the two ships would bring him into the fray in less than thirty minutes, forty-five at the outside.

Prince of Wales

"Captain, Sir. *Scharnhorst* making hard turn to starboard."

"Very well. Make course corrections necessary to keep on her tail to nullify her forward guns."

Moments passed slowly as *Prince of Wales* kept correcting for the turn *Scharnhorst* was continuing to execute. Soon it became apparent that the German ship was going to reverse her course, or possibly go in a circle. Speculation about this maneuver flashed silently between the bridge officers. As the *Prince of Wales* steamed towards the still invisible enemy, they began to encounter the dense smoke screen laid down a bit earlier by *Scharnhorst*. Suddenly, star shells began bursting all about the *Prince of Wales*. Captain Sullivan slowly shook his head and grinned before consulting his radar operator.

"Radar, what position is *Scharnhorst* now?"

"Captain Sir. The radar is quite muddled and I cannot sort out all the blips that suddenly are showing up everywhere. My best estimate is that she is still turning. I will inform you immediately when the screen makes sense. Sorry, Captain, but it's the best I can determine."

Speaking aloud to no one in particular Captain Sullivan mussed, *"Leave it that bloody unpredictable Hun to come up with something different."*

Scharnhorst's shells were still screaming nearby, some very close, which snapped Sullivan out of his momentary lapse. He quickly barked new orders.

"Helm, port thirty. I believe that when we are through this smoke screen, the damnable fog will have lifted enough for us to get a good sight of him. Keep all the guns firing that can bear."

Scharnhorst

"Captain, Sir. *Prince of Wales* turning to port"

Kastanien paused a moment calculating the move by his opponent. They were just past halfway into the circular turn.

"Helm, Reverse course to port. Make the turn as sharp as possible. Steady up on course 225 degrees. Cease making smoke when we are on course. Make speed up to thirty-two knots."

Scharnhorst again wheeled like an overweight ballerina, shuddering a smidgen with the forces of propulsion grappling with momentum. Her forward guns became silent for a few short moments when they could not bear on *Prince of Wales*. After a brief pause, turrets Anton and Bruno rejoined the barrage of high-explosive shells that had never ceased thundering skywards from turret Caesar.

Damage Control Officer Horst Bock reported to the bridge that everything was once more under control. Kastanien, who had been quite naturally busy in the interval, still took a few seconds to thank his efficient damage-control crew for a job well done. Just as the conversation finished, one of the three-quarter ton fourteen-inch shells from *Prince of Wales* detonated with titanic force just forward of turret Caesar. The concussion stunned the crew in the turret for a few moments. No words between Kastanien and Bock were necessary. Bock immediately sprang into action to deal with the newest damage to his beloved *Scharnhorst*. Kastanien ordered second officer Mueller to assess the damage and give him a casualty report.

A few minutes later, Mueller reported to his Captain that the damage was serious but not critical. He also reported that they had suffered eighteen casualties—with six dead, two critical and ten with only minor injuries who would be back on duty within two hours. The fires were out and Caesar would be back in action within minutes. Only one of the gun crew suffered a bad arm injury from the blast.

Prince of Wales

"Captain, Sir. *Scharnhorst* appears to be reversing course."

"Very well. Adjust course to keep after her. Mr. King, signal our destroyers to come out from cover and proceed at top speed on a converging course with *Scharnhorst*. Maybe we can get a fish into her and at the very least slow her down," Captain Sullivan calmly ordered.

Suddenly *Prince of Wales* burst through the oil-black smoke screen into the fog. First Officer Roland King noted that the fog was thinning considerably and promised to be a thing of the past shortly. Captain Sullivan had also come to the same conclusion and ordered the ensign run up the pole in preparation of sighting the enemy thus announcing that the British Navy was here and ready for anything *Scharnhorst* could dish out.

"Mr. King. I believe that we shall soon have visual on *Scharnhorst*. Alert the rangefinder crews to be extra sharp. This exchange of gunfire by radar has been abysmally poor from both sides. When we have visual, our lads will surely ratchet up the percentage of hits—but unfortunately the German will do so as well."

Literally as soon as the Captain finished speaking *Prince of Wales* burst through the last fog bank into a slight chop and dazzling sunshine.

"Captain Sir. I have *Scharnhorst* in sight. She has steadied up on course 225 and is making speed. Hello! She has just raised her flag Sir but I don't recognize it," chirped out Second Officer Jerry Davis.

Captain Sullivan with his huge binoculars already glued to his eyes raised them slightly and grinned before announcing to the bridge.

"Gentlemen. That is the flag we fought against in the last war. I had heard that our good Captain Kastanien is, shall we say, not exactly in step with the new regime in Germany and now wants to do battle with us like when we were almost equal adversaries. Well, good-o. We'll now take on the Imperial German Navy's High Seas Fleet."

Ever inquisitive, Second Officer Davis asked the question that everyone wanted to but were reluctant to do so.

"Captain Sir. Exactly what is the central image?

"An excellent question Mr. Davis. The background is essentially the same, but instead of the swastika in the center of the battle flag, the Two-headed Germanic Eagle clutching the Hohenzollern crown on background of blood red. This was the German battle ensign until the Nazis came to power. For many, many years that was the battle flag of a much-respected German Navy—especially in the last conflict. I feel that we are now doing battle with a worthy opponent rather than a tool of that heinous regime in Berlin. So, I trust I have answered your inquiry satisfactorily and now to the business at hand."

Almost immediately, the *Prince of Wales* rocked from two hits from *Scharnhorst's* eleven-inch guns and three from her 5.9-inchers. All but one hit was aft of the bridge and although the damage was severe, it did not slow down the return fire from the forward (six) fourteen-inch guns and (eight) 5.25 inch secondary batteries. Damage control parties immediately began putting out the fires and carting dead and wounded to the infirmary. The battle was now truly joined.

Scharnhorst

"Launch the second *Arado* immediately. I want her out of harm's way and to deliver a nice little fish lunch to the British. Radio the first *Arado* to circle *Prince of Wales* and report our fall of shot, which might assist Mr. Rost a trifle," Kastanien ordered—in very much the same calm manner that his opponent used.

With sound not unlike racing locomotives, several of the massive fourteen-inch shells from *Prince of Wales* screamed overhead crashing harmlessly into the freshening sea on the starboard side.

"Hard starboard twenty. Mr. Schmidt, in case anything happens to me, always steer into the last fall of shot. I have found that that reduces the enemy's accuracy quite a bit. Moreover, do not maintain a steady course for more than two minutes. No sense in giving them too easy a target."

For nearly fifteen more minutes, the battle raged on, neither side inflicting any seriously crippling damage until one 5.25-inch shell exploded just beneath the bridge of *Scharnhorst*. The concussion and shrapnel momentarily stunned the bridge officers. Captain Kastanien was knocked to the deck but uninjured. Quickly regaining his feet, Kastanien moved to the intercom to the radar room.

"Radar, any sign of *Gneisenau* yet?"

"No, Sir but I have just now picked up two more small blips coming towards us from the port side of *Prince of Wales*."

Kastanien absorbed the announcement, and then stepped out onto the bridge wing with his binoculars. At the relatively close range of the ships, it took only a moment to recognize the new threat. Spritely he stepped back inside and barked new orders.

"Guns, we have two destroyers coming up on us from the port side of *Prince of Wales*. Concentrate all guns on them and blow them out of the water before they come within torpedo range. Helm, turn hard ninety degrees starboard after our guns get off three salvos on the destroyers. Lay down heavy smoke."

In only a few seconds over one minute, twenty-seven eleven-inch 337 kg high explosive missiles of destruction screamed towards the charging British destroyers. Three times that number of 5.9-inch shells joined in the barrage at two relatively tiny ships. In the heightened anxiety of their first engagement with an enemy the two destroyer captains forgot a primary rule of battle at sea. Charging forward at thirty-six knots, they failed to jink to throw off the opponents' gunnery. The first destroyer took an eleven-inch shell directly under the bridge, penetrating to the very bowels of the ship before exploding with catastrophic force. The tiny 1,760 ton *Jervis* blew apart into thousands of metal shards instantly. The second destroyer fared no better. Slightly smaller by a mere 70 tons, the *Kashmir* destroyer took only one hit as well, this one abaft the stack. Again, the "tin-can", as the Americans called destroyers, was rent apart and utterly destroyed by the overwhelming explosive charge of the huge shell. Several of the smaller shells hit home doing serious damage, but were overshadowed by the annihilating effects of the bigger shells.

Prince of Wales

Watching their two greyhounds being obliterated, the officers on the bridge of *Prince of Wales* fell totally silent. The complete destruction of the nearest destroyer sent thousands of small to large chunks of shrapnel screaming in every direction. Many peppered the *Prince of Wales* like pellets from a large gauge shotgun, actually slightly injuring one seaman who was working the damage control forward. Captain Sullivan, himself shocked at the devastating deaths of his fellow compatriots and their once-proud ships, broke the funereal gloom after a pause of several seconds.

"Keep after her with all we've got. Implore the engine room to give us more speed if possible. I want that ship to really *feel* what our destroyers just suffered."

"Sir, engine room states that we are steaming at twenty-nine and one-half knots, but he will give it his everything to squeeze a bit more out of her."

Sullivan mouthed his frustration aloud, "Damnation, *Scharnhorst* is rated at twenty-eight knots; yet we cannot seem to close the gap. Might it be that she is faster than our intelligence has let us know?"

Scharnhorst

After steaming for only six minutes on her new course, Kastanien brusquely issued new orders.

"Reverse course hard. I want to hide behind the smoke."

His orders came none too soon. Mere seconds after *Scharnhorst* wheeled about, several of the deadly fourteen-inch shells from *Prince of Wales* splashed harmlessly into the sea where *Scharnhorst* would have been had she maintained that course. Three minutes later Kastanien again sharply gave new orders.

"Port ninety, through the smoke. Maintain firing. Mr. Rost, we will break through the smoke in a few moments. Do your best to cripple her at the very least before she can do us any serious harm. We will execute a ninety-degree turn to starboard shortly after emerging from the smoke and resume a jagged course of 225 again. We should be closing with *Gneisenau* very shortly. Keep a sharp eye on the radar for any sign of her."

Once again, the blind radar-controlled firing failed to make hits from either side. Suddenly, after a very brief interval *Scharnhorst* burst out of the smoke. The radar operator on *Prince of Wales* had taken careful note of the maneuvers—visually hidden, relaying them to the captain as each one happened.

Captain Sullivan, ever wary of Kastanien's unorthodox machinations, had correctly guessed his opponents move and was ready when *Scharnhorst* suddenly appeared. The forward (six) fourteen-inch guns were ready and immediately began raining shells on *Scharnhorst*. Both sides were now headed towards each other, closing the now twenty kilometer gap rapidly. *Scharnhorst's* six forward eleven-inch guns were blazing away at the *Prince of Wales* with a recycle rate fifty percent faster than the larger caliber British guns—which somewhat evened up the exchange.

Not wanting to get too close to his larger opponent, Kastanien issued the order for a ninety-degree turn to starboard. This shortly allowed turret Caesar to also train on *Prince of Wales*, adding nine more shells per minute to the battle. Captain Sullivan, painfully aware that Kastanien had virtually crossed his "T" immediately ordered a ninety-degree turn to port. Within moments, *Prince of Wales* began opening fire from her four rear turret guns. Now, the air was filled with so many shells that it seemed like a convention of angry locomotives charging willy-nilly all over the sky. The range had shortened to twelve kilometers, which was close enough for reasonably accurate gunnery and both ships were scoring hits. Because of heavy armor-plating, none of the hits, although serious enough, were debilitating to either warship. *Scharnhorst*, being the smaller of the two leviathans, was being rocked with heavier shells and getting the worst of the duel. Kastanien ordered full speed ahead. He needed to increase the range and to get help from his 'sister' ship, which surely had to be coming up soon to assist him.

Prince of Wales

Aboard *Prince of Wales*, the radar and rangefinders announced to Captain Sullivan that *Scharnhorst* was now pulling away at about thirty-two knots. Captain Sullivan, normally a reserved man, pounded his fist on his chair armrest and vented his frustration with an uncharacteristic semi-curse.

"Damn the Germans, they cleverly kept their true speed a close secret. In a few minutes, they will be out of effective range. We must slow her down now or lose her and I, for one, am not going to pursue a faster enemy into the unknown without any escort. Damn it all to Hell."

A trifle shocked by his outburst, the bridge officers glanced at each other with restrained grins. Silently, without any words, Captain Sullivan had shown he was capable of angry emotion and his officers respected him even more for showing his human side. A bit chagrined because of his unprofessional outburst, Sullivan slumped silently back in his captain's chair and watched as *Scharnhorst* slowly but inexorably pulled away from him. Both sides were still scoring hits, but they were becoming fewer and fewer. Soon he knew that only luck and providence would allow a crippling hit to slow or stop the German. Unconsciously Sullivan conceded a grudging respect for the clever Peter Kastanien. He smiled when he thought about the rebellious nature of his counterpart in flying the old German battle flag. *"That would cause Herr Hitler a bit of a tantrum,"* he mused.

As the moments slowly passed, he noted that neither side was making any hits. When the range had opened to twenty miles, Sullivan ordered his guns to cease-fire. His expenditure of ammunition had been heavy and he wanted to make sure that he had adequate ammunition left should he, by a lucky chance, have another go at *Scharnhorst*. For a few moments after *Prince of Wales* guns fell silent, shells from *Scharnhorst* continued to drop harmlessly into the sea and then she too stopped the useless waste of precious ammunition.

Several long minutes inexorably passed very slowly. *Scharnhorst* began to glide over the horizon. Sullivan determined to follow for another hour or two, hoping that his hits had caused some fortuitous breakdown—which would slow his departing enemy. He had been receiving damage reports all along when word came from below decks that all fires and damage was now under control. Captain Sullivan reluctantly asked for the casualty report. Although many had been killed and scores more wounded, it was not as bad as he had feared. For that small favor, he gave thanks to the Almighty.

"Torpedo in the water! Coming in on our port side," screamed the voice from the radar/sonar man.

Captain Sullivan reacted instantly.

"Hard starboard ninety—immediately."

Not as nimble in the water as her opponent, the *Scharnhorst*, *Prince of Wales* slowly made the turn—but not soon enough. The torpedo launched from the second *Arado* slammed into *Prince of Wales* detonating with devastating force. The *Arado* had circled very wide at just a few yards above the waves, making her invisible to the British radar. She had launched her lone torpedo less than half a mile from *Prince of Wales*, virtually assuring a direct hit. The torpedo penetrated the heavy armor and opened a large breach below the waterline causing seriously deadly damage. The rent in the side was too big for any semblance of the pumps to stem the tons of seawater that instantly poured into the stricken ship. In only a few moments, one of the turbines closest to the incoming seawater gave up and shut down. A large portion of the blast was directed upwards smashing everything thing in its way until almost spent, the last of the salt-water lava burst into the bridge. The eruption, although weakened, was enough to stun the officers. First Officer Roland King was the first to recover.

Fortunately, there was no fire and the seawater rapidly drained through the gaping hole in the floor. He immediately staggered over to the supine form of Captain Sullivan. Although he knew nothing about medicine, he knew when he saw the captain's left arm was at an unnatural angle, that the arm was surely broken. Quickly checking the others who were coming around slowly, he determined that the casualty count was a few more broken bones, minor bleeding and doubtless many concussions.

King, realizing he was now temporarily in charge, handed over control of what he knew was probably a seriously wounded ship to Second Officer Jerry Davis—who was the next to recover. Thankfully the intercom was still working so he screamed to sick bay for assistance. The medical team were already on their way. Within a few seconds the wounded were being carted off for treatment. When the medics picked up the captain, he was groggily coming to. Within seconds Sullivan inquired about the condition of the ship and casualties.

As fast as he could, King descended the now-twisted stairs to the lower decks. He needed to find out how badly they were damaged. As soon as he had descended beyond the main deck, he knew for certain that his ship was in extremely serious trouble. Many of the men below decks were dead, many more stunned or wounded. Those that could were streaming up the stairwells, assisting those who needed help. King stopped Chief Engineer Thompson and asked his opinion after telling him the captain's condition. Thompson, a bit shaken, replied with a catch in his voice.

"Mr. King, I don't know yet fully the severity of the damage, but I can assure you that we will remain afloat—at least for a while. We will be much slower until the damage can be patched up. I have a crew working on stemming the incoming ocean and the pumps are all going full tilt.

In the few short minutes after the torpedo hit, the mighty and proud *Prince of Wales* slowed to only ten knots, handling rather sluggishly in the water.

Scharnhorst

"Captain, I have just heard a very loud underwater explosion and the *Prince of Wales* seems to be slowing," blared the intercom from the radar room. "I have also just picked up a faint reading of a ship approaching from the south-west. The new vessel is thirty kilometers away and closing on us rapidly."

Kastanien mulled this new "sighting" for only a few seconds before responding to his radar/sonar operator, "Radio. Send this message in the clear."

"To unknown vessel approaching from our south-west; what is Attila's mate's name?"

The reply was almost instantaneous and only one word. "Sasha"

Huge grins immediately grew on every officer's face, none more radiant than Peter Kastanien's. They all knew that the mystery vessel was none other than their sister ship the *Gneisenau*.

Kastanien then issued new orders, "Hold course until we are almost abreast of *Gneisenau*. We will turn into her and run parallel with her at signaling range. We will not use the radio anymore. Mustn't give any other British warships even the slightest advantage. Recover the *Arados* when we meet up with *Gneisenau* and immediately rearm them with torpedoes. We may have only wounded that British lion and wounded lions are the most dangerous kind. Have the men remain at battle stations but relax a little bit."

Slightly more than fifteen minutes later, the watchers on *Scharnhorst* saw the very welcome sister battleship. *Scharnhorst* turned and within a few moments was cruising at twenty-eight knots at a range of half a kilometer from *Gneisenau*. Signals flashed back and forth until the new plan of attack was formulated and solidified. The two *Sister* ships then split apart and headed back into battle. Soon the *Prince of Wales* came into sight over the horizon. She was smoking a bit, but otherwise looked just as deadly as before. Kastanien ordered the one *Arado* to be launched as soon as she was rearmed. Within two minutes, he was pleased to see his aerial warrior zoom into the sky. He would remember to profusely thank the aircraft crew for a job well done later and make a note of their efficiency in the logbook.

Prince of Wales

The *Prince of Wales* had made decent, but only temporary repairs to her serious damage and was now closing at twenty-two knots. With the underwater breach plugged sufficiently for the present, *Prince of Wales* was back in action. Captain Sullivan, properly patched up, was propped up in his captain's chair—the broken arm awkwardly sticking out, encased in plaster. Fortunately the arm break was simple and clean, requiring little more than resetting. Sullivan had gotten the radar report that there were now two ships approaching rapidly. He had no plausible option other than to assume that *Scharnhorst* had met up with her *Sister.* It was now apparent that the two *Sisters* were splitting up and planned to rejoin the battle with him in the middle.

This would mean that he had to somehow negate one of them, however temporarily, and concentrate on *Scharnhorst,* who he assumed had suffered some battle damage—therefore he should be the least dangerous. *"No easy task given those two captains are very sharp fellows."*

Just then several shells bracketed his ship. One of the Germans was opening fire at extreme range. Once he had verified that the shells had come from the ship on his starboard side, Sullivan barked, "Hard starboard. Engine room; give me all that you have and then some. Guns commence firing. All guns to concentrate on the enemy coming up from our starboard side. Continue turning until our rear turret can return fire. Launch the *Walrus* and have her give us all the information on our adversaries. Make sure the pilot knows to stay out of harm's way if at all possible. The information on their movements is the most important thing."

* * * * *

The Supermarine Walrus *was the amphibious aircraft used by the Royal Navy early in the war. A rather ungainly-looking bi-wing aircraft, it was sturdy enough to withstand the stresses from catapult operations. Many of the serving officers in the Royal Navy thought that this God-awful ugly duckling could not possibly have been designed by R. J. Mitchell, the creator of the magnificent* Spitfire—*but nonetheless it was. The* Walrus *was powered by a single Bristol Pegasus VI radial engine that was housed in a nacelle slung from the centre section of the upper wing with a four-bladed pusher propeller. Armament consisted of two .303 in (7.7 mm) Vickers machine guns. The* Walrus *could only carry a total of 760 pounds of bombs and/or depth charges mounted beneath the lower wings. The* Walrus *was rated at 135 mph, nearly 60 mph slower than her German counterpart, the* Arado. *Although her rate of climb was slightly better than the* Arado, *the British seaplane was simply no match for the German* Arado *in agility or firepower.*

* * * * *

Scharnhorst

"Hard port. Keep us parallel to her so all guns can bear. Maintain a distance of twenty kilometers. Our guns are more accurate than theirs at this range. Radio *Gneisenau* to close on her starboard at maximum speed and pound away when in range of twenty kilometers or less. Signal *Arado* to fire her torpedo at *Prince of Wales* at her port side as soon as she can."

For many long minutes the exchange of shells filled the skies with few hits. *Scharnhorst* was scoring more hits than *Prince of Wales* but neither ship managed a crippling shot.

As the *Arado* was lining up for her torpedo launch, bullets riddled her left wing. Startled, the pilot instinctively dropped the torpedo—immediately hard-banking to the right. He had not seen the *Walrus* bearing down on him. Wounded slightly, the *Arado* quickly dodged out of the line of fire. Without the dead weight of the large torpedo, the *Arado* now had the double advantage of speed and agility over this surprise opponent. The *Arado* began climbing at maximum rate jinking all the while to evade the gunfire. With her superior speed it only took less than a minute before she was out of range. When she was well clear of enemy fire the *Arado* turned sharply.

The hunted now became the hunter. The *Walrus* was slightly above her but the *Arado's* sixty mph advantage soon cancelled that advantage. With (two) 20 mm MG FF cannons in the wings, and a single 7.92 mm MG 17 machine gun in the cowling, the *Arado* quickly closed on the lumbering *Walrus*— shredding the English seaplane's tail section. The

Walrus dove to avoid further damage but its pilot knew he was badly outclassed so he began a desperate dash for protection from the anti-aircraft guns of *Prince of Wales*. The *Arado* pursued him, inflicting serious damage to the left wing. The *Walrus* immediately became too balky to control so the pilot's only option was to land in the slightly choppy sea hopefully ending the air combat. Seeing the *Walrus* was landing, the *Arado* pulled up and away—the pilot reluctant to shoot at a sitting duck. The young *Arado* pilot had learned from his captain that there should always be honor and compassion forwarded to a defeated opponent.

Greatly relieved that the German had ceased firing at him, the *Walrus* pilot quickly dusted off his Catholic upbringing and uttered a few "Hail Maries". He let a large, albeit a bit tense, smile fill his youthful face when the German flew over him executing a slightly sloppy wing waggle— caused by his control surface damage. The *Walrus* pilot's practical training had kicked-in so he kept her engine running to maintain steerage way in the sea.

While the virtually one-sided aerial battle had gone on, the hastily dropped torpedo had plowed forward and struck *Prince of Wales* near the stern. It was apparent that the torpedo had punched through the thinner armor belt and had done very serious damage. *Prince of Wales* had slowed noticeably but her guns were still belching out at full rate. Still feeling the rush of adrenalin from combat, the *Arado's* pilot resumed his reconnaissance role. Less than three minutes later, *Prince of Wales* was hit in the aft smokestack. The *Arado* pilot had actually seen the shell hit and vanish before detonating below decks. The resulting explosion was horrific and much of the aft section of *Prince of Wales* was rent asunder.

Almost immediately *Prince of Wales* slowed to a stop. The eleven-inch shell had penetrated to the boiler room and exploded with cataclysmic force. Coupled with the equally destructive explosion of the torpedo all the turbines were completely destroyed. The eleven-inch shell had penetrated deep enough to blow a huge hole in the soft belly of this great warship. The sea flooded in beyond all control.

Prince of Wales was finished. Her guns continued to fire but with so much damage, none of her shells came even close to *Scharnhorst*. A few moments later the guns of the *Prince of Wales* ceased firing and so Kastanien assumed they had probably ordered abandoning the ship. He also ordered all his guns to cease firing.

"Mr. Schmidt, get me a casualty report as soon as possible. Mr. Bock, get me a damage report and your plans for repair immediately. Radio room, send this message to *Gneisenau* and send it in the clear—no coding. I want the British, especially the *Prince of Wales*, Mr. Churchill and our own HQ to be perfectly clear what we are about to do. Message reads: '*Prince of Wales* is dead in the water and sinking, I am about to attempt a rescue of the survivors. *Gneisenau* will watch over us for any possible trouble.' "

Prince of Wales

On the bridge of the mortally wounded *Prince of Wales* the intercom tube direct from the radio room urgently screamed for the captain. However, Captain Sullivan had slumped in his chair, obviously suffering from shock. Just before he had lost consciousness Captain Sullivan, knowing his ship was finished, had ordered, "Abandon ship."

"What in the 'ell do you want at this time?" First Officer King screamed back.

"Beg your pardon Sir but *Scharnhorst* had just radioed us with an offer of assistance."

"Really now, you don't say? How would this German son-of-a-bitch help but, most importantly why?"

"Sir, they say they will come alongside and take off our survivors if we turn our guns away from them."

"Get the German on the radiophone IMMEDIATELY."

Rather stunned by such a magnanimous offer, First Officer Roland King, now in command of a dying battleship, reflected on the interesting twists that the fates of war conjured up on occasion.

"After pulverizing each other to the death, this sworn enemy of England is willing to rescue those whom he had been trying, quite successfully, to kill just moments ago. One must ponder deeply this interesting development."

Just then, the loud, strident, squeaky voice of radioman John McCambridge smashed into his momentary reverie.

"Sir, Captain Kastanien of the *Scharnhorst* is on your radiophone."

King leaped the short distance for the radiophone, almost ripping the mounting from the bulkhead in his fear-induced haste.

"This is First Officer Roland King, now in command of the *Prince of Wales*. Captain Reginald Sullivan is injured and unconscious. Please restate your intentions."

"This is Peter Kastanien, Captain of the *Scharnhorst*. As you must know, *Prince of Wales* is doomed with a bit more than one hour to stay afloat. If you will turn all your guns away from us, we will come alongside and take off your survivors."

"Thank you very much for your wondrous offer Captain. However, I am quite sure you will understand that I must confer with my remaining officers before I can accept your generous offer. I shall keep this line open and you shall have our reply within three minutes."

"Please hurry, one never knows what might happen to your ship given the extensive damage."

Acting commander King then grasped the ship's intercom with a newfound strength of character and announced in a very clear, strong, emotional voice, "To the officer and crew of the *Prince of Wales*. This is First Officer King commanding. Our Captain Davis is unconscious, thus I have assumed command. Just moments after he gave the command to abandon ship, we received a most welcome, if a trifle unorthodox message from the captain of the *Scharnhorst*. He spoke to me on the radiophone stating that he would pick up survivors—if we turn our guns away from him. I truly believe that he is most sincere as he has nothing to gain from this magnanimous gesture of humanity.

It is as obvious to him as it is to us that our beloved *Prince of Wales* is headed for the bottom. He even stated that we have only about an hour of life left. After conferring a short bit ago with Chief Engineer Thompson, it seems that Captain Kastanien has had vast experience with sinking ships or mystical powers since that was precisely Chief Engineer Thompson's estimate as well. It is my judgment that we take Kastanien's offer—but I sensed and felt that it would be only fair to give you lads a fair chance to voice your opinions. Since time is of the essence, let any objectors either report to the bridge or call on the ship's intercom if you can't make it here within the next two minutes."

King waited a trifle more than two minutes in silence receiving no objections. Much relieved at the prospect of internment vs. an agonizing death from hypothermia or simple exposure, King lifted the radiophone and replied like a true commander.

"Captain of the *Scharnhorst*, we gladly accept your offer of rescue. We are turning main turrets A and B out to the open sea. Turret C is hopelessly jammed where it is. All smaller caliber guns are turned away as much as possible. We will NOT, repeat NOT shoot at you. Please hurry, we seem to be going rather faster than either of us expected. The port-side lifeboats have been smashed beyond usefulness. Please pick us up from our starboard side. Many of my men will be in the liquid deep-freeze if your boats take too long. Captain Kastanien, in case the fates do not allow me the opportunity to shake your hand and thank you in person, please allow me to do so right now. I would also like to add that your English is impeccable. I most sincerely hope I will have the opportunity to know you better since your chivalry has not been seen very much, if at all, since the days of mounted knights several centuries ago. We most gratefully await our shining knight in battleship gray. King out."

Scharnhorst

Kastanien smiled the knowing smile of one whose moral conscience is at peace with itself, despite the cruel, brutal, ugly realities of modern warfare. This warming emotion was replaced in the blink of an eye with a command over the intercom to the entire ship.

"All hands. Attention, attention. This is the Captain speaking. We are proceeding at maximum speed to rescue the crew of the *Prince of Wales*. Gun crews maintain maximum alertness. If she reneges on her promise to desist hostilities by opening fire—even with a popgun, open up with all we've got and blow her out of the water. Rescue crews, man your starboard side launches quickly. Some of her men might be in the water by the time we get there. Rescue them first and then the wounded. Take off men that have not made it to their remaining lifeboats last. Place two men, armed only with Lugers, in each of the boats for the return to *Scharnhorst*."

As *Scharnhorst* neared the stricken British warship, it was painfully apparent that his worthy opponent was damaged far worse than first observed from a distance and truly beyond salvage. It was also apparent that she was going down by the stern more quickly than anticipated. When *Scharnhorst* was a mere three hundred meters away, she slowed enough to just maintain steerageway. Kastanien ordered that *Scharnhorst* maintain station with the sinking warship. Many seamen rushed to the launches and lifeboats and in record time were motoring towards the dying British battleship.

Aboard *Prince of Wales,* similar action was taking place albeit slower since their crew was handling many wounded. Within three-quarters of an hour the *Prince of Wales* was devoid of human life with all of her officers and crew aboard *Scharnhorst.* The wounded were being attended to and the rest of her officers and crew were gathered in the fantail area, watching their once proud battleship slowly sliding beneath the waves. *Prince of Wales* had settled so far in the water that her stern was gone with her prow aimed skyward at a severe angle. Suddenly the loudspeakers blared to life.

"This is Captain Kastanien commanding *Scharnhorst.* To the officers and men of *Prince of Wales*; I have ordered a twenty-one gun salute to your superb battleship. We will only be using our 5.9 inch guns. I wish to say to you that it was a good fight and it saddens to me to see such a great ship go to King Neptune. That is all."

A few seconds after this pronouncement, the crash of guns saluted *Prince of Wales.* As if that were a final signal, *Prince of Wales* turned completely vertical rapidly but still rather graciously slid quickly beneath the ocean's surface. The sodden, dispirited men of *Prince of Wales* all bowed their heads and awaited their future unknown fate. *Scharnhorst* was still barely making way when *Gneisenau* sidled up to her port side a couple of hundred meters away. Once more the boats began ferrying half of the British seamen over to *Gneisenau.* There was simply no way that *Scharnhorst* could accommodate the more than 1,000 rescued prisoners. Many of the moderately wounded were also shipped over to the other *Sister* to alleviate the very heavy workload in *Scharnhorst's* sickbay.

After all the transfers were complete, Kastanien ordered the *Sisters* to head for home. Both he and *Gneisenau* were quite seaworthy, but battered and bruised. To ease the pressure on *Gneisenau's* patched up hull, the *Sisters* began the trip home at a moderate twenty knots. As night approached, Kastanien received a request from Captain Sullivan for an audience. Pleased that his recent adversary would want to see him, Kastanien told Second Officer Mueller to fetch the British captain to the bridge.

After only a few minutes Captain Reginald Sullivan appeared on the bridge, accompanied by a seaman armed with a luger pistol. Kastanien respectfully dismissed the seaman stating that he did not think that a one-armed man would constitute any danger, especially a proper British officer. Captain Sullivan had obviously regained full cognizance, standing ramrod straight, smartly saluting with his uninjured left arm. Kastanien returned the salute, also with his left arm which made the two captains smile.

Sullivan was the first to speak.

"My good Captain Kastanien, I want to thank you profusely for the rescue of my officers and men. It is my understanding that my wounded are being attended to with equally good treatment as your own men. For that I salute you. Your medics even checked out my broken arm to make sure that it was set properly—they said that my medics might have hurried a trifle, being as things were a tad busy at the time. Your boys affirmed that my arm was fixed properly and would mend satisfactorily."

Kastanien, who had silently listened to his British counterpart, then again broke into a genuine grin and spoke, "Captain Sullivan, would you care to join me outside for a chat on this pleasant evening? I promise not to make you walk the plank if you promise not to throw me overboard."

With that quip, both men broke into light laughter and proceeded outside heading back to the fantail. From here they could watch the sunset, which was shaping up to be spectacularly magnificent. Reaching the rail, both men stood silent for several minutes, no doubt musing over the events of the day or just enjoying the pleasant evening with what was now a stunningly beautiful sunset.

Sullivan broke the silence first.

"Captain Kastanien. Once more my heartfelt thanks for rescuing so many of my men. I know that you put your ship and yourself in great danger by contravening normal wartime protocol out here in waters that are filled with deadly predators, seen and unseen. I have instructed all my officers and men to behave like model prisoners and cause you and your crew no problems. I informed them that without your magnanimous generosity they would be fish bait by now. When we are done here, I would like to pass this same order to my men that have been transferred to *Gneisenau*. Again, my most sincere and heartfelt genuine thanks."

"You are most welcome Captain Sullivan. I truly appreciate the fact that we shall not have to deal with several hundred obstreperous captives. I do have some authority, although limited, to insure that you and your crew will be treated with respect when you are interned on shore. I also would like to say that it is an unfortunate shame that our two governments saw fit to be at *odds* with each other. I would have rather liked to have you as an ally versus being the enemy."

"Good Heavens Captain Kastanien, your vocabulary would challenge the legendary lexicon of Winston Churchill. I've had the pleasure of being in meetings with him when he gets wound up and launches into a diatribe on some poor soul—not a pretty sight to see a grown man visually cowed when bludgeoned with words most of us have never even heard of.

"If we were allies with, shall we say, combined navies, then who would be a worthy adversary?"

"Excellent point Captain Sullivan. I would venture to say that possibly the Japanese *might* give us a decent tussle. But they are a very long ways away. The Italians, for all of Mussolini's bombastic rhetoric, are a pathetic joke. We had to send Rommel down to Africa to clean up the disaster that their *superiorly* equipped army had created. The Italians were being demolished by not much more than some untrained nomads on camels with antique weapons.

"As to the Americans, their military has grown up to be a serious enterprise; but their navy is yet to be tested in a shooting war.

"Enough of this idle conjecturing. Please let me be your host at dinner in a little while. I'm quite sure that my galley has taken care of the wounded and is back in the business of feeding a lot of hungry men, yours truly included. I would also like your First Officer Mr. King to join us as he handled the situation admirably when you were temporarily incapacitated."

Captain Sullivan thanked Kastanien in a low gracious voice—such was the high esteem he had acquired for this enemy he had known only a short time. Both the men returned to silently watching the sun sink into the now red-orange sea. Kastanien broke the calm after a few minutes.

"Come Captain, it's time to dine."

With that said the two men silently made their way to Kastanien's cabin. At the door Second Officer Mueller was patiently waiting with a sheaf of papers in hand. He saluted both officers, handed over the papers and excused himself. Kastanien opened the door and motioned Sullivan to be seated while he perused the papers. After only a few moments he announced, "Well, Captain Sullivan it seems that your gun crews did an admirable job of causing some rather extensive damage to my ship. Now the inevitable bad news. *Scharnhorst* suffered eighty-seven dead and two hundred plus wounded. Even worse is the report from your ship. Out of the compliment of 1,422 officers and men we only were able to fish 1,218 from the sea. So, two hundred and four men went down with your ship. I am truly sorry for your losses. Now, that is enough war stuff for now, let us enjoy a pleasant supper."

Kastanien used the intercom to order dinner for four from the galley. He then spoke to the bridge and asked that Executive Officer Hans Schmidt round up First Officer Roland King and join him in his cabin for supper. He also requested Attila be brought to his cabin, if anyone could find him. Captain Sullivan raised both his eyebrows at the mention of Attila and curiosity immediately got the better of him.

"Captain Kastanien, might I please inquire as to who Attila is and the reasoning behind, 'if anyone can find him.'"

Kastanien laughed heartily and decided to mystify his guest.

"Captain Sullivan, Attila is my secret weapon and his whereabouts is his business alone. He is of such incredible value that he is allowed to roam freely throughout the ship, making sure that all is in order. He is under no one's command other than his own. He is our friend and guiding light. We all rely upon him for divine guidance."

Captain Sullivan absorbed this information but could not make sense of it so he remained silent until the mysterious Attila made his appearance. Within two minutes First Officer Roland King entered the cabin after being escorted there by a congenial guard. He was almost immediately joined by Executive Officer Hans Schmidt. Kastanien motioned all to be seated while he stepped behind his desk. In a brief moment he was back at the table with his excellent schnapps and four sparkling crystal goblets. With a touch of theater, Kastanien filled the goblets about one-third full then hoisted his glass. Motioning the other three men to stand, Kastanien spoke, "Gentlemen, a salute to the many men who perished today. May they rest peacefully forever in the arms of the eternal sea."

The four men silently took a drink of the fiery liquid and then Kastanien waved them all to be seated. They spent nearly five minutes in friendly conversation before there came a gentle knock on the cabin door.

"Enter."

Chief Cook Manfried Strass entered first—Attila cradled in his arm. He was followed by three of his staff who carried the delicious smelling dinner. The men quickly set the dinner table with exquisite Royal Bayreuth Bavarian crockery replete with genuine sterling silver utensils. When the plates and bowls were fully laden with the aromatic, sumptuous fare the galley staff quietly departed.

Meanwhile, Kastanien had taken Attila from his chief cook, who assured his captain that the British seamen were being treated more like guests than prisoners. After some sincere words of thanks from the two Englishmen, a grinning Manfried Strass departed.

Kastanien was gently massaging Attila under his chin which triggered the cat to break out in a loud purring melody. Sullivan and King were dumbfounded and speechless.

Kastanien broke the silence.

"Gentlemen, I'd like you to meet Attila, our Honorary Sergeant-at-Arms. Now that my head cook has assured me that Attila has had a proper meal, let us do the same while my good friend here takes a serious nap to digest his dinner."

Sullivan and King, still rendered mute, sat down to what appeared to be a superb meal. Sullivan could not refrain any longer.

"Captain Kastanien that is the most magnificent and largest cat I have ever seen. Is he a regular passenger on your ship?"

"No, no, Captain Sullivan, he is a full-fledged crew member. He is responsible for giving me very accurate weather predictions and maintaining a virtually rodent-free ship amongst his several other duties. He is our good luck charm, making sure that we stay out of harm's way. And he does a superb job at everything. Now let us enjoy our dinner, which looks like an exceptionally special bill-of-fare from my peerless cook."

The excellent dinner was immensely enjoyed by all with the conversation totally about the magnificent cuisine and the wonderful cat, who naturally could have cared less and was curled up fast asleep on the bunk. After another goblet of an especially delightful cordial, Sullivan and King were escorted back to their accommodations and Kastanien proceeded to the bridge. Assuring himself that all was in good order he returned to his cabin and crawled into the bunk with Attila.

Epilogue

Two days later, with most of her wounds hastily patched up but still looking quite presentable despite some blackened smirches smattered throughout the 235-meter length of the graceful battleship, *Scharnhorst*, with a now slightly-limping *Gneisenau*, majestically eased through the breakwater entrance to their new home base in St. Nazaire, France. Captain Kastanien was in his cabin completing his last entries into the ship's logbook when there was an urgent knocking on the door.

"Yes, enter," Was the simple acknowledgement spoken rather sharply by Kastanien.

The door flew open, the highly excited Second Officer Karl Mueller burst into the cabin and spluttered out, "Captain Sir. Executive Officer Schmidt requests you join him on the bridge IMMEDIATELY."

"Good God man. What is so desperately urgent about simply coming into port?"

"Captain, Mr. Schmidt told me that you MUST see for yourself and made me promise not to blurt out what's happening on shore."

Kastanien, who was at first slightly irritated with his second officer, couldn't help but lift himself from his chair laughing the good laugh.

"Mr. Mueller, I fear you have given most of the surprise away, however I shall do my best to keep your credibility with Mr. Schmidt."

Mueller froze when the import of the Captain's words sunk in—then he visibly relaxed when his beloved captain laid his hand rather heavily on Mueller's shoulder and gave it a gentle squeeze.

"Karl, let us make to the bridge and see what the fuss is all about."

Arriving on the bridge in just a few seconds, Kastanien was dumbstruck with the sight on shore. Several thousand people were crowding every niche that could garner even a tiny glance at the great battleships that were returning victorious from an adventuresome journey into harm's way. Kastanien spoke not a word, even though his mouth was agape with the sight. He silently opened the door to the port bridge wing. The smooth water inside the protected breakwater easily carried the tumultuous sound of the cheering crowd to him—reverberating in waves throughout the previously somber bridge.

The unusually mild weather, blessed with abundant sunshine, had no doubt assisted in swelling the crowd to monumental proportions. Kastanien quickly recovered himself, dashed back into the bridge snapping out orders like a Maxim machine gun.

"Good heavens, it's a welcoming committee, the likes of which I've never heard of, let alone seen—even at Party rallies in Berlin. Make haste Mr. Schmidt; have all the crewmembers, except those absolutely essential to docking operations assemble, lined up along the entire length of the port side in their best, cleanest uniforms. I want them parade smart. This includes the British officers and those of our men in the infirmary who can make it. Mr. Gott, slow us down to three knots to give the men ample time to change and assemble. We only have about two kilometers to the dock. At our current speed of five knots, we'd get there much too soon. Signal *Gneisenau* to do likewise in all respects."

The bridge officers, who had been equally stunned by the awesome sight on shore, briskly issued orders of their own which turned the victorious battleship into a beehive of frantic activity. The ship's superb grapevine worked overtime at record-breaking speed with this news. The blaring announcement from the ship's public address system could not be heard by all, especially in the extremely noisy engine rooms; so a first-rate vocal communications system had long ago been developed by the crew to keep up on every scrap of news. Within less than two minutes, every single crewmember immediately knew and grasped the importance of the monumental event about to take place.

This time, probably the first time in recorded history, the grapevine news-machine suffered no individual skewing of the facts. The last man to know was told exactly the same thing as the first. The superbly trained, battle-hardened seamen of *Scharnhorst* and *Gneisenau* rapidly scrambled through this new, unfamiliar kind of exercise with extreme efficiency. Kastanien had not left the bridge to freshen up as he had much earlier donned his captain's best uniform, anticipating the normal debriefing summary that always followed immediately on any warships return. Most of his officers were also attired in their best, just in case they were needed at the forthcoming meeting. Within fifteen minutes, the decks of the two battleships port side-rails rapidly filled with smartly dressed seamen, each one standing at ease but erect as a telegraph pole. The two ships were still over three-quarters of a kilometer from the docks when radio operator Eric Weisboch burst into the bridge.

"Captain Sir. Grossadmiral Dönitz requests you please speak with him on the radiophone immediately."

"Requests? My, that is a bit unusual Mr. Weisboch. Lead the way."

"Yes Sir. He was most exceptionally polite. I have never met or spoken to him but I have heard that politeness is—shall I say—not one of his stronger attributes."

"Yes, you may say it because I have met him a few times and I would most heartily agree with you. However, it's best that we keep that opinion to ourselves. Agreed?"

"Yes Captain. Here is the radiophone for you. Shall I leave the room for your privacy?"

"No, that won't be necessary."

With muddled emotions, Peter Kastanien took the simple device from his radioman.

"Grossadmiral Dönitz. This is Captain Peter Kastanien speaking."

Kastanien listened in silence for less than two minutes before handing the radiophone back to the radioman.

"Mr. Weisboch. That was definitely not the Karl Dönitz that I have met before. This one seemed to have real warm blood coursing through his arteries. Just goes to show that one cannot judge an Admiral, especially our Grossadmiral Dönitz, by his demeanor while he goes about his duties. Once again, keep these opinions between us and be prepared for a few surprises when we dock. Operate your post until you feel the ship slow even more as we approach the dock. Then join the officers on the port bridge wing."

Radioman Eric Weisboch smartly saluted his captain, who responded likewise and headed immediately back to the bridge.

The brilliant spring sunshine refracted from millions of small wavelets created by the slow passage of the two gray leviathans. The sun was halfway down the western horizon, which enhanced the scintillating, shimmering display much like fireworks infused on water as the slightly mauled, but victorious battleships, *Scharnhorst* and *Gneisenau* slowly edged their way into the waiting dock with its jubilant crowd cheering even more vociferously.

Today was a very joyous one for the German Kriegsmarine.

Made in the USA
Middletown, DE
04 November 2016